THEOLOGY
of the
NEW TESTAMENT

THEOLOGY
of the
NEW TESTAMENT

by

Karl Hermann Schelkle

English Version by

William A. Jurgens

III
MORALITY

THE LITURGICAL PRESS

Collegeville, *Minnesota*

THEOLOGY OF THE NEW TESTAMENT

Volume One: CREATION: World — Time — Man

Volume Two: SALVATION HISTORY — REVELATION

Volume Three: MORALITY

Volume Four: THE RULE OF GOD — CHURCH — ESCHATOLOGY

THEOLOGY OF THE NEW TESTAMENT — 3 MORALITY — is the authorized English translation of *Theologie des Neuen Testaments — 3 Ethos* by Karl Hermann Schelkle, copyright © 1970 Patmos-Verlag, Düsseldorf, Germany.

Nihil obstat: William G. Heidt, O.S.B., S.T.D., *Censor deputatus. Imprimatur*: ✠ George H. Speltz, D.D., Bishop of St. Cloud.

Printed by the North Central Publishing Company, St. Paul, Minn.

FOREWORD

In Jesus Christ and in his co-humanity God is revealed to the world. And it is in this co-humanity that God continues to be present in a world given to secular pursuits. God and gods are real, insofar as faith is lived (1 Cor. 8:5f.). It is the reality of God which brings the future into the midst of our lives. Faith must justify itself before the world and make God manifest, yes, real. The New Testament exhibits, in its primitiveness, an authoritative example of "truth in love" (Eph. 4:15f.). Christian existence in the New Testament manner is not, however, a law given for all time, but instruction and example, the sense and purpose of which is to be evolved ever anew so as to be realized under new circumstances. For that reason the clarification of the historicity of the New Testament kerygma is as urgent as is its relevance to the present hour. "New and old" (Matthew 13:52) shape the treasure of doctrine. In the universal unrest and disorder of the Church and of theology, reflection on the primitive charter of the New Testament may well be of decisive importance.

The present sketch of New Testament morality, as the third part of a *Theology of the New Testament,* follows immediately upon the first part, which appeared in 1968 (English version in 1971): *Creation (World — Time — Man).* Part Two *(Salvation History — Revelation)* and Part Four *(The Rule of God — Church — Eschatology)* are still to follow. The plan of a unified New Testament theology permits the discussion of individual exegetical questions only to a very limited extent. Even the literature can be mentioned only selectively. It is up to the whole to carry with it and justify the individual parts. I believe, at any rate, that such a project is worthy of the attempt.

— *Karl Hermann Schelkle*

CONTENTS

II. BASIC ATTITUDES

III. OBJECTIVES

IV. VARIOUS AREAS FOR CONSIDERATION

THEOLOGY
of the
NEW TESTAMENT

§ 1. CONCEPT AND HISTORY OF THE THEOLOGY OF THE NEW TESTAMENT

1. THEOLOGY AS "WORD CONCERNING GOD"

The etymological meaning of *theology* is "word of God," in the sense of "word about God." In the term *theology*, representing λόγος τοῦ θεοῦ, θεοῦ is an objective genitive. In man's eyes, God's intangibility and incomprehensibility but contribute to his majestic sovereignty. It is, therefore, the conviction of every theology, and of the Christian theology more especially, that man cannot speak of God until God has first spoken to man, and when God has revealed and disclosed himself to man. Any word about God is possible to man only if he has first heard the word which God himself has spoken, and so long as he continues to listen to that word. Theology, therefore, as an attempt at scientific reflection on God's revelation, is science within faith.

The theology of the New Testament,[1] then, can be defined as "word about God" on the basis of the word in which God reveals himself in the new covenant — which, indeed, assimilates to itself the old covenant — and which word is set down in the book of the New Testament as attestation to this revelation.

a) Holy Scripture and word of God.

Since it is the task of theology to testify to the word of God, understood as the word spoken by God,[2] a question arises as to where and how this word was spoken, and where and how it is now to be heard. For the Bible, both Old and New Testaments, it is an unquestionable certainty that God did speak and does yet speak his word to men. In the Old Testament this word of God was spoken as the word of the law, of prophecy, and of history.

The word of God proves itself to Israel and to the world by means of the authority which it demonstrates by its being fulfilled in judgment and in salvation. Israel discovers the word of God over and over

3

as the determining factor in its history. By a reflective consideration of the past, leading back stepwise to the very beginning, recognition of the power of the word in history leads gradually to the knowledge and affirmation of the fact that God created the world by means of his word.

In the New Testament, Jesus and the Apostles acknowledge the word of God which was directed to Israel under the old covenant. The New Testament reports about the instructions which came to men in its own time. On that point, however, the New Testament is constant in its declaration that Christ is the final, all-validating, all-embracing Word of God. "Oftentimes of old and in many different ways did God speak to our fathers through the prophets. And now in these final days he has spoken to us in the Son" (Heb. 1:1-2a). It is in Christ that God's "yes" to all his promises is found (2 Cor. 1:19f.).

What was primarily spoken word pressed forward to become scripture. Lawgivers (like Moses) and prophets recorded the oracles of God which they were promulgating. The New Testament recognizes the Scripture of the old covenant as having been prompted by the Spirit (Matthew 22:43; Acts 1:16; Heb. 3:7; 2 Peter 1:21). A ripe testimonial which was spoken originally of the Old Testament may be taken today as applicable to the whole of Scripture: "From your childhood until now you have known the Sacred Scriptures, which are able to instruct you for salvation through the faith which is in Christ Jesus. All Scripture, written under God's inspiration, is useful also for teaching, for reproving, for correcting, for instructing in righteousness, so that the man of God may be perfect, equipped for every good work" (2 Tim. 3:15-17).

Jesus himself never set his word down in writing. We might bear in mind that many who are esteemed by mankind as among its great ones expressed their teachings only orally, leaving the writing down thereof to their disciples; so it was with Jesus, with Buddha, and with Socrates. Disciples of Jesus wrote down in the Gospels his sayings and discourses. In other writings they applied the gospel to the circumstances of the community, as did the Apostles, for example, in their letters.

Paul, being an Apostle, declares his conviction that the word of God reaches out ever anew in the Church through his own word:

"You received from us the word of God's message, accepting it not as a human message, but, as it truly is, the message of God, which surely is doing its work among you, the faithful" (1 Thess. 2:13). The remark of St. Augustine, however, is likewise valid: "Even John did not speak of the matter as it really is, but only as he was able; for it was man who spoke of God" (*On the Gospel of John,* 1:1).

Though we call Sacred Scripture the word of God, it is delivered, nevertheless, quite tangibly in human language, whether in Hebrew or in Greek. God's word is always spoken to us by men and in their language. Indeed, unlike men, God has neither mouth nor tongue. And were he to speak, how should man understand the language of God? How can the Infinite speak a finite word, or the Eternal an ephemereal word? When we talk about the word of God being spoken to men and to us men, it is clear that our manner of speaking makes use of imagery and analogy.

The Bible itself recognizes that the word of God does not find expression in the same way as does speech among men. There are numerous narratives in the Old Testament which recount how God revealed himself to men amid thunder and lightning and various phenomena of nature. Witness the promulgation of the ten commandments on Sinai — God made them known in the midst of clouds and smoke, with thunder, lightning, and earthquakes (Exod. 19).

Yet, in the same Old Testament we find the narrative of the vision of God imparted to the prophet Elijah on that same Mount Sinai (1 Kings 19). With the king threatening him with death, and persecuted by the unfaithful of Israel, Elijah concealed himself in a cave on Sinai and wanted to die. There God spoke to him: "Go forth and stand on the mountain in the presence of the Lord." And a powerful storm came, splitting the mountains and shattering the rocks. But the Lord was not in the storm. After the storm came an earthquake. But the Lord was not in the earthquake. After the earthquake came lightning and fire. But the Lord was not in the fire. After the fire came the whispering of a gentle breeze. When Elijah heard it, he covered his face with his mantle, went out and stood at the entrance of the cave. And the Lord spoke to him: "Up! On your way again! In Israel there are seven thousand who never bowed their knee to Baal and whose mouth never kissed him."

Such an account as this, in which God speaks with the prophet and treats him like one friend with another, we might label as myth. More accurately, however, this account counteracts the mythology of the manifestation of God in the phenomena of nature. Contradicting the old Sinai story, it says expressly that God appears and speaks, not in fire and upheaval, but in a soft whisper, which naturally is no longer an externally audible word. What, then, is the truth? Where does God reveal himself? In fire and earthquake or in gentle exhortation? Scripture reports the one as well as the other. The one as well as the other — and, in fact, both together — that is the whole truth.

We can adduce an example by comparison of the Old Testament with the New. In the Law of Moses the letter of divorce was permitted and prescribed, by which a man was permitted to dismiss his wife. Along with the rest of the Law, the letter of divorce is designated as "God's commands, statutes, and ordinances" (Deut. 11:1-4; 30:16). According to the Gospel narrative (Mark 10:2-12), Jesus was questioned about this provision of the Law. He answered: "By reason of the hardness of your hearts did Moses write you that commandment. From the very beginning of creation, however, God made them man and woman. . . . And the two will be one flesh," i.e., they become like one person.

Jesus terms the letter of divorce, which in the Old Testament was referred to as a statute of God, a law of Moses. And he criticizes this law of Moses on the basis of the primeval divine will, made known when God first created man and woman (Gen. 1:27; 2:24). Not every word of the Bible is literally and verbatim the law of God; there are also humanly imperfect words therein. The will of God is often to be found in hidden depths.

Sacred Scripture is both word of God and word of man. A richly significant simile says that the Bible contains the word of God after the fashion of the incarnate Word of God lying in the manger.

Besides, Sacred Scripture is only in part direct verbal discourse. In lengthy sections it is only the narrative thereof, telling us how God summoned man and how he dealt with him. Our first task is to draw therefrom the recognition of how and who God is, and more and more, what his word means.

b) Interpretation of Scripture — import of the word.

How is this living word of God to be understood in the Scriptures? We have only to listen with the judgment of faith, a task which is never completed but requires constant renewal and fresh pursuit. To travel the path from reading Scripture to hearing the word, on to that critical point of decision where we must pass from hearing the word to obedience to the word, we have two distinct aids to guide us: scientific exegetical endeavor and the community of the faith.[3]

The Bible is a text from Jewish and Greek antiquity. As such it is a text which poses for us many questions of the same sort as those which must arise with any profane text of the same antiquity. The efforts required in providing solutions to such problems are laborious and involved; and exegesis knows no dispensation therefrom. Scientific theology is obliged to undertake this work for the whole Church, which wants to read the Scriptures, to hear and to proclaim them. Exegesis must come to know many words and concepts, examining them carefully, in order to achieve understanding in its encounter with but even a single word of revelation. It may perhaps come at last to the admission that while this particular word is indeed known and used at the present time, its special meanings and the totality of its implications are strange and cannot be understood by our world.

The word of God has been spoken through thousands of years of historical time and has been accepted by hearing and believing men, each according to the understanding of his own time; and it bears testimony still for us. It finds utterance in one way in the writings of the Old Testament at the beginning of revelation, and in another way in the New Testament; and again, in the New Testament, differently in the four Gospels and in the letters of the Apostles. Christ speaks in divine simplicity; in the Apostles' reports, reasoning and demonstration are applied. There speaks the Holy One; here speak men, who have experienced every breach and burden of sin and who stand in need of redemption.

Within the New Testament, theology unfolds itself as reflection upon faith and upon the gospel proclamation. The words of Jesus himself are interpreted and developed in the process of handing them on. They are adapted to new problems. The Gospels are not purely and simply historical accounts of the life and teaching of Jesus; they are a testimonial to faith in him and revelation about him, who now is Shepherd and Lord of the Church. The Gospels are essentially post-paschal in their entirety. Even in those accounts which treat of the pre-paschal Christ, there is a concomitant announcement of the resurrection.

Never are the Gospels only history as such; they are always theology. This is true especially of the last Gospel, that of John, in which history, interpretation, and kerygmatic announcement all make their presence abundantly clear. None will dispute the fact that the letters of Paul and the other Epistles too, in their doctrinal content, bear witness to the faith of the Church. In our interpreting of the Scriptures, we recognize significant distinctions in the manner of development among the various New Testament writings. We recognize distinctions between what is original and what is derived, between declarations of essential importance and those which are merely peripheral.

Every difference of the New Testament writings notwithstanding, and while we can speak of the distinct theologies of the Synoptics, of Paul, and of John, still it is *one* theology, *the* New Testament theology, of which we speak. The New Testament writings as a group are bound together in unity by two very real facts: they all revolve about Jesus Christ, and they all have their origin in the Church. The New Testament witness concerning Jesus Christ develops and unfolds from the proclaiming Jesus to the proclaimed Christ. The proclamation, however, is set forth in different ways by the various witnesses. New Testament Christology — and we can say the same of Old Testament theology — is not a systematic dogmatic unity, but a unity (not, however, a sameness) of history.[4]

The unity of the New Testament has its foundation, after all, in the one Church. This is true even though, as the New Testament itself predicted would be the case, the unity of the Church is never realized in its ideal, but was in fact hindered and encumbered from the very beginning by opposition and factionalism. It is, nevertheless, indisputable that faith and proclamation began within the confines of the Church, wherein they were produced by the Church; and it is here that Scripture in its diversity was written. This source of the New Testament theology is contained in the canon of the New Testament.[5]

The canonical Scriptures are the proper source for a presentation of the theology of the New Testament, although the writings of the Fathers of the Church, especially the earlier Fathers, are to be considered along with them. The New Testament canon is the fruit of a lengthy period of development. Looking back upon our past, we now are able to recognize the requirements of apostolicity, catholicity, and inspiration as rules and norms for the acceptance of Scripture.

Apostolicity demands that the writing have been composed by one of the original Apostles; or, there is a broader sense in which apostolicity is acquired by association with these same original Apostles. Thus the Gospels of Mark and Luke belong to the canon, both Mark and Luke having been regarded from earliest times as followers of the Apostles. This viewpoint is important for us, since for many writings authorship by an Apostle is questionable. The possibility of an ancient pseudepigraphy is to be considered in the case of several of the Pauline Epistles (especially the pastoral letters and even more so with Ephesians, Colossians, and Second Thessalonians), as well as with the Catholic Epistles. No undue value, then, should be placed upon the question of "authenticity." In any case, the Epistles are authentic testimonials to most ancient tradition.[6]

Catholicity is determined through acceptance by all communities. Church Fathers like Origen, when traveling, made inquiries about this catholicity.

Just as afterwards the Old Testament was acknowledged as inspired (2 Tim. 3:16; 2 Peter 1:20-21), so too a similar conviction prevailed about the special gifts of the Spirit (Acts 2:4; 15:28; 1 Cor. 7:40) and the wisdom (2 Peter 3:15f.) which marked the Apostles. This is the biblical beginning of a knowledge about the inspired character of the New Testament, which is manifested afterwards even at a very early time (e.g., in the *Muratorian Fragment*; and in Irenaeus, *Adversus haereses*, 3, 11, 7f.).

The canon finds its ultimate basis in the fact that the Church received into the canon those writings in which it recognized authentic witness. Its spirit and the spirit of the writings meet and recognize each other. This spirit may be understood historically and sociologically as the enduring and genuine estimate of its conformity to its ideals which a community has of itself. To the Church itself that spirit is the divine Holy Spirit, who is conferred on it and who protected the same spirit in the Holy Scriptures. Paul presupposes such a criterion when he says: "If anyone thinks he is a prophet or a recipient of the spiritual gifts, let him recognize that what I write to you is a command of the Lord" (1 Cor. 14:37).

The harmonious consciousness of faith within the congregation manifested itself already in the New Testament in self-strengthening patterns and formulas of faith, such as our exegesis recognizes more and more in the texts. The Passion and resurrection history of Jesus in the Gospels, like the Passion and resurrection theology of the Apostles, is sustained by the single interpretation of the Cross, which in the Gospels is stated more in descriptive passages, and in the Epistles more in didactic passages.

The Pauline Epistles contain more than a few credal or liturgical texts (Rom. 1:3f.; 1 Cor. 11:23-26; 15:3-5; cf. Eph. 5:14; Col. 1:15-20; 1 Tim. 3:16), which the Apostle found already existing in the Church and which he repeated in his letters (see below, ch. 6). The same Church already distinguished the authentic teaching from heresy (Matthew 24:5, 11; 1 Cor. 11:19; Gal. 2:4; 2 Peter 2:1). The New Testament Church is intent on the preservation of the unity of its faith and doctrine.

The canon of the biblical books was acknowledged definitively in the early Church about the year 400 (with some variation of time between the East and the West). For the Catholic Church, it was confirmed by the Council of Trent, although some questions raised within the Council remained undertermined. The Reformation had already expressed its criticism of the traditional canon, and along those same lines a passionate discussion about the canon has arisen in modern Protestant theology.[7]

No one wants, however, to break up the traditional compass of the New Testament. What is sought is a central canon, a canon within the canon, wherewith a norm might be found for the separation of the essential from the less important, and the original from the derivational. An exposition of the New Testament theology, though it cannot erase the differences in the separate writings, will nevertheless have the duty, and pursue the goal, of recognizing and displaying the unity of the New Testament within its very diversity. If we emphasize differences and seem to relegate unity to the background, it is only because by so doing we are forced to increase our depth of understanding.

Ultimately, and in consequence of the unity of Old and New Testaments, we must speak not merely of a New Testament theology but of a biblical theology. The God of the old and new covenants is one and the same God. This unity is in fact disclosed to us in the very name of Jesus (Jehoshua), which means "Yahweh redeems." The New Testament itself testifies to this unity. Its many references to the Old Testament bear witness to the consciousness that the new era recognizes itself as the fulfillment of the old. God, who in times past had spoken to our fathers, now spoke in this final period through his Son (Heb. 1:1f.). Turning toward Christ inaugurates understanding of the Old Testament (2 Cor. 3:15f.). From the very beginning, even in the oldest formulas of faith (1 Cor. 15:3f.), the Church furnishes proofs "according to the Scriptures." The exposition of New Testament theology, then, must always be accompanied by a backward glance toward Old Testament theology.

How this is to be accomplished will vary in different instances, but we can generalize to a certain extent. The differences and contrasts between the Old and New Testaments are not to be overemphasized. This was done to some extent by the Fathers of the Church in their unhistorical and allegorical interpretations, which found everywhere in the Old Testament symbolic allusions to the New.

All modern exegesis seeks to attain a grasp of the Old Testament primarily in the way in which it understood itself and in its relation to history. The dealing of God with men attested to therein, however, is of concern to men of every time; for it is the same God who reveals himself in the old era and in the new. A segment of modern (Protestant) exegesis lays great emphasis upon the points of contrast. In extreme cases the Old Testament would be preparatory and introductory to the New Testament only as a witness to the failure of human religions and of moral endeavor.[8]

Other exegesis recognizes in the history of the Old Testament a growing inclination toward the New.[9] The New Testament itself often explains the Old in such a way. Paul cannot escape the fact of his having been deeply conditioned by the history of Israel. His conviction that the Old Testament leads away from the work of men to the grace of God is fundamentally correct (Rom. 1:17; 10:5-13). So, too, in respect to Christian theology, modern Old Testament exegesis is satisfied that it is valid to explain the Old Testament ultimately in the order of promise and fulfillment in reference to the new covenant in Christ. The unity of the Sacred Scriptures, Old and New Testaments, is, in the last analysis, that unity of which Hugh of St. Victor speaks when he says: "All of divine Scripture is but a single book; and this one book tells of Christ and is fulfilled in Christ" (Migne, PL 176, col. 642D).

Working in Scriptural exegesis often presents difficult enough questions both for the individual and for the whole Church; and this was perceived even while the New Testament was yet being written. The Second Epistle of Peter, written in the late Apostolic period, speaks of the fact that the Church is being disturbed and grieved by conflicts in the interpretation of Scripture: ". . . just as our dear brother Paul also has written to you, in accord with the wisdom granted him — as also in all his letters, speaking in them about these things. In those letters are some things difficult to understand, which ignorant and unstable readers distort, just as they do the rest of the Scriptures, unto their own destruction" (3:15-16). From the very beginning the Church is charged with the need and necessity of interpreting her Sacred Scriptures.

In listening to the Scriptures, exegetical interpretation is certainly one aid; but there is another also — the congregation of faith in the community of the Church. As "word of life" (John 5:24), and life-begetting like the Sacrament, the Scriptures create the Church, through which they themselves in turn remain a living thing. We understand this Church to be the great, one, holy, catholic, and apostolic Church, to which, with our Catholic Church, the Greek Church too, and all the baptized are related. "The essential content of Sacred Scripture is eternally present to the Church, because it is her heart's blood, her soul, her breath, and her all" (Johann Adam Möhler).

Scripture interpretation in the Church is interested in the knowledge and faithfulness of the entire community of saints, embracing all times and countries. Here we may quote the statement which Martin Luther wrote as his hermeneutic legacy: "No one can understand Vergil in his *Bucolics* and *Georgics* until he has been a shepherd or farmer for five years; nor Cicero in his *Letters* until he has been actively engaged in community affairs for twenty years. Let no one think he has tasted sufficiently of the Holy Scriptures until, along with the prophets, he has ruled the congregation for a hundred years. . . . We are beggars. We surely are."

"The word that was heard is of no avail if it does not unite itself with those who hear it, by means of faith" (Heb. 4:2). Every aid to hearing and understanding leads us on, to the point where faith becomes the critical factor. To explain the Scriptures is itself, in the last analysis, a science within the faith; and faith itself is not dependent in any way upon knowledge, as if it were a consequence thereof; rather, it comes about "through Christ, as an assurance in respect to God" (2 Cor. 3:4); and ultimately, it is a gift of God (Phil. 1:29).

2. New Testimony Theology and Other Theological Disciplines

What the special preserve of New Testament theology is can perhaps be best explained by showing how it is distinguished and differentiated from other theological disciplines.

It is obvious that New Testament theology is very closely bound up with New Testament exegesis, the latter dealing with the interpretation of particular passages of the Scriptural text. The exegesis of verse and pericope is taken from New Testament theology, set in order and understood in context. If New Testament theology presupposes and builds upon exegesis, it can also, for its own part, be of service to exegesis. Exegesis must not isolate individual passages. New Testament theology helps it to understand the separate part within the structure of the whole. On the other side, as exegesis progresses it is quite irresolute in compelling New Testament theology to make a critical examination of its comprehensive exposition, to promote and deepen it ever more and more. New Testament theology extols the content of the texts; and even to the present time its function is to make this content known.

New Testament theology is not part and parcel with Church history, as if it were but a history of the Church in the New Testament era. Certainly New Testament theology and Church history both search into the same documentary records of the New Testament. But each of these branches of study proceeds toward its separate goal. New Testament theology does its work with the purpose of lifting out revelation from the word handed down by means of Scripture. Church history, when it investigates the New Testament, seeks to reconstruct, in accord with the New Testament, the complete internal and external history of the primitive Church. It wants to be able to display, as evidenced in the primitive Church and, in fact, in the Church in every period of time, the workings of the word in and on the world.

Neither is New Testament theology the same thing as dogmatics. The task of dogmatics is to give a systematic presentation of the realities disclosed through the word of God, appropriate to the earlier as well as the modern ecclesiastical announcement of doctrine, in its history and in its orderly construction. The sources of dogmatics, then, are Scripture and Tradition — if indeed one may be permitted to distinguish between the two. New Testament theology and dogmatics are consequently distinct according to the range of their sources. They are also distinct as regards the goal of their scientific endeavors. New Testament theology writes principally about the findings of exegesis. Dogmatics systematizes ecclesiastical doctrine in view of the actual conditions, spiritual or otherwise, prevailing in history or at present within or without the ecclesial body. Dogmatics seeks, then, with the assistance of its conclusions, to advance beyond the traditional store of ideas and to give fresh development to the teachings of faith. All of this is beyond the boundaries of New Testament theology.

Much the same may be said of the relation of New Testament theology to moral theology. New Testament theology writes also about the New Testament doctrine in regard to Christian living. And moral theology likewise treats of the same. Moral theology, however, is the scientific exposition of the Church's whole body of doctrine on morals and life. The source material of moral theology is not only the New

Testament but the whole experience and tradition of the Church Moral theology, then, seeks to gain an understanding of the totality of modern life as it affects both the individual and society, and to set it in order, bringing the light of Christian principles to bear upon it. This goes far beyond the aims of New Testament theology.

Neither, however, can the relation between New Testament theology on the one hand and dogmatics and moral theology on the other be so defined as to make the task of New Testament theology the searching out and assembling of biblical passages to serve as propositions for dogmatics or moral theology, thereby laying the biblical foundations for the modern systems of dogmatic and moral theology. Ever since the golden age of Scholasticism, dogmatics has had the following structural arrangement: an introduction with deliberations on the nature of dogmatics and theology, followed by sections on God, one and triune; on creation; Christology and Soteriology, comprising a doctrine of redemption; and then the doctrine of grace, of the sacraments, and eschatology. Were New Testament theology to borrow this same order of categories, it would only be forcing itself into a foreign system. Considerable portions of our dogmatics are only hinted at, remaining as yet quite undeveloped in the New Testament.

On the other hand, much that is treated in great breadth and depth in the New Testament is given only summary exposition by our modern dogmatics (e.g., the doctrine of the Word). Much the same may be said in respect to systematic moral theology and the New Testament. An arrangement and systematization of New Testament theology cannot be imposed upon the New Testament from without but must be extracted from the New Testament itself. To apply modern systematic schemata to the New Testament is to do violence to the latter.

Nevertheless, New Testament theology will often give some thought to systematic theology and take it into account. It is of value to New Testament theology to view its questions in the perspective of latter ecclesiastical developments. In that way it can recognize which problems are included in the still simple biblical teaching; and from the history of doctrine, which interpretations of the biblical witness are possible. Ultimately, New Testament theology and systematic theology serve a common end — the exposition of the word and the revelation of God.[10]

The New Testament sum total of Christian faith and life, in comparison to the multifaceted dogmatics and moral theology developed in modern times, is necessarily undeveloped and incomplete. To offer but a few examples: the New Testament does not teach seven sacraments as unequivocally as does our modern dogmatics. Many propositions in the doctrine on grace were first proposed and decided in the course of historical development. Mariology, which constitutes a significant part of our modern dogmatics, is not yet articulated in the New Testament with anything of the intensity that it has today. The New Testament doctrine on state and society is incomplete because the problems and possibilities of the forms of society and government which history has since introduced were not yet known to the New Testament writings. The world of modern science and technology poses to the faith for consideration and resolution questions and problems which could not yet have been thought of in the New Testament.

If New Testament theology is undeveloped theology, its lack of completeness is not of such a kind as to cause it to be regarded as defective and of less value than the modern, more systematized theology. It is much more in view of historical rather than theological considerations that New Testament theology has its incomparable significance and value. The New Testament is the oldest documentary record of the Church. It is here that the faith and life, being and spirit, of the Church in all its primitive purity and initial perfection are described and certified. Purity, intensity, and strength of authority are properties of the New Testament.

In any spiritual movement the source remains normative for all future time; and the life of such a movement will remain forceful as long as it continues to acquire new strength from its roots and beginnings. Consequently, then, every later period must continually seek to acquire anew that faithful understanding of God, world, and man that is borne witness to in the New Testament, in order to gain a mastery in the same faith over the new questions and problems posed by a new era.

The New Testament, however, is in a still very much deeper sense normative for the Church, inasmuch as it was produced through the Spirit (2 Tim. 3:16; 2 Peter 1:21), an inspired document attesting to the faith. The doctrine of inspiration is not only a declaration of the fact that Scripture was written in the Spirit; rather, inspiration signifies that Scripture remains ever powerful in the strength of the Spirit. For the Church, therefore, Scripture is incomparably more normative and creative than any other book.

Since the New Testament is not only a report but a more significant account, and not only a directly challenging kerygma but a progressively pondered understanding of the faith and a body of apologetic, dogmatic, and ethical teaching, surely the New Testament is itself full of theology.[11] The word *theology* is not to be found in the New Testament; but be that as it may, what it signifies is there. An exposition of the theology of New Testament does not, therefore, undertake something inappropriate, nor does it impose something foreign upon the New Testament; rather, it lifts out and sheds light upon what is actually enclosed within the New Testament. It makes clearly intelligible what is contained therein and continues and correlates what was begun therein. And then dogmatic theology enters in, to carry on where New Testament theology leaves off.

Some expositions of New Testament theology may discuss whether Jesus himself, his word and his work, constitutes a part of New Testament theology or whether he is but the presupposition thereto, while New Testament theology first begins to exist with the pondering upon Jesus in the congregation and, before all else, with Paul and John. But if theology is the word about God, the word of Jesus and the revelation of God which comes to pass in him is the beginning and foundation of New Testament theology. It is on the basis of this revelation that the new word about God first becomes possible. If Christ is really the Word of God (John 1:1), then he is not only part, but the very center, of New Testament theology.

Finally, New Testament theology will not only describe the New Testament report but will interpret it. It will inquire after its content and the purposes of the forms of its declarations, which forms are perhaps unfamiliar to us; and it will relate the New Testament declarations to our modern questions and to our time.

3. History of New Testament Theology

"Bring along the books, especially the parchments," the Paul of the Pastoral Epistles asks a friend (2 Tim. 4:13). Certainly the term "the parchments" refers to the Old Testament Bible. We might understand the remark as an apostolic admonition to the Church, which, in its sojourning with all peoples in all times, has always brought along its books, and the Bible especially, known simply as "the book."

The books always required clarification. And thus exegesis has been practiced in the Church from the very beginning. The Bible, Old and New Testaments, already contains much in the way of interpretation; again and again matter already given is taken up anew, explained, and carried further. To begin with, if through the centuries the Bible was read personally by only a comparatively few Christians — indeed, few possessed the biblical books — nevertheless, it worked its powerful influence in the Church through various intermediaries. It was read in the Mass and explained in homilies. In mosaics, paintings, and stained glass the principal events of Old and New Testament salvation history were depicted in the churches, to be viewed by all. Theology regarded itself purely and simply as the science of the Bible. Until well into the Middle Ages, every teacher in the Church was also — in fact, principally — an interpreter of Holy Scripture. Toward the end of the Middle Ages, Duns Scotus, in his own time a teacher of the first rank, declared: "Our theology treats of nothing except that which is found in Scripture or which can be deduced from Scripture" (*Opus oxoniense*, prol., qu. 2).

In the radical changeover from the Middle Ages to modern times, there began also a new era for the Bible in the Church. The Renaissance, which rediscovered the Hebrew, Greek, and Latin manuscripts in the libraries, turned its attention to the Bible in its ancient languages. In 1516 Erasmus of Rotterdam published from the manuscripts the first printed edition of the Greek New Testament. The Reformation regarded the Bible as the solitary source and norm of revelation and of faith.

In the retinue of the Reformation came biblical theology, in its narrower sense, as part and proper division of exegetic theology. As the single source for the faith, the Bible was henceforth loosed by the Reformation from the connection which it had previously had with Tradition. The new dogmatics no longer continued the theology of the Fathers and of antiquity; rather, a new beginning had to be made and a new foundation laid. To this end the biblical passages for dogmatics were assembled together and interpreted in a connected fashion. Such collections were called *Collegia biblica* or *Vindiciae sacrae*. This happened in the seventeenth century. The designation "biblical theology" was first used as a book title in 1629 at Kempten by Wolfgang Johannes Christmann for his book *Teutsche Biblische Theologie*.

In the seventeenth and eighteenth centuries, Pietism made the concerns of biblical theology its own. In conformity with the general aim of Pietism, biblical theology was supposed to bring to acceptance the unvarnished doctrine and person of Christ, which Pietism found lacking in a Protestant theology that had become scholastically orientated. Under the far-reaching influence of Pietism, Carl Haymann, cathedral preacher and superintendent in Meissen, published his *Versuch einer biblischen Theologie* in 1708. A fourth edition of his work appeared in 1768.

The efforts surrounding biblical theology were then continued by the historical-critical biblical science of the Enlightenment. It wanted to treat New Testament doctrine like a historical report, extracting it from its sources; but soon it brought biblical theology into conflict with the prevailing dogmatics, in opposition to which it claimed to be the expositor of the genuine and historical Christianity in its primitive purity. Pertinent to this development was the address of Johann Philipp Gabler, given in 1787 at the University of Altdorf: *Oratio de iusto discrimine theologiæ biblicæ et dogmaticæ regendisque recte utriusque finibus*.

The first Catholic theologian who recognized, even if it was not yet written, the necessity of a biblical theology, was Johann Sebastian Drey. In his work *Kurze Einleitung in das Studium der Theologie mit Rücksicht auf den wissenschaftlichen Standpunkt und das katholische System* (Tübingen, 1819; reprinted at Frankfurt am Main, 1966, pp. 74–84), he demands, in addition to the biblical history, a biblical theology which is to be "the compilation of the doctrine of Christ and his Apostles. . . . Biblical theology must be regarded as the groundwork of all theological science." Drey, with his insight and challenge to theology, was far ahead of his time. Even today his challenge has not yet been met.

In the history of theology, Johann Anton Bernhard Lutterbeck deserves to be mentioned for his work *Die neutestamentlichen Lehrbegriffe* (2 vols., Mainz, 1852). The work provides, in a strongly educative spirit, a detailed exposition of the New Testament surroundings and historical period, along with sketches of the Petrine, Pauline, and Johannine doctrine and their content. About one hundred years ago, Karl Werner, of the theological faculty of Vienna, gave his lectures entitled *Lineamenta theologiæ biblicæ Novi Testamenti*. Theophilus Simar must be mentioned with respect on account of his *Die Theologie des heiligen Paulus* (Freiburg im Breisgau, 2nd ed., 1883). The first Catholic book with the title "New Testament theology" is the work of A. Lemonnyer, *Théologie du Nouveau Testament* (Paris, 1928; new edition by L. Cerfaux, Paris, 1963). The first Catholic work of such title in German was supplied by M. Meinertz, *Theologie des Neuen Testaments* (2 vols., Bonn, 1950). It could say of itself: "This book is the first complete and detailed exposition of New Testament theology from the Catholic viewpoint." Others deserving of mention are: J. Bonsirven, *Théologie du Nouveau Testament*, (Paris, 1951), a book that gives special attention to the relation of the new covenant to the old. R. Schnackenburg, *Neutestamentliche Theologie* (2nd ed., Munich, 1965), gives a critical and continuing bibliography of the whole area of New Testament theology. There appear therein in increasing numbers monographs on New Testament concepts or even on larger areas such as Christology, eschatology, theology of John, of Paul, etc.

General theological as well as biblical encyclopedias take New Testament theology into account. In our own times Protestant theology, continuing its work, has produced significant presentations of the theology of the New Testament, thereby doing a service even for Catholic exegesis. To be mentioned among recent works are: P. Feine, *Theologie des Neuen Testaments* (8th ed., Berlin, 1951); R. Bultmann, *Theologie des Neuen Testaments* (6th ed., Tübingen, 1968); H. Conzelmann, *Grundriss der Theologie des Neuen Testaments* (2nd ed., Munich, 1968); W. G. Kümmel, *Die Theologie des Neuen Testaments nach seinen Hauptzeugen* (Göttingen, 1969).

Among English-language works we might make mention of F. C. Grant, *An Introduction to New Testament Thought* (New York, 1950); A. Richardson, *An Introduction to the Theology of the New Testament* (London, 1958); F. Stagg, *New Testament Theology* (Nashville, 1962).

4. Method of Procedure

Basically there are two possibilities which present themselves in the drafting of a New Testament theology. One possibility is to treat the epochs of the New Testament proclamation according to their leading figures, each in a separate section; Synoptics, Primitive Congregation, Paul, John, Late Apostolic Writings. Such is the plan of most presentations, including those of M. Meinertz, J. Bonsirven, R. Schnackenburg; and such too is the plan of the presentations of the Protestant theology of P. Feine, R. Bultmann, H. Conzelmann, and W. G. Kümmel. The disadvantage of this plan is that it does not allow the great themes to be presented except in a disjointed fashion, and does not show their progressive development throughout the New Testament.

The other possibility is to pursue ideas and themes of the New Testament proclamation through to the end of the New Testament, and to treat the areas of faith and life comprehensively. Obviously, in this plan the actual theology of important biblical books and epochs or of authoritative Apostles (like Pauline theology or Johannine theology) could not be presented as a unit. A thematically planned New Testament theology might perhaps be organized in the following manner:

    I. Creation (World, Time, Man);
    II. Revelation in History and in Salvation History (Jesus Christ and the Redemption; God, Spirit, Trinity);
    III. Christian Life, (New Testament Morality);
    IV. God's Dominion, Church, Consummation.

The treatment of the individual themes, greater and lesser, would then follow the historical development within the New Testament itself.

I. BASIC CONCEPTS

§ 2. MORALITY AS OBEDIENCE DICTATED BY FAITH

Two considerations can be set down beforehand for the sake of introducing an explanatory distinction in respect to the New Testament morality: the first concerns philosophical ethics [*Ethik*] and biblical morality [*Ethos*]; the other, Old and New Testament morality.[12]

1. PHILOSOPHICAL ETHICS AND BIBLICAL MORALITY

In primitive times the gods were the guardians of justice and of morals. Morality has its basis in religion. Philosophical ethics is detached from this oldest of arrangements; and it erects its system fundamentally out of rational deliberation and insight into the spiritual-moral tendency of man and the ethical problems which he meets in his time and world. The basis and point of departure for this ethics is human reason. The law governing men is man himself, just as he is encountered both as an individual and as a member of the community.

Socrates and Plato, the great teachers of Greek ethics, made their ethics conform to the idea of the good. The good is the highest idea, and God himself. Through the power of *eros*, man is moved to the performance of the good. Whoever recognizes the good will do what is good, for the good draws men irresistibly along. This philosophical ethics remains religiously determined. The good is the holy and the divine. Platonic ethics is strongly community-oriented and politically interested. Ethics ought to realize the ideal of human community. Plato founded ethical idealism, which remained immutable.

23

In the Stoa, the ethics of which became vastly significant for the Western world, the ethical ideal is to live in conformity with nature, in accord with reason, the logos. The human logos participates in the pantheistically conceived divine logos, which is the world-reason. The law of nature is an expression of the eternal law of God. Even this ethics, then, is based in religion. The ethics of the Stoa continues to exist in the teaching that there is a natural law; this teaching came to have a special importance for Catholic moral theology.

In the evaluative ethics of more recent times, the ethical system is drawn up as a system for the man of prudent standards, and it is a system which is both discovered and realized through actual behavior. Such, perhaps, can be perceived in the ethics of German idealism, as well as in the ethics of Immanuel Kant, and afterwards, to mention a very important name, in the ethics of Max Scheler. Existentialism is experimenting with a new presentation of ethics. Man is met within the I-thou relationship. Ethics is in reference to one's fellowman. It demands a structured submission to the community.

In modern ethics man understands, as it were his basic principle, that he is himself his own law. His ethics is autonomous. This does not mean willfulness or licentiousness, but simply that man is himself really *law*. Nor does autonomous ethics in any way mean atheism. Kant requires religion as postulate for the realization of ethics. Accordingly, duty appears to be divine command. Deep relationships were formed between German idealism and (Protestant) theology. Autonomous ethics could certainly continue on to the abandoning of religion, and in part it did in fact expand in that direction. Thereafter ethics was said to be godless, and ethics was also said to be the only true religion.

Whether a purely autonomous ethics is within the realm of possibility is a question, not for biblical theology, but for moral philosophy. Scholars will continue to argue whether moral law, when it is discovered, is really derived from the autonomy of man or whether it does in fact depend in a less obvious way upon religion and its adjuncts.

The New Testament and the whole Bible in general gives no systematic presentation of moral conduct; but it does contain more than a few reflections upon moral regulations and a great deal of admonition, by way of general principles as well as by concrete examples. It is better, therefore, to speak, not of biblical ethics, but of biblical morality. Systematic Christian ethics is founded thereon. Biblical morality, in its establishment and in its goal, does not claim to be rationally demonstrable; rather, it is morality out of obedience to the word of God, morality on the daring venture of faith, as daring as faith itself. Biblical morality and Christian ethics as well are theonomous. Dogmatics and ethics as well are parts of the Christian teaching of faith. Accordingly, the basis and goal of moral conduct are determined in conformity to the biblical understanding thereof.

The basis of moral conduct is reverential fear in the face of God's majesty and obedience to God's word, his command and call. Obedience does not first inquire after the justification of commands, in order to obey only if it understands the necessity of a command; rather, it obeys in faithful submission to the will of God. The goal of moral conduct is the showing forth of the order and honor of God (". . . so that men may see your good works and give praise to the Father, who is in heaven"— Matthew 5:16).

That God's will is the measure of morality is among the properties of God adduced by both Old and New Testaments. He is holy; indeed, one only is holy, God (Lev. 19:2; 1 Peter 1:16). He is good; indeed, one only is good, God (Mark 10:18). Since the moral man recognizes and believes that God is the Holy One and he that is good, he knows that he himself is not, in view of God's command, handed over to caprice but is submitted to salvation, and that this moral law does not impose extraneous control on him but is able to set free his inmost being while perfecting it.

If biblical morality is obedience, we must consider the nature of this obedience. It is not an obedience toward man, but obedience as giving heed to the directing and saving word of God, an obedience not in compulsion but unto freedom. In treating of New Testament morality, therefore, it is necessary to speak not only of obedience but also of freedom.

Biblical morality is not unrelated to natural and philosophical ethics. A distillate of the wisdom poetry of old Oriental cultures (of Egypt and Mesopotamia) is to be found in the collected proverbs of Israel's wisdom. Greek philosophy works its influence on Hellenistic

Judaism. Now the teaching about virtue is given a rational basis; it is an "order" that is necessary and has its own precious worth. The admonitions continue to be referred to God, since it is he that produced the creation-like arrangement of the universe (Prov. 3:13-26). The Law of Moses was conceived as the perfected expression of the natural moral law: "We believe that the Law originates with God; but we know also that the Lawgiver of the world gives his Law in accord with nature" (4 Macc. 5:25). Philo carried out in breadth and depth the synthesis between the Torah and the law of nature.[13]

Paul accepted the then current concept of the natural law but inserted it into the context of the belief in creation. Accordingly, the law of nature is God's dictum to man and God's operation in man. Paul speaks expressly of the natural law: "If the [pagan] peoples, who have no law, do by nature what the Law prescribes, these, who have no law, are law unto themselves. They show forth the requirements of the law, as written in their hearts. And their conscience too bears testimony" (Rom. 2:14-15). Even the pagans know the moral law as the law of nature, as demonstrated by their actions, and even by their accusing consciences. Greek ethics is aware of *conscience*, both the word and the concept (see Vol. 1, p. 137, of the present work).

Paul even presumes the existence of a natural order when he condemns homosexual conduct as being "contrary to nature" (Rom. 1:26). He argues in the tradition of Stoic ethics, according to which the observance of the law implanted in us by nature constitutes moral conduct, since the Divinity, in which the world is grounded, is manifest in nature. Drawing on the intellectual heritage of Stoicism, Cicero (*De legibus*, 2, 4, 10) says: "The true and highest law, forceful in commanding and in forbidding, is the Supreme Divinity's design of right reason." The passages cited from Paul can be grouped together along with Rom. 1:18-23, according to which, reason is able to recognize God's divinity. Through the medium of Hellenistic Judaism (Wis. 13:5), no doubt, Paul is, even in this instance, under the influence of Stoic philosophy (see Vol. 1, p. 23, of the present work). Nevertheless, men have perverted the proffered possibility of coming to a recognition of God and of the moral law. They became idolators (Rom. 1:23), and all, Jews and Gentiles alike, stand subservient to sin (Rom. 3:9-20).

The hortatory character of the Apostle's letters opens them even wider to the influence of Hellenistic ethics. The New Testament borrows the word and concept *moral virtue*. It borrows conventional rules and regulations for its tables of duties to one's neighbor, as in the catalogues of virtues and vices (see below, ch. 17). Paul treats of fundamentals when he says: "Whatever is true, whatever honorable, whatever just, whatever pure, whatever agreeable, whatever praiseworthy, if there be any virtue, anything laudable, give thought to these" (Phil. 4:8). Also included in this list are concepts from Stoic doctrine in regard to virtue. The influence of secular social ethics is especially clear in the Pastoral Epistles, for example, when they characterize the Christian faith as piety (see below, ch. 18).

In the later history of moral theology, the influence of philosophical ethics on the moral doctrine of the Church increased and became even deeper.[14]

2. MORALITY OF OLD AND NEW TESTAMENTS

The morality of the Old Testament and of the New Testament is a morality of obedience. The Israel of the Old Testament and early Judaism as well had a clear recognition of this characteristic of the Jewish moral command. The basic axiom holds good: "It was told you, O man, what is good and what the Lord demands of you: To do only what is just, to love what is good, and to walk humbly with your God" (Micah 6:8). God's word provides the basis for the moral law. This law is the right and the good. It is realized in constant and faithful association with God. Israel perceived the morality of obedience not as a burden but as honor and grace, since the will of God was manifest to it. The pagan lives in the dark (Ps. 147:19-20). The extraordinarily long Psalm 119 (from the post-exilic period) is a unique testimonial to Israel's thanksgiving for the law and her joy therein. As God's living word, it is grace and salvation without end.

For the New Testament period, Rabbinic literature is able to clarify Judaism's moral conduct and its understanding of the Law. The commandments are obeyed because they are divine commands. Rabbi Johanan († *ca.* 80 A.D.) prohibits any critical questioning about the content of the laws of purification, at the same time declaring it a matter of indifference: "Neither can a corpse make unclean, nor can water make clean. For he that is holy has said: A statute I have fixed, an ordinance I have decreed. No man is authorized to transgress my ordinance. For it is determined: This is the way of my Law." It suffices for this ethic, therefore, to know that God has so commanded. That is why the command is good and why the deed in accord with the law is good.

From the standpoint of faith, this conduct is thoroughly righteous. But still, there are hazards therein. A morality based on obedience can turn into empty legalism. And the demands of such a morality can be insisted upon so long, and only so long, as a command perdures. What is not written down in statutory fashion seems not to be required. It is also possible to infer and conclude that all that is commanded can be considered as equally important and equally essential, because it is just as certainly a divine command. Perhaps on the one hand, commands of worshiping and demands of morality and of social justice, and on the other hand, ritual and ceremonial prescriptions in regard to cultic practices, or even unimportant legal usages, since they are all God's laws, are not formally distinguished one from another. They appear side by side, all under the same sanction (Exod. 34: 14-26; Lev. 19; Ez. 18:5-17).[15]

In the extracting of moral directives from the Old Testament, certain weighty and complicated basic questions arise. The God of the old covenant is the God also of the new. Like biblical theology, so too is biblical morality one, whether in the Old or New Testament. New Testament moral doctrine, therefore, harks back again and again to the Old Testament. Nevertheless, there is much that is morally possible in the old covenant which is clearly impossible in the new; witness the laws on polygamy, on slavery, and on the regulating of punishments. The cultural, social, and religious viewpoints and conditions have changed fundamentally from the Old Testament to the New, and from the New Testament to our own times. Often enough it is possible to extract from the Old Testament assertions which are frankly contradictory to New Testament morality; and in the light of these contrarieties what is proper to New Testament moral teaching is made clear.

In quoting the Old Testament, the New Testament often employs methods of interpretation to which we can no longer subscribe. Indeed, our method must be to search out what is behind the texts, in order to discover the will of the living God; and this is the method employed by Jesus in the Sermon on the Mount.

By way of example, we might recall how Israel, after the annexation of Canaan, found a new lifestyle. In Egypt and during the desert sojourn, Israel had come to know Yahweh as God of war and as Leader in the wilderness. Now Israel withdrew into Canaan and changed its manner of living from the nomadic to the agricultural. The fields, the vineyards, and the labor of the farmer were under the protection of the gods of Canaan, Baal and Astarte. Would not Israel invite the anger of these gods if she declined to worship them? Would not the fruitful fields dry up if the gods who bestowed this fruitfulness were no longer adored? For Israel it was a perilous problem.

Against this temptation prophets and priests did battle, exhorting Israel to be faithful to her God. A part of Israel opted for the manner of life of the Rechabites (Jer. 35:1-19). They rejected the new culture and continued, as formerly in the desert, to dwell in tents, believing that thus they would keep faith with the God of their fathers. By far the greater part of Israel, however, chose otherwise; they understood that their task was to keep faith with Yahweh, the God of their fathers, even under this new style of living. Israel, in obedience to the God of the covenant and in reliance on him, attained to the essential understanding of how to live and carry on in her new circumstances; and she erected a new order of affairs on the foundations of her old faith.

In the new covenant a new world is created through the words and works of Christ and through the mission of the Spirit. Moreover, the very existence of each and every man is given a new basis. From this new being a new behavior must follow. The believer attests his belonging to the living Christ first in his creed and in praise of God in words, and then even in his conduct in the world. According to the New Testament, faith in Jesus Christ demands that a certain direction be applied to the life of man in this world — therefore, a specific morality. That is why there are so many assertions to be found in the

New Testament which bear witness concerning the new behavior expected of the Christian and which admonish him to such conduct in
the faith. The ethical precepts are not something apart from the dogmatic propositions; rather, both together constitute a unique testimonial of faith.

3. MATERIAL AND FORMAL ETHICS

A presentation of New Testament morality must deal with fundamental questions. It has been denied that it is even possible to construct an objective New Testament ethics, devoted to a content of
norms and commands. The New Testament, it has been maintained,
exhibits no individual injunctions, but only the command of love.
Whoever loves, knows in individual concrete cases what is demanded
of him. The norm is sufficient: . . . as oneself. To set up commands
and prohibitions is but legalistic moralizing. The concrete, moral
"thou shalt" is inseparable from the suggestion of personal decision.

In a Pauline ethics, however, it is certainly true that the Spirit
given to every Christian is the basis and ordering of his moral conduct. Does not the evidence of the New Testament, with its many
hortatory texts, militate against such a denial of a concrete ethics?
Certainly love is the great command, in which all others are included
(Matthew 22:34-40; Gal. 5:14). Nevertheless, the one command of
love is interpreted both by Jesus (Matthew 19:18-21) and by the
Apostle (Gal. 5:19-24) in specific actions.

The denial of a material ethics — as, for example, in R. Bultmann [16] — is certainly a part of the basic existential interpretation of
the New Testament. It shares both in the triumphs and in the uncertainties of the existential interpretation. In ethics it voices the essential
concern that morality must realize the good in free, personal choice.
Nevertheless, as norm and duty, the good is higher than and prior to
the person and his situation. Admittedly it is seldom easy to determine the norm with certainty; and the situation of man in his daily
business affairs is rarely entirely unequivocal. Thus there remains
great latitude in the area of judgment; and it is here that a decision
must be risked. Law and system reach their limits at the point where

man stands directly in the presence of God. Order must not become rigid system or statutory casuistry. That would be Pharisaism, against which Matthew (23:4, 16-36) warns us.

In evaluating a purely formal ethics, it must not be forgotten that the philosophy of Immanuel Kant produces an after-effect in which formal obligation is elevated to the principle of morality ("Behave in such manner that the maxim of your will can be considered each time as the principle of universal legislation"). The moral worth of the person demands, therefore, that the moral will itself be law. Just as duty and moral good are here equated, so too with the New Testament command to love, understood as formal morality.[17]

I. INSTRUCTION AND CHALLENGE OF JESUS

As in Israel, so too for Jesus [18] the moral life is ordered by God's command. It is articulated fundamentally in the decalogue and in the chief commandment of love. In replying to a questioner, Jesus referred to the list of commandments: "You know the commandments. Thou shalt not kill; thou shalt not commit adultery; thou shalt not steal; thou shalt not bear false witness; thou shalt not defraud. Honor father and mother" (Mark 10:19). To the question about the chief commandment Jesus responds with Deut. 6:4-5 and Lev. 19:18, "Thou shalt love the Lord thy God. . . . Thou shalt love thy neighbor" (Mark 12:29-31).

Nevertheless, along with every conformity between the old and new covenants, it is necessary also to determine what is distinctive. Certainly the morality of both covenants is a morality of obedience. But the New Testament morality is new and different in this respect, that the foundation and bearing of its obedience is different from that of the old. This newness can be characterized as follows:

1) The Old Testament command is interpreted by Christ with a view to the demands of completeness and subjectivity.

2) Obedience is understood as emanating from Jesus, the new Image of God.

3) Obedience is demanded with extreme urgency in view of the nearness of the kingdom of God.

4) Obedience is defined as the imitating of Jesus.

5) Obedience is now made possible as life in the Spirit.

These five characteristics are equally validated in regard to the teachings of Jesus in the Gospel and in respect to the preaching of the Apostles.

1. The Demand of Completeness and Inwardness

In the written law and in the interpretational traditions surrounding it, Israel found the unqualified will of God; and she endeavored, through a precise fulfillment of the law and commandments, to attain to righteousness. The risk of mishap in the externals of this legalism was great and could not always be avoided (see above, p. 28).

The preaching of Jesus presents a vigorous opposition to the legalistic view of the law. In this contest he did not have to combat behavior prompted by ill-will and a spirit of contempt for the law; rather, he had to struggle against an interpretation of the law which claimed and actually believed itself to be the product of zeal for the law. Jesus refused to regard man's relationship to God as a relationship in law. Man is obligated not merely to the extent of the written law. He is fully constrained, and he cannot excuse himself before God on the grounds that he has observed the written law and is in all other respects free. That is the sense of the antitheses in the Sermon on the Mount: "You have heard that it was said to the ancients. . . . I, however, say to you . . ." (Matthew 5:21-48). The "ancients" are not those who were at that time well-advanced in years, not parents and grandparents, but the generation of the fathers. To them was it said on Sinai: "Thou shalt not kill. . . ." And the legal doctrine drew therefrom the conclusion: This only is forbidden.

Jesus, however, explains that the mere letter of the law is not nearly sufficient. Even angry intent is forbidden, because it is as wicked as the deed itself (Matthew 5:21-26). And again: Whoever shuns adultery but tolerates lustful desire in his heart has neither understood nor fulfilled the commandment, for it enjoins total chastity (Matthew 5:27-32). Jesus demonstrates to casuistry that it selfishly twists the law and turns the law to sterile legalism. He warns about this abuse and demands that the sense of the law be fulfilled. So with the thought underlying just and proportionate punishment: an eye for an eye, a tooth for a tooth (Matthew 5:38-41). Somewhere in the ancient Orient this law may have been devised to bridle a man's immoderate vengeance, and non-biblical casuistry may have used it as a right to vengeance.

Jesus demands anew the sense of the law, which desires justice and is productive of gentleness and a spirit of forgiveness: "Resist not the evildoer! Whoever strikes you on the right cheek, turn to him the left also" (Matthew 5:39). The letter of divorce was also subject to abuse.

Although it was in itself already an infringement against the pristine ideal of marriage as established by the hand of the Creator, it should have served equally well to circumscribe the arbitrariness of the husband and to protect the rights of the wife, since it forbade the husband to dismiss his wife on mere caprice and demanded grounds and orderliness in such an event. The thrust of the law, therefore, was marital fidelity. Nevertheless, out of the letter of divorce had developed the alleged right of the husband to free himself from the obligations of marital fidelity. Jesus therefore demanded anew the sense of the law — radical fidelity (Matthew 5:31-32).

The law of love enjoined: Thou shalt love thy brother, thy fellow countryman — in short, each and every human being. Those who were other than fellow countrymen were formerly outside the narrow circle of tribal limits. And now the commandment had come to be interpreted as enjoining love of neighbor and hatred of others. Jesus, however, explains that whoever is amiable only toward his friends does not know what love really is. Total love commands the loving even of one's enemies (Matthew 5:43-47). The Sermon on the Mount, therefore, declares forevermore: God does not bind man only to the extent that behavior is prescribed by formal commands, leaving the intent of a man free beyond that point. The demand of God goes far beyond the demand of law with its casuistry. It demands the good will of man toward all men. And in the face of this demand there is no excuse and no possibility of escape.

The law, with its many commands, should not hedge a man in, cramping and crippling him. It should free him to the truth and help him to salvation. Therefore Jesus repeatedly urges consideration of the spirit and intent of the law as opposed to its juridical-casuistic interpretation. He insists on the spirit of the law of purification, which is directed not to external but to internal purity. "You clean the outside of the cup and the dish, but the inside is full of rapacity and greed. Blind Pharisee! First purify the inside, then the outside will also be clean" (Matthew 23:25-26).

Jesus insists on recognition and fulfillment of the purpose of the law, which is directed to the salvation of man because God wills this salvific healing. That is why Jesus heals on the Sabbath. A command like that of the Sabbath, and commands in general, can and must be tempered to what is salvific. "The Sabbath is for the sake of man, and not man for the Sabbath" (Mark 2:27). Jesus insists on the deed as essential and on the doing of what is essential. This the law does too: "Woe to you, you Scribes and Pharisees! You pay tithes on mint, dill and anise, and leave undone the weightier matters of the law, right judgment and mercy and fidelity. These things you ought to have done, while not leaving the others undone! You blind guides, you that strain out the gnat and swallow the camel" (Matthew 23:23-24).

Jesus demands love as the tempering of the law. In response to the question about the greatest commandment, he says: "Thou shalt love the Lord thy God with thy whole heart, and with thy whole soul, and with thy whole strength. Thou shalt love thy neighbor as thyself. On these two commandments depend the whole law and the prophets" (Matthew 22:37-40). The morality of obedience is established anew. Jesus requires obedience, total obedience, to the spirit of the law.

2. The Obedience of the Child to His Father

The morality of the New Testament is obedience to God. Jesus reveals and announces that God is Father (see Vol. 1 of the present work, pp. 103–106). The new image of God includes a new morality. It is the attitude of the child in the presence of and with the Father in heaven. The disciple must be like the child who is prepared to give wholly of himself, with no thought of any right to payment or reward. "Whoever does not accept the kingdom of God like a little child, will not enter into it" (Mark 10:15).

Since God is the Father, the child knows his word and his will as the ordering of his life. Submission to God's will is not forced, but takes place in confidence and in love. The child of the Father dissociates himself from everything that God's will opposes, from everything that is sin. The condition of childhood demands a struggling after the good, because God is good, and his goodness constitutes his being. Thus the command to love is given a new foundation: ". . . so that you may be sons of your Father in heaven, who makes his sun to rise on the evil and on the good, who sends his rain on the just and on the unjust" (Matthew 5:45). This holds good for the whole area of moral endeavor in general: "Be perfect, as your Father in heaven is perfect" (Matthew 5:48).

3. THE KINGDOM OF GOD

The kingdom of God is in the process of arriving — indeed, it is already present. It is still hidden, but present nevertheless in Christ and in the community called by him. "The kingdom of God is among you" (Luke 17:21). And still that kingdom belongs to the future. The Church, therefore, is instructed to pray unceasingly for its coming: "Thy kingdom come" (Matthew 6:10). Now the total arrival of God presses on from the very edge and brink of the world and time. The kingdom, then, is a power that decides the present. Man stands forever in the apprehension of God's arrival, an event which for him is both judgment and salvation.

In the Gospels, as also in the Epistles and in the Apocalypse, the eschatological reckoning calls for readiness, watchfulness, prudence, sobriety, probity, and hope. All the problems, qualities, and values of man stand in the light and under the judgment of this future event: nature and world, poverty and riches, marriage and family, culture and genius. "As it was in the days of Noah, so too will it be in the days of the Son of Man. They ate, drank, married, bought and sold, planted and built, until Noah went into the ark. And the flood came and destroyed all" (Luke 17:26-27). The world is now as it was then — in the moment before God's entry. In the face of this, everything else loses its overweening importance. It demands the renunciation of possessions, the setting aside of home and family, indeed, even of oneself: "If anyone comes to me and does not hate his father and wife and children and brothers and sisters, yes, his very life, he cannot be my disciple" (Luke 14:26-27).

There is now but one thing necessary, and this must determine a man's behavior. The disciple must be prepared to set all else aside for the sake of this: If your hand scandalize you, if your foot scandalize you, give them up (Mark 9:43-48). It may even be necessary, in order to enter into the kingdom, to be celibate (Matthew 19:12). Whoever loses sight of these conditions is as much a fool as the rich grain-farmer. He counts on earthly possessions and believes he can be secure therein; and he forgets to take into account that which is critical, the fact that at any moment his life can be demanded of him (Luke 12:16-20). Only one thing matters — that a man gain entry to God's kingdom. Indeed, it is not as if, in view of his virtues, a man might merit the kingdom — it is always a gift. But faith and fulfillment of God's will are conditions of entry. The disciple, therefore, must take pains to go in through the narrow gate that leads to life (Matthew 7:13). The important thing is to seek first the kingdom of God and his justice (Matthew 6:33). Thus it is that the relentless approach of the kingdom of God determines the moral life of the disciple.

4. The Following of Jesus

The Gospels report both how the multitude and how the narrower circle of Jesus' disciples followed after him; and those reports are in fact a summons to join in this following. The import of this summons is that, from the external, tag-along sort of following that the multitude practices, this following must become a deeper sort, a following of Christ in the only true sense, as a life-companionship with the Master. When the young man comes to Jesus and says to him, "I want to follow you," Jesus replies to him, "Go back, sell what you own, and give it to the poor. Then come and follow me" (Mark 10:21). In this instance "follow" means to share with Jesus in his life-style of poverty and resignation to the will of God.

"Following," then, signifies following in being of service: "Whoever wishes to be great among you, let him be your servant; and whoever wishes to be first, let him be the slave of all. For the Son of Man has not come in order to be served, but to serve" (Mark 10:43-45). Such following demands constant self-abnegation and a readiness for total renunciation: "If anyone wishes to follow after me, let him deny himself and daily take his cross upon himself and follow after me" (Mark 8:34; for an explanation of the words, see below, ch. 12).

The Gospel of John also speaks of Christ's being the ethical model for his disciples. After doing them the service of washing their feet, Christ says: "I have given you an example, that as I have done to you, so you also should do" (John 13:15). And more about the central commandment of love: "A new commandment I give you, that you should love one another; as I have loved you, you also ought love one another" (John 13:34). And in general: "Whoever loves me keeps my word" (John 14:23). The morality of the disciple and of his daily conduct is founded on the following of Jesus and on obedience to his word and example.[19]

5. Life and Conduct from the Spirit

Certainly the post-Pentecostal preaching of the Apostles was the earliest development of the doctrine about the Spirit who operates in the lives of the faithful. Nevertheless, the Gospels, which know that "the Spirit had not yet been given, because Jesus had not yet been glorified" (John 7:39), already point out the future period of the Spirit. John the Baptist points ahead to the baptism which the coming Messiah will dispense in Holy Spirit and fire (Matthew 3:11). The promise designates moral purification and renewal as gifts of the Spirit. Jesus himself says that in the necessity wrought of persecution the Spirit will be word and strength of the disciples: "For it is not you who are speaking, but the Spirit of your Father who speaks through you" (Matthew 10:19-20). The Spirit is the faculty of bearing witness, of being strong and of persevering. He it is who performs the actions of the moral life.

The doctrine of John's Gospel is even more closely developed. Face to face with Nicodemus, Jesus discloses that the rebirth in water and Spirit makes possible the entry into the kingdom of God: "That which is born of the flesh is flesh. That which is born of the Spirit is spirit" (John 3:6). Man is by nature flesh. The existence which belongs to him is naturally mortal; its mode is perishability and nothingness. Through the Spirit man becomes a new creation, yes, he becomes himself spirit; and spirit portends the divine world hereafter. Thus man is withdrawn from his nothingness, and his life and work acquire true value. In his farewell discourse in John's Gospel,

Jesus promises the Spirit of truth, who will teach the disciples and be their Advocate (John 14:26; 15:26; 16:5-10). Thereby the morality of the New Testament first becomes truly a new testament, since it not only commands and requires but also imparts the capability of fulfilling what is demanded. Therefore the command now no longer works unto sin and judgment as in the Old Testament; rather, the command itself is gospel, truly good tidings of salvation.[20]

II. PREACHING AND DOCTRINE OF THE APOSTLES

The preaching of the Apostles develops the moral doctrine of the Gospels to the fullness of the New Testament witness. As with the whole of the New Testament announcement, so too with the moral doctrine thereof, it is not to be expected that the word of Jesus and the preaching of the Apostles will be simply and in every respect identical. Differences of methodology, of persons, of times — all these things are bound to produce their effects.

Christ speaks in sublime simplicity, with a primitiveness born of clarity and truth, in obvious union with the Father, and as master of every situation. The Apostles cannot speak in such manner. They are theologians who reflect, reason out, and demonstrate. Paul is a prime example. He reasons laboriously with syllogisms, clarifying and proving his propositions for himself and for others. Through questions and doubts he continues on to arrive at understandinig and to reach a lucidity of expression. No man can boast of having been Jesus' teacher; but the Apostles have received many suggestions and helps. Paul makes use of words, concepts, and notions of diverse origins, the heritage of traditions, both Jewish and Greek.

One other critical distinction, even for ethics, is that which is evidenced in their sayings, and proceeds from the disparity of persons, from the difference in the being and in the lives of Jesus and the Apostles. Christ is the sinless one, whose innermost quality of being untouched by sin is attested to by the Gospels as well as by the preaching of the Apostles: "Who among you can convict me of even a single sin?" (John 8:46). "He knew no sin" (2 Cor. 5:21). The Apostles are all converts who have, sad to say, experienced sin in their own lives and have passed through violations and catastrophes, coming finally to faith and renewal of life. They are obliged to speak as Paul does: To wish is within my power, but to accomplish is not. . . . Wretched man that I am, who will deliver me from the body of this death! (Rom. 7:18, 24). Christ is the Son, who lives in the unity of the Father. The Apostles are men in the midst of men, the guilty in the midst of the guilty. That is why an ethical message and admonition from the mouth of Jesus must be different from an admonition from the mouths of the Apostles.

Finally there is necessarily a difference because of the changing times. Jesus and the Apostles live and speak in different eras. In the preaching of Jesus the redemption is announced as belonging to the future; messianic salvation is still hidden. Not so in the era of the Apostles. The salvational event has already been completed in the incarnation, death, and resurrection of the Lord. The Apostles are looking back upon it; they must think of it and speak of it in its aftermath, in the new era. The reconciliation has already taken place. Now there is righteousness, salvation, Spirit, new life in Christ. And this new reality of salvation points beyond itself to its consummation in the future. This new situation is to be announced and coordinated with the message proclaimed by the Apostles. In consequence of this necessary development, the doctrine of the Apostles about moral life in accord with the gospel has its origins in the preaching of Jesus.

Under the presupposition of these distinctions, the doctrine of the Apostles can be described from a viewpoint similar to that of the moral instruction of the gospel.[21]

1. THE OLD TESTAMENT WORD OF GOD

The Old Testament moral commands retain their validity even in the preaching of the Apostles. "Christ is the end of the law" (Rom. 10:4), and the gospel is freedom from the law (Rom. 7:6; Gal. 3:10-13). Nevertheless, in many instances Paul strengthens his admonitions with Old Testament passages (Rom. 12:16-20; 1 Cor. 5:13; 2 Cor. 8:15, 21; 9:7-10; Eph. 4:25; 6:2-17; Phil. 2:15). That the law is at an end is valid for the totality of the Old Testament ritual law (Rom. 14:14, 20; Col. 2:16f.). Certainly the moral law of the Old Testament is abolished as a way to salvation through works; but it remains as a norm for living. But even in this capacity it must be viewed with a critical eye. The Old Testament law must not turn into a deadly legalism (2 Cor. 3:6). The spirit of the law and the core around which its provisions center is love; and the law of love must be fulfilled (Rom. 13:9). Paul interprets the law, even as Jesus did, according to its substance.

Later Epistles pursue their hortatory ends by means of the Old Testament (Heb. 3:7-11; 12:5-6, 12-13). The elegantly hortatory Epistle of James draws heavily upon Old Testament Jewish tradition. The Catholic Epistles make even further use of the body of Old Testament sayings (1 Peter 2:17; 3:10-12).

The moral command of the Old Testament is valid for the New Testament to the extent that the figures of the Old Testament are examples for the Christian. Abraham is an example of the faith by which man is justified (Gal. 3:8-9; Rom. 4:1-22). Sara is an example for Christian women, who are her daughters (1 Peter 3:6). The Old Testament witnesses to faith from Abraham to David are examples of faith for Christians, who have "a swarm of witnesses before their eyes" (Heb. 11).

2. Sonship from God

The preaching of the Apostles likewise speaks of the fatherhood of God and of the sonship of men, and says that this relationship constitutes a new moral dimension: "Indeed, you have not received the spirit of bondage, productive of fear; rather, you have received the spirit of sonship, in which we cry, 'Abba, Father dear!'" (Rom. 8:15). To stand in the relationship of sonship to God implies the obligation of allowing oneself to be led by the Spirit of God, as by a father. "Whoever are led by the Spirit of God, they are sons of God" (Rom. 8:14). The proximity of God demands purity and integrity.

After Paul has called attention to the fact that, in accord with the Old Testament promise, God will be the Father of his sons and daughters, he goes on: "Since we are the possessors of these promises, we want to purify ourselves of every defilement of flesh and spirit" (2 Cor. 7:1). The sons of God must bear a resemblance to the Father: "Be imitators of God, as beloved children; and walk in love, even as Christ has loved you" (Eph. 5:1).

The First Epistle of John draws out in an emphatic manner the ethical inferences of the declaration of our filiation from God. Sonship to God and sin are incompatible opposites. "Whoever is born of God does not sin, because God's seed is in him. He cannot sin because he is born of God" (1 John 3:9). The believer is, through God's own begetting and by God's own seed, a child of God. As long as God's seed, the basis of our sonship, is lively and active in the man who is justified, such a one cannot sin. More especially, however, for John the hallmark of sonship with God is love. For, if God is love, love must characterize his children too: "Everyone who loves is born of God and knows God. Whoever does not love has not known God. For God is love" (1 John 4:7-8).

3. The Expectation of the Last Days

The critical passage of time has ushered in Christ, and the new world has dawned. The resurrection of Christ is the beginning of the new creation (1 Cor. 15:20, 23). The eschatological period of salvation has begun and is now announced (2 Cor. 6:2). Certainly salvation belongs even yet to the future (Rom. 8:9, 14; Gal. 5:5). Nevertheless, the speedy return of the Lord will bring all things to consummation (1 Cor. 16:22; Phil. 3:20; 1 Thess. 4:13f.). Between the present and the future of salvation, life goes on. Christ belongs to the new creation (2 Cor. 5:17); but the new life is hidden with Christ in God (Col. 3:3).

Christians wait and hope (Rom. 8:19-25). They are "joyful in hope" (Rom. 12:12). But expectation and hope do not make men indolent in this world. To be sure, it had been the error of some Christians in Thessalonica, in view of the proximate arrival of the Lord, to regard everyday tasks and duties as unimportant. The expectation of the day of the Lord, however, should not bring about fanaticism, but should engender watchfulness and sobriety, faith and love (1 Thess. 5:6-8). A stern challenge states simply: "Whoever does not work, neither shall he eat" (2 Thess. 3:10).

The Christian takes part in the trade and commerce of the world, but in the freedom of the "as-if-not." "The time is foreshortened. Therefore shall those who have wives be as if they had not; those who weep, as if they wept not; those who rejoice, as if they rejoiced not; who buy, as if they possessed nothing; who use the world, as if they used it not. For the shape of this world is passing away" (1 Cor. 7:29-31). This passage in Paul is reminiscent, both in its measured phrases and even in its actual words, of a similar passage in Luke (17:26f.). What Christ says there, Paul says here: in view of the eschatological expectation everything comes to judgment. The clock of the worlds is far advanced. The night is at an end. At any moment Christ's coming may occur, with the suddenness of the dawn. Christians dare not let themselves be taken by surprise in the midst of works of darkness. They must do now the works of the day of Christ. "Let us lay aside the works of darkness and put on the armor of light" (Rom. 13:11f.). They must always and in all things be "children of the light and of the day" (1 Thess. 5:5). They who wish to take part in the coming kingdom must keep themselves free of sin and depravity (1 Cor. 6:9-10; Gal. 5:19-21). Were it not for the belief in a resurrection, it would be logical to enjoy life to its fullest, with no thought of responsibility in its enjoyment (1 Cor. 15:32).

The consciousness of impending answerability is a strong motive for a moral life. We wish, says Paul, to be outside the body and at home with the Lord. "It is, therefore, to our credit, whether near to him or far away from him, to be pleasing to him. For indeed, we must all appear before the judgment seat of Christ" (2 Cor. 5:9-10). If the Christian is pleasing to the Lord at the present time, he may hope to be with him in heaven in the time to come. In expectation of the day of Christ, Christians ought to grow in understanding and love. "Make an investigation of the things that matter, so that you may be upright and blameless for the day of Christ, and filled with the fruit of righteousness" (Phil. 1:10-11).

The First Epistle of John also indicates that life is eschatologically determined. Thus he admonishes us: "Little children, abide in him, so that when he appears we may have confidence, and not be ashamed when he comes" (1 John 2:28). "Everyone who has this hope in him makes himself holy, just as he too is holy" (1 John 3:3). He on whom this hope is founded is Christ, who, as the just one, is likewise the holy one (1 John 2:29). The life of one who believes and hopes must be in conformity with the being of the Lord, who is the object of our faith. Therefore the disciple too must be holy.

As to the expectation of the last days, the Apostle may have deceived himself about the actual time of Christ's return, thinking, or at least hoping, that his reappearance was very near. Nevertheless, what is essential remains: the belief in the approaching advent of God perdures, and the Church lives in the expectation of the arrival of the Lord. With that, the freedom of the future life is opened to her.

4. Christ's Word and Example

In the Church of the Apostles the gospel of Christ has to be announced as word of Christ and as word about Christ (1 Cor. 9:14; 2 Cor. 2:12; Gal. 1:7; Col. 1:5-6). "Let the word of Christ dwell among you abundantly; in all wisdom teach and admonish one another" (Col. 3:16). The word of Christ was announced by the Apostles; and now it is called to mind and strengthened in the community by the Spirit. The community is to weigh it and interpret it in teaching and admonishing. The behavior of the community must bespeak the gospel; and thus will the gospel be brought to efficacy.

In the mind of Christians, Paul lives from earliest times onward as the Apostle who dispensed the teachings of Jesus. In one instance the Acts of the Apostles so describes him. Paul's ship has put in at Miletus, and he has invited the elders of the community of Ephesus to Miletus. He recalls for them how he has worked among them: "In all things I have shown you that one must assist the weak and be mindful of the word of the Lord, who said: 'To give is more blessed than to receive'" (Acts 20:35).[22]

Nevertheless, in his letters Paul says very little of the man Jesus, of his teachings, or of his earthly history. It must be remembered, however, that the letters of Paul do not repeat his mission preaching, but settle questions and problems of existing congregations.[23] At the same time, from the Epistles of Paul it is easily seen that the Church of the Apostles taught the new morality in accord with the word and example of Jesus. For Paul, a question was settled if he knew what the Lord had said about it. This was true for the fundamentally important question of the regulations on marriage in the Church. "As to the married, not I, but the Lord commands that a wife is not to separate from her husband" (1 Cor. 7:10). Paul appeals to the Lord's saying about marriage which is preserved in the Gospel (Matthew 5:32; 19:9).

Even the mission is to be arranged in accord with the word of the Lord. "Thus also the Lord has directed, that those who announce the gospel should have their living from the gospel" (1 Cor. 9:14). His remark is similar to what is recorded in Matthew 10:10 and Luke 10:7. Another saying of the Lord is handed down in the Church as the institution of the celebration of the Lord's Supper (1 Cor. 11:23-25). In 1 Thess. 4:15 Paul quotes an apocalyptic saying of the Lord.

This harking back of Paul to the sayings of the Lord allows us to surmise that collections of such sayings had already been assembled, and were valued as a norm for the community. Although they were of the greatest authority, they were accorded no precise legal standing. Paul takes the saying of the Lord about marriage and develops it further in accord with historical exigencies, e.g., in the situation of a separation of the spouses taking place in spite of the prohibition thereof (1 Cor. 7:11), and in the case of mixed marriage between a Christian and a pagan (1 Cor. 7:12-16).

Since Paul appeals now and then to sayings of the Lord in order to provide a basis for the morality of the Church, it might be possible, even in places where he does not reveal his source openly, to accept the interpretation that even in these instances his admonition is determined by statements of the Lord. Perhaps this is the case with the command concerning love of one's enemy: "Bless those who persecute you; bless and do not curse" (Rom. 12:14) depending upon the saying of the Lord in Matthew 5:44. Or when Paul designates the command about love as the sum and substance of the law: "The commands, 'Thou shalt not commit adultery, thou shalt not kill, thou shalt not steal, thou shalt not covet,' and every other command is contained in this saying, 'Thou shalt love thy neighbor as thyself'" (Rom. 13:9), it calls to mind the saying of the Lord about the great commandment (Matthew 22:35-40). Paul's remark about faith moving mountains: "And if I have all faith so that I could remove mountains, and have not love, I am nothing" (1 Cor. 13:2), calls to mind a similar saying of Jesus (Mark 11:23). When Paul says that he is convinced "in the Lord Jesus" that nothing is in itself unclean (Rom. 14:14), it is reminiscent of the saying of the Lord that repeals the Old Testament laws of purification (Mark 7:15). Paul's demand that what belongs to the government be given to the government (Rom. 13:7) is strikingly similar to the saying of the Lord about the government (Mark 12:17). Furthermore, 1 Peter 2:13-17 may very well be dependent upon this same tradition.

It is not only by the word of Jesus that the new morality is determined, but also through the character of Jesus and by his life as model for his disciples. Paul repeats his admonitions again and again that the character of Jesus is a call for Christians to imitate him. The truth and truthfulness of Jesus oblige his disciples to similar behavior. "Our message to you is not 'Yes' and 'No'. For the Son of God, Jesus Christ, was not 'Yes' and 'No'; rather, it was the 'Yes' that was in him. As many as the promises of God are, the 'Yes' is in him" (2 Cor. 1:18-20).

Christ, as the fulfillment of all God's promises, is the revelation of all God's truth. He is also the revelation of God's truth, however, in his own personal truthfulness. Even this must be a model for the disciple: "The truth (i.e., the truthfulness) of Christ is in me" (2 Cor. 11:10). Christ is the revelation of God's benevolence and love for men, since he himself is benevolent and loving of mankind: "The goodness and loving kindness of our God and Savior has appeared to us" (Titus 3:4). The goodness, gentleness, and mildness of Jesus must be put into practice also in the community: "I admonish you by the goodness and gentleness of Christ" (2 Cor. 10:1).

Christ is a model for self-renunciation in love. His image must be effective in the Church. So says Paul, in admonishing the Christians of Corinth to be generous: "You know the graciousness of our Lord Jesus Christ, who, though he was rich, became poor for your sakes, so that you might be enriched by means of his poverty" (2 Cor. 8:9). Christ is the obliging example of the desire to serve: "Let not each one look to his own interests, but each to the welfare of the other. Have and dispose your mind in Christ Jesus. He, who was in God's form, emptied himself, inasmuch as he took on the form of a slave.

He humbled himself, in that he became obedient even unto the cross" (Phil. 2:4-10). Christ subjected himself humbly to the law and became our servant. It follows therefrom that we ought to "receive one another, even as Christ has received us" (Rom. 15:7).

In a special way is the sorrowing Christ a model for the Christian. "Each of us ought to please his neighbor, doing him good by edifying him. For Christ too did not serve his own pleasure, but as it is written: 'The reproaches of those who reproach you have fallen upon me'" (Rom. 15:2-3). In this passage Paul quotes Psalm 69, the psalm about the Passion, which also is woven into the Gospel (Mark 15:6f.) in its narrative of the sufferings of Jesus. Paul, then, draws attention to the Passion of Jesus. It too serves as a model for the Christian. Christians must forgive one another in memory of Christ who wrought forgiveness on the cross and who now, as the glorified one, presents them to the Church: "Bear with one another and forgive one another, if anyone has a grievance against another; even as the Lord has forgiven you, so also should you forgive" (Col. 3:13). Equally to the point is the admonition: "As beloved children, be imitators of God and walk in love, as Christ also loved us and delivered himself up for you as an offering and sacrifice, to ascend to God in fragrant odor" (Eph. 5:1-2).

The First Epistle of Peter gives impressive warning that the sorrowing Christian must follow the sorrowing Christ. Christ suffered innocently, doing good to others. In this he has left behind a model for our imitation. The Christian must follow in his footsteps (1 Peter 2:21-25). Christ is the mighty hero who goes on before and opens the way. To be the second to go on a path is much easier. And Christ, who suffered as the just one for the unjust, is the example referred to in the passage: "It is better to suffer for doing good than for doing evil" (1 Peter 3:17f.).

The Epistle to the Hebrews has in mind the suffering Christ as an example for imitation when it says: "In patience let us run the course laid out for us, looking to the author and finisher of faith, Jesus, who, in place of the joy which was his, bore instead the cross, heeding not its shame" (Heb. 12:1-2). "Jesus suffered outside the gate, in order to sanctify the people by his blood. Let us, therefore, go outside the camp to him and bear his reproach. For we have here no abiding city; rather, we seek the city which is to come" (Heb. 13:12-14). The letter understands in symbolic fashion what is primarily a purely historical account, that Jesus died on the cross outside the walls of the city. It takes it as portending that Jesus died as an outcast from the society of men. And to this it attaches the admonition that we too must be prepared to relinquish worldly honor and share with Christ his shame.

The disciple is obligated to give of himself even as Jesus gave of himself. "In this have we come to know his love, that he laid down his life for us. We too are duty-bound to lay down our life for the brethren" (1 John 3:16). The whole moral admonition can be summed up: "to walk worthy of the gospel of Christ" (Phil. 1:27); and the ultimate goal of this morality is: "to grow up to the measure of the stature of the fullness of Christ" (Eph. 4:13).

Again and in a deeper way Christ becomes the image and basis of the Christian life through the sacraments of the Church. Baptism is to die and rise again with Christ. It brings about and carries out in each of the faithful the death and resurrection of Christ. In consideration of having received the sacrament, it is afterwards the duty of the baptized to realize his baptism in his life. The action and actualization invested in the sacrament of baptism by God is to be laid hold of and carried out anew, again and again, in the moral commitments of daily life. "If it be that you have died and have risen with Christ, now shall it be that you are dead to sin and alive to God in Christ" (Rom. 6:6, 11).

The Lord's Supper is a sacrament of divine communion. The one Bread unites all in one body with the Lord and in one body with each other (1 Cor. 10 and 11). The communion which God has effected ought not be disrupted or destroyed by man. The one body of the Church, however, is disrupted by lack of charity (1 Cor. 11:17-34). Union in the body of the Lord is destroyed by the sin of unchastity, which unites one to another body (1 Cor. 6:16), and by idolatry, which represents and produces communion with the demons (1 Cor. 10:14-22). It is the moral duty of the Christian to actualize in faith and in brotherly love the communion effected by God.

Paul refers to the work which God effects as "new creation." "Neither circumcision nor foreskin is of any account, but only new creation" (Gal. 6:15). And again: "If one is in Christ, he is new creation. Behold, he has become a new thing" (2 Cor. 5:17). What happened is creation, not merely development or advancement of something already existing, not the mere perfecting of virtue already present and natural and achieved by a man through his own capabilities. God creates a new thing. Still, this reality may be hidden: "Your life is hidden with Christ in God" (Col. 3:3). But it is God's reality, and therefore it is truth most real. To live morally is to shape our actions each day after the pattern of this divine activity.

When, therefore, Paul says of the new creation that it subsists "in Christ" (2 Cor. 5:17), he gives utterance to that comprehensive phrase which is essential for the New Testament morality. "To exist in Christ" indicates the communion of being and of life which the Christian has with the Lord. It is precisely in this communion that moral striving and moral living are accomplished. This existing-in-each-other is ever anew the source of moral strength. It is this existing in Christ that directs the daily life of the faithful to faithful surrender to Christ (Eph. 1:1; 1 Tim. 1:14); to the accomplishment of truth and truthfulness (Rom. 9:1; 2 Cor. 1:19; Eph. 4:21); to the witnessing of faith (2 Cor. 2:17; 1 Thess. 4:1); to the service of love (Rom. 8:39; 1 Cor. 16:24; 1 Tim. 1:14); to the determination to endure (1 Cor. 15:58; 2 Cor. 13:3). Paul says about all of this that it takes place "in Christ."

Christian existence is subject to a twofold developmental pressure. From above, the power of the dawning kingdom with the reappearance of Christ presses in upon the world and time. And from within there is the pressure of the spiritual power of Christ, which is in the Christian, and in which Christ wants to take shape. Life is lived in the midst of these pressures.

The Synoptics invite the disciples to "follow after" Jesus. The term is not found in Paul nor in the other Apostles. In the Synoptics it was always understood quite literally, in the sense of the disciples actually going along behind the Master. Thus it was only suited to assert the relationship to the historical Jesus, and did not seem to be suitable for expressing the attachment in the Spirit to the glorified Lord. Therefore, though the term may be lacking in Paul and in the Apostolic Epistles, the idea is nevertheless present, if "following after" is given the meaning of carrying out the life of Jesus in faith and of living by the word and character of Christ. The import of such "following after" is depicted by Paul in broad strokes and with new depth when he gives shape to the life of the faithful through the word, life, and sacrament of Christ.

5. Life in the Spirit

Not until the era of the Apostles, after the pouring out of the Spirit on Pentecost, could the reality of the Spirit in its depth and fullness be conceived. Now the Spirit fills the Church. He is given by means of baptism as well as by the word (Acts 1:5; 1 Cor. 12:13) and is received in faith (Gal. 3:2, 5).

In sources other than the Pauline Epistles the efficacy of the Spirit is seen, not exclusively but nevertheless most clearly, in extraordinary and wonderful occurrences, such as ecstasy, the gift of tongues, miraculous gifts (Acts 2:4; 8:39).

Indeed, Paul himself was an ecstatic (2 Cor. 12:1). He thanked God for the charism of speaking in tongues (1 Cor. 14:18). But it is Paul who recognizes the operation of the Spirit not only in prodigies (1 Cor. 12:8-11), but even more in the commonplace of Christian living. Again and again, notably in Rom. 8:1-27 and Gal. 5:16-26, Paul describes the Spirit as the strength as well as the stature and manner of the new life. Whoever does not have the Spirit does not belong to Christ (Rom. 8:9). The Christian is moved by the Spirit (Rom. 8:14) and is therefore obligated to the Spirit (Rom. 8:12). Those who are in the Spirit think only of the things pertaining to the Spirit (Rom. 8:5), and they walk no more according to the flesh but according to the Spirit (Rom. 8:4; Gal. 5:16). The Spirit is not fanaticism and unbounded enthusiasm. Certainly the true Spirit is easily confused with a foreign and false spirit (2 Cor. 11:4). The genuine Spirit is the Spirit of Christ (Rom. 8:9). He in whom the Spirit dwells cleaves to Christ (1 Cor. 6:17).

The hallmark of the Spirit is that he serves to edify the community (1 Cor. 14:3f.). Even the Spirit has his order. It is "the law of the Spirit of the life in Christ Jesus" (Rom. 8:2). The Spirit is Christ, present and efficacious in the community (2 Cor. 3:17). The Spirit effects sonship: "God gives the Spirit of sonship, in which we cry 'Father!'" (Gal. 4:6). The prayer in which "the Spirit pleads in God's presence for the saints" is an operation of the Spirit (Rom. 8:26f.).

As Holy Spirit, the Spirit is aloof and alien to sin: "Do you not know that your body is the temple of the Holy Spirit?" (1 Cor. 6:19). The Christian, therefore, must hold himself aloof from all unchastity. In the basic conduct of moral living the Christian encounters the Spirit as freedom: "The law of the Spirit has set us free from the law of sin and death" (Rom. 8:2); as peace and joy: "The kingdom of God is righteousness, peace and joy in the Holy Spirit" (Rom. 14:17; 15:13).

The Spirit is effective in individual moral actions. He is the Spirit of meekness (1 Cor. 4:21) and of all moral steadfastness: "Bear the fruits of the Spirit, which are these: love, joy, peace, patience, kindness, goodness fidelity, meekness, continency" (Gal. 5:22-23). He is the Spirit of faith (Acts 6:5; 11:24; 2 Cor. 4:13) and of love (Rom. 5:5).

After tallying up the gifts of the Spirit one after another in a lengthy list (1 Cor. 12:4-11), Paul finally admonishes: "Strive after the even greater gifts of the Spirit" (1 Cor. 12:31). These greater gifts of the Spirit are love (1 Cor. 13) and prophecy, i.e., the teaching, aiding, and edifying word (1 Cor. 14).

§ 3. SIN AND GRACE

I. SIN

Sin is a concept of differing import in the various religions and in their histories.[24] Sin and guilt are moral and chargeable lapses of men against divine and human law. But sin and guilt are also ritual and cultic transgressions which a man can commit unwittingly and involuntarily; thus animals and things can be guilty. Even these sins, however, are punished by the divinity, or at least they require expiation.

In Greek tragedy the problem of guilt found a celebrated and deeply effective presentation. Even here, however, guilt is not necessarily subjectively imputable blame, but includes what is objectively horrible. By divinely decreed fate Oedipus kills his father and then marries the woman who is, unbeknown to him, his own mother. Subjectively innocent, he becomes tragically guilty. The tragic hero can only submit faithfully; it is not given him to escape his guilt by conversion and to come back home to the communion of God.

Religions seek after the origin of sin, and the quest is easily expanded to a search for the origin of evil in the world. Among the basically possible and even actually attempted answers are these: Dualistic ideologies can suppose that from the very beginning there were two divine powers in the world, Good and Evil, in constant conflict with each other. The origin of evil can also be wrongly attributed to the will of God, as if he created evil as a kind of test for man. To be sure, such a god as this would be supporting demoniacal inclinations. Or on the other hand, it is man who is guilty, who desires and chooses the evil.

Israel's tradition shares in the universal history of religion. Even the religion of Israel recognizes and punishes trespasses that are committed without intent, and demands their expiation (Lev. 4-5; Num. 15:22-29; 35:11, 15). Oza but touched the ark of God in order to steady it and he must forthwith die for it (2 Sam. 6:6-7). Nevertheless, the history of religion will say, and quite rightly, that sin, considered as personal, moral guilt in the face of a personal God, is an essential concept of biblical religion. What is central to biblical faith is that the sinner stands before God and receives forgiveness from God's love.

The old Yahwistic narrative of the lapse into sin in Gen. 3 explains the origin of sin as guilty infringement against the will and command of God by the man, even though the inducement thereto (in the seduction practiced by the serpent) comes from outside the man (see the present work, Vol. 1, pp. 92-97). The preaching of the prophets deepens the consciousness of sin and guilt. They know and declare that the distinction between good and evil is "in the heart," i.e., in man's responsibility (Jer. 4:4; 5:23; Ez. 11:19). To Israel it was said: "Man looks at outward appearances, but the Lord sees into the heart" (1 Sam. 16:7). The prophet is obliged to pass condemnatory judgment on the people: "This people draws near to me only with its lips, but its heart is far from me" (Is. 29:13). Sin is defection from God's covenant for the sake of strange gods. The fathers already so defected, and the present generation behaves even worse (Jer. 16:10-12).

In the language of the Old Testament, sin is called hardening of the heart: "I send you to a child with insolent face and hard heart" (Ez. 2:4). Sin is characterized as an inflexible and stiff neck (Exod. 32:9; Deut. 31:27; 2 Chr. 30:8; Is. 48:4), as resistance against God's law (Jer. 17:23; 19:15). Sin is the breach of the moral order of God 1 Sam. 15:23; Hos. 4:1f.; Jer. 7:3-24). Sin is dishonoring of God (Is. 1:4; Mal. 1:6) and infidelity toward his election and love (Is. 24:5; 48:8; Jer. 3:20; Ez. 16:59; Hos. 3:1). As opposed to God's wisdom, sin is foolishness (Deut. 32:6; Is. 29:14; Jer. 5:4). The Psalms (32, 38, 51) attest to experience and knowledge of the nature of guilt and sin. In the period of the New Testament, Israel was oppressed by a grave and universal consciousness of sin.

In the judgment of the community of Qumran, man is lost in sin: "I belong to impious mankind, to the body of wanton flesh. My sins, my transgressions, my iniquities, together with the waywardness of my heart condemn me to communion with the worm and with all that walk in darkness" (1 QS 11:9f.). The godly men of Qumran submit to numerous purificational exercises and baptisms. But they know that the external rites are not enough. What is required is a new and much more rigorous observance of God's law (1 QS 3:4-6).

4 Esdras too bears witness to such a consciousness of sin: "All men are full of sin, burdened with guilt" (7:68). This provides internal evidence for believing that 4 Esdras was written after 70 A.D. and under the influence of the political catastrophes of Israel, which were interpreted as punishment for sin. Properly speaking, it is in this time that Israel first begins to ponder more frequently and more penetratingly the biblical history of the fall. Its reflection concludes to the doctrine of inherited death and, if not of inherited sin, at least to that of the continuously and disastrously effective original sin of Adam

(see Vol. 1 of the present work, pp. 34–37). With deep longing Israel awaits its Messiah, who will purify his people of all sin; thus in the *Psalms of Solomon* (17:33, 36): "He makes Jerusalem quite holy and quite pure, as it was in the beginning. . . . In his day no injustice anymore takes place with them, when all are holy and the anointed of the Lord is now their king." Likewise in the *Testament of Levi* (18:9): "In its priesthood sin is at an end, and lawlessness no longer does evil." (The same expectation is expressed in Matthew 1:21 and Luke 1:68-75.)

The New Testament follows logically upon the old covenant. Jesus announces that God is the Father, whose goodness is manifest in his works (Matthew 5:45). Before this Father man recognizes his sinfulness and his removal from God, while at the same time he longs to be with God. This becomes accomplished fact by the coming and by the word of Jesus. Sin is understood as becoming guilty before God and before man. The prodigal son, on his return, confesses: "I have sinned against heaven and before you" (Luke 15:18). Sin is a guilt-bearing offense against one's neighbor: ". . . if your brother sin against you" (Matthew 18:15). Sin can be understood as one and the same transgression against God and man, insofar as it is directed against the one ordering of God, which is love, — since, indeed, the love of God and of neighbor are brought together in one commandment (Mark 12:30-31).

Jesus purifies and deepens the concept of sin inasmuch as he recognizes only moral and not cultic transgressions. He rejects purificational usages as external. The heart is the place where evil is wrought (Mark 7:14-23). It is not purification of vessels but interior purity that is required (Matthew 23:25f.; see also ch. 15 below). Jesus, however, says that the ruination of sin is universal in occurrence. He calls his generation "adulterous [25] and wicked" (Mark 8:38).

All are guilty of death (Luke 13:1-4). For Jesus it is not that everything is sin and only sin; but he discovers sin in everyone. One only is good, and he is God (Mark 10:18). Nevertheless, even of this generation Jesus' requirements are the highest: "Be perfect, as your Father in heaven is perfect" (Matthew 5:48). This is not a possibility of such kind that man need only will it and he is restored. It is God only who can forgive sin and save man. The kingdom of God, which is now upon us, spells the conquest of sin and the restoration of the world. Forgiveness takes place because Jesus, as the Messiah, enters into the communion of sin and takes sin upon himself. He gives his own life as the price of man's ransoming (Mark 10:45; see the present work, Vol. 2, section entitled *Christ the Redeemer*). New Testament morality is not possible except on the basis, and in the context, of the asserted salvational deed of God. Therefore this salvation is not just a single and solitary occurrence; rather, it is continually a new event of grace.

The Johannine writings say that the world, originally God's creation and loved by God even yet (John 3:16; 15:9), is perverted by sin into a world of disaster and death (see the present work, Vol. 1, pp. 148–152). The wickedness of the world was manifest in its rejection of God's revelation (John 3:19). This rejection of Christ and of the Son of God is the essential sin (John 1:5, 10). "If I had not come and had not spoken to them, they would have no sin" (John 15:22). The Spirit will convince the world of sin (John 16:8-9). If the gifts of Christ to the world are truth, light, and life, sin produces the opposite of each: lies (John 8:55), darkness (John 3:19), and death (John 8:21, 24; 1 John 5:16).

Sin is *injustice*, as the denial of the divine justice (1 John 5:17); and *lawlessness*, as being in opposition to the divine will which imposes an order of conduct (1 John 3:4). In the last analysis, sin is hostility to God — indeed, complete opposition to God; it is the work of the devil (John 6:70; 1 John 3:8). The Son, however, liberates from sin (John 8:36). John the Baptist introduces him to the world as "the Lamb who takes away the sin of the world" (John 1:29).

There are antithetical statements in the First Epistle of John: "If we say that we have no sin, we are deceiving ourselves, and the truth is not in us" (1 John 1:8); and, "Everyone who is begotten of God remains in him" (1 John 3:9; 5:18). The reasoning is probably to be understood in this way: the Christian comes to acknowledge that he is always a sinner and that he requires pardon over and over again (1 John 1:9). The heart too accuses the faithful (1 John 3:20). But he is confident also that he receives forgiveness constantly, since the power of God, to which the believer holds fast, is his support (1 John 5:18). "Whoever abides in him, sins not" (1 John 3:6). Christ is always the advocate with the Father (1 John 2:1), and the Christian must be willing to settle his relationship to God through him. As the Holy One, Christ overcomes all sin (1 John 3:5). He is the atonement for all the sins of the whole world (1 John 2:2).

The actual condition of the Church is this: it is holy and, at the same time, it is sinful. Perhaps it is in opposition to a gnosis which declared the congregation to be sinless that the First Epistle of John makes this affirmation. The redemption must ever purify and preserve the Church. But the Church must itself cooperate if it is to abide in grace. "Whoever keeps his commandments abides in God and God in him" (1 John 3:24). The members of the congregation must assist each other in overcoming sin: "When someone sees his brother commit a sin which is not unto death, he should ask, and he will give him life" (1 John 5:16).[26]

The Apostle Paul describes the operation and nature, gravity and seriousness of sin as it takes effect in reference to and in connection with flesh, law, and death. The "flesh" is primarily the natural life of man, although not necessarily something evil. Like any other man, the Christian too lives his natural life "in the flesh." What is crucial is whether "in the flesh" only assigns the area of potentiality within which life is lived, or whether it signifies at the same time a life according to the flesh. "Though we walk in the flesh, we do not carry on our struggle according to the flesh" (2 Cor. 10:3). When a man is living according to the flesh, he is attempting to derive his life from the world of the natural and earthly and to maintain it therein. In this very attempt, however, the earthly is disclosed as the transient and perishable. It is folly, therefore, for a man to decide to live thus; or worse, it is sin, because this turning toward creation is a turning away from the Creator, who is the giver of life.

This false confidence, moreover, is false self-confidence, in that it is an attempt to procure and safeguard life by one's own energy and achievement. Thus the aspiration of the flesh is inimical to God (Rom. 8:6f.). Flesh and sin become one, in such a way that man's proper self is annihilated: "I am carnal, sold into the power of sin" (Rom. 7:14). Hence, flesh is by no means merely the life of instincts and physical passions. Certainly the physical appetites pertain to the flesh. But even the intellectual, moral, and religious endeavors of man

can be carnal. Even in this area man can attempt to do his own work
in opposition to that of God.

Sinful folly and sinful purpose can operate in two ways: in the
frivolity that scorns the divine order, as in the case of pagans; and
even in the industrious zeal to fulfill commands and ordinances, as
with the Jews. Zeal may be no more than a striving to win justification through one's own efforts. That is why Paul warns the Galatians,
who want to revert to the justification of the Law: "You have begun
in the spirit, and now you want to finish in the flesh" (Gal. 3:3).
Such zeal "is not to be held in honor, but is done for the gratification
of the flesh" (Col. 2:23).

The sinfully autocratic behavior of man finds its expression in self-
adulation. It is characteristic of the Jews, who pride themselves in
the Law (Rom. 2:17, 23), and of the Greeks, who glory in their own
wisdom (1 Cor. 1:29-31). The other side of this glorying, however, is
the anxiety of man, who is apprehensive about himself. It is inevitable that a man, if he wants to live by his own efforts, must live in
anxiety as to whether or not his efforts will be effective. From such a
situation as this the Christian is exempt: "You have not received a
spirit of bondage so as to be again in fear, but the spirit of sonship"
(Rom. 8:15).

Sin forms an alliance with the Law. "The Law is holy and the
commandment is holy and just and good" (Rom. 7:12). It is "given
for the sake of life" (Rom. 7:10). Nevertheless, sin spoiled and perverted the Law. The Law produces in man the recognition of sin;
indeed, it brings a self-awareness to sinning and ushers in the sin
(Rom. 3:20). "Sin made use of the commandment and thereby produced all manner of lust in me. When however, the commandment
came, sin awakened to life. I, however, fell victim to death; and thus
it came about that the commandment, which ought to lead to life, led
me to death. For sin made use of the commandment and deceived
me, and with its help it killed me" (Rom. 7:7-11). The Law made
sin become immeasureably sinful (Rom. 7:13). Sin became universal,
and everything is shut up under sin (Gal. 3:22) — not merely the pagans, who had no written law, but even Judaism, and in spite of the
Law (Rom. 11:32).

Finally, sin forms an alliance with death. Man is called unto life.

But through sin man loses his way and plunges headlong into death: "The command, which was given me for the sake of life, became my death" (Rom. 7:10f.). The coin with which sin pays its servant is death (Rom. 6:16, 23). Here death is to be understood primarily — just as Rom. 5:12 indicates — as death in the natural sense of dying. But this death is confirmed and made final by the sentence of perdition which, on judgment day, God will hand down upon the sinner (Rom. 2:6-11). Thus it is true: "If you live according to the flesh, you will die" (Rom. 8:13). Paul summarizes the forces of disaster: "The sting of death is sin, and the power of sin is the Law" (1 Cor. 15:56). As a venomous beast deals out his poisonous bite, so does death kill man by means of sin.

Paul portrays sin as a personal, demoniacal being. Sin "came into the world" (Rom. 5:12); "it gained the mastery" (Rom. 5:21). Man is like a slave bought by sin (Rom. 6:17; 7:14). Sin dwells in a man and acts in him in such a way that the man loses to it his own existence as a person (Rom. 7:20). This is not all mythology, such as that, perhaps, by which men of old believed that the devil took possession of men; nor is it only metaphorical and rhetorical language; rather, it is the description of an existential reality.

II. GRACE

The Old and the New Testaments speak penetratingly of sin, the better to announce grace,[27] which forgives and saves. One of the oldest declarations about the God of Israel reports: When Moses on Sinai called on Yahweh's name, Yahweh passed before his face and called: "Yahweh, Yahweh is a merciful and gracious God, patient and rich in favor and fidelity, who extends grace to the thousandth generation, who forgives guilt and wickedness and sin" (Exod. 34:6). This declaration is repeated in substance again and again (Num. 14:18; Jer. 4:2; Joel 2:13; Pss. 86:15; 103:8). God deals with man "in accord with his great mercy" (Pss. 51:3; 69:17; Neh. 9:19, 27-31). God's favor and grace are realized in respect to the people in the covenant, in respect to the individual in protection and aid of every kind. In the older parts of the Old Testament, God's favor and grace are extended primarily to the whole people, e.g., in the election to the covenant (Gen. 9:8-17); in the promise of the people's conversion (Amos 5:15; Jer. 3:12); or finally, after doing judgment, in new healing (Hos. 2:23; Is. 60:10). In the last days, however, grace is extended broadly over Israel and beyond to the Gentiles (Is. 42:1; 45:20-25; 49:6).

In the post-exilic congregation the promise of grace is applied increasingly to the pious individually. This bespeaks the universal development by which the individual now first begins to emerge independent from the collectivity of the people. In earlier writings, the pious individual expects even earthly gifts; later, however, it is largely spiritual goods. God's favor is the salvation of the sinner (Ps. 51:3-19). A psalm (36:6-11) probably of late origin praises God's goodness toward men and beasts. His favor signifies: "With you is the source of life. In your light we behold the light." God's grace is promised to those "who are upright of heart."

In the intertestamental era such texts as the *Psalms of Solomon* (2:33-36) speak with deepest confidence of God's grace. The Qumran scrolls, too, bear witness to a trust in God's grace, and finally in a manner which is like a preview of Paul's message, e.g., in 1 QS 11:12-15; 1 QH 4:31; 7:30. The Qumran community understands itself as a covenant of grace (1 QS 1:8; 1 QH Frag. 7:7). In conformity with the expectation of the Qumran congregation, the grace of God is bestowed on the godly, who expend themselves with a new earnestness and with all their strength for the sake of the Law. The sinner is lost. The New Testament says, however, that even the sinner receives grace.

The usual New Testament term for *grace* is χάρις.[28] It is also used outside the New Testament for the favor and kindness of men as well as of the divinity: in Hellenism, for the favor of the gods; in the worship of the monarch, for the grace of the king; and even in Jewish linguistic usage, for the kindness of God (thus in the Septuagint, in Hellenistic Jewish Wisdom literature, and in Philo and Josephus).

Perhaps it is Paul who introduces the word χάρις into New Testament Greek. It occurs often in his Epistles and in writings influenced by him (not only in the Pastoral Epistles, but also in Luke, in the Epistle to the Hebrews, and 1 Peter). The thing signified, however, is present in the New Testament, even where the word χάρις is lacking. As words of much the same meaning we can point to ἔλεος and οἰκτιρμός.

The Sermon on the Mount, with its beatitudes (Matt. 5:2ff.), says that God's mercy and grace are active now; and this is confirmed by what follows, the numerous accounts of cures, which have their probative force in the fact that the cures are worked in the body as well as in the soul. God's mercy is apparent in the forgiveness of sin which Jesus promises and actually imparts. That it is now the time of visitation rich in grace is the import of the proclamation of the kingdom of God. The Gospel of Luke speaks of the grace of God and of its coming upon Mary (1:28, 30), as well as upon Christ himself (2:40, 52). Peace and God's saving will now hold sway over the elect (Luke 2:14).[29]

The Acts of the Apostles announces the grace of God and its coming upon the Church (4:33 *et passim*). The gospel is the "word of grace," inasmuch as it brings about the imparting of grace (Acts 14:3; 20:24, 32). The Lucan writings, however, speak also of the grace of Christ. In its own soaringly descriptive manner, the Gospel reports: "All marveled at the words of *charis* (grace, in the sense of charm) which came forth from his mouth" (Luke 4:22). The words of Jesus are powerful in moving, in touching, in healing. Christ favors (graces) with cures (Luke 7:21). At the Council of Jerusalem, Paul attests: "We believe confidently that we are saved through the grace of our Lord Jesus" (Acts 15:11).

The Gospel of John uses the word "grace" four times in its prologue. As the revelation of God, Christ is his pouring-out of grace and favor. From his fullness, Christ gives grace for grace. Grace is now the antithesis of the Law (John 1:14-17). Christ is salvation, in the sense of redemption from sin (John 1:29; 1 John 2:2).

It is Paul who plumbs the depths of sin; so too is he the greatest theologian of grace. The description of sin ends in discovering grace as its final aim: "Where sin abounded, grace abounded still more" (Rom. 5:20). Law and sin lead man to death, in order at last to bring him face to face with God's grace. God's aim, in respect to man, is justification, not sin; life, not death. Beyond the desperation of death man attains to God, who is the Creator and who, as such, imparts life and is the only one who can take life away from man.

God shows himself as the Creator of life even in the matter of grace. He is believed in, therefore, as the one who raises up the dead and who calls into existence that which did not exist (Rom. 4:17). When Paul found himself so grievously afflicted that he gave himself up for dead, it was "in order that we might not trust in ourselves, but in the God who raises the dead" (2 Cor. 1:9). Grace is made manifest in the fact that life has overcome death. God has grace: "God has presented Jesus Christ as a sign of propitiation through faith in his grace" (Rom. 3:24-25). God gives and effects his grace now.

The Son of God has sent grace into the world: "God's gift and grace has been richly distributed to the many through the grace of the one man, Jesus Christ" (Rom. 5:15). The grace of God is present in Christ and is his own. "The call takes place in the grace of Christ" (Gal. 1:6). In the initial and concluding greetings of his letters, Paul wishes this grace to the Church (Rom. 1:7; 16:20; and similarly in the others). The mission and the person of Christ can be designated simply as grace: "Recognize the grace of our Lord Jesus, who became poor for our sakes" (2 Cor. 8:9). The grace of God and Christ's giving of love are the same (Gal. 2:20f.).

Just as God effects grace, so too does he give Christ. It is "the grace of our God and Lord Jesus Christ" (2 Thess. 1:12). The concepts "love of God" and "grace of Christ" are interchangeable: "The grace of the Lord Jesus Christ and the love of God. . . be with you all" (2 Cor. 13:13). The grace of God is his royal and powerful dominion in the world: "As sin reigned in death, so now shall grace reign by justification unto eternal life through Christ our Lord" (Rom. 5:21). Grace, as the power of God, determines that life: "By God's grace I am what I am, and his grace in me was not in vain" (1 Cor. 15:10). God's grace will always, in this life, be productive, so long as faith gives it a place to work. Even in incapacity and in the inability to achieve anything by one's own efforts is God's grace made evident: "It was the outcome of faith, so that it might be according to grace"

(Rom. 4:16). If the Galatians want to create their own justification by their works, they have "fallen out of grace" (Gal. 5:4).

The preaching of grace is in sharp contrast to the Law and the works of the Law (Rom. 3:21f.; 4:4; 11:6). One who has been called and who has been the recipient of God's gifts must "remain in the grace to which he has attained" (Rom. 5:2). It is also possible to receive grace in vain (2 Cor. 6:1). Grace creates in Christ the beginning of the new life, which should continue to be strong through a whole lifetime. Grace and justification mean the same thing (Rom. 5:17). The one grace (*charis*) is the basis of the manifold gifts of the Spirit, the charisms (Rom. 12:6; 1 Cor. 1:4-7). Even Paul's apostleship is a personal grace (Rom. 1:5). The Pauline concept of grace is reminiscent of the Johannine concept of life. Grace changes the command "Thou shalt" to the pledge "You can and you may."

The tidings of grace are found even more richly in biblical theology developed under the Pauline influence. God's grace is conceived as grace through Christ. "The glory and riches of God's grace" are our lot in the beloved Son (Eph. 1:6f.). Grace is received in faith (Eph. 2:8). Now has the saving grace of God appeared; it allows us to look forward impatiently to the ultimate hope (Titus 2:11-13). Grace is given in Christ Jesus (Titus 3.6-7; 2 Tim. 1:9). Having been received, it produces faith and love (1 Tim. 1:14).

Grace becomes effective in the charism of the grace of office (1 Tim. 4:14; 2 Tim. 1:6). Through its High Priest, Jesus Christ, the Church has access to the throne of God, which, through the mediation of Christ, has actually become for us a throne of grace (Heb. 4:16). The letters of the Apostles borrow the initial greeting of Paul's letters, "grace and peace" (1 Peter 1:2; 2 John 3; Apoc. 1:4). The salvational work of Christ was promised from the beginning (1 Peter 1:10); and now the grace of God which has been given determines a mode of life and gives direction to hope (1 Peter 1:13). Grace is given in the Church in an abundance to each (1 Peter 4:10; 5:10). Christians stand in it (1 Peter 5:12). Grace is eternal life (1 Peter 3:7). Christians must grow in the grace and knowledge of Christ (2 Peter 3:18).

As a dogmatic concept grace has become for us too bound up in formulae; indeed, it is benumbed. In our daily speech, grace still has about it something of a feudal ring, when a lower lord paid homage to his grace, a higher lord. A proverbial expression such as "grace precedes justice" means that justice is to be tempered by mercy, grace being in this instance an act of compassion. In the fullness of the biblical concept grace is much more — it is new creation as God's love and life.

§ 4. REWARD AND PUNISHMENT

The New Testament speaks of the relation of sin and forgiveness in which man finds himself in the face of the personal God. If men stand before the living God in guilt and grace, then there must eventually be a meting out of punishment and reward.[30] Punishment and reward are, in fact, God's definitive transaction with men.

It would be a misunderstanding of the gospel to hear in it only the tidings of the forgiving Father-God. The gospel announces also the majesty of the holy God who makes demands of men and judges them. Jesus speaks of punishment: "What does it profit a man to gain the whole world, only to be punished by the loss of his life?" (Mark 8:36).[31]

Jesus likewise speaks of the reward ($\mu\iota\sigma\theta\grave{o}s$) for doing what is good. "Your reward will be great in heaven" (Matthew 6:1, 20). It is not the rich and famous who should be invited to table — they can repay the invitation on earth — but the poor and sick; and God will repay it at the resurrection of the just (Luke 14:12-14). With the summoning to judgment and with the admonition to keep this judgment in mind, Jesus requires a certain ordering of actions — of what is done and what is permitted to be done. "I tell you, for every idle word that men speak, an accounting must be made on the day of judgment" (Matthew 12:36). Christ serves notice of the "Gehenna of fire" (the fire of hell).[32] Whoever wrongs his brother "shall be forfeited to the fire of hell" (Matthew 5:22). "It were better for you that one of your limbs be given up for lost, than that your whole body should perish in the fire of hell" (Matthew 18:9). For this reason the gospel admonishes the fear of God: "Do not be afraid of those who kill the body, but cannot kill your life. Rather, fear those who can destroy both body and life in hell" (Matthew 10:28). Jesus threatens the unfaithful cities: "Woe to you, Chorazin! Woe to you, Bethsaida! . . . It will be more tolerable for Tyre and Sidon on the day of judgment than for you" (Matthew 11:21-22).

The admonition and warning about the judgment, in which individuals will be judged, is repeated in parables based on the kingdom of heaven. At the consummation of the ages the angel of judgment will separate the good and the wicked. The wicked will be "thrown into the furnace of fire. In that place there will be the weeping and the gnashing of teeth" (Matthew 13:47-50).[33] In the apocalyptic parables the same formula appears repeatedly (Matthew 24:51; 25:30). The arrival of the Son of Man at the judgment will bring with it the separation of the wicked and the good: "They will go away into eternal pain; the righteous, however, into eternal life" (Matthew 25:46).

The preaching of Jesus, in describing the world beyond, makes use of words and representations which are qualified by temporal limitations. Though he uses such, it is not his intention thereby to shed any light upon the where and how of the judgment — something which, quite certainly, Jewish apocalyptic does attempt to do with the broad portraits it paints of the judgment. Jesus takes advantage of the parable form for his declarations. His announcement is not apocalyptic but certainly eschatological. It is vital for him to bring man before the judgment, yes, to situate him right in the judgment. In this way he brings strongest motivation to bear upon his ethics. At the same time, nevertheless, there is certainly the possibility to be reckoned with, that familiar and traditional phrases have been placed in the mouth of Jesus.

With his teaching of reward and punishment as repayment in accord with one's actions, Jesus shares in the Old Testament and contemporaneous Jewish belief. In both instances this tenet is the result of a particular concept of God, while at the same time there are certain important differences which must be noted. The conviction that, by virtue of the operation of the Godhead, good behavior will result in prosperity and success while sin and frivolity are unable to produce either peace or prosperity, is certainly common to every religion; and so too it pertains, from the very beginning, to the traditional belief of

Israel. Judaism expected reward even in the form of earthly reward; indeed, it concentrated to very high degree on the earthly reward. The just receive their reward, and the wicked their punishment, in the here and now.

The Deuteronomic historical writing is relentless in viewing Israel's whole history in accord with this principle. History becomes a grand but gloomy documentation of God's justice. In Deuteronomy a promise is frequently attached to its command: "so that it may be well with you, and that you may live long upon the earth." The idea of repayment is central to the prophetic preaching, even as promise of reward, but certainly more often as threat of judgment thrown in the face of presumptuous security. In the Wisdom literature the disciple is informed again and again that the good may expect reward, and the evil, punishment. The conviction of divine repayment with punishment and reward is an expression of the living belief in God's constant dominion over men.

In later books of the Old Testament and in the apocrypha, the reward is spiritualized, as, for example, in the doctrine of immortality found in the Wisdom books. The reward is eternal communion with God (Ps. 22:25f.; _Ethiopic Henoch_, 58:1-6). The rule of the Qumran community (I QS 4:7) says: "The sons of truth will have abundance of peace so long as days endure, and fruitfulness of seed with all eternal blessings and eternal joy in everlasting life, and a crown of glory and a resplendent robe amid light perpetual."

The conviction about the reward, however, quite often becomes perverted finally into a calculating attitude toward the reward and for the sake of the reward. From then on the shaping of his future lies in man's own hands. God becomes more man's servant than his Lord. There were voices raised against this attitude, but they were few and far between. Antigonus of Socho (_ca._ 200 B.C.) warned: "Be not like those servants who serve their master only for the sake of a reward, and heaven will be yours." The protest itself makes it abundantly clear that the usual conception and expectation were otherwise. Faced with life's reality, faith might doubt and despair of God's justice. Job, therefore, opposes such a false religious spirit. It is not true that prosperity and fear of God, misfortune and sin, must be always in direct accordance with each other. God governs in complete freedom (Job

38:1–42:6). The arithmetical *quid pro quo* concept of reward continued beyond this time. In the New Testament era, 4 Esdras 5:38 says: "If the work is performed, the reward is forthcoming. Good deeds awake, wicked sleep no more." It implies oppressive anxiety as a consequence of unforgiven guilt.

If Jesus follows the Old Testament concepts of God's reward and punishment, the differences between the Old Testament and Jesus are nonetheless great and deep. As the one who is truly personal and living, God is the creator, sustainer, and support of man. God is the one who creates and gives, man is the one who receives. God calls man and is Lord over man, and man owes him obedience. Therefore man is the one who is accountable, therefore is he subject to God's decree of judgment, whether to reward or to punishment. This is but the expression of the fact that the temporal and earthly life of man is indissolubly dependent upon God.

In the sayings of Jesus, God is the Lord of man in an even more strict sense than in Jewish theology because God is free and is neither bound nor can he be bound by any claim of man. No work of man puts God in his debt. The disciple of Jesus knows that his performance never measures up to the absolute challenge of God. God alone is good (Mark 10:18). Before such a God as this man can never advance any claim. He is comparable to the slave, who has only his duty to perform and can do no more. "When you have done all that is commanded you, say: 'We are unworthy slaves. What we must do, we have done'" (Luke 17:7-10). In the presence of God, man can say of himself nothing else but what the tax-collector says: "God, be merciful to me, a sinner" (Luke 18:13).

But God is also the Father, who wants to adopt man, even the sinner, as his child. Moral conduct, therefore, never wants to hoard up profit; rather, it is submission in confidence and love; it does not reckon, does not go to law, does not demand. The consciousness of sonship impels one to moral conduct so simply and self-evidently that the thought of reward never occurs — it cannot and may not occur. To reckon on reward is out of the question. If, nevertheless, there is talk of reward, then the reward is always freely given and gratuitous. This is the substance of the parable of the workers in the vineyard. First of all it depicts in minute detail the agreement entered into in respect to the reward. But human order and justice are turned about. The last receive as much as the first. Payment and reward are given, however difficult it may be to understand, in one and the same measure to all, who view the relationship of God to men as the same as that between a precisely reckoning distributor of work and those who accept employment.

The substance of the passage is the message of God's love, gracious in giving. It is not justice that counts out a deserved recompense; rather, God's love is poured out over and above the good will of men (Matthew 20:1-15). The reward is never to be expected, because it can never be earned by good behavior. God's recognition of man takes the latter by surprise. "The just will answer: 'Lord, when did we see you hungry . . .?'" (Mathew 25:34-40). Repudiation will likewise be surprising (Matthew 25:41-45). Jesus does speak of the reward; but still, every thought of payment is excluded. To put it simply: the reward is promised to him who is obedient not for the sake of the reward. This paradoxical truth is expressed in such a saying as that of Luke 17:33: "Whoever seeks to gain his life will lose it. And whoever loses his life will gain it."

Ultimately, what is the reward? It is decidely other-worldly. Here and in the present age, distress and oppression are the lot of the disciple. "If they persecuted me, they will persecute you" (John 15:20). God himself is the reward in his kingdom. "Yours is the royal dominion of heaven" (Matthew 5:3, 10). "Come, you blessed of my Father! Take possession of the kingdom" (Matthew 25:34). In that God responds to the confidence of man, he himself becomes the priceless gift. To do good for the sake of the reward is the same thing, then, as to do good for God's sake. God is the recompense. This recompense is always accompanied by forgiveness and love.

The expectation of punishment and reward is a certainty to the other New Testament writings as well. "Whatever a man sows will he also reap, either corruption or eternal life" (Gal. 6:7f.). "We must all make an appearance before the judgment seat of Christ, so that each one may receive recompense for what he did during his life in the body — be it good or evil" (2 Cor. 5:10). "It is not the hearers of the law who are righteous before God, but the doers thereof who will be justified" (Rom. 2:13). Paul concludes his admonitions with words

both of threat and of promise: "Do you not know that the unrighteous will not inherit the kingdom of God. Be not deceived!" (1 Cor.
6:9f.). The unrepentant is warned: "By your stubbornness and your
impenitent heart you are storing up wrath for yourself on the day of
wrath and of God's just judgment" (Rom. 2:5). Punishment is designated simply as death (Rom. 1:32; John 5:24; 8:51).

Paul speaks likewise of the reward. The reward is the kingdom
of God (1 Cor. 15:50). It is described also as "glory, honor, immortality, eternal life" (Rom. 2:8, 10). God remains the judge. The Christian
belief in the graciousness of God is certainly not of a mind that there
is no wrath of God nor that there is no impending judgment; rather,
it indicates a hope of being saved from the wrath of God. "Since we
are justified by his blood, we hope to be saved by him from wrath"
(Rom. 5:9).

The sense of the Pauline teaching becomes evident when the Apostle, in explaining the history of Abraham, says that Abraham obtained justification on the basis of faith without works, "not as his
due, but as a grace" (Rom. 4:4). Paul speaks of the reward, just as
did Judaism and as did Jesus. For Paul, too, there is value to the Old
Testament Jewish teaching, from which he accepts the schema of
punishment and reward. But he subjoins to it the new concept of
grace. With the realities of faith, presented precisely by Paul in the
concepts of faith and grace, the Jewish schema is in reality split.

An example serving to clarify this is Paul's statement: "The reward
of sin is death, but the grace of God is eternal life" (Rom. 6:23).
Death, to be sure, is the reward which man has earned; eternal life,
on the contrary is never deserved, but always a gratuitous gift. Paul
characterizes his work and his life as "grace of God with me" (1 Cor.
15:10). For this cooperation the Apostle expects the reward which is
certainly forthcoming. The word "reward" remains, but its implications are different. In this regard Paul says that it is never possible for
a man to make any boast before God; he can boast only of that which
God has done through Christ (Rom. 3:27; 2 Cor. 12:9). In similar
vein, Eph. 2:8f. says: "For by grace in virtue of faith have you been
saved, not of your own doing. It is God's gift, not because of works —
let no man boast of that."

Paul is just as unequivocal when he says that God will judge according to works (Rom. 2:13; 2 Cor. 5:10) as he is when he says that justification takes place without works (Rom. 1:17; 3:24, 28). Is the teaching of Paul split into two parts? Is there a religion of works and law, and a religion of grace? Did Paul teach such irreconcilable notions, without ever becoming aware of it himself? Certainly God's grace justifies those who cling to the faith. Faith alone can make blessed; but this faith, if it is genuine, is never alone; rather, it is productive of deeds (Gal. 5:6). Therefore Paul can say that the gospel does not abolish God's commandment, but actually fulfills it completely, inasmuch as the demand of the law is faith and love (Rom. 3:31; 8:4).

The gospel, in making provision for the judgment, in no way detracts from the concept of God. With the judgment, works are still required. Certainly it is still true that the righteousness which alone can enable man to withstand the test in God's presence is never merited but is always a gift freely bestowed. Man's part of the work is always overshadowed by the much greater part which belongs to God: "It depends not on the one who desires, nor yet on the one who runs, but on God, who shows mercy" (Rom. 9:16). If these be antitheses which do not permit our resolving them fully, it remains God's secret how, in his fullness of power, the gift of righteousness is to be related to that severity of judgment which demands fulfillment of the law. God's sovereignty can have possibilities between justice and mercy of which we know nothing. Ultimately it must be conceded that all human reasoning lags far behind the reality of God.

Modern ethics has explained well enough that the reward incentive pertains to a lower degree of morality. The good has within itself its own reason, its own nobility, its own reward. Freedom and magnanimity are made something lesser through reflection on a reward. Morality takes a step toward eudaemonia. "Eudaemonia is the euthanasia of all right morality" (Immanuel Kant). It may perhaps be difficult to reject such questions and objections entirely. In accord, however, with the writings of the old and new covenants, Jesus speaks unequivocally and in forceful terms of reward and punishment.

On this point there is a distinction to be made between Holy Scripture and the revelation contained therein. If this writing is a religious text, it is to be subjected to philosophical criticism. We will then, perhaps, come to the conclusion that it voices an as yet incomplete ethics. Even Jesus was not able to free himself entirely of an older tradition. He remains bound to a people and a time. But if Scripture speaks God's words, and if Christ speaks as God's Son, then philosophy, man's sense of religion, and ethics are to be subjected to Scripture's criticism. Thus we find in Scripture God's word as to what religion really is: it is not mortification and descent into nothingness; but neither is it, as many religions would have it, enthusiasm or mystical union with the Godhead. Revelation says, then, that moral intent and behavior, as the pre-eminent fruits of faith, are required by God's word and command.

Moral action is the religious goal of human life. But this goal, which is designated in Scripture as the kingdom of God or as eternal life, is so incomparably and inexpressibly great that no man can achieve it of himself; on the contrary, it can only be given as a reward infinitely greater than all other rewards. The idea of reward has its place within the message of the coming and already dawning kingdom of God, which man can but accept as a free gift. "It is your Father's will, to give you the kingdom" (Luke 12:32).

Is it possible, then, that revelation says ultimately: In that ostensibly highest human ethics there lies the possibility of pride beyond all measure? Does it not belong to God alone to desire to do what is good purely for the sake of the dignity of what is good? That means to do what is good in the pure freedom of the self-existent and to have sovereign creativity in respect to the good. It means "to be like unto God." The reward concept is ever a call to humility. Along with his capability of recognizing and desiring the good, man is still but creature. The fruit of his action, the meaning of his decision for the good, does not result of itself, but is given by God as recompense.

II. BASIC ATTITUDES

§ 5. CONVERSION AND REPENTANCE

The first word spoken by Jesus in his public ministry was, according to the Gospels, "Be converted!" (μετανοεῖτε — Matthew 4:17–Mark 1:15). If this was, in point of time, the first word of Jesus' preaching, it was in fact, in order of importance, his first challenge. He must reproach his audience with being "a wicked and adulterous generation" (Matthew 12:39). It is quite proper, then, that his first word be "Convert!" [84]

What does the word μετάνοια mean? How is it to be translated — as contrition, repentance, conversion? In profane Greek literature the principal meaning of the word is "change of mind," "repentance." What it means in the New Testament, however, is to be inferred largely from the Old Testament.

For the English concepts *conversion* and *repentance* the New Testament sometimes uses forms of the words μετάνοια and μετανοεῖν (thus largely in the Synoptics and in the Apocalypse), and sometimes forms of ἐπιστροφή and ἐπιστρέφω (principally in Acts, the Pauline Epistles, and in 1 Peter). In Acts 3:19 and 26:20, μετανοεῖν and ἐπιστρέφειν are used in conjunction with each other. The New Testament words go back to an important Old Testament term, *shub* (to turn about), from which *teshubah* (return) is formed later. The Septuagint renders the terms in question with ἐπιστρέφειν ἐπιστροφή), whereas the more recent Greek versions also use μετανοεῖν (μετάνοια).

In Hellenistic Judaism this use of the word μετανοεῖν is unequivocal; thus in Sir. 48:15: "In all of these things the people did not repent (οὐ μετενόησεν). Nor did they leave off from their sins, until they were

73

driven out of their land and were scattered over all the earth." Similarly in Sir. 44:16, Henoch is said to have been "an example of penitence (ὑπόδειγμα μετανοίας) for all peoples." Numerous further examples are to be found in the Wisdom Literature, in the *Testaments of
the Twelve Patriarchs*, and in Philo and Josephus.

The prophets of Israel, through the whole period of their operation,
issue their call to repentance with the word *shub*. The earliest prophets, like Hosea and Amos, lament the fact that God's solicitous love
is scorned (Hos. 1–3; Jer. 2:2; 3:1). The people and their leaders refuse to be converted to God from their disbelief and infidelity. A
national catastrophe will be their punishment (Hos. 5 and 6; Amos
4).

In conversion and repentance Israel must turn away from idols,
as well as from injustice and immorality and from contempt for the
commands of God (Jer. 7). When Israel converts to the Lord, he will
help her and heal her, building up and planting in her (Hos. 6:1;
14:2f.; Jer. 24:5-7). "Let the godless abandon his way and the wicked
his thoughts and let him be converted to the Lord, and he will show
mercy to his own and to God, for he is bountiful in forgiveness"
(Is. 55:7). Conversion is the turning away from strange gods to the
true God. Baal and his like belong to the world and pronounce it
holy. To follow them is to enjoy life in avarice and carnal pleasure.
To return, therefore, to the God of Israel, who is the moral God, is to
turn from sinfulness to justice and morality (Deut. 31:18; Josh.
22:16-29; Judg. 2:19; 1 Kings 9:6; Jer. 7:9).

Nevertheless, conversion cannot simply be willed by man in order
to be brought about; rather, it is God's salvation only that can
loose man from his error and turn him to God. "If you allow me to
be converted, I will surely be converted; for you are my God" (Jer.
31:18). Later prophecy interprets the whole history of Yahweh's dealings with his people as God's call to repentance and conversion. God
always advances to meet man's turning to him. It is really true:
"Turn unto me, and I will turn to you" (Zech. 1:3; Mal. 3:7).

It is really conversion to God that is meant when, after the exile
and in the period when the Law was so highly prized, conversion
is demanded in terms of "return to the Law" (Neh. 9:29). The *Eighteen Benedictions* (5) pleads: "O Lord, bring us back to thee! We

would be converted. Renew our days as once they were! Glory be to thee, O Lord, thou who lovest repentance!" According to Rabbinic writings, repentance is a condition for the coming of the Messiah. And the Messiah himself will likewise convert men to God.[35]

The Qumran community is a community of repentance. It is the covenant of those "who are converted to the truth and who abstain from all wickedness" (1 QS 6:15). The godly wish to "raise up God's covenant . . . and be converted to his covenant" (1 QS 5:22). In Qumran numerous ablutions and purifications were practiced. Nevertheless, "they cannot be purified who do not repent of their wickedness. There is impurity in all who transgress his word" (1 QS 5:13f.). Conversion is return "to the Law of Moses with one's whole heart and with one's whole soul, complying with all that he has enjoined, and complying with all that was revealed to the priests in respect to the Law" (1 QS 5:8f.). The New Testament injunction of repentance will not be dependent upon Qumran; rather, Qumran and the New Testament both come out of the same temporal-historical situation. In both, total conversion is demanded as a condition for salvation.

The conversion demanded in Qumran is a renewed and stricter commitment to the Law of Moses as taught therein and as interpreted in the community's rule of life. In the Gospels the word of Jesus demands conversion to the original law of God as opposed to its Mosaic codicil (Mark 10:5-9) and without — yes, against — its later traditions (Mark 7:8-13). It is logical that conversion in Qumran demands entry into the insular community, while sinners remain abandoned to their fate. Jesus requires that men acknowledge ever anew that they are sinners and that they constantly renew their conversion (Luke 7:50; 15:7, 10). Here entry into a juridically segregated community neither helps nor heals; rather, it is the totality of faith which acknowledges that salvation is possible only as God's gift (Luke 18:14).[36]

This long history of a word and its concept brings us to the import of the New Testament terms. With the New Testament, μετάνοια does not signify merely a change of mind restricted to intellect; nor is it only remorse, orientated to the past and rooted in feelings; nor is it only that repentance which will repair past injustices. In the New Testament, μετάνοια signifies conversion as a radical turning of the whole man to God. It is virtually synonymous with ἐπιστρέφειν. ἐπιστρέφειν, however, tends to emphasize the visible and external act, while μετανοεῖν stresses more that which is beneath the surface, the processes of thinking and willing.

The following considerations may prove a useful elucidation of the above. In the same period in which the New Testament was written, Epictetus (*Diss.*, 2, 22, 35) says that "the wise man knows no μετάνοια (regret or remorse)." Seneca (*Letters*, 115, 18) declares: "Philosophy will give you the greatest gift there is, namely, you will never experience regret." The etymological significance of *metánoia* is "change of *nous*, or mind." The mind need change only in regard to what was previously accepted falsely, foolishly, or wickedly; having now a better understanding, it must change. The wise man, however, is neither foolish nor wicked. Therefore he never has need of *metánoia*. Though it is quite logical that Stoic philosophy knows no *metánoia*, both philosophy and religion as well known of a conversion (ἐπιστροφή). In his image of the subterranean cavern, Plato (*Republic*, 514A–521C) portrays man's inevitable turning about from shadows to light, from the world of becoming to being. Later religious philosophy admonishes that the soul ought to be turned toward the good, toward the divine (thus in Epictetus, Marcus Aurelius, Porphyry, and Plotinus). Mystery cults oblige their adherents to a new, pious, and moral life.[37]

In the presentation of the gospel, the history of John the Baptist as herald of the advent of Jesus stands as an introduction. The accounts about Jesus and about the Baptist betray frequent similarities. If both issue a call to *metánoia*, this might be attributable simply to the historical process, the Baptist and Jesus both having taken up the call to conversion directly from their milieu and from the situation of their times. John "announced the baptism of repentance for the forgiveness of sins" (Mark 1:4; cf. Matthew 3:11). Matthew places a similar message in the mouth of Jesus: "Be converted! The kingdom of heaven is at hand!" (Matthew 3:2 = 4:17).

Just as with the prophets, John's call to repentance is accompanied by threatening allusions to the nearness of judgment. Nevertheless, this judgment is not, like that of the prophets, a punishment of God; rather, it is the final judgment before the initiation of God's dominion (Matthew 3:7). John demands the conversion of those who in Israel are regarded as sinners and who are typified as tax-collectors (publicans) and soldiers. The conversion which is demanded is a turning away from greed and power and a turning to God, in that it is a conversion to the approaching kingdom of God (Luke 3:10-14). Conversion is also demanded, however, of those who are faithful to the Law, the Pharisees and Sadducees (Matthew 3:7-10). Even they are on a false path, and their lives are wrongly ordered. Even they are far from God, lost and in sin. Man in general, in the condition in which he first meets and encounters the word of God, is on a false path, far removed from God.

Both the concept and the aim of conversion are contained substantially in the declaration of Jesus' message: "Repent, and believe in the gospel" (Mark 1:15). If the use of the word *gospel* suggests a later structure, still, the saying is valid, that faith is the fulfillment of conversion — faith, however, as the confidence of a child in his father, and as a reliance on God's salvation in his Christ. Conversion takes place first in a coming home to the love of God. Therefore, the very call to repentance is a gospel, and the call to conversion is a call to joy. Even in heaven there is joy over the sinner who repents, more than over the righteousness of the just (Luke 15:7, 10).

Even of the individual act of repentance it is correct to say that repentance is joy. In the style of action up to the present time, in penitential works there was no thought of the nearness of God's kingdom. "Can the wedding guests fast as long as the bridegroom is with them" (Mark 2:19). Fasting, so long a sign of sorrow and renunciation, is now for the disciples an expression of joy. "When you fast, anoint your head and wash your face" (Matthew 6:17). Only where there is joy can the New Testament call to conversion be accepted and understood.

Like the penitential preaching of the prophets, the New Testament says that the return of man to God must precede the turning of God toward man. Nevertheless, this turning of God toward man has now taken place in Christ, yes, Christ himself is this turning, as the beginning of God's kingdom among men and as the event of God's forgiveness. Because God's dominion is coming, man is able to come to God. "Be converted, *because* the kingdom of God is approaching."

Even the linking of the command to become like a child is an indication that conversion is not a human work but a grace. "Unless you turn about and become like little children, you will not enter into the kingdom of heaven" (Matt. 18:3). Just as the child knows that he must take an inferior position when in the company of adults, so too, to be like a child means to be humble and to recognize that the disciple can accomplish nothing of himself but can only consent to accept what is given. Only one who receives can enter into the kingdom. Indeed, that is why there is talk again and again of the *inheritance* of life (Mark 10:17) and of the kingdom (Matthew 25:34). An inheritance is always something given. *Metánoia*, according to the mind of Jesus, signifies the attempt to live by the gift of God.

Even though it is God's action that is critical, nevertheless, man's own proper share in this activity is by no means unnecessary. Along with God's turning toward man in the kingdom, there is required also a total conversion of man to God. The admonitions and summonings, however, are no longer in the character of legislative command; rather, they but inaugurate the possibility of their fulfillment. Thus the command issued in the preaching of the Baptist finds validity even in the gospel: "Bring forth fruit befitting a conversion" (Matthew 3:8).

According to the gospel, this fruit can be characterized as a new morality, that of the Sermon on the Mount, as well as imitation through discipleship. Conversion tolerates no halfway measures: "If anyone comes to me and does not hate father, mother, wife, children . . . , yes, his very life, he cannot be my disciple" (Luke 14:26). Nor does conversion allow of any recanting. Once undertaken, there is no turning back; the only direction is forward. Whoever dallies with even so much as the thought of reverting, like the plowman who glances over his shoulder, is not worthy of the kingdom (Luke 9:61f.).

There is no release from the urgency of the summons. Upon hearing the news that Galilean pilgrims had been killed while offering sacrifice, and that at the pool of Siloam a tower had fallen and in so doing had struck down eighteen men, Jesus answered: "Unless you repent you will all likewise perish" (Luke 13:1-5). All are subject to death and guilty of death. Even a righteousness of the just is self-deception and error. Only total conversion bespeaks the truth of the human situation. What is required is resignation of one's own self and total surrender to God, who will be gracious to the sinner. Therefore does Jesus say of his mission: "I have not come to call the righteous, but sinners to conversion" (Luke 5:32).

Jesus' call to repentance points consistently to a judgment upon impenitence. "Then Jesus began to threaten the cities in which most of his mighty works had been done: 'Woe to you, Chorazin! Woe to you, Bethsaida! If the mighty works done in you had been done in Tyre and Sidon, they would have repented long since in sackcloth and ashes" (Matthew 11:20f.). In the miracles of Jesus the mercy of God is evident, that mercy which now seeks men out. Man must allow himself to be found and to be saved. He must heed the call of God, answer him and follow him.

The penitential preaching of Jesus is more powerful and incomparably more crucial than any preaching up to that time. If the men of Nineveh turned over a new leaf at the preaching of Jonah, then the present generation must do even more, because here there is one who is greater than Jonah (Matthew 12:41). There can no longer be any excuse to neglect conversion and repentance.

What the biblical call to conversion entails may be seen even more clearly in the preaching of the Apostles, which broadens and develops that admonition. As soon as the Twelve were sent out by Jesus, "they preached that men must be converted" (Mark 6:12). The resurrected one bade that "conversion unto the forgiveness of sins should be preached in his name" (Luke 24:47). In his Pentecost preaching, Peter says: "Be converted, and be baptized every one of you" (Acts 2:38). In the Church, conversion becomes visible and effective in the reception of baptism. The sacrament, however, has personal decision as its prerequisite. Thus even in the temple Peter says: "Do penance and be converted, so that your sins may be blotted out" (Acts 3:19). He sounds the moral goal of conversion. Thereafter if this be a summons, it is, nevertheless, a grace. God "gives to Israel conversion and forgiveness of sins" (Acts 5:31). And this preaching is directed also to the Gentiles: "Now God has granted conversion unto life even to the Gentiles" (Acts 11:18).

On the Areopagus, Paul preaches that God bids all to be converted before the coming judgment: "God has overlooked the times of ignorance; but now he orders all men to act wisely, because all men

everywhere must be converted" (Acts 17:30). The glorified Christ, in
his appearance near Damascus, lays down the aim of the mission
preaching which is committed to Paul's care: ". . . that they may turn
themselves from darkness to light, from the power of Satan to God"
(Acts 26:18). In Miletus, Paul himself says of his own mission work:
"I have borne witness before Jews and Gentiles as well about conver-
ion to God and about faith in our Lord Jesus" (Acts 20:21). Even
here conversion is completed through the positive complement of
faith (as in Mark 1:15). In the presence of Agrippa, Paul declares that
he preached to Jews and Gentiles that "they should be converted and
turn to God and do works worthy of their conversion" (Acts 26:20).
Once more the moral demands of conversion are emphasized. In the
Acts of the Apostles, the Church of Christ is simply the one which
"has turned to the Lord" (Acts 9:35; 11:21; 15:19).

The concept and word *metánoia* is found also in the Epistles of
Paul. Thus in his admonition to Israel: "Do you presume upon the
riches of God's goodness, his patience and forbearance? God's kindness
will lead you to conversion" (Rom. 2:4). God grants and works conversion, which, however, calls men to make their own decision. Even
to the Church among the Gentiles it is said: "You have turned away
from idols to God, to serve the living and true God" (1 Thess. 1:9).
Paul was obliged to grieve the Corinthians repeatedly by his reproofs.
But this grieving "brought about a conversion unto salvation" (2
Cor. 7:9f.). Paul fears that when he comes to Corinth again he will
have to bear a great deal of grief on account of those who sinned previously and have not turned away from the impurity, lechery, and
debauchery which they have practiced (2 Cor. 12:21). Paul is probably
referring to sins committed when the Corinthians were still pagans.
But for Christians the duty of conversion goes on and on. There is
the duty of the bishop: "With mildness shall he set his opponents
aright, that God may perhaps grant them conversion unto the recognition of truth" (2 Tim. 2:25).

Although Paul's actual use of the word *metánoia* is comparatively
infrequent, he uses other words and forms to express the same concept. Conversion is demanded as withdrawal from the world: "Do not
be conformed to this world, but be transformed by the renewal of your
mind" (Rom. 12:2). He speaks of the death of the old man and the

resurrection of the new in baptism and in the additional personal ratification of baptism (Rom. 6:1-11; Col. 2:11f.). The idea of "conversion" or "turning about" is evident also in the terms "new creation" (2 Cor. 5:17; Gal. 6:15); "new life" (Rom. 6:4; 2 Cor. 5:15); and "new man" (Eph. 2:15; 4:24).

The work of God precedes any human doing, but a necessary concomitant is life in the spirit. Ultimately the summons to conversion is contained in what is for Paul the essentially important expression of faith, in which the turning from death to life is accomplished. Conversion remains the constant duty even of Christians. The inner man, who is none other than the new man, "must be renewed from day to day" (2 Cor. 4:16).

The Gospel of John does not use the word *conversion*. It is characterized, however, by pairs of antithetical terms: light and darkness, truth and lies, love and hate, death and life, God and world. Faith is the turning from one to the other (John 5:24). The gospel teaches and requires rebirth (John 3:3-7). Even in this it gives expression to the summons to conversion. And like the summons to conversion, this too is a gift of God. "No one can come to me unless it is granted him by the Father" (John 6:65).

The admonition to repentance and conversion in the latest writings of the New Testament is no longer merely the proclamation of mission preaching to Jews and Gentiles but an urgent concern within the Church. In the Epistle to the Hebrews, the possibility of the penitence of a Christian is questionable when he has fallen away from his first conversion in baptism. "It is not possible for those who have *once* been enlightened, who have tasted of the heavenly gifts, who have become partakers of the Holy Spirit, and who have tasted of the powers of the world to come, if they be fallen away, to be renewed again unto conversion [unto repentance]" (Heb. 6:4-6). Apostasy from faith is not only estrangement from the Church and exclusion from her communion, but it is forfeiture of former vocation and sanctification, and of the communion of God. Repentance seems impossible in this Epistle, especially on the part of man, because such wickedness, according to human estimation, no longer permits any hope. The subjective impossibility of repentance is also an objective ordering of salvation, since divine judgment is effected conjointly in man's guilt.

A warning can be found in the history of Esau, who, after the sale of his birthright, "found no opportunity for conversion, though he sought it with tears" (Heb. 12:17). It is not quite clear whether the text means to imply that Esau sought a change of mind on the part of Isaac, or, indeed, on the part of God; or whether he sought a remorseful conversion of himself. Apparently it is this last which is intended. If the divine gift is spurned in contempt, then conversion is no longer at man's disposal; but in any case, it remains a free gift of God.[38]

2 Peter 3:9 bespeaks a view in some way opposed to that of the Epistle to the Hebrews: "God wills that all should attain to conversion [repentance]." History knows that only after many altercations, yes, long struggles between antithetical necessities and bases, did the Church find an order of penance and the ability to establish it.

The Apocalypse of John is urgent in its admonitions to conversion. Again and again the call to repentance goes forth in the letters to the seven churches of Asia Minor (Apoc. 2:5, 16, 21f.; 3:3, 19). If the admonition goes unheeded, the Lord of the community will, upon his arrival, execute judgment. The Apocalypse has to announce, nevertheless, that men will be brought to reflection and conversion not even by the severest of calamities, which will only bring them to blaspheme God the more (Apoc. 9:20f.; 16:9, 11).

From the beginning of the gospel (Mark 1:15) even to the last book, the Apocalypse, the call to conversion goes out. It is the summons to a redemption to be accomplished again and again, redemption from being lost in the world, to a homecoming in purity and joy, in faith and in the love of God. Along with God's repeated call, however, there is also his repeated promise, to accept man upon his returning home. Life can be summed up in the saying: "What must we do? Be converted!" (Acts 2:37f.).

§ 6. FAITH

Lexicography and the history of religion show that the words *faith* and *to have faith* (πίστις and πιστεύειν) have the intensive significance of religious faith first and only in the Greek Bible, both Old and New Testaments.[39] In the classical Greek language, πιστεύειν means "to presume something, to have confidence in someone, or to hold something as true." The Greek does not *believe* in the existence of his gods; but he *knows* that the gods exist, since he continually sees them and has experience of them as those powers (spiritual, in the sense of supernatural) with which the world is filled.

In the later period of Hellenism, nevertheless, πίστις occasionally takes on a religious import. In the *Corpus Hermeticum* (1, 32) the *mystes* says: "I believe and confess that I am going to light and life." In a prayer to Isis (probably of the first century A.D.), her worshipers are termed "those who call upon you in consequence of their faith." The Greek translation of the Old Testament, the Septuagint in particular, uses the word with a minimal emphasis on its religious import. With words built on the stem πιστ-, it translates various Hebrew words, of various word-stems, which in some way signify: to assent to or give consent to God, to place one's confidence in him, to say "Amen!" to him. In this way the Greek Old Testament has conceived as the essence of the Old Testament religion one and the same set of circumstances of faith, which it has characterized and brought into prominence through but a single word-family. It is followed in this by later translations, even by many of those in modern languages.[40]

In the Old Testament, the word and concept *faith* is first encountered in the history of Abraham. "Abraham believed (*i.e.*, had faith in) God," who promised him a son (Gen. 15:6). Paul explains this at some length: Abraham hoped against all hope, and that was reckoned to him as righteousness. Abraham is the grand example of faith (Rom. 4:3). To believe or to have faith means, in this instance, to trust in God's word and promise. Faith is effected as agreement of intellect, confidence of man, obedience of will. The prophets speak of the mighty power of faith. It is in faith that the people of God finds its life and its security. This is expressed in the saying: "If you will not believe, you shall not endure" (Is. 7:9 — in Luther's translation: "If you do not rely on Yahweh, you will have no support"). "Whoever believes will not falter. This is the firm foundation stone, which Yahweh lays in Zion" (Is. 28:16). Not a few of the Psalms (35:5-11;

40:1-6; 46; 56:4f.; 91) are witness to firm faith, even if the word itself is not used.

With her deliverance from Egypt, Israel "believes" or "has faith" in the power of God in her history (Ps. 106:12 = Exod. 14:31). Delivered from her need, she says: "I have believed, for which reason I now can say, 'I was once bent low'" (Ps. 116:10). Paul (2 Cor. 4:13) finds in the passage just quoted, testimony to the one Spirit who effects faith in the old and in the new covenant as well. Faith builds on God's word: "I believe in your commands" (Ps. 119:66). Use of the term *to believe* in the sense of *to have faith* is not infrequent in the Wisdom books, e.g., in Sir. 2:8; "You that fear the Lord, believe in him; and your reward will not be made void"; see also Wis. 12:2.

As long as Israel lived within her own boundaries and shut off from other peoples, she took her Yahweh-religion as a matter of course for her nation. From earliest times, of course, the prophets had to guard the people against the temptations presented by the worship of Baal. When, however, the ancient Judaism began to be spread abroad in the diaspora, she found herself in opposition to her heretical surroundings. Now she understood that the essence of the biblical religion was the worship of *one* God in the imageless, pure spirituality of faith.

The Jewish religion recognized and perceived the way in which it was different from other religions, whose essence was cultic and often pompous solemnities, as in the kingdoms and religions of the Near East, which solemnized the divine power vested in the potentate. Again and in another way Israel perceived the special character of her religion in contrast to that of Greece, whose religion was the cult of beauty, of humanity, and of intellectual knowledge; or in contrast to that of Rome, whose religion was an expression of the unity of the state (as especially is the case in the cult of the emperor).

In her confrontation with the overwhelming Hellenistic culture and in the struggle to hold her own under the foreign domination of Rome, Israel came to recognize her faith as a possession most peculiarly her own. In her impotence among the great political powers, she set up her faith as religious power. In the later books of the Old Testament, faith is ever more consciously, ever more openly identified as that which distinguishes Israel from the Gentiles. This is the case with the books of Maccabees (2 Macc. 7:14; 8:18), in the Wisdom literature (Wis. 15:3), as well as in the extra-canonical writings, e.g., 4 Esdras 13:23; "God will protect the afflicted if they have works and faith in the Most Sublime and Almighty"—and note the phrase "works and faith," which is otherwise than Paul in Rom. 3:24.

If *faith* originally signifies the subjection of the whole nation to God's command, the individual gradually emerges from the collective bond of the nation, and the godly man can give expression to what is ever his own proper experience of his God, referring to it as to *faith*—a process which becomes possible especially with the prophets (Is. 28:16; 40:31) and in the Psalms (46; 91; 116). The Greek Bible solidifies the word and concept *faith* in the thought and piety of Judaism. In the New Testament era, Philo (*Abraham*, 46) is able to speak about faith and to describe the existence of the believer in a way which corresponds to our own notion of faith: "The only true and certain good is faith in God: comfort in life, abundance of good hope, release from pain, rich yield in goods, renunciation of evil intent, recognition on account of godliness, happiness as one's lot, universal betterment of the soul, which depends upon the author of all things, who can do all and wills the best."

The Qumran texts, in the meantime, do not, properly speaking, know the biblical concept of faith; in any case, what they speak of is "fidelity" to the Law. That which is characteristic of the New Testament comes into view by way of the contrast between what the *Commentary on the Book of Habakkuk*, found at Qumran, understands by the words of the prophet, "The righteous man shall live by his faith" (Hab. 2:4), and what Paul understands by the same text. According to the Qumran scroll (1 QpHab 7:18–8:1), God will save those who keep the Law, because of their obedience to the teacher of righteousness and to the new efforts which he demands in respect to the Law. According to Paul (Rom. 1:17; Gal. 3:11), however, it is not Law nor works of Law which justify, but faith, which accepts Christ's work of salvation.

The New Testament can enter into the Old Testament understanding and consciousness of faith. But its own concept and its own preaching of faith become something else, something new, inasmuch as the word and concept *faith* are now employed with a totally unaccustomed frequency, as well as with a more intense precision of meaning. Now the spirit and power of faith become that by which a man's life is brought to fulfillment, just as they can be the order and law of a community. This happens because still another force is released from within the Christian faith, the force which is "love, in which faith is effective" (Gal. 5:6; see also chs. 8 and 9 below).

What faith is might also be discovered by contemplating a kind of living evidence in opposition to the New Testament. In the midst of one of the most important wildernesses of Palestine, in the Plain of Sichem, standing erect even today, are the ruins of old Samaria, from Roman times until today called Sebaste (Sebastia), i.e., City of Augustus. Still intact are the magnificent substructures and outer staircases of the Temple of Roma and Augustus, which once stood there. The remains of the column-lined street which led up to the heights and the temple thereon, and the rows of columns themselves, cast only a shadow of the former glory of the temple and the city. Here in the midst of Israel a flourishing heathen priesthood served its alien gods with pompous processions and sacrifices. Jesus and his disciples looked up from the paths they trod and saw this and other pagan temples. In such circumstances, what might their thoughts have been? Probably that which is expressed in one of the sayings of the Lord: "When you pray, do not raise a din the way the pagans do. They think, you see, that their torrent of words will assure their being heard. Do not be like them! For your Father knows what you need even before you ask him" (Matthew 6:7).

In the Gospels there is recorded repeatedly a saying of the Lord as to what faith is *not*. In a harsh saying, Jesus describes the men to whom he is speaking as an unfaithful and perverse generation (Matthew 17:17; 12:39; 16:4). The Jews who were standing around him pronounced twice each day the Jewish confession of faith, the *Shema'*: "Hear, Israel, there is one God and none other besides him." And in spite of this, Jesus calls them a faithless generation. It means simply this: One can repeat a confession of faith again and again, and still be a faithless man. Faith is not an external confession.

What faith is, in the mind of Jesus and in the New Testament sense, is exposed by the history of Peter and of how he walked on the water (Matthew 14:28-31).[41] Difficult as it is to determine the literary and form-critical character of the pericope, it is nonetheless to be candidly regarded as a didactic narrative clarifying the nature of faith. The disciples are traveling at night on the Lake of Gennesaret. While they are toiling, and at about the fourth watch of the night, the Lord appears to them. They are terrified and cry out in fear. At the beckoning of the Lord, Peter climbs out of the boat. The word of the Lord prepares the way and Peter strides across the unfamiliar depths. Faith makes the place upon which the believer can step and on which he can depend. But faith is not simply a matter of saying "yes" once and having it hold good forevermore. It is continually put to the test and abandoned and must every instant be affirmed anew. Peter sees the storm and becomes frightened; and because he calls for help he begins to sink. The opposing reality becomes stronger than his fiducial bond with Christ, until this bond is severed and Peter sinks into the waves. Jesus seizes him and holds him fast. To believe means to depend upon a reality which is more real than the world itself. In accord with all practical experience, it was not to be accepted that the water would support him. Faith attends more to the word which promises that water will support him than it does to practical experience. Faith is the decision hazarded upon the word of promise in the midst of a menacing world. Afterwards there is often enough a sinking and a crying out for help. Faith is existence in fear and doubt, but without fearing ("Fear not!") and without doubting ("O you of little faith, why did you doubt?").

Another saying of the Lord speaks again about the power of faith: "Have faith in God! Truly, I tell you, if anyone should say to this mountain, 'Up with yourself and cast yourself into the sea,' and does not waver in his heart, but believes that what he says will happen, it will be done for him. Everything is possible for him who believes" (Mark 11:22-23). It is, nevertheless, impossible for mountains to uproot themselves. But in the totality of its resignation to God's will, faith partakes in God's almighty power. It is not a resigned surrender of oneself to reality, but the winning of a power over reality. Its passivity is highest activity. Everything is possible to one who believes (Mark 9:23), because to God everything is possible. Disbelief knows that it has not this faith. From afar off it can but look into a land of possibles, which to it is closed.

Another of the Lord's words says, in regard to faith: "Whoever causes one of these little ones, who believe in me, to stumble, it would be better for him if a millstone were hung around his neck and he were cast into the sea" (Mark 9:42). The saying emerges from a concrete event, when Jesus placed a child in the midst of the group and indicated this actual child. But from its simple and most natural sense, the saying proceeds to a deeper meaning. In the presence of adults and so far as adults are concerned, children are of lesser importance. They expect the gifts of adults, and are able to accept them with pure joy. In this respect the child is an archetype of the believer, who knows that before God he is of no importance and expects all things as God's gift to him.

In the gospel it is often said of faith that it heals and saves. "Your faith has saved you" (Matthew 9:22; Mark 10:52; Luke 7:50; 17:19) is the conclusion to the narratives of the cures worked by Jesus. And therewith it is ever apparent that in this physical healing the salvation of the whole man is intended and does take place.

How, then, is faith to be understood in the sayings of Jesus? It is the conviction that God is ever at hand, if only man is prepared to turn to him. And that God is ever the rich and powerful gift, if man will but permit himself to be recipient. The power which faith has to stir and to move is, for man, a redeeming power unto salvation. Man comes to such faith, however, not by his own design, his own will, his own capability; rather, his being moved from disbelief to belief can come only as a gift of God. That is why the father of the boy who was possessed cries out: "I do believe! Help thou my unbelief!" (Mark 9:24). To the disciples "is given the secret of the kingdom of God" (Mark 4:11). It was not flesh and blood but the Father in heaven who by revelation enabled Peter to recognize Christ Jesus (Matthew 16:17). The Father "hides his secret things from the wise and clever, and uncovers them to the unsophisticated" (Matthew 11:25).

In the older Gospels, those other than John's, Jesus does not expressly require faith in the Christ himself.[42] Inasmuch, however, as the Gospels at times refer the genesis of faith to an encounter with Jesus, and since his saving help is the result thereof (Mark 5:34), faith therefore arises from — and as faith, is vested in — the healing power of Jesus. And insofar as the teaching Christ requires faith in his word, which reveals the heavenly Father (Matthew 11:25-27) and announces the approaching kingdom (Mark 4:11); and insofar as he demands the imitation of his person (Mark 8:34), in that same measure also this faith that he demands is not only the faithfulness of the man whose confidence is in the Father, but it is directed even to Christ himself, and commences in association with him.

Prompted by the inner necessity of progressing from the pre-paschal to the post-paschal era, the Church of the Apostles proclaims the faith as faith in Christ, his word, his work, and his person. Nevertheless, this faith does not remain concentrated on Christ alone, but through him it is turned again toward the Father. Faith recognizes and grasps the dealing of God in Christ, or, as Paul puts it: "Because we know that a man is not justified on the basis of works of the Law, but only by faith in Christ Jesus, we have become faithful to Christ so as to be justified by faith in Christ" (Gal. 2:16). To believe means to be open to the salvational dealings of God which take place in Christ. Faith is "having confidence toward God through Christ" (2 Cor. 3:4). Faith is heeding and answering the word that God speaks in Christ to the world: "Faith, therefore, comes from hearing; the message which is heard, however, comes from the preaching of Christ" (Rom. 10:14-18).

Like the gospel, Paul too says that faith is gift and grace of God. "God gives the measure of faith" (Rom. 12:3). Faith is a charism (1 Cor. 12:9). It is effected through the (divine) Spirit of faith (2 Cor. 4:13). "It has been granted you not only to believe in Christ, but to suffer for him" (Phil. 1:29). If God works in a man unto faith, the man is not thereby relieved of his responsibility; rather, it is only now that his responsibility becomes clear. "With fear and trembling work out your salvation. For it is God who works in you, both willing and working in accord with his salvific will" (Phil. 2:12f.). Man must not forget that in the work of salvation God is his partner and he is God's partner.

The word of God, to which man responds in faith, reaches him in preaching. It is not the bare account of a historical event that should conduct a man to knowledge; nor yet a thesis, the correctness of which one perceives, so that he must then accept it; rather, the preaching of faith is challenge and summons, and more, it is promise.

The acceptance of the word, therefore, is not merely a matter of perception and understanding, but of acknowledgment and obedience. This idea puts its mark upon the formula devised by Paul about the "heeding of faith," i.e., the "obedience of faith" (Rom. 1:5; 16:26; Gal. 3:2, 5).

As response of man to God's word, faith is from its very beginnings decision and action, and thus it progresses of itself to other areas. Faith must stand the test as "faith, which works in love" (Gal. 5:6). Faith must be productive of works (1 Thess. 1:3). It is fulfilled in the "joy of faith" (Phil. 1:25). Without love any talk of faith is empty chatter (1 Cor. 13:1). All this notwithstanding, faith never merits salvation, which remains always a free gift. "We believe that a man is justified by faith apart from works of the law" (Rom. 3:28). Probably Paul is speaking in this instance primarily of the works of the Old Testament Law. But still, in the overview of these works, works in general make their appearance. The way of law, however, not only does not lead to the goal because no one can pursue it to the end, because no one is able in fact to fulfill the law; instead, the way of law is erroneous from the outset because it is an attempt to achieve righteousness through works. It is directed toward self-adulation (Rom. 2:17; 1 Cor. 1:29). It is sinful because it is an attempt at self-maintenance and self-righteousness.

As a sinner, man stands ever with empty hands before his God. He must renounce every claim and can but permit himself to be the humble recipient of gifts. This happens when, in the faith of Christ, he applies himself to works. It is then and thus that man is justified by faith apart from works. Faith is radical obedience, in that the believer completely renounces every claim of his own. It is this faith that is spoken of when it is said, "faith alone makes blessed." Nevertheless, this faith, if it is full and genuine, never is alone but is always "effective in love" (Gal. 5:6; see also ch. 14 below).

Faith is lived and experienced personally. The disciples beseech the Lord: "Increase our faith!" (Luke 17:5). Paul speaks of the same matter, but with a different emphasis. Many are "weak in faith" (Rom. 14:1). Faith "increases itself" (2 Cor. 10:15).

In the history of the Church, Paul has become in a special way the Apostle of faith. Nevertheless, there is in the Church another most

excellent Apostle, John,[43] who speaks of faith with scarcely less pene-
tration. In John, too, the believer enters into salvation through Christ.
In the Gospel of John this Christ is announced with new words and
concepts. He is the shepherd, the gate, the bread, the vine, the light,
the word. He is "the way, the truth, and the life" (John 14:6).

The history of religion shows that similar words and concepts were
important even to the contemporaneous religious milieu, especially to
the gnosis. These religions promised their adherents similar benefits
of salvation. The Gospel of John is couched in the conceptualizations
of its time. It recognizes, therefore, the hankering after these benefits.
But the Gospel states at the same time that the world has until now
provided false solutions to these quests for life and to these longings
after salvation. It opposes Christ to the false gods which the world
has produced, and announces that he is the fulfillment of its every
quest.

To believe, therefore, means to have nothing to do with the then
current standards, judgments, and solutions. Faith demands the surrender of false security and lies; it demands a readiness to accept the
new truth and the new life which Christ gives. Faith is a decision
against the world and for God's salvation. Since Christ is the sole
and total revelation of God, faith is essentially the confession of Jesus
as Christ and as love of God (John 20:31). This faith is light and
life (John 12:46). It dispenses eternal life (John 3:15; 5:24). Jesus
himself demands this faith in his mission and in his person (John
6:29; 10:37f.; 12:36). To believe in the Son, however, is to believe
also in the Father (John 12:44f.; 17:8). Genuine faith is that which
abides in the love of Jesus (John 16:27) and keeps his word (John
8:51; 14:15).

The preaching of the Church will spread this faith abroad throughout the world (John 17:20f). Faith does not need the presence of
Jesus, in the sense of a simultaneity of presence (John 20:29). This
faith is an overcoming of the world. "This is the victory that conquers
the world, our faith" (1 John 5:4). John too says that faith is the work
of God in man, as an effective decision of man. "No one can come to
me unless the Father, who sent me, draws him" (John 6:44). God's
drawing of man means his gracious dealing with man whereby man
makes his decision. God's drawing takes place in man's approaching.

If man does not conclude to the proper response, his unbelief is culpable and sinful (John 9:41; 15:22).

It holds good for Paul, as well as for John and for the whole of the New Testament, that faith and knowledge are not exclusively antithetical to each other. As teacher, Jesus is concerned with the perception and understanding of his listeners and disciples (Matthew 13:11, 51; 15:10; Luke 10:11). His revelation dispenses a knowledge of the Father (Matthew 11:27). But little faith can result from lack of understanding (Matthew 16:8-11). Paul speaks of the knowledge of faith in two different senses: of the knowledge about salvation history, which knowledge is transmitted through revelation and word: "We believe, and do therefore preach as one who *knows*, that he who raised the Lord Jesus will raise us also with Jesus" (2 Cor. 4:13f.; cf. Rom. 6:8f.); and of that knowledge which discloses to the believer a new understanding of himself: "We glory in our tribulations, because we *know* that tribulation makes for patience" (Rom. 5:3; cf. 2 Cor. 5:6; Phil. 1:19).

With John, too, knowledge and faith are bound together in the unity of a single act. Both words, then, can appear in the sequence *to believe — to know* ("We have believed and have known that you are the holy one of God" [John 6:69]), as well as in the sequence *to know — to believe* ("They have known and have believed that you sent me" [John 17:8]). It is not the case, therefore, that faith, as the simpler element, proceeds to knowledge, as the more profound; nor is it as if faith were to supplement knowledge. If, indeed, faith meets itself in the midst of knowledge, still, knowledge remains ever in faith. New Testament faith, then, is not a blind leap into dark paradoxes and contradictions; but neither is it a philosophy. To question is not prohibited to faith; no, much more, it is commanded. It must progress continually in perception and knowledge of God (Col. 1:9f.). Faith and knowledge are an antithetical unity.

The problem of the doubt of faith already occupies the attention of the New Testament. A saying of the Lord speaks of the doubt in a divided heart (Mark 11:23). The narrative about Peter's walking on the water depicts the temptation of doubt (Matthew 14:28-31). Of prayer and faith, James says: "Let him ask in faith and doubt not; for the doubting man is like a wave of the sea that is driven and tossed by the wind. He is a double-minded man" (i.e., a man with a divided soul — James 1:6-8). The appendix added to Mark at a later time speaks in alarming and moving intensity about the lack of faith prevalent in the Church. The resurrected Christ must censure his disciples severely on account of it. Overcoming its own disbelief, the Church must proclaim the gospel (Mark 16:11-16).

In the New Testament texts adduced this far, faith is presented as the subjective faithfulness entered upon by a man, the power by which something is believed. At the same time, however, faith has its own specific content. For Paul, faith is always faith in Jesus as the Lord, and the confession thereof: "If with your mouth you confess that Jesus is the Lord, and in your heart you believe that God has raised him from the dead, you will be saved" (Rom. 10:9). Faith is already understood also as the objective quantity of a confession and as a norm. Faith has a content which is embraced; thus in Rom. 12:6; Gal. 1:23; Eph. 4:5; and more prominently in the Pastoral Letters: 1 Tim. 2:7; 3:9; 4:6; Titus 1:1. When Paul writes: "I have handed down to you what I too received, that Christ died for our sins according to the Scriptures, that he was buried, and that he was raised up on the third day, and that he appeared to Cephas and then to the twelve" (1 Cor. 15:3-5), we already perceive clearly the formula of the confession of faith still in use in the Church today.

There are more than a few examples of the New Testament's striking a familiar note of accord with the modern formulation of the Church's *Credo* (especially Rom. 1:3f.; 4:25; 6:3-5; 14:9; 1 Thess. 4:14; further, Acts 10:38f.; 1 Peter 1:20f.; 2:21; 3:18f.; and even Mark 8:31; 9:31; 10:33f.). The oldest confession of faith, then, is quite rightly called "The Apostles' Creed" because in both the content and form of its essential parts it goes back to the time of the Apostles.[44]

Toward the end of the New Testament era, the concept of faith becomes more objectified. The last Epistles to be added to the New Testament bear testimony to this. The Epistle of James already finds it necessary to oppose a misunderstanding according to which faith is only an intellectual activity which can be isolated from the rest of life: "What use is it, my brethren, if someone says that he has the faith, while he has no corresponding works? Can the faith save him?" (James 2:14). And further: "You believe that there is but one

God. And you do rightly. Even the demons believe and shudder" (James 2:19).

The Epistle to the Hebrews emphasizes the importance of faith. At the very opening of that chapter which produces such a cloud of witnesses to the faith, faith is defined as "a pledge of what is hoped for (*or* a standing by what is hoped for?) and being fast convinced of things, though they are not seen" (Heb. 11:1). The Letter states further, that we receive in faith the teaching about the existence of God and about the divine creation of the world (Heb. 11:3, 6). Certainly faith is not a philosophical perception, since it must obey the word of God (Heb. 4:2). Faith is based on Christ, who is the prototype of faith as "leader of faith" (Heb. 12:2). He is the spokesman, the functioning high priest, through whom the congregation is sanctified to the service of God (Heb. 9:11–10:25). Faith places the whole man in the presence of God; therefore the admonition: "With undefiled hearts in the fullness of faith let us come into God's presence" (Heb. 10:22).

The Epistle to the Hebrews is in harmony with early Judaism and Qumran, inasmuch as in their writings also the necessity of preserving the faith is emphasized. This is understandable, given a period in which the faith of the Synogogue as well as that of the Church was obliged to prove itself in its accomplishments, in the face of numerous persecutions. In this way faith becomes a way of life and a virtue. On the other hand, however, there is also a relationship between the Epistle to the Hebrews and the late Apostolic writings, in which the blending of kerygma and morality presumes in the manner of its expression that the Christian is not already given a new and eschatological existence, but must win for himself the prerequisite thereto.[45]

The Epistle of Jude, verse 3, purposes to defend "the most holy faith, which was once for all delivered to the saints [i.e., the Church]." The faith is the rule of faith. Nevertheless, this faith is delivered to all the saints, and all are answerable for it. It is not as if it were tendered only to an administrative body governing the faith and charged with managing it for all the others.

In the Second Epistle of Peter (3:2), Christians are charged to hold fast to "the predictions of the holy prophets, and the commandment of the Lord and Savior, announced through the Apostles." The content of the faith is the teaching of the prophets, who predicted Christ, and the teaching of the Apostles, who proclaim the gospel of Christ: therefore, the Old Testament and the New. The Apostles are authoritative intermediaries between Christ and the Church. The gospel of Christ, however, is designated and understood as the law of Christ. This understanding is accentuated juridically and morally. The faith is understood more and more as the sum total of the fiducial knowledge handed down in the Church. The ever personal faith comes to pass in the individual's acceptance of the norm of faith. Biblically understood, faith is never the bare intellectual act of holding the teaching of the Church as true. Not only is it much more than that, it is really something quite otherwise — it is response to God's word in an act of personal confidence therein.

In the course of time the question as to the nature of faith has become a question which stands between the Churches and is debated as a controversial question between Catholic and Protestant theologies. It is certaintly true that when the term "true faith" is used, the current Catholic understanding tends to take faith more in the sense of the objective doctrinal content of the faith as confession, while the Protestant understanding looks more to the subjective, personal discharge of faith as faithfulness.

The history of the dogma and doctrine of the Church demonstrates, nevertheless, that for the great teachers of the Church, like Augustine and Thomas Aquinas, the concept of faith definitely includes also the subjective, personal faithfulness. The concept of the true faith as orthodoxy is consolidated in the counter-Reformational position of the Church, which formulated Catholic dogma and emphasized its differences from that of the Reformation. It will be our task even in this to learn from the ancient truth: the New Testament in its entirety and the Fathers of the Church.

In the gospel there is a remark of Jesus, couched as a question, melancholy in its implication of a negative reply: "Will the Son of Man, when he returns, find faith on earth?" (Luke 18:8). Is it really true, as one occasionally reads or hears, that in our time the world is losing or has already lost the substance of faith? Perhaps the number of the unchurched has increased in our time beyond what it was earlier; or perhaps such lack of attachment has only become more a matter of public knowledge than it was earlier. In any case, being un-churched must not be equated with radical disbelief. Who knows how much faith there may yet be, a faith of which one is scarcely conscious, but a faith still, if it be no more than a kind of longing cry: "Lord, I do believe! Help thou my unbelief!"

A certain confession of unbelief says: "As long as the public opinion of the West perdures, to the effect that the only thing that can save the world is the holding of the postulates of the Christian faith as true, it will perforce lengthen the era of faithlessness and will continue to drive new generations to cynicism, to superficiality, and to apathetic helplessness" (G. Szczesny, *Die Zukunft des Unglaubens*, Munich, 1958, p. 220). This assertion might be justified if Christian faith meant repeating past history and holding fast to yesterday's metaphysics, and proving the validity thereof with a system of theses which, to be sure, we sometimes mistook and do yet sometimes mistake for the Christian faith itself (which can happen, perhaps, for the reason that the witness which the faith gives about itself is insufficient). But that statement is not right if Christian faith means continually to surrender yesterday and today for the sake of winning ever anew a tomorrow which is God's promised gift.

Let it be noted that in its presentation of the faith, the New Testament employs not only words of the same root as πίστις, but also πείθεσθαι (to obey, to believe), and πεποιθέναι (to trust [in God]), and related words. We find them above all in Paul, and then also (under Pauline influence?) in the Lucan writings. In the majority of instances they have the purely human meaning that they have in profane Greek literature. In this sense, πείθεσθαι, derived from πείθειν (to persuade) = to be convinced; πεποιθέναι = to trust in men.

The following passages are theologically significant: "Wrath and judgment will overtake those who do not obey the truth, but obey wickedness" (Rom. 2:8); and: "Who has hindered you from obeying the truth?" (Gal. 5:7). Israel is a "disobedient and recalcitrant people" (Rom. 10:21, quoting Is. 65:2). Jews and Gentiles alike are disobedient to God (Rom. 11:30-32; Heb. 3:18; 11:31). Sinners are flatly desig-nated as "sons of disobedience" (Eph. 2:2; 5:6). As in other places in Paul (Rom. 1:5; see above, p. 89f.), these terms are employed in de-scribing faith as obedience, and the lack of faith as disobedience. The same mentality can be seen in Acts 17:4: "Some were persuaded [came to the faith]"; and Acts 28:24: "Some were persuaded of what was said, but others remained in disbelief."

In the New Testament the primary meaning of πεποιθέναι is in reference to trust or confidence between men. Nevertheless, the concept is characteristically modified, so that it becomes "confidence in the Lord" (Gal. 5:10; Phil. 2:24; 2 Thess. 3:4). The Christian communion of faith deepens and consolidates trust among men. Paul speaks also of trust in God. The Apostle had to endure extreme peril, "so that we might not trust in ourselves but in God" (2 Cor. 1:9). Even in Phil. 1:6, the reference is probably to trust in God and not in the community. A lengthier formulation is encountered: "In Christ we have trust and confidence of access through faith in him" (Eph. 3:12).

While the Old Testament, especially in Psalms and Isaiah, often speaks of confidence in God, the New Testament uses the formula sparingly. This relation to God is designated more often as faith. Does *faith* express surrender to God in a more radical way than does *confidence*, in which there may yet be a partial reservation of one's own desire and of trust in personal performance? Well, Paul warns us about false confidence: "We glory in Jesus Christ and put no confidence in the flesh, though I myself have reason for confidence in the flesh also" (Phil. 3:3-4). Jesus speaks of those "who trust in themselves, that they are righteous" (Luke 18:9). Not infrequently Paul uses the word πεποίθησις, but only in its profane meaning (2 Cor. 1:15; 8:23; 10:2).

§ 7. HOPE

The theology of hope has been much discussed in treatises and in lectures.[46] If one inquires after the bases of hope, several can be adduced. Our world, and above all our young people, live in apprehension and fear about the future. One of the new fears is the threat of the extraordinary destructive forces that can be unleashed. For generations the socialist ideology sought to lead the present forth to a better future; and now its answer to the quest for a future has been renewed

and urged again by socialism and communism, which offer a utopian
vision of prosperity. The realization of this prosperity must begin immediately and without delay. Out of this there has developed a science of what is to come, a futurology.

Christian faith wants the gospel, its message about the questions
and needs of our times, to be heard. It may be that the message of
salvation, presented in a very individualistic manner, will become the
salvation of individual souls. With that consideration we are now
constrained to turn our consideration to the social, indeed to the cosmic, content of the message.

That hope is a basic attitude sustaining men's lives is a point of
common knowledge to Greek culture, Judaism, and Christianity.
Hope is determined in different directions, according to its own content. Hope is never merely a discovering of the future; and what is
hoped for is never merely a succession from the present. Hope is
rather a creating of the future. "What should and must be, is the foundation of what is."

Plato speaks of the hope which shapes and determines the life of
man. "For our whole lives through we are filled with hopes" (*Phile-
bus*, 39E). Our striving after the noble and the good "procures for us
our greatest helps for the present . . . and effects our greatest hopes
for the future; and if we preserve our reverential fear of the gods, it
will lead us back to primordial nature and, through the healing of
our weakness, make us happy and blessed." In the face of death the
wise man is "of good hope" (*Apol.*, 41C; *Phaedo*, 64A). He has
"great hope of acquiring there what he has striven after here" (*Phaedo*,
67B).

The Mysteries of Eleusis bestow upon the *mystes* "blessed hopes in
respect to death, that they will enjoy a better life" (*Ael. Aristides*, 22,
10). According to Porphyry, the Neo-Platonist, there are four values
which are determinants in life: faith, truth, love, and hope. "It is
necessary for a man to believe that his sole salvation is return to God.
Whoever believes this must strive with all his power to know the
truth about God; whoever has come to know it must love him whom
he knows; he who loves, however, must, while he lives, feed his soul
on noble hopes" (Porphyry, *Letter to Marcella*, 24).

In the literary and epigraphic witnesses to the cult of the emperor, he is lauded as the "savior." Among the more celebrated are inscriptions to Augustus, in which it is said that he is the savior who fulfills the hopes of former times and who has uncovered new hopes for the future. Such proclamations are not foreign to the language of the New Testament.[47] The New Testament allows the validity of hopes of worldly expectations, takes them up and fulfills them, as Paul says: "What you worship as unknown, this I proclaim to you" (Acts 17:23).

Antiquity, to be sure, first established the theory of atheism, then presented it to man, who renounced all hope and contented himself with death as the end of it all. As a prefatory motto to his book *Winter in Vienna* (1958), an abysmal contradiction of hope, Reinhold Schneider quotes a saying of Epicharmus: "Mortal man must harbor mortal thoughts; for mortals know no immortality."

To the Old Testament, hope, in its true and proper sense, is that hope which is directed toward God — the hope, therefore, which is included in and proceeds from faith. This hope is valid for the whole nation as well as for the individual. As is the case always in the history of Israel, so here too the individual is for the most part spontaneously relegated to the background behind the collectivity of the nation. In the time of the fathers, God concluded a covenant with Israel, promising the land and, what is more, the messianic kingdom of the final age. Accordingly, the hope of the early period was directed toward the promised land (Gen. 15:7-17:8; Exod. 3:8, 17; 6:4; Deut. 1:8).

Joshua finally entered into the promised land. After the capture of the land, hope was vested in the expectation of the ever-present protection of God, who will not abandon his people (Is. 55:3; 61:8; Ez. 16:59-63). Certainly this protection often enough seems not to be visible or practicable in the manifold afflictions which time and again threaten Israel's very existence. And Israel comes to expect this help more and more as a future redemption from every evil and as a future period of permanent good fortune. This is what the prophets point ahead to. Again and again they unveil hope as a divine new beginning (Hos. 12:7; Ps. 40:2). God, in his trustworthiness, will not disappoint this hope (Micah 7:7; Ps. 42:6).

At the same time, however, the prophets have to contend with presumptuous hope, because Israel, in view of its sins and outrages, has merited not God's blessing but his curse. The message of hope, therefore, holds good only for a purified Israel or for a purified remnant of Israel (Is. 8:16-18; 46:3; Amos 3:12). After the collapse of both kingdoms (of the northern kingdom, Samaria, in 722; and of the southern kingdom, Jerusalem, in 587), prophecy promises that God will found a new covenant, that the Messiah will purify and redeem his people, after which Yahweh's kingdom will be established over Israel and the whole world (Jer. 31:31-34).

Where hope is not such a hoping in God but a hoping in human plans and remedies, it will prove deceptive. God will stir up this deception and change it into fear and terror. There is warning of this in the preaching of the prophets. Israel and Judah, the northern kingdom and the southern, allied themselves with foreign powers. Because of their common wickedness, they will suffer a common fate; they will be ripped asunder in the catastrophe (Amos 1 and 2). The riches and wealth amassed by social injustice will be reduced to poverty (Amos 3 and 4). The wail of the death dirge will sound over the house of Israel (Amos 5). False confidence in possessions and strength and gods will perish in the fire of judgment (Zeph. 1-3). Again and again the prophetic conviction is voiced that the leaders must founder and the people be dragged down if trust is placed not in God but in their own ability and the help of peoples and powers (Ps. 32:10; Hos. 10:13f.; Is. 30:1-5; 36:6-9; Jer. 2:7; Ez. 29:6f.; 2 Kings 18:24). The prophets warn about trusting in political alignments and grand economic alliances. The hope of fools (i.e., the godless) will be frustrated (Prov. 11:7).

In Israel the hope of the individual is based upon the hope of the whole people. True hope is that which counts on God. "In conversion and rest is your salvation; in quietness and trust, your strength" (Is. 30:15). "You are my refuge, a strong tower against the enemy" (Ps. 61:4). "My Lord, my God, you are my hope; from my youth have I trusted in you" (Ps. 71:5; cf. Pss. 16:1; 37:5-7). Confident hope in God sets one free of anxiety in the face of the world, in that it is made secure in the fear of God. "The eye of the Lord rests on those who fear him, on those who confidently trust in his kindness" (Ps. 33:18). "Remain all the time in the fear of the Lord;

for surely there is a future and hope will not be cut off" (Prov. 23:17-18).

The personal hope of the godly is the expectation first of all of assistance against the oppressive difficulties of daily life. But more and more God's help is thought of as an eschatological futurity which will put an end to every difficulty forever. "On that day men will say: Behold, this is our God, in whom we hope, that he might help us. This is the Lord, in whom we confidently trusted. Let us be glad and rejoice on account of his help" (Is. 25:9). "I think thoughts of salvation and not of disaster, to prepare for you a future full of hope" (Jer. 29:11). Since hope is directed toward a future which comes from God, it is clear that the early present is temporary and preparatory.

Even the Qumran scrolls promote and extol hope. It is hope in God's favor in the judgment and unto eternal life. "I know that there is hope for one who turns away from his misdeeds and abandons his sins" (1 QH 6:6). "There is hope for him whom you have formed from the dust by eternal counsel" (1 QH 3:20f.). "There is hope on account of your power. For no man is just" (1 QH 9:14; similarly, 1 QH 11:30f.).[48] In the New Testament era, Judaism is filled, yes, often convulsed, by apocalyptic messianic expectations and revolutionary movements arising therefrom, all of which founder.

In the New Testament the terms for hope (ἐλπίς, ἐλπίζω) are of frequent occurrence in Paul, in Hebrews, and in 1 Peter; in the other books they occur only occasionally. A word-group of lesser importance is formed around δέχομαι (to accept, to wait for). The rare word ἀποκαραδοκία (earnest expectation) occurs only twice, in Rom. 8:19 and Phil. 1:20.

In the Synoptics, the word ἐλπίς has the significance of religious hope in Matthew 12:21, which is a quote from Is. 42:4 ("In his name do all the Gentiles hope"). The passage declares that the Old Testament hope has been fulfilled in Christ. Except for usages with no special religious significance in Luke (6:34; 23:8; 24:21) and John (5:45), the word *hope* is otherwise absent from the Gospels; the concept itself, however, is certainly there. The message of Jesus, being an announcement of the future kingdom of God, is a message of hope. In this way the beatitudes of the Sermon on the Mount are a message of hope. They promise the poor and meek eventual satisfaction, comfort, mercy, and possession of the kingdom.

The basic attitude of hope is, in the Synoptics as well as in the rest of the New Testament, coupled with the required practice of patient endurance, ὑπομονή. In perseverance and steadfastness in the midst of every trial, hope awaits the final salvation (Mark 13:13; Luke 8:15; 21:9). If the word and term *hope* are lacking in the Gospels, certainly the concept is there. The arrival of the expected Messiah is the fulfillment of former hope. Simeon and Anna were awaiting messianic comfort (Luke 2:25, 38). Through his disciples John the Baptist inquired of Jesus whether he was the expected one (Matthew 11:3). At the heart of the matter is the fact that it is no longer so necessary to speak of hope as of its fulfillment.

In the preaching of the Apostles, then, the new hope is proclaimed as the expectation of full revelation and of the consummation of what was begun. The Church now looks ahead to the "coming of him who has come." In this sense, the word and the concept *hope* are of essential importance to the Apostle Paul. Though it may not always be expressly stated, it is nevertheless a constant presupposition that hope is to be understood theologically, Christologically, and eschatologically. It is to be understood theologically because it is not a hope in just any kind of help, but in the expectation of God's gift. This hope is Christological, inasmuch as it has already been initiated in the work of Christ, and will be fully realized with the Lord's parousia. Eschatologically it is understood as that hope which is fulfilled only at the end of the ages, although until that time it has its beginning of realization already in the present.

The term and the conceptual content of hope are disclosed in chapter 8 of Romans. Romans 8:24 constitutes a broad definition of hope: "In this hope were we saved. A hope, however, which one sees already fulfilled, is hope no longer. What use were it to hope for what one already sees? But when we hope for what we do not see, then we await it in patience." "In this hope" does not mean that believers have the hope of someday being saved; they are already saved, in that, by God's doing, they are already promoted into the expectation of the future. Hope is always directed to the future. The object of hope is never presently experiential. Otherwise, it would no longer be hope but possession.

Howevew, this signifies in no way a lessening, but actually makes for an increase, in the evaluation of the benefits which are the object of hope. Whatever is presently visible is in the category of the known. Hope is directed toward benefits which are greater than any that are presently tangible. It does not choose the visible, as being something manifestly secure, while regarding what is not visible as something uncertain and to be relinquished. Even the invisible, the greater thing, is regarded as a certainty; and it is for this hope reaches out.

In general, hope cannot tend toward the visible because all that is visible is temporal. "We look not to the things that are visible but to the things that are invisible. For the things that are visible are ephemeral, but the invisible are eternal" (2 Cor. 4:18). Christian hope does not look to what is visible and perishable; it does not even depend on what is perishable. There is testimony to this in the example of Abraham, "who, against all hope, believed in hope" (Rom. 4:18). Abraham found that he could no longer count on what was naturally given and available. Then trust in a future given by God made its entrance. Hope is so very much based on the unavailable and invisible that, from the world's point of view, it can only seem to be a paradox.

New Testament hope is dependent upon the salvational deed of God effected in Christ. "We have hope through Christ toward God" in consequence of the righteousness and splendor which now are effected by God and which shape the new covenant (2 Cor. 3:4-12). This is the foundation of hope: that God has in fact established the new covenant. The hope of the old covenant has been fulfilled. To this was prophetic hope directed, and on this does Christian hope now stand firm.

The knowledge that the Old Testament Scripture has been fulfilled serves to strengthen our hope: "Whatever was written in former times was written for our instruction, that by steadfastness and by the encouragement provided by the Scriptures we might have hope" (Rom. 15:4). Hope is founded on the work which God has begun. "Hope cannot disappoint. For God's love is poured out into our hearts

through the Holy Spirit, who has been given to us" (Rom. 5:5).
Probably the Apostle is thinking of the situation of the judgment.

The believer will not be brought to disgrace in the judgment by
the discovery that his hope has been a deceit. The love of God, given
to us, is surety against that. Paul is certainly not speaking here of
man's love directed to God — there is no depending on that, just as
in general man's will cannot be depended on — but of God's love
directed toward man. The basis of its security lies in this, that God
has set the beginning in motion by his election and love. The Spirit,
however, is the agent of God's work (so too in John 14:26; 2 Cor.
3:8).

The root and basis of hope is faith in God's work. "In hope, Abraham believed against all hope" (Rom. 4:18). Faith and hope are mentioned in close connection with each other: "Enabled by the Spirit, we
await in faith the fulfillment of the hope of righteousness" (Gal. 5:5).
If, in accord with the New Testament, faith is God's gift, so too is
hope. "It is God himself who has loved us, and by grace has given us
eternal comfort and good hope" (2 Thess. 2:16; cf. Rom. 15:13).

Other attitudes are bound up with hope, which together determine
the Christian way of life. Hope begets patience: "If we hope in that
which we do not see, we await it in patience" (Rom. 8:25). Patience
is what distinguishes genuine hope from the mere phantom thereof.
The latter flares up and collapses. It proceeds from the bubbling up
of sentiment and from the fleeting images of phantasy. Genuine hope
is concerned with reality and is firmly grounded thereon. That is
why it is strong in patience, the ability to "abide thereunder". Hope
and patience are bound together: "We are constantly mindful of the
strength of your faith, of your painstaking love, of the patience of
your hope in the work of our Lord Jesus Christ, in the presence of
our God and Father" (1 Thess. 1:3). The trilogy of faith, hope, and
love is matched to the series strength, concern and patience. The deed
must proceed from the mental disposition. In the last analysis, however, none of it is man's achievement; all is the gift of Christ, in his
communion.

Paul pursues the origin of hope even farther back. If Christ is the
revelation of God in the world, hope is ultimately God's operation.
Certainly faith is now persecuted. This persecution, however, does

not destroy faith and Church, but serves to awaken hope. Thus Paul builds the chain: tribulation — endurance — proven virtue — hope (Rom. 5:4). Hope is the well-spring of joy (Rom. 12:12), as well as of candor (2 Cor. 3:12). Hope is certainly stress and waiting, but not uncertainty and fear; rather, it is confidence and security of existence, founded in God. Confidence in regard to a consummation in the arrival of the Lord unites present and future. "It is my eager expectation and hope that I shall in no way be confounded, but that Christ will always, as even now, be publicly glorified in my body, whether by life or by death" (Phil. 1:20). Paul speaks of eager expectation and of hope. If this represents human uncertainty, it will nevertheless be annulled in the face of faithful hope. It can be fulfilled in the ordinary death of the individual; but it will be made manifest at the coming of Christ. "From heaven we await the Savior, the Lord Jesus Christ" (Phil. 3:20).

In the eschatological view, even now hope withdraws us from the world. "We await the blessed hope and the appearing of the glory of our great God and Savior, Jesus Christ." This expectation, however, causes us "to renounce godlessness and worldly lusts, to live soberly, justly, and piously in this world." So much the more do we do this, "because this Savior, Jesus Christ, gave himself for us, to free us from all lawlessness" (Titus 2:11-14).

This great hope not only fills pious people, not only does it motivate men, but it embraces all creation. "Creation was subjected to futility, not of its own volition but by him who subjected it in hope. Creation too will be set free of its bondage to decay, unto the freedom of the glory of the children of God" (Rom. 8:20f.). Fear and longing are the primitive phenomena of every life; and Paul wants to explain the basic reason why this is so. This condition is not of God's original creating, but is a guilty encumbrance, certainly not incurred by irrational creation itself, but as sharing in the guilt incurred by man. The lament of nature is for Paul a sign that the creation waits in hope of its redemption and glorification. "It champs at the bit" (Rom. 8:19). What Paul is saying may become more understandable for us if we bear in mind that he partakes of a long tradition. The expectation of a transformation of creation is as old as the Bible. In the era of messianic salvation there is to be a new heaven and a new earth (Is.

65:17). This idea is more closely delineated in the Old Testament apocrypha and in the Rabbinic traditions. Even the New Testament speaks occasionally of this hope (besides Rom. 8, see also Acts 3:21 and Apoc. 21:1).

Paul unites the apocalyptic expectation with the conviction that the history of creation cannot be separated from the destiny of man. Creation has in man its meaning and its focus. Man's history with God is the history of all creation. This is as true in relation to the fall (Rom. 8:20) as it is in relation to the redemption (Rom. 8:19). Adam's decision to transgress is the beginning and origin of death not only for mankind but for the totality of creation. Therefore, when man is liberated from death unto glory, the curse is removed even from irrational creation; and it too will regain the glory of paradise. Even in this Paul participates in late Jewish tradition. A certain Rabbi says: "Things were created in their perfection, but after the first man had sinned, they were spoiled; and not before the Messiah comes will they be restored to their proper condition."

Paul's teaching leaves us with some questions. Since it appears to us that birth and life, suffering and death, take place in accord with the laws of nature and in the natural course of events, how are we to understand them as the consequence of a primitive decision and deed of man? Paul goes back to Gen. 1–3 and understands these narratives as a literally historical account of a succession of events: the creation of the world, of man, and original sin. According to the accepted knowledge of science, the history of man is preceded by a natural history through an incalculable length of time, filled with a horrible struggle for existence and frightful catastrophes.

Our interpretation understands the primitive history of Gen. 1–3 not as history but as an etiology which wants to explain, in the context of the biblical belief in God and creation, the existence in which we find ourselves (see the present work, Vol. 1, pp. 3–13).

Here Paul has arrived at the limits of the knowledge possible to him in his time. Paul says this much about the problem at least: the redemption of man is not a redemption *from out* the world — that is an Oriental or even Platonic doctrine of redemption — but a redemption *along with* the world. If man is redeemed from futility and transitoriness, then, along with him, all creation is so redeemed. Death cannot cease to exist in respect to man only. Life and death cannot continue to exist side by side. Therefore, death must be vanquished in all creation. And not only this, but creation must attain to the freedom of the glory of the children of God. The freedom here spoken of is not to be understood as freedom of being, which is the perfection of being. Glory, however, is not just some sort of beauty or some kind of luster, but the appearance of God, which was manifested in the old covenant as a splendor over Israel (2 Cor. 3:9; 4:6).

These expectations are united now in the broadly conceived cosmic Christology. In Christ, creation took its beginning, in him it has its continuance, and in him it is perfected, now and in the future (Col. 1:16f.; Heb. 1:2f.). Even hope abides, and is brought together in Christ. It is nought else but the consummation of that which was begun in him as the work of salvation and is present still. "Christ in you, the hope of glory" (Col. 1:27). "Jesus Christ, our hope" (1 Tim. 1:1). The history of Christ is the foundation and shape of all Christian hope. Accordingly, it is in a double sense the hope of resurrection. Resurrection is both the grounds and the goal of hope.

Hope determines the Christian so essentially that Paul can designate Christians simply as "those who are rejoicing in hope" (Rom. 12:12), while the pagans are those "who have no hope" (1 Thess. 4:13). Even the pagans make for themselves images and representations of life and death. Even they construct hope for themselves. But their hope is unfounded, spurious, and cannot abide. Hopelessness and paganism are synonymous: "You were without hope and without God" (Eph. 2:12). The true God is guarantor of true hope. Accordingly, the biblical God is called "the God of hope" (Rom. 15:13). This God can bestow hope because he possesses the fullness of life. "We have hoped in the living God" (1 Tim. 4:10). Dead idols give no guarantees of life.

In Acts, the terms *hope* and *to hope* are concentrated and narrowly focused on a solitary point of eschatology, the universal resurrection of the dead. This is the "hope" about which a discussion took place between Paul, the Sadducees, and Israel collectively (Acts 23:6).

The concept and understanding of hope are developed in the Epistle to the Hebrews,[49] wherein the property of hope is presented more as the maintaining of hope than as the content of hope. Faith and hope are closely united: "Faith is the pledge [50] of what is hoped for and a conviction of things which one does not see" (Heb. 11:1). The passage has the form of a definition. Form-critically, it may be labeled as a principle or axiom which formulates Christian doctrine. Like faith, hope too is directed to a world which is not visible. The reality hoped for is not visible and not available; only through the revealing word is it unlocked, only with the gift of the further word is it clarified. It is thus that hope is able "to enter into the inner shrine, behind the curtain, where Jesus has gone as a forerunner" (Heb. 6:19f.). In the old covenant, only the high priest was permitted to enter into the holy of holies, and that but once a year; but now, since Christ has opened it, the entryway to holiness is open to every Christian (Heb. 9:11f.; 10:19f.).

Hope is certain of attaining to the heavenly world. The congregation is "God's house, if we hold fast our confidence and pride in our hope" (Heb. 3:6). Confidence and pride signify ability and power both to preserve hope in eschatological salvation and to be joyful in confessing this hope. Hope cannot but be jubilant on account of its riches and the certainty thereof. Hope begets confidence and jubilation. Life in faith is directed toward and reaches out "to the hope which is set before us" (Heb. 6:18). Each one, however, should "demonstrate his zeal even to to the fulfillment of hope at the end" (Heb. 6:11). The zeal of the congregation must perdure until it has received the total content of its hopes in the final consummation. "Let us hold fast to the never-wavering confession of hope" (Heb. 10:23). The confession to which the congregation is to hold fast is designated as hope. Accordingly, hope and faith are one and the same (cf. Rom. 10:9f.).

The content of faith, guaranteed by God, is unshakeable. The Epistle to the Hebrews is able to designate Christian faith, condition, and existence straightforwardly as hope. In comparison to Judaism, Christianity is simply "the better hope" (Heb. 7:19). For this hope is certain; it leads and reaches more certainly to its goal. In a figure much used even to the present day, hope is described as the "anchor of the soul,[51] sure and fast" (Heb. 6:19). Just as a ship flees from a storm at sea back to its harbor and lies there at anchor, peaceful and secure, so the believer flees from the world to his God. Hope bestows peace and security upon the soul. The soul is protected against the onslaughts of enemies from without; and within itself, against doubt and fear. Hope is the core of Christian life and the power which shapes it.

In Romans (4:18) as well as in Hebrews — and prior to these, already in Jewish tradition — Abraham is the archetype of faith. Of him it is said: "By faith Abraham was obedient, and he went out to a place which he was to receive as an inheritance; and he went out not knowing where it was that he was to go" (Heb. 11:8). This is always the manner and way of hope: it knows not whither it goes. It knows that its future is God, and more than this it does not know. But this is enough. Indeed, "it is not yet apparent what we shall be" (1 John 3:2).

The First Epistle of Peter treats repeatedly of Christian hope. "God has given us a new birth unto living hope through the resurrection of Christ from the dead, to an imperishable inheritance" (1 Peter 1:3-4). The opposite of living hope is a hope which is dead, i.e., which is fruitless, in that what is hoped for is not and will not be realized. Christian hope is certainly living hope. It is not a mere uncertain and indefinite longing; rather, it is assured and certain. It is living hope, because its foundation and its goal are in Christ, who, as the resurrected one, is Lord of life. Christians are reborn to living hope.

Since First Peter quite frequently refers to baptism, in this instance too rebirth may be an oblique reference to baptism. Still, redemption through the salvational work of Christ and faith itself can be designated in general as new birth. The goal of hope is the heavenly inheritance. If this benefit belongs to the future, it is nonetheless assured, and shares not at all in the threat which is otherwise common to all human benefits. Christians are "faithful to God, who raised Christ from the dead" (1 Peter 1:21). Christ is the basis of faith and at the same time the enduring communion between God and man. It is through him that "faith and hope are to be directed toward God" (1 Peter 1:21).

Faith and hope are united in the sense that faith can perdure only so long as it is productive of hope. Faith can endure the weighty problem, in the anticipation of its solution. Christians must be firmly prepared to answer anyone "who requires an accounting for the hope which is in you" (1 Peter 3:15). In accord with the situations which the Epistle envisions, questions about hope might be asked out of curiosity and hostility, or out of friendliness and a willingness to reform. The accounting is required on the subject of hope. Hope, therefore, is almost the same as faith, which but emphasizes the fact that faith is operative in hope. The hope which is "in you" may be in reference to the Christian community, but it can also signify the hope of each individual Christian.

There is a significant text in the Second Epistle of Peter, although that writing, originating toward the end of the first century, was probably written, in view of ancient pseudepigraphical practice, under the name of the Apostle Peter so as to indicate its purpose of carrying Apostolic teaching further and of applying it to new problems. The letter says: "We await with earnestness the coming of the day of God. . . . According to his word we await a new heaven and a new earth, in which righteousness will dwell" (2 Peter 3:12-13). In the context, probably the apocalyptic traditions of the world at large are made use of, and this even at the risk of propagating the mythological idea of a world conflagration; nevertheless, when the goal and content of hope are declared to be quite intangible and purely intellectual, it comes as a renunciation of every mythology.

It is no mere chance that the Johannine writings have little to say about hope, and the Gospel of John, nothing at all. These writings regularly speak very forcefully of salvation as an event of the present time (John 4:23; 5:25). There is an admonition concerning hope in 1 John 3:3: "Everyone who thus hopes in him is made holy, just as he is holy." The one to whom this hope is directed is Jesus (1 John 3:2). As the one who is righteous, he is the holy one (1 John 2:29). The life of the man who believes and hopes must bespeak the nature of him in whom faith is vested. One who hopes, then, must be holy.

In the Gospel of John, Christ is the way, the truth, the life, the light, the bread, the true shepherd, the eternal Word of God. In the milieu of the Gospel and at that time, especially with the beginning gnosis, one spoke of the hope for these good things. The Gospel in no way reproves the longings of men. Their hope is well-founded and good. Now they are promised true and complete fulfillment of their hopes. Along with other already mentioned New Testament texts, these are allusions to the problem of the relation between natural and God-given hope. Natural hope is of two sorts: that which is man's ordinary and constant experience, and that which is a systematic conceptualization of a utopian future. The redeemed hope, however, can take in the unredeemed.

Terminology distinguishes, in respect to faith, a *fides qua creditur* (faithfulness, faith as the power or virtue by which something is believed) and a *fides quae creditur* (the content of faith, faith as the body of believed doctrine). So too one can distinguish between a *spes qua speratur* (the keeping of hope) and a *spes quae speratur* (the content or object of hope). The content of hope embraces, in conformity with biblical eschatology and apocalyptics, the ever-personal eschatology of death, judgment, heaven, and hell; and the events of the cosmic eschatology of parousia, resurrection, general judgment, and consummation of all things. In this schema, eschatology promises the *what* of these happenings, while apocalyptics portrays their *how*.

To exegetic and dogmatic theology it is not an easy question, how the apocalyptic and eschatological portrayals of the New Testament are to be understood. What part of it is imagery, and what part declaration of faith? The declarations are assuredly couched in an imagery far removed from us. The eschatological portrayals in the Bible are employed in a similar or even in the same way as in the contemporaneous apocalyptic writings. As an addition to texts long known, the Qumran scrolls have come to light only recently. The images are evidently, then, attempts at presentation qualified by a specific period of time. This is the direction, at any rate, of our basic assumptions.

Eschatological declarations are declarations about a world beyond time and space. In all our declarations, however, we must necessarily make use of the categories of time and space. With this in mind, it is apparent that all eschatological declarations are necessarily couched in figurative language. Probably it was Immanuel Kant more than anyone else who brought this into prominence in the philosophical and theological consciousness. Theological reflection has long been earnestly occupied with the problems of the hermeneutics of eschatological declarations.[52]

As representative of modern existential theology we might mention Rudolf Bultmann's *Die christliche Hoffnung und das Problem der Entmythologisierung*. Its final sentence reads: "The thrust of the mythological imagery of hope, laid bare in the process of demythologizing, is this: it speaks of the future, which belongs to God, as the fulfillment of human life." In this interpretation the biblical declarations about the consummation of all things (Rom. 8:20f.) seem probably to have been proposed mythologically. On the other hand, more recent interpretations emphasize, contrary to this "rape of eschatology," the futurity of biblical and Christian expectation. These interpretations are expressed in forceful language by Jürgen Moltmann in his *Theology of Hope* and in the discussions engendered by this book. Moltmann says: "Without a cosmological eschatology, the eschatological existence of man cannot be asserted" (p. 60). Christian theology must be the "teaching of Christian hope, which embraces as much the object hoped for as the hope which it excites" (p. 111). Hope has its starting point in Christ's resurrection from the dead. "A Christian faith which is not faith in the resurrection can be called neither Christian nor faith" (p. 150). "The hope born of cross and resurrection changes the futility, the contrariety, the agonizing of the world into its *Not yet*, never allowing it to evaporate into its *Nothing*" (p. 179).

A Church filled with eschatology will endeavor with all its strength to orientate mankind and the world to the future. The future must become a force in the present. The proclamation of hope must become a watchword to the modern world, which is moved and excited by the problem of the future. In the face of the world, the Christian must "give an account of his hope" (1 Peter 3:15). Secularized hope finds powerful expression in the work of Ernst Bloch, *Das Prinzip Hoffnung*. The work of many years, it unites disparate ideas, considerations, and prophecies. It has even taken Jewish apocalyptics and the Christian expectation of salvation and brought them together, although in a materialistic and atheistic ideology. In an all-embracing evolution, man and world push forward and drive on to the future perfection. Its content is for us a still hidden utopia. In man, however, there is an ever-present, groping consciousness of hope in work. It must be raised to consciousness. Bloch acknowledges the principle of hope, in spite of the fact that it flies in the face of the totality of historical experience. This principle of hope must be the heritage of religion — another way of saying, according to Bloch, that it is the heritage of mythology. Still, is this utopia not just a new mythology?

In our time, biblical theology and a humane philosophy of hope, individual as well as social problems and attempts at their solution, are in literary as well as spiritual communication with each other. Both flow into the public history of the striving after a renewal of society.

§ 8. LOVE OF GOD

Aristotle teaches that it is meaningless to speak of a love of the gods for men, because there is nothing lacking for the gods' own blissfulness (*Ethica Nicomachea*, 8, 7, 4; 9, 9, 1). Likewise he says: "It is absurd for anyone to say that he loves Zeus" (*Magna moralia*, 2, 11, 7, 1208). This holds good for the whole Greek religion, and is typical of all natural religious sentiment.[53]

The Greek religion, it is true, worshipped love as divine in the form of Aphrodite; and other religions too, in similar fashion, have personified the power of love. But they only wish to say thereby that love is such a mighty and sublime power that man experiences it as a demoniacal power. It is, nevertheless, only the God of biblical faith who loves man. One can say, no doubt, of extra-biblical divinities: this god is dispenser of mercy; or, this god is kindness. Mercy and kindness devote themselves to the one who merits them. God's love is otherwise, and it is more. It does not inquire after the merit of its beloved. In the human concept of love, there is always a movement toward that which is recognized as filled with worth, and is thereby aspired to as worthy of love. The one who loves seeks, by a giving and a taking, the enrichment of himself out of the worth of the one who is loved.

According to this concept, whatever else he can do, the God of philosophy most assuredly cannot love. Conceived as the absolute, he possesses all that is good. According to Plato, God is purely and simply the Good. To such a God, then, love, inasmuch as it is a striving for increment in something valued, is impossible. The love which the biblical God possesses, however, is not greedy of worth; rather, it gives worth and creates worth. It turns itself toward the worthless, yes, even to what is of negative worth, to the sinner, and makes what was unworthy of love worthy of love. The essence of biblical and Christian religion is love, which moves everything. From God, who *is* love, it goes through Christ to the world. The divine gift of love is poured out further in the love of neighbor. Through this great communion of love, love turns back to its divine source.

The Old Testament describes first of all the loving rule of God over men, and speaks in later texts, even expressly of the love of God for men. The creation of the world and the shaping of man are the work of divine goodness. "God saw that it was good" (Gen. 1:4, 10, 31). God concluded a covenant of blessing with Noah (Gen. 9:1-17), with Abraham (Gen. 15:18) and the fathers (Gen. 26:3-6; 28:13-15), and finally with the whole people of Israel on Sinai (Exod. 24:8; 34:10). In the election of Israel, God showed her his special grace and favor (Deut. 14:2). Israel's Lord is "a merciful and gracious God, long-suffering, abounding in grace and fidelity, keeping favor unto the thousandth generation, forgiving of guilt, iniquity, and sin" (Exod. 34:6f.).

In the Canaanite milieu of Israel the Baals, the lords and gods of nature and of life, were worshipped in fertility rites and love feasts (Judg. 6:25). Even kings of Israel and many of the people were adherents thereof (1 Kings 16:31; 19:18; Jer. 11:13). The prophets combatted Israel's lapse into idolatry (1 Kings 18:21-40; Jer. 2:23; Ez. 6:4-6; Hos. 13:1). It is, then, somewhat of a risky venture for the Old Testament to describe the relation of God to his people as love. The basis of Israel's being chosen is the paradoxical quality of divine love (Deut. 7:7f.; 10:15). The prophets have to proclaim this love. The relationship between God and Israel is like a marriage contract. Indeed, Israel has broken the contract and has become a whore; but even yet God does not abandon his people (Hos. 2:19-23). "When Israel was still young, I won her dearly. Out of Egypt I called my child" (Hos. 11:1). "With an everlasting love, I love you. That is why I have kept you in favor so long" (Jer. 31:3).

The Psalms speak further of God's faithfulness to his covenant (Ps. 89:4f.); but now there is another element, his love of each individual: "The Lord lifts up those who are bowed low, and he loves the righteous" (Ps. 146:8). God's mercy extends to all his creatures (Ps. 145:9-16). If stronger and stronger emphasis is placed on God's justice, still, Israel never forgot the message of God's mercy (4 Esdras 7:132-139). The pious of Qumran praise God: "The mercy of his mercifulness he has manifested to us from eternity to eternity" (1 QS 2:1).

The God who loves expects the love of Israel in return. In the marriage covenant, Israel is obliged to love and to be faithful to Yahweh (Hos. 1–3; Is 54:4-8; Jer. 31:32). "I, the Lord, your God, am a jealous God, who visits the guilt of fathers upon the children, grandchildren, and great-grandchildren of those who hate me, but shows mercy to the thousandth generation of those who take care to love me and keep my commandments" (Exod. 20:5-6). The love of man for God is of obligation in view of the covenant. Love for God, therefore, can be spoken of as a commandment; thus in the great commandment, which is repeated even in the New Testament: "You shall love the Lord your God with your whole heart, with your whole soul, and with all your strength" (Deut. 6:5).

While the commandment to love appears already in Deut. 6:5 in connection with the demand that the Law be fulfilled (Deut. 6:1-7), in Deut. 10:12 the commandment reads: "You shall fear the Lord, your God, so that you walk in all his ways, to love him, and to serve the Lord, your God, with your whole heart and with your whole soul." Fear of God and love of God are one and the same. Obedience and service, therefore, are required. Nevertheless, the most profound kind of fidelity to God is love: "I think of you and remember how you were devoted to me in your youth, how you loved me when you were yet a bride, how you followed me in the wilderness" (Jer. 2:2). In the Psalms, God's communion is understood as love. "The Lord protects all who love him" (Ps. 145:20; cf. 18:1; 31:24-25; 91:14; 116:1). Wisdom too speaks of the bond of love: "They who are faithful in love shall abide in him" (Wis. 3:9).

Post-biblical Judaism knows likewise that "the Lord is true to those who love him in truth" (*Psalms of Solomon*, 14:1). About 100 b.c. the *Letter of Aristeas* (229) says that to love God is itself his gift: "The highest beauty is piety. Love is your strength. It is, however, the gift of God." As Israel before it, the Qumran community knows that it is itself the chosen and beloved of God (1 QS 1:22; 2:2-4; 3:26). Under Oriental and Greek influence, Rabbinic Judaism at the time of the New Testament speaks of love as the essence of the relationship with God. It supports the mystical interpretation.[54]

The most precious possession which the New Testament has received from Israel is its knowledge about the love of God. Even Jesus attests this consciousness of the love relationship between God and man. He makes God manifest as the only one who is good (Mark 10:18), the dispenser of mercy (Matthew 18:33; Luke 6:36), as well as the loving Father (Matthew 5:45; 6:9) who seeks out men like a shepherd after his straying sheep (Luke 15:4-7) and who receives his prodigal son (Luke 15:11-32). As the beloved Son (Mark 1:11), Christ now makes the Father's love known and real. In order to explain his office in regard to sinners, that God seeks them out and receives them back again, Jesus recounts the parables about the lost things (Luke 15:2f.). In this service of Christ, his drawing of the poor, the sick, and sinners to himself, God's love is experienced (Mark 2:5). It is now the messianic time of salvation, when, for the sake of the love of God, sin is forgiven and peace is imparted (Luke 7:47, 50).

Man is challenged by God's love. Even in the present messianic era of salvation the old commandment of the love of God holds good. The Gospels (Mark 12:28-34)[55] tell of an encounter of Jesus with the literate Jewry of his time, on which occasion Jesus teaches the commandment of love. To the question as to the first commandment, Jesus answers: "The first is: 'Hear, O Israel, the Lord, our God, is one Lord. You shall love the Lord, your God, with your whole heart and with your whole soul and with your whole mind and with your whole strength.'" The commandment of loving God is the first commandment both for Israel and for the gospel. Loving God is externalized in the bond of faith, in prayer, and in the communion and celebration of divine service (Luke 2:49). To love God, however, also means to be in God's service. Greed for other good things is far removed therefrom: "No one can serve two masters. You cannot serve God and Mammon" (Matthew 6:24). Love toward God can be endangered by the burden of earthly misery, so much so that when this misery reaches its high point in the eschatological period, the "love of most men will grow cold" (Matthew 24:12).

In the saying of the Lord: "Be merciful, as your Father is merciful" (Luke 6:36), it is intimated that God's merciful love goes forth first to men. This is stated in the parable, when from a distance the father spies his lost but now returning son, and hastens to him and welcomes him with love (Luke 15:20). After the salvational work of Christ, the Church of the Apostles makes itself known; and similarly now that

God's love has become, as it were, an invitation to man, man is able to respond to God's love.

The beginning of every love relationship between God and the world proceeds initially from God, who, with his love, seeks out man; and thus the stimulus of love has begun. "God has shown his love for us, in that Christ died for us while we were yet sinners" (Rom. 5:8). With a note of personal intimacy, Paul says: "The Son of God loved me and gave himself for me" (Gal. 2:20). In Christ, God's love was and is devoted to the world: "Nothing will separate us from the love of God in Christ Jesus, our Lord" (Rom. 8:39).

This love holds the Church in its embrace: "The love of Christ holds us fast, because we believe that one has died for all, and therefore we all have died" (2 Cor. 5:14). The love of Christ for his Church is comparable to the love of marriage partners (Eph. 5:22). God's love is ever effective in the matter of election. Paul is at home with the Old Testament belief in election. The faithful are "the beloved of God, his chosen ones" (Rom. 1:7; Col. 3:12). "In love he has predestined us to sonship through Jesus Christ" (Eph. 1:5). Love brings forth new life: "God in his great love with which he has loved us — we who were dead in sin — has made us alive together with Christ" (Eph. 2:4). "The love of God is poured forth into our hearts through the Holy Spirit, who has been given to us" (Rom. 5:5).

The love which the Apostle speaks of here is not man's love for God, but God's love, which comes to man beforehand and which fills him. It is God's purpose that this love be turned back to him. God evokes love creatively. "If one loves God, one is known by him" (1 Cor. 8:3). Awaked by God, love flows back from man to God: "Now that you have known God, so much the more shall you be known by God" (Gal. 4:9; cf. 1 Cor. 13:12; Phil. 3:12). Before a man can love God, he must invariably first be called to it by God. "God turns everything to good, for those who love him, those who are called according to his purpose" (Rom. 8:28). Since it is God only who can effect love, the Apostle's blessing is: "May the Lord direct your hearts to a love for God and to steadfastness in Christ" (2 Thess. 3:5).

Paul speaks often and in a penetrating manner about faith. But his message and his intention must not be regarded too narrowly. Faith is the way, love is the goal. The goal is more important than the way, the deed more important than the word. Faith is an outstretched hand eagerly grasping for grace. But the Apostle has a still greater thing to say: we attain to God. Paul speaks in such a way that love too is included when he describes the relationship of man to God as one of faith. And ultimately he ranks love above faith: "Now, however, there abide these three, faith, hope, and love. The greatest of these is love" (1 Cor. 13:13).

Faith, hope, and love comprise Christian existence. The greatest of these is love, because it remains forever. It conquers death (Rom. 8:37). It is the bond which never shall be broken (Col. 3:14). "Love never ceases" (1 Cor. 13:8). Love for God finds its ultimate fulfillment: "What no eye has seen, what no ear has heard, what the heart of no man has conceived, all this has God prepared for those who love him" (1 Cor. 2:9). That love embraces and perfects faith is said also in the blessing: "May Christ dwell in your hearts by faith, so that you, being rooted and grounded in faith, may be able . . . to know the love of Christ, which surpasses knowledge" (Eph. 3:17-19). Christ's love is present in the Church and in the world, and fills them. But it is incomprehensible, and ultimately it excels and surpasses all experience and knowledge.

In John's Gospel it is love that moves God and the world, and chains them together. The innermost circle of love unites the Father and the Son. The Father loves the Son because the Son carries out his mandate and expends his life for the redemption of the world. "The Father loves the Son and has given all things into his hand" (John 3:35). "For this reason the Father loves me: because I surrender my life" (John 10:17). The Son also loves the Father; and the world should perceive how great this love is by the fact that the Son behaves as the Father has charged him (John 14:31). The love of God for the world and for man is apparent in the mission of the Son: "God so much loved the world, that he gave up his only Son" (John 3:16). The Father's love embraces even the disciples along with the Son: "The Father loves you because you have loved me and have believed that I came forth from the Father" (John 16:27).

God is beginning of love: "Love consists in this, not that we have loved God, but that he loved us and sent his Son as an expiatory sacrifice for our sins" (1 John 4:10). Love turns back from the disciples to the Father. "He first loved us. We must, therefore, also love him" (1 John 4:19). Man first responds to God's love by faith: "We have known and have believed the love which God has for us" (1 John 4:16).

Love for God, however, must also be effective of obedience to God's word (1 John 2:5) and of love for the brethren (1 John 3:17). Love for God is not compatible with love for the world. "If someone loves the world, the love of the Father is not in him" (1 John 2:15). With the passage "God is love" (1 John 4:8, 16), the being of God can be characterized as turning toward men, inasmuch as his dealings with men and his treatment of them is always an externalizing of his love. This is manifested in salvation history by God's surrendering of his Son for our salvation (1 John 4:9, 14), and constantly in the action of God's love by which we are made children of God, our Father (1 John 3:1), and by which God is in us and abides therein (1 John 4:16).

That God is love is not an abstract philosophical declaration, but a declaration pertaining to salvation history. In view of the close connection between John's Gospel and the First Epistle of John, it may perhaps be said additionally that the essence of God is love, because Father and Son from eternity onward are one in love (John 14:31; 17:24). The communion of faith and of love for God will never cease. "Whoever abides in love abides in God, and God abides in him" (1 John 4:16). The Christian, therefore, is confident even while awaiting the judgment. The love of God for us would not have accomplished its purpose, and our love were not yet perfected, if faith were to be as fearful before God as it is before a human court of justice. So it is true: "There is no fear in love" (1 John 4:18). This is both promise and admonition. God's children must renounce and overcome everything that stands in the way of the God-given communion of love in order to become fully truth and reality.

Even the Apocalypse of John speaks of the Church's love of God: "I hold this against you, that you have abandoned your first love" (Apoc. 2:4). "I know your works, and indeed, your love and your faith and your service and your patience" (Apoc. 2:19).

In the Bible, Old Testament and New, man's love of God is the highest of moral conduct. Accordingly, great Christian teachers like

Augustine, Thomas Aquinas, and Francis de Sales tell us that loving God brings perfection to the Christian life. Following the example of the Scholastics, theology even today refers to love for God as the "formation of the virtues" (*forma omnium virtutum*). Love gives the virtues their configuration, unity, and perfection. It is able to do this because it imparts to all the moral activities of man their relationship to God.

The ecclesiastical ordering of life bases contemplation (*vita contemplativa*), both as act and as state, on the great value placed on the love of God. This sense of values held good for centuries. Other traditions may have united themselves to the biblical heritage. Neo-Platonist mysticism may have found entry there. When God is designated "the highest good, most worthy of love," Neo-Platonic terminology is being used. That along with alien words some alien concepts also found entry is beyond dispute. But the essential remained — the biblical doctrine about the love of God.

It is difficult for more recent Protestant ethics to hold fast to the old interpretation; in fact, it even rejects it. This is taking place under the influence of the philosophy of Immanuel Kant. He is sharply polemical in maintaining that it is utterly impossible to serve God in any other way than by fulfilling one's obligations to other men. The only truly worthy service of God would be the love of neighbor. This problematic viewpoint finds its most forceful expression in the modern prattle that God, as a metaphysical being, is dead and can be found and loved only in relation to men.

On the other hand, biblical ethics, Protestant as well as Catholic, emphasizes that the Pauline and Johannine testimony about the love of God (both as love of God for man and the corresponding love of men for God) must not be foreshortened or passed over.

It need scarcely be mentioned that a violation of love of neighbor cannot be covered over by an ostensible love of God. The gospel says that a man cannot absolve himself of his obligation to his parents by a sacrificial offering (Mark 7:11f.). The gospel repeats, as a saying of the Lord, the words of the prophet: "I desire mercy and not sacrifice" (Matthew 9:13 = Hos. 6:6). Love of God is genuine only when it proves itself in love of brother (1 John 2:5; 3:17). To shun one's neighbor on the pretext of devotion is to build a temple to false gods.

We may cite two remarks of Karl Barth. The first (in *Erklärung des Römerbriefes*, Zollikon-Zürich, 2nd ed., 1929, p. 303f.) demands a rigid separation between what is genuine and what is spurious: "The love offered to God is *agape*, and as such it is distinguished from every kind of *eros*, even religious *eros*, by the lightning sword of death and eternity, which announces that here the new man, who neither woos nor allows himself to be wooed, stands in the presence of the God with whom, in distinction to Baal and his like, no manner of erotic love is to be set in motion." Nevertheless, Barth is at variance with Protestant theology's vocalized denial that man can love God in any genuine sense of the term *love*. One can attempt to escape from the obligation of love of neighbor in a falsely understood love of God, or from the love of God in a falsely understood love of neighbor. "The sons of God renounce every inclination to such an escape" (*Die kirchliche Dogmatik*, I, Zollikon-Zürich, 4th ed., 1948, p. 480).

§ 9. LOVE OF NEIGHBOR

To the question as to which is the principal commandment, Jesus replies: "The first is, 'You shall love the Lord your God with your whole heart. . . .' The second is this, 'You shall love your neighbor as yourself.' There is no other commandment greater than these" (Mark 12:29-31).[56] In giving utterance to the twofold commandment of love, Jesus quotes from the Old Testament: the commandment of the love of God is from Deut. 6:5; that of love of neighbor is from Lev. 19:18. According to the Gospel accounts, Jesus was on this occasion in conversation with the teachers of the Law, who immediately concurred with him. In the twofold commandment they find nothing surprisingly new.

According to Luke 10:27, it was even the teacher of the Law himself, and not Jesus, who formulated the commandment. This presentation probably has its origin in Luke's redacting. For him, the conversation over the principal commandment introduces the parable of the Good Samaritan. In the Lucan composition Jesus puts a special emphasis on the realization of a commandment already known, the commandment of love. Mere knowledge of the commandment, seeing that it can be taken very lightly, is worthless. The collective evidence of the Synoptics demonstrates that the New Testament is aware of the fact that in respect to this commandment it is at one with the tradition of Israel.

Israel read in its Law: "You shall not hate your brother in your heart. . . . You shall not take vengeance on your countryman, but you shall love your companion as yourself" (Lev. 19:17-18). The love of' neighbor embraces primarily the community of Israel, since foreign peoples have not yet entered upon the scene. The consciousness of descent from a common forefather makes brothers of countrymen. The love of neighbor is brotherliness. The communion of countrymen is preserved in God's covenant. It is in God that love of neighbor has its deeper basis; and for that reason it is commanded in his name (Lev. 19:10, 18, 34). Service of God and love of neighbor are one. "It has been told you what is good and what the Lord requires of you: to do nothing but what is just, and to love kindness and to walk humbly before your God" (Micah 6:8).

In the further development of the Law, love of neighbor is extended even to the strangers who dwell in the land (Lev. 19:34; Deut. 10:19), even if not to foreigners passing through the country. But to them, of course, the obligation of hospitality to a guest holds good. The stranger is received into the mercy of God along with Israel (Ez. 47:22). The traditions from the period of the fathers report an exemplary practice of hospitality (Gen. 18:1-8; 19:1-8; Judg. 19:11-30).[57]

To be sure, the law of reprisal (*lex talionis*) held good in Israel: "Fracture for fracture, eye for eye, tooth for tooth" (Lev. 24:17-21). This law, however, is not a commandment to vengeance but to a just compensation for violated rights. For a bodily injury, the culprit is not to be slain. It is better in general to practice forbearance rather than hatred, which is destructive: "You shall not hate your brother in your heart. . . . You shall not take revenge, nor bear a grudge against your countryman" (Lev. 19:17-18).

Even an enemy is not excluded from deeds of succour: "If your enemy is hungry, feed him; if he thirsts, give him to drink" (Prov. 25:21). "Good sense makes a man slow to anger, and it is his glory to overlook an offense" (Prov. 19:11). When God wants to do good to a man, he reconciles him with his enemies (Prov. 16:7). Even the *Letter of Aristeas* (227), dating from about the year 100 B.C., commends the love of one's enemy. God can grant a man the power to do so.

In a portion of late Judaism, nevertheless, the concept of neighbor and the commandment of loving one's neighbor were defined somewhat narrowly. Samaritans and foreigners were excluded from the obligation of love. In the period of the New Testament, the pious kept apart from sinners, Pharisees from non-Pharisees (John 9:34).

In Qumran the eschatological hour of decision forbade any communion with sinners. In accord with God's avenging will, the sons of darkness are to be hated (1 QS 1:10; 9:21; 10:19-21). The godly man, however, will refrain from any personal vengeance (1 QS 10:17f.). Within the Qumran community love was required, and certainly it was practiced. The consciousness of brotherhood (1 QS 6:22; 1 QSa 1:18; 1 QM 15:4; *Damascus [Zadokite] Fragment*, 8:17; 9:16) is a living thing. "In the communion of truth, all shall be of becoming humility, of merciful love, and of just thinking" (1 QS 2:24). The fragmentary *Damascus* or *Zadokite Document* (14:13-17) portrays the investigative solicitude of the community, which seeks to omit nothing: "Their wages for at least two days per month are to be given into the hands of the overseers and judges. From this a portion is to be given for the benefit of the orphans; and it is to support the poor and the needy, the old man who is dying, and the homeless, and him that has been made captive by a foreign people, and the virgin who has no relatives and whom no one desires in marriage, and the slave, whom no one in the brotherhood will hire." [58]

On the other hand, Judaism in the Hellenistic diaspora extended the concept of neighbor. The Greek translation of the Old Testament speaks, in Leviticus 19, not of the love of countrymen, but universally of one's neighbor. The commandment of the love of neighbor is expanded as much in the current of religious proselytizing among the Gentiles as it is under the influence of Hellenistic ideas of humanism (Sir. 13:15, in LXX). In isolated instances late Judaism combined love of God and love of neighbor in a single commandment: "Love the Lord and your neighbor" (*Testaments of the Twelve Patriarchs*: Dan. 5:2f.; Issachar 5:2; 7:6; Zebulon 5:1).

Philo, in *De specialibus legibus* (2, 63), says: "There are two basic
teachings, under which innumerable individual doctrines and propositions are ordered: in relation to God, the commandment of divine
worship and piety; and in relation to man, that of love of neighbor
and righteousness." According to Philo, in *De virtutibus* (102–174),
the love of neighbor is to be practiced in its broadest extension in the
following succession of steps: countryman, proselyte, foreigner, enemy,
slave, animals, plants, every other creature. So Philo requires even love
of one's enemy. The New Testament, however, cannot make such distinctions as he does. It knows no gradations in love; for every other
man is one's neighbor.

Charitable beneficence and love of neighbor were practiced abundantly in Israel (and beneficence is one of Israel's claims to honor even
today). The Rabbis encouraged charitable deeds with sayings such as
these: "The world consists of three things; teaching of God, service of
God, and performance of deeds of kindness"; or, "Beginning and end
of the Torah are works of the love of neighbor." The following tale is
well-known, and was written down shortly before the time of Christ.
A Gentile who wanted to become a proselyte came to Rabbi Shammai
and demanded of him that he teach him the sum-total of the Torah
within a specified length of time, no longer than he could stand on
one foot. Shammai, of course, refused him. Thereupon he went to Hillel, who accepted him and summed up the whole Law in the nega-
tively formulated Golden Rule: "What you would not want done to
you, do not to your neighbor. That is the whole Torah. The rest is
explanation. Now go out and learn that."

Shammai's refusal was not unreasonable. All the commandments are
ultimately of God's ordinance; all, therefore, are important and holy.
That Hillel permits a question as to the principle of the Torah is
probably no mere fortuity. He came from the diaspora and therefore
had contact with Greek thought, which invariably seeks after the
order and principle of things. The conviction of the Rabbinate to
which he gives expression may also be important for the clarification
of the New Testament narrative. Jesus is questioned as to the principle
of the Torah. The teacher of the Law "tested him" (Matthew 22:35).
The question is tendentious, even as Shammai saw it.[59]

Although the New Testament commandment of love accepts that

of the Old Testament, it does not simply continue the old. Even here there is something new. This can be verified by three considerations:

a) The forceful emphasis placed upon the commandment of love, and the uniting of love of God and love of neighbor into a twofold commandment, are new and distinct. In the Old Testament the two commandments are found in the midst of many others, and widely separated from each other. Their union in the New Testament is evidence that the two commandments together form a single entity. Faith in God and love of God are the foundation and source of the love of neighbor. Faith declares that the world is God's creation and man is God's child, and they are therefore worthy of being loved.

The second commandment, however, determines the sense of the first. It is in love of neighbor that obedience and love in respect to God are authenticated. It is not possible to offer sacrifice to God while living in enmity with one's brother (Matthew 5:23f.; Mark 11:25). Jesus repeats the words of the prophet: "I desire mercy and not sacrifice" (9:13 = Hos. 6:6). The codicil to love of neighbor, "as yourself," in both the Old and the New Testaments, is not a limitation placed by the commandment, as if self-love were to be the measure of love (as Christian moral theology has occasionally taught!). The sense of the term is not that of limitation, but of the removal of limitation. Thus, as the care which an egotistical man lavishes on himself and his affairs knows no bounds, so much the more should be the care which he bestows on others.[60]

b) The uncompromising extension of the commandment of love to every man without distinction and even to one's enemy is new. Even Judaism extended the command of love beyond the narrow circle of its own community, and commanded love of enemy. In Israel (as, indeed, always and everywhere) the realization of the commandment may have lagged somewhat behind the ideal, so that the issuing of a new call was thoroughly justified. The nature and basis of Jewish theology and ethics, however, was certainly not love, but righteousness. This is, in any case, verifiable for the period of the New Testament.

The parable of the Good Samaritan points up the difference between the viewpoint of official Judaism, represented by priest and levite, and Jesus (Luke 10:29-37). The teacher of the Law asks: "Who is my neighbor?" He thinks that he has the right to choose and to set a limit. But the conclusion of the narrative turns the question against the questioner when Jesus asks: Who is it that has behaved like a neighbor toward the stricken man? You dare ask nothing; rather, it is always you who are asked, you upon whom requirements are placed. You are always the one close by, the neighbor, even in respect to strangers and aliens. Your service must be selfless. It is not friends, brothers, and relatives that one should invite — those who can return the favor — but the poor, the crippled, the lame and the blind (Luke 14:13-14).

In the telling of this parable, as well as in express command (Matthew 5:43-47), Jesus extends the commandment of love to include even one's enemy. Jesus knows that with this command he is flying in the face of accepted interpretation and practice. His use of antithesis shows as much: "You have heard that it was said, 'An eye for an eye, a tooth for a tooth' (Exod. 21:24f.). But I say to you, 'Do not resist one who is evil.'. . . You have heard that it was said, 'You shall love your neighbor and hate your enemy.' But I say to you, 'Love your enemies . . . , so that you may be sons of your Father in heaven.' "

In the Psalms there are in fact frightful outbursts of hatred against the enemy (Pss. 33; 55; 58; 129; 137:7-9). Without hesitation the petitioner execrates his enemies as enemies of God (Ps. 139:19-22). The members of the Qumran community are likewise expected to hate those opposed to the community as enemies of God (1 QS 1:9f.; 10:19-21). Since Jesus tells his listeners that they have been taught to hate their enemies, and since there is no such commandment to be found in the Old Testament, while in Qumran hatred of enemies is expressly demanded, exegesis must ponder the possibility that Jesus may have formulated his command about love of enemy in reference to Qumran.[61]

c) The reason given with the commandment of love is new. It reads: "Love your enemies . . . , so that you may be sons of your Father in heaven, who makes his sun to rise upon the evil and the good" (Matthew 5:44-45). "Be merciful, even as your Father is merciful" (Luke 6:36). The message about a Father bounteous of his mercies is a new message (see the present work, Vol. 1, pp. 103–106). The Old Testament and Judaism emphasize throughout the doctrine of a just God. The New Testament is the gospel of the God who is filled with forgiveness at this very moment, the message about the forgiveness taking place right now in Christ, the message revealing God's love. For the sake of this love of God, and because it is swift to forgive, the disciple too can and must forgive. The disciple belongs to the publicans and sinners, who now obtain forgiveness. Were he not now to forgive, his situation would be like that of the unmerciful slave, whose great debt was remitted, but who would not himself remit the small debt of his fellow slave (Matthew 18:23-35). The disciple is obliged to pray: "Forgive us our debt, even as we have forgiven our debtors" (Matthew 6:12).

Forgiveness and love are now commanded anew for the sake of Christ, who himself exhibits the love of God and neighbor. He is one with all who suffer want. The things that are done to them will be revealed in the final judgment as having been done to Jesus himself (Matthew 25:31-36). In the unprotected child, it is Jesus himself who is received (Mark 9:37). As the Son secure in the love of the Father, Christ is the servant of all. The example of the Lord constitutes an obligation upon the disciple. "Whoever among you would be great must be your servant, and whoever among you would be first must be the slave of all. For even the Son of Man came not to be served but to serve, and to lay down his life as a ransom for the many" (Mark 10:43-45). In the Gospel of John this new rationale of love is treated in greater depth (see below, p. 134).

The New Testament commandment of love is to be considered not only in its relationship to the Old Testament, but also in comparison to its contemporaneous extra-biblical world, i.e., in comparison to Greek and Roman ethics, wherein we find the human relationship of love treated. The Greek language and culture has three words for *love*. ἔρως signifies passionate love, in which the one who loves covets the other for himself. φιλία signifies the inclination and solicitous love of the gods for man, and of friend for friend. ἀγαπᾶν means to be fond of something or someone, to like to do something, to show love toward someone, often of the superior toward the inferior. This is the expression of the love that gives of itself.

Although ἔρως and ἐρᾶν are important words in Greek culture, they are not found in the New Testament; and φιλία seems to occur therein more characteristically in a derogatory sense, e.g., φιλία τοῦ κόσμου (James 4:4). In distinction thereto, it is biblical literature only (and consequently, ecclesiastical literature) which recognizes the noun ἀγάπη. In profane Greek literature the verb ἀγαπᾶν occurs, to be sure; but the noun ἀγάπη has not as yet been authenticated in literature prior to its use in Scripture. Its first literary occurrence is in the Old Testament Bible, where it is employed in the Greek translation. Probably it was borrowed from the common speech of the (Egyptian) people; and this word was chosen because it did not have the contextual overtones which accompany the words ἔρως and φιλία. In its own way, then, lexicography confirms the fact that Christian love is something new.[62]

Plato, in the *Symposium* (203), employed a myth to demonstrate what *eros* is. At a celebration of the gods, *Penia*, Miss Poverty, spies *Poros*, Mr. Riches. Their encounter and union begets Longing, or *Eros*. *Eros* is that movement which arises between the rich-in-worth and the impoverished-in-worth. It is the striving for fulfillment and perfection, the yearning after that which is lacking, and the hankering to obtain the valuable; and to add to oneself through this devotion is its highest fulfillment. The object of *eros* can be a person, or even a thing or an idea. It is the worth thereof that is loved. What is yearned for in this love is the enhancement of one's own fullness of life and being.

It is otherwise with New Testament love. For biblical and New Testament love there is no other object than the *thou*, either the thou of God or the thou of man. Love is not a mere sterile relation to a thing of desirable worth; rather, it is an ever personal relationship. Man, therefore, is by nature and vocation a personality in no way self-sufficient, neither belonging to himself nor having any power of his own; rather, he is a person by creation, dependent upon the power of God. The Bible further states that from his very creation man is ordered toward society with others. Created as man and woman, human beings are from their very origin drawn to each other. In this respect both the Old and the New Testaments recognize *eros* as a creation of God (Gen. 2:24; Mark 10:7). The basic situation in which man finds himself is not one of free self-sufficiency, but one of answerability.

The love which Christianity knows is otherwise than *eros*, because instead of coveting, it gives. It is God who initiates the first stimulus of love, because he creates in love and he devotes himself to unfathomable redemptive love of his creature, even though the latter is a sinner. "While we were yet sinners, Christ died for us" (Rom. 5:8). By devoting himself to the worthless, God makes it valuable. The poor man who is made rich by God's love must no longer love covetously, as if to enrich himself; for now he can himself love with that kind of love which gives. He devotes himself to the poor man, in order to make him rich.

If *eros* is obliged to say: "I love you because you are so valuable," then *agápe* can say: "I love you, because you are there." The love that Christianity knows is distinct also from sympathy and love generated by emotion and sentiment. Sympathetic love is a love which chooses and prefers its object; and the basis and criterion for its choice is its own profit. The biblical love of neighbor is not love of a chosen one. A neighbor is not this one or that one with whom one feels a bond of sympathy, but every man with whom one comes into contact and who is in need of help.

Emotional and sentimental love knows, besides hate, which is the opposite of love, a third thing — indifference. The biblical love of neighbor recognizes no such possibility. When one person meets another, they cannot retreat into indifference. There is only love or rejection. Because this love is not a selective emotion, the New Testament commandment says simply: "Thou shalt love." It is a challenge to the will and to man, who is faced with having to make in the sight of God a decision in respect to his neighbor. If love is understood as sentiment, it makes nonsense of the commandment. If love is commanded, the love that is intended must be a bearing of the will.

Christianity recognizes love even in those forms which Greek culture calls friendship and *eros*. To biblical morality, these too reflect men's high evaluations of created reality. God's love for the Son and for his disciples is expressed with the term φιλεῖν (John 5:20; 16:27). Christ addresses his disciples as friends (Luke 12:4; John 15:13-15). Love for Christ the Lord is prerequisite for community and, ultimately, for salvation. "If anyone does not love (φιλεῖ) the Lord, let him be accursed!" (1 Cor. 16:22). Even brotherly love is designated by φιλεῖν. "Greet those who love us in the faith" (Titus 3:15). The members of the community are united with one another as friends (φίλοι — 3 John 15).[63]

Christian morality recognizes even *eros*. But it is the task of this morality to reclaim a relationship between *eros* and *agápe*. *Eros* is not to be held in suspicion, not to be disparaged, not to be suppressed. If such has happened at various times and in various places in the history of the Church, it can but be regarded as a disavowal of the belief that God's creation is a good work. *Eros*, however, must be redeemed from self-seeking covetousness to a giving out of the fullness of love. This is expressly stated in the Apostles' admonition, as we shall shortly see.

In the milieu of the New Testament, the Stoa teaches a humanistic command of love. In the classical antiquity of Greece, the city was once the prototype of culture and of the ordering of life. The city-states, however, lost their significance in Hellenism. The Roman Empire embraced the whole known world, and in a world-empire the idea arose of a world-citizenship. This view of man and the world is taken up again and presented philosophically in the Stoa. At the time of the New Testament this was happening especially in the writings of an Epictetus and a Seneca. According to these writings, all men, in their reason, partake of the divine world-reason. They are all of the same sort, all children of God and brothers among themselves. Man's love is universal and must embrace all. "Let man be holy to man" (Seneca, *Letters*, 44; *De beneficiis*, 3, 28). "Where there is a man, one has the opportunity to do good" (Seneca, *De beata vita*, 24, 3). Inner participation is required. "A good deed is done not with the hand only, but is completed in the soul" (Seneca, *De beneficiis*, 1, 5, 2). Love does not draw a line at the ungrateful, nor does it stop short of slaves and enemies. "If you wish to imitate the gods, show your benefactions even to the ungrateful. For the sun rises even on the wicked, and the seas stand open even for pirates" (Seneca, *De beneficiis*,4, 26, 1). This morality of the Stoa must not be underestimated.

Nevertheless, the Stoa's universal love of man, like all philanthropy, is different from biblical love of neighbor. The Stoic love of man is practiced for the sake of man's intrinsic worth, while the biblical love of neighbor reaches out to another through the love of God. In the final analysis, the Stoic sage's love of one's fellowman is not mere self-less service, but it is also of advantage and profit to the one who practices it. This love ought to free and perfect the sage himself. He will hate no man, for "the wise man hates not the erring" (Seneca, *De ira*, 1, 14, 2). "Only the discerning man has the capacity to love" (Epictetus, *Diss.*, 2, 22, 3). He loves, however, "for his own benefit" (*ibid.*, 1, 22, 13). It is said without embarrassment, "I am my own neighbor" (*ibid.*, 4, 6, 11; 3, 4, 10). Love of neighbor is a way for the wise and noble man to assure his own peace and dignity.

The Apostle Paul develops the gospel of love further, and at the same time expresses it anew in relation to the new post-paschal and Pentecostal situation. The law of God, which commands love, is presented anew as the word and law of Christ. "Bear one another's burdens, and thus you will fulfill the law of Christ" (Gal. 6:2). Christ is, by his life, the teacher of love. The incarnation of Christ is both fact and prototype of service. With a hymn which Paul found already at hand and which he borrowed from the congregation, he says: "Let all look to that which is in the interest of others. Have this mind among yourselves, which also was in Christ Jesus, who was in the form of God . . . , but emptied himself and took the form of a slave and became like unto men. . . . He humbled himself and became obedient unto death" (Phil. 2:4-8). Paul sums it up: "You know the grace of our Lord Jesus Christ, who, though he was rich, became poor for your sake, that you might be made rich by his poverty" (2 Cor. 8:9).

Paul knows about the service of love of the Man, Jesus Christ. The kindness of Christ places an obligation upon the Apostle as well as the congregation. Paul conducts himself accordingly, and he admonishes the Corinthians to do likewise. "I admonish you by the meekness and gentleness of Christ" (2 Cor. 10:1; cf. Titus 3:4). Even the Christ of the Passion is an example for imitation: "As the Lord has forgiven you, so you also must forgive" (Col. 3:13).

In 1 Cor. 13, Paul sings a canticle, as it were, in praise of love. In this passage the love of God and the love of neighbor are conceived as a unity. Love has no equal. It is "the still more excellent way" (1 Cor. 12:31). Charismatic gifts, faith and understanding, heroic deeds of self-abnegation are nothing without love. All these things amount only to self-seeking if a man has not love. "Love does not seek its own way. . . . It bears all things, it believes all things, it hopes all things, it endures all things" (1 Cor. 13:1-7).

To the Christians in Thessalonica Paul writes: "You have no need of any written instruction about love of the brethren. For you yourselves have been taught by God to love one another" (1 Thess. 4:9).

How did this instruction come about? Paul can hardly mean instruction through the Old Testament word of God. Did this teaching take place through the word of God in preaching, in which the word of God is heard (1 Thess. 2:13)? Or was the word imparted by the divine Spirit, spoken in that intimate area between God and believing man where the agency of no third person is required?

Faith must beget love. Paul often mentions faith and love in connection with each other. He greets the congregation, stating that he remembers their "work of faith, labor of love, and steadfastness of hope" (1 Thess. 1:3). Paul thanks God that the Church at Colossae has distinguished itself "by faith in Christ Jesus, and love for all the saints" (Col. 1:4; cf. Philemon 5). "Faith must be effective in love" (Gal. 5:6). Indeed, man is justified by faith alone (Rom. 3:27). Genuine faith, however, never is alone, but always carries love along with it.

Like Christ himself (Mark 10:19), Paul too says, in words borrowed from the Old Testament (Deut. 5:17-21), that love is the fulfillment of the Christian life: "The requirement of the Law is summed up in this saying: 'You shall love your neighbor as yourself. . . . Love is the fulfilling of the Law'" (Rom. 13:8-10). Love must be devoted first of all to the congregation. The congregation has a special claim thereto. "Let us do good to all men, and especially to those who are of the household of the faith" (Gal. 6:10). Again and again Paul admonishes the Church to preserve and prove its love (Rom. 15:5; 2 Cor. 8:24; Gal. 5:13f.; Phil. 2:3). Love pours forth from the Apostle to the congregation, and from the congregation back again to the Apostle (2 Cor. 8:7; 12:15). The reception of love comforts the Apostle and refreshes the saints (Philemon 5 and 7). "Let all things be done in love" (1 Cor. 16:14). This must be the order and law of the Church.

In the Roman congregation, peace was endangered by the opposition between the strong, who were convinced they were permitted to eat anything, and the weak, who ate only vegetables (Rom. 14:2). Even if it is a correct principle that everything is clean, still, the first rule must be love, which can relinquish its claims even when in the right. "If your brother is troubled, you are no longer walking according to love" (Rom. 14:15).

In Corinth an excess of enthusiasm threatens to throw the congregation into disorder. It will have to give an account of itself on the criterion of love (1 Cor. 14:1). Only that which edifies the congregation is good (1 Cor. 14:12). And love is also ordered to the understanding and to the rights of the individual. Freedom is obliged to exercise a certain deference toward a brother (1 Cor. 8:12f.). "Knowledge puffs up, but love builds up" (1 Cor. 8:1). Contempt for a brother is outrage against Christ (1 Cor. 8:12).

The communion of marriage partners must be determined by love: "You men, love your wives, as Christ loved the Church and gave himself up for her" (Eph. 5:25). "Let the young wives love their husbands and children" (Titus 2:4). Love rules in the Christian home.

Obviously the New Testament could have no thought of abolishing slavery as a legal institution. But the social structure is altered when the Christian slave is regarded as a "brother, both as Christian and as man" (Philemon 16). It is a constant rule in all things: "Let no one seek what is in his own interest, but the interests of others" (1 Cor. 10:24).

The Church is already the "kingdom of the Son of love," of the last days (Col. 1:13). A decision for love is always at the same time a decision for Christ the Lord. The Church has its law and its composite of ordinances. Even love cannot violate the law, and the Church cannot in general negate the law and abolish it. But at least its ideal is the ordinance of love.

Love draws no line at the boundaries of the congregation. "Let all men experience your gentleness" (Phil. 4:5). "May the Lord make you increase and become ever richer in love for one another and for all men, even as is our love for you" (1 Thess. 3:12). Love will even prevail over the enemy. It may not win him over from evil, but it will at least endeavor to overcome evil with good (Rom. 12:14, 21). "Take care that none of you repays another's evil with evil in turn, but be considerate always of how you will do good to one another and to everyone" (1 Thess. 5:15; cf. 1 Peter 3:9). Love is "the bond of perfection" (Col. 3:14).[64]

This love, nevertheless, is not such a virtue as a man might realize of himself, if only he wills it. Much more, it is a gift of God. Love is only possible in the "new creation in Christ" (2 Cor. 5:17). Love is understood as a gift of God when it is characterized as "fruit of the Spirit" (Gal. 5:22) and as "love in the Spirit" (Col. 1:8).

If this love is only possible, now at least it *is* possible, because the Christian is first loved by God in Christ. Having had love bestowed upon himself by God, he can now bestow it on others. "Be kind to one another, merciful, forgive one another, even as God in Christ has forgiven you. Be imitators of God, as [his] beloved children, and walk in love, even as Christ loved you and gave himself up for you" (Eph. 4:32 — 5:2). The forgiveness which God has shown the world for the sake of Christ's self-renunciation not only makes it possible for the Christian himself to be forgiving but in fact obliges him to be so.

Christians are God's children because when Christ became their brother he imparted sonship to them (Gal. 4:4f.). Christ is the first among many brothers (Rom. 8:29). Brotherhood and brotherliness must now unite all. Those who are beloved of God must love in turn. They become imitators of God, and imitators again of Christ, when they complete their lives in love. This is the finest thing that can be said of the Christian life. The words of the Apostle call to mind the words of the Lord that children of God, children of the Father, must be lavish with their love, even as he is (Matthew 5:45).

According to the Gospel of John, the love of God for the world is made manifest by the mission of the Son (see above, ch. 8). God's love should be the beginning and foundation of love in the world. Jesus loved his own with a great depth of love (John 13:1). Out of love he laid down his life (John 15:13). After washing his Apostles' feet, Jesus admonishes them that they should find in this action a very special example: "If I, then, your Lord and Teacher, have washed your feet, then you must wash the feet of each other. For I have done this for you as an example, that you also should do for each other as I have done for you" (John 13:14f.).

Love, then, is the law of discipleship: "This is my commandment, that you love one another, even as I have loved you" (John 15:12, 17). Love is now commanded anew and made possible anew. That is why Jesus can say: "A new commandment I give unto you, that you love one another; even as I have loved you, that you love one another" (John 13:34). Love is, in the face of the world, the hallmark of the community. "By this will all men know that you are my disciples, if you have love for one another" (John 13:35).

The Johannine Epistles repeat in a kind of solemn monotony the commandment of love. Love of brother is the commandment of Christ (1 John 3:23; 4:21). Christians have heard the commandment of love from the time when they first became Christians (1 John 2:7). In accord with the example of Christ, Christians must be prepared to sacrifice their lives for others (1 John 3:16). Whoever hates his brother belongs to the kingdom of the devil (1 John 3:10). Whoever loves his brother abides in the kingdom of light (1 John 2:10) and life (1 John 3:14). Just as in the saying of Jesus (Mark 12:29-31), so too in the admonition of the Apostle, the love of God and the love of neighbor are one: "If any one asserts: 'I love God,' and at the same time hates his brother, that man is a liar. Whoever does not love a brother, whom he sees, cannot love God, whom he does not see" (1 John 4:20). Love for God is perfected in love for brother (1 John 4:12, 16-17). The brotherly love of which First John speaks so often is an application of love of neighbor. Love, however, is not restricted to the community of faith but is extended to all. The Christian is a brother; but so too is every man (1 John 4:20).

The Apostle seems to be reflecting on the history of the command- ment of love: "Beloved, I am writing you no new commandment, but the old commandment which you had from the beginning. The old commandment is the word which you have heard. But then again, I am writing you a new commandment, which in truth is in him and in you. The darkness has passed away, and the true light is already shining" (1 John 2:7-8). The commandment of love is an old com- mandment. The Old Testament gives voice to it, and it was not en- tirely unknown to the ancient and non-biblical world. But it is never- theless a new commandment. There is a new basis for the command- ment. And the obligation as well as the possibility of keeping the commandment are new (John 13:34). The world is new, God's true and bright world. Love is not only practicable in this redeemed world — it is in fact its hallmark.

The Epistle of James, too, knows the commandment of love as an old but still current command: "If you really fulfill the royal law, according to the Scriptures: 'You shall love your neighbor as yourself,' you do well" (James 2:8). According to the context of the passage in the letter, it is an offense against universal love to show favoritism to the rich. It is a question to what extent this utterance of James is dependent upon the Gospels, or whether James is dependent, like the gospel, on the similar old Jewish tradition. Accordingly, it can scarcely be decided whether the commandment of love in James 2:8 is the product of Old Testament Jewish tradition or of Christianity. It is not even certain why this commandment is referred to as the royal law. Does it mean to say that the commandment adduced in Lev. 19:18 has royal rank among the other commandments, just as in Mark 12:31 it is designated as the greatest commandment? Or is the whole law, since it is given by the Divine King, a royal law from which only the commandment of love is cited here?

The New Testament certifies that the primitive congregation understood and practiced love as service and help, regarding this already as the duty of the whole congregation. The celebration of the Divine Service exhibited the bond of union in the community. The common meal, which was both Sacrament and actual feeding, united all. This unity must not be destroyed (1 Cor. 11:17-34). The meal was called (later?) simple *agápe*, which means "love" (Jude 12f., and in some manuscripts, 2 Peter 2:13). In the divine service a brotherly kiss was given (Rom. 16:16; 1 Peter 5:14). Christians recognized themselves as brothers and sisters, and called each other such (Acts 21:7, 17; Rom. 1:13; 16:1; James 2:15; and elsewhere).[65]

The ideal of the primitive congregation demanded solicitude for the poor, even a voluntary community ownership of goods (Acts 6:1-6; 8:32-37). Paul interested himself in the congregations on behalf of the collection for the mother-community at Jerusalem (Rom. 15:26f.; 2 Cor. 8–9; Gal. 2:1-10; Acts 21:10-17; 24:17). Zeal of this kind is "proof of the genuinity of faith" (2 Cor. 8:8). It is the concern of the Epistle of James to admonish to good works (James 2:15f.). The congregations are prompt in providing hospitality, such as was required especially in view of the needs of the missions (Rom. 12:13; 1 Tim. 3:2; Heb. 13:1f.; 1 Peter 4:9; 3 John 5-8). In this we have the beginnings of a congregational ordering of the service of love.

III. OBJECTIVES

§ 10. FREEDOM

According to the New Testament, freedom [66] is one of the essential determinations of moral personality and of moral life. It is Paul more than anyone else who attests to this. He includes under this heading the freedom of man from law, sin, and death as the powers of wickedness which have done violence to men until now and which want to do him further violence. The esteem which the New Testament proclamation places on freedom takes up a long history and leads it on to its conclusion.

The Old Testament concept of freedom relegates it to the political and legal sphere. Often it treats of the political freedom of the people. Israel had lost this freedom in the period of its Egyptian servitude. Moses led the people out of the house of bondage (Deut. 7:8) into freedom, even if this meant immediate insecurity and misery (Exod. 12–13). Israel remembered her being freed from the bondage of Egypt every year in the Passaḥ. The ancient narrative was read aloud and explained by the father of the family.

The exodus from Egypt was the manifesto of political freedom, particularly in a time when Israel had lost that freedom. In the midst of great political catastrophes the northern kingdom of Israel had lost its independence with the conquest of Samaria by the Assyrians in the year 722 B.C., and the southern kingdom of Judah in 586 B.C. with the destruction of Jerusalem and the deportation of the people in the Babylonian captivity. The Lamentations of Jeremiah bewail the loss of national freedom. The sayings concerning salvation addressed to the exiles in Babylon promise release and redemption (Is. 43:1, 14; 44:22f.; 52:3); and they are to be understood as meaning at one and the same time release from political captivity and redemption from guilt.

137

Israel defended its political independence again in the wars of the Maccabean period, when both her political and her religious freedom were at stake. The freedom and redemption sought for is again primarily her political freedom (1 Macc. 4:9-11). In the New Testament era, freedom was lost again under the foreign domination of the Romans. To this period belongs the petition of the *Eighteen Benedictions* (10) : "Blast loud the trumpet for our release."

Israel knew the problem of freedom even as a juridic and personal problem in the distinction between free men and slaves. Even in Israel there were slaves, though by law their lot was essentially better than it would have been in other nations.

In general, however, the problem of freedom was not experienced as a personal problem in Israel. The godly man recognizes himself as bondsman of God. But to be slave of God bespeaks no lack of freedom; rather, it is an honor, a vocation to the most estimable service. Among the Orientals, to be in the service of a mighty prince is great honor. The pious man finds his joy in obedience to God (Ps. 40:9; 119:47).

Israel's faith, which recognized that man is totally subject to the domination of God, never posed the question as to how human responsibility was to be fitted into such a schema.[67] In all events, the latest writings of the Old Testament and the post-canonical books make it clear that in Judaism questions about the responsibility of man did arise, and they had their origin in the uncertainties of which the Greeks were aware, in respect to man's freedom of will. Thus Sir. 15:11-20 repels the assertion that God is the author of sin. Much more to the point, as Creator of man, God surrendered to him the making of his own decisions. If a man but will, he can keep the commandments. Before man lie life and death. Whichever he chooses will be given him.

According to 4 Esdras 7:71f., men experience the just punishments of God because, in spite of their possessing *reason*, they behave godlessly. And according to 4 Esdras 8:55f., they have — those, that is, who are going to perdition — "by their own choice" been contemptuous of the Almighty and have spurned his law. *Ethiopic Henoch* (98:4) explains that sin was not sent upon the earth, but that man himself created it. Philo (*Quod omnis probus liber sit*) presents individual freedom in the sense of Stoic philosophy, even if the examples which he adduces are from Israel's history.

The term and concept of freedom have a long history in Greek literature and culture. Originally freedom was understood as the government's independence of external political influence, an independence in which even the citizenry shared. It is with this sense in mind that Xenophon (*Memorabilia*, 4, 5, 2) has Socrates say that freedom is "a beautiful and majestic good for the individual as well as for the state." For the Greeks the sign and proof of freedom is freedom of speech ($\pi\alpha\rho\rho\eta\sigma\iota\alpha$). Nevertheless, even Socrates and Plato have pointed out that this freedom of the citizenry is not capricious and licentious, but a freedom to be exercised within the order of the community. For the sake of the dignity of the law, Socrates declined to make use of the opportunity offered him of escaping from his imprisonment. For the sake of the dignity of the law, he preferred to die.

The Greek finds this freedom realized only in the Greek democratic *polis*. He pities and scorns everyone who has to live under any other kind of civil arrangement. This political arrangement in Greece came to an end in the third century B.C. A political freedom in the sense of what had until then been the ideal never arose again. Freedom was now understood as a personal ideal. It withdrew into the subjectivity of the individual. Philosophy asked how a man might be free even when he was oppressed by the ruling powers, even when he was in chains. The Stoa in particular, by far the most recognized philosophical school of the time, posed the question of who might be free. And the answer was: "He that can think is free." And Epictetus said time after time: "In thinking, man is master over his emotions and passions." Because he thinks, he is free even of the ideas and views of the crowd. In thinking, man is at one with pure nature, understood as divine. This is what Stoic philosophy holds out as the way to freedom.

Greek philosophy recognized also that there are very weighty philosophical problems involved in the question of man's freedom of will. The question was posed whether or not there are causeless occurrences within the free choice of man. And if man is not free, how can he be held responsible? Socrates, Plato, the Stoics, and the Epicureans occupied themselves with this problem.

Philosophy did not attempt a solution to the question of life. Constraint in regard to his existence and destiny weighed heavily upon the man of the late period of antiquity. The times experimented in order to find other ways, ways of religion, ways out of constraint into freedom. The mystery religions promised to open such a way. Initiation into the mysteries should impart release from the world. The consecrated initiate understood that in his religion he was set free of the wicked world. He was newly born to a new life beyond the control of persons and powers.

The gnosis taught that man, in the condition in which he finds himself, is not free, because he is set down in a wicked world and made subject to it. He who accepts the teaching of the gnosis can experience redemption. Man deceives himself about his own condition. He does not know that he is bound, with no hope of salvation. The revealing word permits him to recognize that he lives without freedom. Release is given and effected by the redeemer, who teaches his own, collects them, and leads them home. Man himself, however, must assure that he is his. He must not lose himself again and again in the wicked world, but must abstain from it. The gnosis, therefore, requires asceticism, such as abstinence from food and sexuality.

To the question of who it is that is free, the Greeks provide various answers. The Greek is free in comparison to the barbarians. The thinking man is free in comparison to one who is entangled in error. The redeemed man is free in comparison to the man who remains in his misery.

The New Testament knows the concept of freedom in the political and in the social sense. Nevertheless, political freedom as the freedom of Israel from foreign domination is of no interest to the New Testament. The saying of the Lord, "Give to Caesar what is Caesar's and to God what is God's" (Matthew 22:21), repulses every error of a political messiahship. The New Testament recognizes the existing government (Rom. 13:1-7; 1 Peter 2:13-17). The Christian has unassailable freedom as a citizen of the heavenly government (Phil. 3:20). Christians are children of the free Jerusalem (Gal. 4:26-28; Heb. 12:22). The freedom of the faith and of the Church is such that no one can disrupt it, no one can take it away.

The New Testament knows also the concept of freedom in the social sense, according to which a man is free if he is a slave to no earthly master (John 8:33; 1 Cor. 7:21; 12:13; Gal. 3:28). The New Testament does not intend to make any change in this situation, at least in its legal aspects. The gospel is no manifesto of social revolution (see below, ch. 22). The New Testament uses the word and concept of freedom mostly in the religious and moral sense. In this, however, the understanding of freedom is quite different from that of Greek philosophy. In this Greek sense, freedom is not to be encountered in the Synoptics. Release does take place now, however, when Jesus teaches and lives freedom from the Law, even be it in the radical deepening of the Law, as in the Sermon on the Mount (Matthew 5:27-48). Freedom becomes a reality when Jesus conquers demons, sickness, and death. Christ brings redemption to what was lost in sin and death (Mark 10:45). Freedom finds its voice in the proclamation of the kingdom of God. For that kingdom is the free, safe world.

The whole of the New Testament states that man, whether he knows it or not, has lived until then in a complete lack of freedom. He is cowed beneath the powers of sin and death, which are operative through the Law. Men are "slaves of sin" (Rom. 6:20). The wages of sin, however, is death (Rom. 6:23). Man strives greedily for security, fulfillment, and betterment of his lot in life. In truth and in reality, nevertheless, the end of his achievements is always death (Rom. 8:6). The Law, however, which in itself is the holy and just will of God, effects all this in man's present sinful existence. It causes sin to expand to overwhelming proportions, and man experiences in his members, as it were, a law of sin (Rom. 7:23).

The Law, moreover, becomes the occasion and basis for sin not only when it provokes man to contradiction and violation of itself, but even when man wants to fulfill the Law. For he follows the Law only to establish for himself a reputation for righteousness and in order to have in the face of God a claim to reward and life. Fulfillment of the Law, therefore, can be itself a kind of self-seeking (Rom. 10:3; Phil. 3:9; Col. 2:23). Of himself and on his own, man is without hope, locked up "in the law of sin and death" (Rom. 8:2). According to the New Testament, and contrary to the hopes of the Stoa, it is in no way possible for a man to free himself from evil by the control and discipline of himself.

Release now came about, however, through an event external to ourselves, through the deed of Jesus Christ, who took upon himself vicariously the curse of sin and death to which man had fallen heir (Rom. 8:3; 2 Cor. 5:21; Gal. 3:13). "Unto freedom Christ has set us free" (Gal. 5:1). This freedom is not at all a means now available to man for a self-determination which had previously miscarried; rather, it is ever an action of God done to man, which man takes hold of in faith. Man can and must now realize this freedom which has been given him. The believer is able to attain to this freedom for himself when he hears the call to freedom and follows it (Gal. 5:13) and permits the Spirit of life to be operative (Rom. 8:9). This takes place in the community of the Church through the reception of baptism (Rom. 6:1-11) and in obedience to the teaching (Rom. 6:17f.).

This freedom is in no sense unbridled license. Paul had previously to apply himself to the misunderstanding of his teaching. He says that the fact is quite to the contrary: "Freed from sin, you have entered the service of righteousness" (Rom. 6:18). Indeed, this freedom is such that man can enjoy it only in the service of God and of neighbor (Gal. 5:13). Paul himself serves as an example; as an Apostle, he becomes the slave of all (1 Cor. 9:19). So greatly does this freedom differ from lawlessness that Paul can say of the new existence that it is directed "toward the law of the Spirit of life in Christ Jesus" (Rom. 8:2). The disciple now fulfills "the law of Christ" (Gal. 6:2). This law is, to be sure, "the perfect law of freedom" (James 1:25). The liberty of the law becomes ever true and real in the fulfillment of the law of freedom. As a right which is consequent upon freedom, Paul mentions the liberty of faith in candor of speech before God (2 Cor. 3:12; Eph. 3:12), as well as in speech before men (2 Cor. 7:14; Eph. 6:19).[68]

Freedom, as something to be lived and realized, shows its dynamic power where it counts, in overcoming opposition and obstacles internal and external to man. Paul describes freedom not only and not so much as a freedom *from* something, but as a freedom *for* something: as freedom *from* law *for* the gospel; as freedom *from* the flesh *for* the spirit; as freedom *from* sin *for* grace; as freedom *from* death *for* life. In its full perfection freedom is not as yet possible, not yet realized. The Spirit is its earnest-money (Rom. 8:23). In its fullness it will come only as an eschatological gift. The totality of creation will be set free from the bondage of corruptibility unto the children of God (Rom. 8:21). Freedom is not only personal but cosmic liberation (see above, ch. 7). Ultimately, however, this eschatological expectation is bound up with the work of Christ in the Gospels, inasmuch as it is he that is our assistance in every physical need, indeed, it is he that conquers death. Liberation is not merely inner grace and forgiveness but physical salvation. The resurrection is the conquest of death and decay. The end and goal is a sound world and new creation.

John (8:31-36) is at one with this theology of Paul. Here "the Jews" represent the man who does not believe. He is "the slave of sin" by his very nature, even though he may not know it and regards himself as free. The slave, i.e., the man who is lost, "does not remain in the house in eternity." Only the truth, which is Christ, and the surrender of the Son can make the Jews free unto life. The Jews will attain to freedom if they abide in the word of Jesus. Here freedom is already a present event as well as a future gift.

The concord between Paul and John is significant. It makes it a certainty that this is not the doctrinal course of an individual Apostle, of Paul alone or of John alone, but that it is contained in the New Testament preaching of salvation. It is under the influence of Pauline theology that 1 Peter can say — and indeed, this Epistle in general is influenced in a high degree by Paul — : "Live as free men; and not as those who use freedom as a pretext for wickedness, but as servants of God" (1 Peter 2:16).

If in the New Testament, and as distinct from the Old, the term and reality of personal and moral freedom is of extreme importance, this message will make its impression on the contemporaneous Greek world, in which freedom was a precious possession. The surrounding world became for the New Testament an inducement to recognize in the gospel true freedom and to proclaim it. "In the idea of inner freedom antiquity and Christianity meet each other, and at the same time, part company. For in the one, inner freedom is obtained by the strength of its own ability to reason and by the use of its own powers; and in the other it is the gift of God's liberating grace" (R. Bultmann).

The New Testament offers a solution to what is for every morality a question of fundamental importance, the relation between law and freedom. The law which is surmounted in the gospel is, to be sure, primarily the Old Testament Law. But along with the Old Testament Law, the gospel focuses its sights to some extent on the ever-present hazard of legalism in general. It is overcome by right and virtue of freedom in the Spirit.

Pertaining also to the problem of freedom, and especially for us today, is the problem of the freedom of the will. Theology has interrogated both the Old and the New Testaments as to what they have to say about man's freedom of will. In so doing, however, an attempt is made to extort from Scripture the answer to a question which, to be sure, is not within its competency. For freedom of will is, in this sense, a philosophical problem.

In the controversies of the Reformation and counter-Reformation the problem was set down in the formulas *De libero arbitrio* (Erasmus) and *De servo arbitrio* (Luther). Proofs for both viewpoints have been found in the theology of Paul. Paul teaches a judgment according to works, in which man is rewarded or punished according to merit or guilt. The same holds good for pagans, Jews, and Christians. All are under the wrath of God (Rom. 2:5-6). "We must all appear before the judgment seat of Christ, so that each may receive according to what he has done in the body, be it good or be it evil" (2 Cor. 5:10). This presupposes that man is able to choose responsibly. Nevertheless, the situation in which man finds himself is such that by his own will and ability he never can attain to righteousness. He cannot of himself obtain release from his condition of being lost. Only God's saving will can lead him forth from death to life. In actual fact, he alone is free, who is situated in redemption. He alone is withdrawn from sin and death, and made free unto life. In this way the proposition *De servo arbitrio* can be given a basis.

According to the biblical doctrine of man, God-given deliverance moves man's will. In this situation of freedom, he is responsible under grace.

The idea and ideal of freedom has had a many-faceted history in the Church, with the Church, and even against the Church. Was the freedom proclaimed by the New Testament, and especially by Paul, intended to be a spiritual and religious freedom, given a further understanding in the preaching of the Church? Perhaps this has happened to some extent. Biblical freedom was united in the course of time with other concepts, especially with freedom understood in a political sense. The biblical proclamation of freedom can extend its operation in many directions, until at last and in the most extreme instance, in the name of freedom, freedom *from* the Church is demanded!

§ 11. PEACE AND JOY

There are two basic and related attitudes mentioned in the New Testament, sometimes separately and sometimes in connection with each other: *peace* and *joy* (Rom. 14:17; 15:33; 16:20; Gal. 5:22). To begin with, both are works of God and his gift to men. And both must be realized in the community as well as in each individual.

I. PEACE

In profane Greek literature, peace (εἰρήνη) denotes various situations: political peace, peaceful intercourse between men, peace of soul. In the New Testament era, the peace which reigned in the Roman Empire seemed to be the fulfillment of the universal yearning for peace.[69]

The biblical concept of peace has its basis in the Old Testament concept of *shalom*, a term which, in its etymology, includes the basic significance of well-being, as well as the attitude of contentment flowing therefrom. The concept embraces wealth in earthly and spiritual goods, prosperity and consummate good fortune. But since it is God who "works weal and creates woe" (Is 45:7), for the godly man peace, in the totality of its fullness, is a gift of God (Lev. 26:6; Ps. 85:9-14). Peace is security in the protection and favor of God (Ps. 122). The prophetic announcement promises peace as redemption by God: "I harbor thoughts of weal and not of woe" (Jer. 29:11). "Peace, peace to the far and to the near!" (Is. 57:19).

Peace becomes a messianic-eschatological concept. The Messiah is called "Prince of Peace" (Is. 9:6). Peace and righteousness will come upon the people along with the kindness and glory of God (Is. 45:8,

17, 24-25). If peace is a gift for the whole nation, it can at the same time be promised to or withdrawn from the individual. "My soul is bereft of peace, I have forgotten what good fortune is" (Lam. 3:17). In the New Testament era, Israel was expecting peace as an eschatological gift of salvation: "Judgment will fall upon men. Peace will be concluded with the just, protection and peace will be imparted to the elect; mercy will descend upon them; they will all belong to God, and he will make peace with them" (*Ethiopic Henoch*, 1:7f.).

The Rabbis praise peace among men. To establish peace is an estimable work.

Since the Septuagint translated *shalom* almost without exception by εἰρήνη, in the Bible the Greek word had imposed upon it the overtones of the Hebrew word.

The community of Qumran saw itself as the community of salvation pertaining to the last days. Peace and salvation, therefore, are to be its lot, if here and now, as the community of the sons of light, it will take up the battle against the sons of darkness (1 QM 1:9-11). Its salvation will be subjected to purification as if by the fire of a smelter (1 QM 17:1). But still, "God destroys not the peace of those who serve him" (1 QH 9:11). "The protection of his peace is ever present" (1 QH 9:33). Salvation is promised in the blessing of the priest: "May God lift up his gracious countenance to you with everlasting peace" (1 QS 2:4). The vision beholds already the heavenly hosts: "The covenant of your peace have you engraved with the graver of life, so as to rule over them in all the days of eternity" (1 QM 12:3).

Even in the New Testament, *peace* can mean, according to the context, eschatological well-being, to which, certainly, peace pertains. At the time of Jesus there were such greetings in use as: "Peace be with you!" and "Go forth in peace!" Jesus too used these formulas, in which soundness of life and being is meant. This is the meaning of the word he speaks to the woman whom he healed (Mark 5:34; Luke 8:48), as well as the word addressed to the sinful woman (Luke 7:50). The fullness of this sense of the word is apparent in the peace-greeting with which the disciples are charged: "When you enter any house, say immediately, 'Peace be to this house!'" (Luke 10:5).

Peace is an objective gift which can be accepted or turned back again (Matthew 10:13; Luke 10:6). Now that Jesus has entered Jerusalem, peace has been prepared in heaven. Jerusalem, however, did not know "the things that make for its peace" (Luke 19:42). Still, the peace of the Savior is not such as the world understands, not even that which the disciples were expecting. "I have not come to bring peace, but the sword" (Matthew 10:34). Neither Jesus nor the disciples wish to establish discord. Nevertheless, the gospel can bring division into families (Matthew 10:35-36). It will bring forth persecution of the disciples (Matthew 10:17f.). But more important than all this, there remains the salvation promised and given to the disciples.

The knowledge of a later generation announces salvation as an accomplished event already in the Lucan history of the childhood of Jesus. The Canticle of Zechariah expects of the prophet John that his service will be "to guide our feet into the way of peace" (Luke 1:79). The angel proclaims "peace to men of [God's] good will" (Luke 2:14).

In John's Gospel, peace is the gift given to the disciples. "Peace I leave with you, my peace I give to you. Not as the world gives peace do I give it to you" (John 14:27). If there is here the faint sound of the usual departing wishes, there is nevertheless much more intended. It is not merely an idle wish for prosperity, but a promise of salvation in full measure. The unbelieving world does not know this peace. The peace which the world has, if any, is of another sort. The disciples will experience grief and oppression in and from the world (John 16:20-22, 33). They must not allow themselves to be led astray in striving after worldly peace, so as to find their satisfaction therein.

True peace is, as a gift of Christ, a contingency beyond anything the world can offer. When the gospel further states: "Let not your hearts be troubled or dejected" (John 14:27), it is thereby made apparent that the peace of the disciples will be experienced as peace of heart. The disciples receive it by accepting the domain of salvation presented to them. Peace is given by the Lord and is secure in him: "I have said this to you, that you may have peace in me" (John 16:33). Even in the uncertainty attaching to belief, the disciples abide in peace, in the midst of but beyond all the unrest of the world (John 16:32). When the resurrected Christ presents his greeting of peace repeatedly (John 20:19, 21, 26), it is a hint that peace is a fruit of the cross and a gift of the Glorified.

The preaching of the Apostles has to announce that in the work of salvation God has henceforth created peace between himself and the world, and makes it effective in the world and in the Church. Now "the gospel of peace" is proclaimed (Eph. 6:15). God is "the God of peace" (Rom. 15:33; 1 Thess. 5:23; Heb. 13:20), and Christ is "the Lord of peace" (2 Thess. 3:16). Between the heavenly and the earthly worlds, God has "established peace in the blood of the cross" (Col. 1:19-20). This cosmic pacification embraces all things. The salvation which guards all men is now given in Christ. "The peace of God, which surpasses all understanding, will guard your hearts and minds in Christ Jesus" (Phil. 4:7). The peace of Christ reigns in hearts (Col. 3:15). This peace is not a human work, but a "fruit of the Spirit" (Gal. 5:22). "The purpose of the [divine] Spirit is life and peace" (Rom. 8:6). Peace is God's mercy (Gal. 6:16).

Paul accepts a profane usage when he begins his letters with wishes for peace. But he gives it an entirely new content: "Grace be to you, and peace from God our Father and from the Lord Jesus Christ" (Rom. 1:7; and similarly in many other places). In accord with epistolary style, Paul can also conclude his letters with wishes of peace (2 Cor. 13:11; Gal. 6:16; Eph. 6:23; Phil. 4:9; 2 Thess. 3:16).

Peace and happiness are productive of right ordering in respect to God. "Since we are justified on the basis of faith, we have peace in respect to God" (Rom. 5:1). Peace is also sanctification (1 Thess. 5:23). God will consummate our safe-keeping: "The God of peace will soon crush Satan under your feet" (Rom. 16:20). Here at the end of the Epistle to the Romans, Paul wants, certainly, to recall again the warnings which he was obliged to issue against false doctrines and schisms. To that end he refers again to his remarks about peace. Unrest is at bottom a work of Satan, the counterpart of the God of peace.

Peace will be consummated when Satan is vanquished. Paul describes the final conquest with a mythological image from Gen. 3:15, which notes that the serpent's head will be trampled on. God will force Satan beneath the feet of the faithful so that they can trample on him. This will happen soon, for the time of the world, in which Satan is yet allowed to carry on his pernicious works, will soon be at an end. The final consummation is near indeed (Rom. 13:11-13). Peace is the final goal of each man. "May glory and honor and peace come upon every man who does good, on the Jews especially and on the Greeks also" (Rom. 2:10). Peace is "incorruptibility," i.e., immortality (Rom. 2:7).

In the term *peace*, when it is applied to the relationship between men, there is a concept of considerable social importance. Jesus himself concludes his talk about the proper bearing of a disciple with the remark: "Keep peace with each other" (Mark 9:50). Those who have understood the message of Jesus are peacemakers among men (Matthew 5:9; 2 Cor. 13:11; 1 Thess. 5:13). Peace with God is peace among men, since Christ, as peacemaker, has reconciled to unity in his person those who are far off and those who are near, i.e., the Gentiles and the Jews (Eph. 2:14-18). "The kingdom of God is not eating and drinking, but righteousness and peace and joy in the Holy Spirit" (Rom 14:17). Paul had spoken of the opposition between the strong and the weak in Rome. The strong ate meat without scrupling over it; the weak ate only vegetables (Rom. 14:2). But all this is unimportant. One thing only is essential: that there be righteousness, peace, and joy in the community.

The kingdom of God is still in the future; and yet, it is secure already in the present. Those who are justified will one day live in God-given righteousness in peace and salvation. The future kingdom is even now symbolically present in the unity of the Church effected by the Spirit abiding therein. It must come about and be realized even now. Christ has effected righteousness, peace, and joy, and dispenses them evermore. The Christian, therefore, must endeavor to assist in bringing peace. In this way he serves to edify one and all (Rom. 14:19).

This peace is the bond and unity of the congregation (Eph. 4:3). The God of peace wants peace among men. The peace of Christ should be in every era, in all places and in all ways (2 Thess. 3:16). There are, therefore, certain concrete questions to be decided, for example, in regard to the marriages of believers with unbelievers, whether the bond remains or is to be loosed. "God has called you in peace" (1 Cor. 7:15). This is true also of the arrangement of divine service, which must not be disturbed by fanaticism: "God is not a God of confusion but of peace" (1 Cor. 14:33).

The gospel of peace seems to be summed up in the wish with which

Paul closes his Epistle to the Romans: "May the God of hope fill you with all joy and peace in believing, so that by the power of the Holy Spirit you may abound in hope" (Rom. 15:13). Thus the good things of salvation are recited again: hope, joy, peace, faith, power, and spirit. God reveals and makes available and guarantees hope. As a foretaste of future salvation he gives even now joy and peace; every man ought to be filled to overflowing with them. Again Paul expresses his good wishes: "May the God of peace be with you all! Amen!" (Rom. 15:33). In the blessing and in the vision of Paul, there is a grand harmony encompassing God and his Church.

As in the letter to the Romans, so too in other Epistles of Paul (1 and 2 Corinthians, Galatians, and Philippians), the description of quarrels and confrontations in the communities lets it be known that the New Testament Church has not yet been able to realize its ideal of peace. Even the Epistle of James warns about passions, parties, and strife, which have their origin in a false and arrogant quest for wisdom (James 3:14-18); and he warns further against wars and enmity, even murder, which "come from the passions which are at war in your members" (James 4:1-10). Is the letter exposing real situations in the community, or does it simply borrow themes and formulations from proverbial literature? Whatever be the case, the letter wants to point out that the situations which it portrays are of universal experience and can at any time become actual events. The development of the communities in a Greek milieu, which would tend then and there to cause a rupture between simple faith and pneumatic wisdom, might well be the occasion of some apprehension along these lines. In any case, it is true enough that "the fruit of righteousness is sown in peace by those who make peace" (James 3:18).

In the Pastoral Epistles, the bishop is admonished to "be solicitous for righteousness, faith, love, peace among all who call upon the Lord with a pure heart" (2 Tim. 2:22). In their society Christians must "strive after peace and holiness" (Heb. 12:14). They must expend some efforts "to be found in peace" (2 Peter 3:14).

The Acts of the Apostles describes the Church as having the realization of peace (Acts 9:31; 10:36; 15:33). In this presentation the eschatological good becomes an already historically present sociological good.

II. JOY

In the world of his God and in the presence of this God as Creator and Redeemer, the man of the old covenant is moved and filled with joy.[70] Joy in the work of creation is self-declaratory. Even if this is not expressly stated, certainly admiration for creation goes along with the content of the creation narrative in Gen. 1–2:4. The Psalms (8; 19:2-7; 24; 29) announce the praises of creation. Creation itself praises the deeds of God (Pss. 65:12-14; 89:6), and it is called upon to praise God (Ps. 145:10) and to rejoice: "Let the heavens rejoice and the earth be jubilant" (Pss. 96:11; 97:1). Creation shall celebrate its God (Is. 35:1; 44:23). God himself "rejoices in his works" (Ps. 104:31), and the psalmist acknowledges: "I will rejoice in the Lord" (Ps. 104:34).

Joy in creation is disclosed as joy in the good things of creation. The harvest is joy (Ps. 126:5f.; Is. 9:3), and so too is the vintage (Is. 16:10). Wine produces joy (Judg. 9:13; Ps. 104:15; Sir. 31:27). Rich possessions make for joy (Ps. 37:11). Woman gives joy to a man by her charm and virtue (Prov. 5:18; Sir. 26:2, 13). The delight of the bridegroom in his bride is an image of God's delight in Israel (Is. 62:5). Children are the joy of their parents (1 Sam. 2:1; Ps. 113:9). Joy is conducive to health (Prov. 17:22). But the wise man knows that joy can be such an internal and personal thing that another is incapable of understanding it (Prov. 14:10). It is God who preserves or takes away (Jer. 7:34) the joy of his people.

The Old Testament preacher, Qoheleth, sees and experiences life's disillusionments. But even he speaks of the joys of this fleeting life, of the joys of labor and work (3:22; cf. Deut. 12:18), of union with a beloved wife (9:9), even of joy in food and drink (3:12f.). He praises this joy in the midst of hardship (8:15). And all of this is joyfulness of heart, given by God (5:18f.).

The work of the Creator is continued in history. Even the activity of God in history is cause for joy. Israel shall rejoice in her Creator, and Zion in her King (Ps. 149:2). God showed kindness, joy, and favor to Israel; for this reason all should rejoice (Ps. 98:4). God comforts his people in their homecoming out of a strange land; for this reason heaven and earth should rejoice in exultation (Is. 49:13). The coronation of the king (1 Kings 1:40) and conquests and escape from the enemy are celebrated in joyous festivities (1 Sam. 18:6; 1 Macc. 5:54; 2 Macc. 15:29, 34-47).

The covenant is security for God's lasting work of salvation; and for this, Israel gives joyful thanks (Pss. 95:1f.; 145:7f.). In its worship Israel is certain of God's presence. Israel must have no part in liturgical orgies (Hos. 9:1). Still, it celebrates its feasts in joy and gladness (Pss. 42:5; 68:4; 100:2). God himself has prepared these feast days so that all will be glad and rejoice (Ps. 118:24). In a spirit of triumph shall the sacrificial meal be celebrated, and with thanks to God for his blessings on human accomplishments (Deut. 12:7; 28:47). The Old Testament mentions Passover (Is. 30:29; 2 Chr. 30:21-25), the Feast of Weeks (Deut. 16:10f.), and the Feast of Tabernacles (Ps. 81:2-4) as especially joyful feasts. At the Feast of Tabernacles after the return from exile, Ezra expresses the joy thereof: "The joy of God is your strength" (Neh. 8:10).

Within the national community, the pious experience God's joy even personally. They have their joy in the Law of God (Pss. 1:2; 19:9). It is their delight even in the midst of oppression (Ps. 119:143). Those who are poor and who seek God can rejoice in God's grace (Ps. 32:10f.), in God's justice (Ps. 51:10, 14), and even in God himself (Pss. 34:3; 69:33; 70:5; 105:3). Even in dire straits, one who petitions God is comforted in his salvation (Hab. 3:18). The prophet exults over his own salvation: "I will rejoice in God, and my soul shall exult in God. For he clothes me with the garments of salvation and covers me with the robe of righteousness, like the bridegroom, who sets a garland on his head, and like the bride, who adorns herself with trinkets" (Is. 61:10).

Occasionally there is actually expressed what is more often allowed to remain in the background of the invitation to joy. Life is harassed by the comfortlessness of the expectations of what lies beyond in the underworld. "Do everything that you can. For in the underworld, whither you are going, there is no doing, no planning, no longer any understanding or wisdom" (Eccl. 9:10; cf. Ps. 88:11-13; Job 10:21f.). This, then, is the reasoning behind the admonition to enjoy life and its good things as long as they last (Eccl. 5:17, 19). Nevertheless, there is hope to be found, even in the face of death. The petitioner rejoices and exults in the assurance that God will lead him through death and into life (Ps. 16:9-11, which, in Acts 2:25-28, is understood as having been spoken of the resurrected Christ).

Joy will be complete in the messianic era of salvation. Thus the prophetic expectation and message: "You make their exultation great and their joy powerful. They rejoice before you as one rejoices at the harvest, as one exults at the division of booty" (Is. 9:3). In the period of Israel's captivity in Babylon, the hope of release and of returning home appears as a prototype of the messianic joy (Jer. 31:7-14; Baruch 4:22f.). Heaven and earth will exult when God redeems Jacob and is glorified in Israel (Is. 44:23; 49:13). The nations will gather around in joy (Is. 56:6f.). God is creating Jerusalem as a new creation, to the joy and gladness of his people (Is. 65:18). Israel is already called upon to welcome its Messiah-King with jubilation (Zech. 9:9).

Either the messianic joy passes over into eschatological joy, or else it is this already. Salvation, joy, and exultation will then be imperishable. "Everlasting joy covers their heads, joy and exultation will be their lot; sorrow and sighing shall flee away" (Is. 51:11). The final everlasting salvation is prepared not for Israel only, but for all peoples. "I am coming to gather peoples and tongues, and they shall come and view my glory" (Is. 66:18). "A new heaven and a new earth will I create, and they shall remain in existence" (Is. 65:17; 66:22). The original majestic creation, paradise and Eden, will be set up again. "Joy and delight is to be found there, songs of laud and praise" (Is. 51:3).

Rabbinic theology and piety are joyful and exultant in praising God's salvational actions in history, at present, and in the last days. The pious of Qumran exult about God in prayers and songs, on account of his mercy and the revelation of his secrets (1 QS 10:9-17; 11:12-19). Even God's chastisements become joys and delights (1 QH 9:24). God's truth is ever a joy to the soul of his servant (1 QH 11:30). He rejoices in God's mighty hand and exults over his assistance and his salvation (1 QM 13:12f.). The certainty of ultimate triumph is a joy even now (1 QM 14:4; 18:6). The ensigns of the final war will bear the inscriptions "God's Works of Salvation" and "Joy of

God" (1 QM 4:13f.). After the victory God's creation will be filled with "everlasting majesty and everlasting joy" (1 QH 13:6).

Even extra-biblical texts know about religious and especially cultic joy. In the mystery religions, as the Christian apologete Athenagoras (22) recounts, the manifestation of the divinity was met with the cry: "Let us rejoice" A prayer of a *mystes* has come down to us in a papyrus: "We rejoice because you have appeared to us; we rejoice because you have divinized creatures by your recognition." According to the *Corpus Hermeticum* (13:8, 18), after the rebirth, joy takes possession of the soul and sorrow withdraws. And the one who is reborn prays in thanksgiving: "I praise the spiritual light. Praising, I rejoice in the joy of the spirit." A Mandaean text reads: "The king in the heavenly city of light . . . rejoices in a joy without affliction and his whole kingdom rejoices with him." In the *Odes of Solomon* (31:3, 6; 32:1) the Redeemer proclaims joy, and the faithful receive it from him. The Lord is their joy (7:1f.; 15:1).

The New Testament never speaks expressly of joy in creation. This being the case, it may be stated quite emphatically that the Old Testament is the Book of Creation, while the New Testament is the Book of New Creation.

The words which the New Testament uses in portraying joy are, in verb and noun pairs, χαίρειν and χαρά (the most frequently used), ἀγαλλιᾶσθαι and ἀγαλλίασις, εὐφραίνειν and εὐφροσύνη. These terms appear often enough even in the Greek translation of the Old Testament. While each of these terms originally had its own distinct emphasis, these emphases are scarcely distinguishable any longer in their New Testament usage. Here the terms are used in connection with each other (Matthew 5:12; Luke 15:32; Acts 2:26; 1 Peter 4:13). The more proper significance of ἀγαλλιᾶσθαι is the jubilation (originally cultic) over God's eschatological, salvational activity. Even profane joy can be signified by εὐφραίνειν (Luke 12:19; 15:29; 16:19; Acts 7:41), which, however, serves also for expressions of joy in salvation (Rom. 15:10; Gal. 4:27; Apoc. 18:20). From joy there can come about even a kind of glorying in joy (2 Cor. 1:14; 1 Thess. 2:19).

In the New Testament, joy is joy over already present or soon to be accomplished messianic salvation. The forefathers, like Abraham (John 8:56) and David (Acts 2:26), were already full of joy at the prospect of this era. Now is the lofty era [*hohe Zeit*] of consummate joy. "How can the wedding [*Hochzeit*] guests fast while the bridegroom is with them?" (Mark 2:19). The Messiah himself rejoices in doing his work for men (Matthew 18:13). He exults in the Holy Spirit on account of the Father's revelation (Luke 10:21).

Now the world will be set up again in soundness, which is demonstrated by the expulsions of demons and miraculous cures. The people respond to these cures with expressions of joy (Luke 5:26; 13:17; 18:43), just as they do at the raising of a dead man (Luke 7:16). The conversion of a sinner elicits joy (Luke 15:5-10). The preaching of the gospel is listened to with joy (Mark 4:16), and the kingdom of God is joyously welcomed (Matthew 13:44). Even the disciples rejoice, because they are able to vanquish demons. Certainly they ought to rejoice much more over the fact that their names are inscribed in heaven (Luke 10:17-20). Even in the midst of persecutions the disciples can rejoice (Matthew 5:11-12). They expect to enter into consummate joy (Matthew 25:21-23).

At his entry into the city of Jerusalem, the Messiah is greeted with joy (Luke 19:37-38). The mighty miracle of the resurrection awakens not only fear but great joy as well (Matthew 28:8; Luke 24:41; John 20:20). With the knowledge that came later about the beginning of the era of salvation, the Gospels speak already in the infancy histories of the joy with which the Child-Messiah was received into the world (Matthew 2:10; Luke 1:14, 44; 2:10).

John the Baptist was exultant because he was to introduce the Messiah to the community (John 3:29f.). The joy given to the disciples is the joy of Jesus (John 15:11). The joy which Christ has in unity with the Father is also the joy of the disciples (John 17:13). This joy is a gift; but at the same time it must always be earned by the disciples until it is brought to eschatological perfection (John 15:11). The disbelieving world does not understand this joy. It finds its joy in rejecting and persecuting Jesus and his congregation because they are a constant offense and reproach to the world (John 17:14). Their existing in an inimical world is the source of the disciples' sorrow. Their joy, therefore, is always in opposition to the world, and must be maintained in the face of opposition (John 16:20). The disciples will rejoice because they will see Jesus again (John 16:22; 20:20).

Joy begets faith, which, however, is not effected once for all time but must be ratified over and over again, and for which there is the promise that the Savior's gift will be given again and again. The believer can himself let his joy be ruined; but it cannot be wrested from him by an inimical world, because the basis of his joy is not in the world, not even in the faith of the disciple himself, but ultimately it is in its being gift of the Lord (John 16:22). Genuine joy is without end.

The Gospel of John speaks further of the joy of the community. The Church finds in its mission work the joy of the harvester of a later generation who reaps the fruits previously sown by another (primarily Christ himself — John 4:36).

Christ at his departure sends his disciples back in joy (Luke 24:52-53). The words of the gospel (Acts 8:8; 13:48), like baptism (Acts 8:39; 13:52) and the faith itself (Acts 16:34), fill the Church with joy. "In exultation and purity of heart" they celebrate the Eucharistic banquet (Acts 2:46). Enthusiasm marks the presence of the Lord experienced at this banquet, through which presence their final union with him is anticipated. In joy the missionaries render service (Acts 8:39; 11:23).

Like the Acts of the Apostles, the letters of the Apostles too portray the community as filled with joy (2 Cor. 8:2; Phil. 1:25; 2:29). Joy ought always be realized in brotherly companionship and unity (1 John 1:4; 2 John 12; 3 John 4). Paul calls upon the members of the community to rejoice always (Rom. 12:15; 2 Cor. 13:11; Phil. 2:18; 1 Thess. 5:16). As co-members of the community (Rom. 12:5), Apostles and community must help each other to be joyful (Rom. 15:32; 2 Cor. 2:3; Phil. 2:2). Israel and even the pagan peoples will rejoice over the expansion of the Church (Rom. 15:10). The Church exults like a mother blessed with children (Gal. 4:27). The community is the honor and joy of the Apostle (Phil. 4:1; 1 Thess. 3:9). The Apostle serves the joy of the Church (2 Cor. 1:24; Phil. 1:25), and at the same time he shares in her joy (Rom. 16:19; Phil. 2:17f.).

The foundation for joy is the grace of the Father, who has established the Church in the kingdom of his beloved Son (Col. 1:12f.). The present messianic salvation is noted as the origin and source of joy; joy is characterized as "joy in the Lord" (Phil. 3:1; 4:4), or as "joy in the Holy Spirit" (Luke 10:21; Acts 13:52; Rom. 14:17; 1

Thess. 1:6). As presence of God, the Spirit is the basic cause of joy. Joy is a fruit of the Spirit (Gal. 5:22). Christ, anointed with the oil of joy on account of his righteousness, is the foundation of the joy among his disciples (Heb. 1:9).

Joy is connected with the other salvational experiences: with faith (Phil. 1:25); with love (1 Cor. 13:6; Gal. 5:22; Philemon 7); with hope, since present joy is in reference to the future (Rom. 12:12; 15:13); with comfort (Acts 15:31); with peace (Rom. 14:17; 15:13; Gal. 5:22); with truth, when truth signifies God's revelation (1 Cor. 13:6); with prayer (1 Thess. 5:16; Phil. 1:4); and with thanksgiving (Col. 1:11). Joy operates in the Church in the service of love (2 Cor. 8:2; 9:7). The life and situation of the Christian can be designated as the presence of the kingdom of God or as "righteousness and peace and joy in the Holy Spirit" (Rom. 14:17).

Righteousness and peace, however, are not man's own accomplishments; rather, it is God's gift which establishes man in salvational righteousness before God and in peace with him. Thus, joy too is much more an objective work of God than its subjective reception, even if it can be realized only in an existing person; this latter fact, however, accounts for the admonition to be joyful.

Paul speaks of joy even in its simple, everyday meaning. Besides the formulas of greeting, as in 2 Cor. 13:11 and Phil. 3:1, such declarations as in Rom. 15:32; 16:19; 1 Cor. 16:17; 2 Cor. 2:3; 7:7, 13, 16; Phil. 2:28; and Philemon 7 can be noted. All of these are texts which speak of joy in human companionship and society (comparable declarations in Phil. 4:10 and 1 Thess. 3:9 have a religious ring to them through mention of God or Lord.) This may be of some interest for a study of the psychology of Paul. To him, community is a joyful necessity. Even the long list of greetings in the final chapter of Romans is expressive of this aspect of Paul's character (Rom. 16:1-16, 21).

True joy is not utopian, i.e., it does not overlook or deny prevailing reality. Nevertheless, joy is stronger than any oppression. The joy of the disciples remains in spite of sorrow and affliction (John 16:20). The Apostles bear witness in joyful martyrdom. Punishments which ought to be ignominious they regard as honors bestowed (Acts 5:41). Joy is indestructible. Paul experiences this joy as "sorrowful, yet always rejoicing" (2 Cor. 6:10), as "abundant joy in the midst of afflic-

tion" (2 Cor. 7:4), as "joy in being weak" (2 Cor. 13:9). He is full
of joy, even if he "is to be offered up at the sacrifice and at the liturgy
of the faith" of the congregation (Phil. 2:17).

The Christians in Thessalonica accepted the word "in great affliction, with the joy of the Holy Spirit" (1 Thess. 1:6). The Church in
Macedonia rejoices in trial and affliction (2 Cor. 8:2). It is not only in
spite of and in the midst of oppression that the faith rejoices, but even
on account of it. The oppression and misery of the Apostle work unto
salvation for the Church (Col. 1:24 cf. 2 Cor. 4:10; 13:9). The Christian rejoices over opposition, because opposition is productive of steadfastness and constancy (James 1:2f.). In the certainty of future salvation, Christians are able even now to rejoice in every trial (1 Peter
1:6).

Present joy is promise and assurance of future glory. Earthly joy, of
course, is an entirely different matter. Those who laugh now will
mourn and weep later (Luke 6:25). The joy of the world is deceptive
and counterfeit (John 16:20). It is perhaps a primitive, malicious
pleasure (Apoc. 11:10). In the face of the impending consummation,
such present things as possessions, marriage, sorrow, and joy are fleeting (1 Cor. 7:29-31). As sinners, everyone ought to take warning: "Be
sensible of your misery and mourn and weep! Let your laughter be
turned to weeping and your joy to dejection" (James 4:9). Nevertheless, the promise of eschatological beatitude still holds good: "Rejoice
and be glad Your reward is great in heaven" (Matthew 5:12). The
Lord will call the faithful servant into his joy (Matthew 25:21-23).
After their sorrow the disciples will possess this eschatological joy
(John 16:20, 22).

In the expectation of the arrival of the Lord, the community in
Philippi should be full of joy (Phil. 4:4f.). At the reappearance of the
Lord, the community will be the crown and joy of the Apostle (Phil.
4:1; 1 Thess. 2:19). If the Church now shares in the suffering of the
Lord, it will come to share also in his glory (1 Peter 4:13). They who
believe now, without having seen, will exult in unutterable and radi-
ant joy when they have attained to the goal of salvation (1 Peter 1:8f.).
In present miseries Christians should be mindful of this, just as they
bear persecutions in the consciousness that they will have a better and

abiding possession (Heb. 10:34). With Christ they must accept the cross in place of joy in order to become perfect with him (Heb. 12:2). God will, by his power, one day present believers "without blemish before the presence of his glory with rejoicing" (Jude 24). The heavens already rejoice over God's judgment and salvation (Apoc. 12:12; 18:20). One day the Church too will celebrate, in jubilation and joy, the marriage of the lamb (Apoc. 19:7).

§ 12. RENUNCIATION AND ABNEGATION (ASCETICISM)

In the history of ethics, an attitude of pronounced reticence or rejection in respect to the basic impulses of life, which stimulate man from within and without, is called asceticism.[71] The terms *renunciation, abnegation* and *mortification* are more biblical.

The word *asceticism* come from Greek ethics. The primary significance of the term ἀσκεῖν is simply "to work, to practice, to exercise." The meaning soon becomes divergent. The term can mean physical exercise (much like γυμνάζεσθαι or ἀθλέω), and it can also mean spiritual training. Thus it designates the purifying and refining abstinence which looses and redeems from corporality and from the world, in particular the technique of the wise man's spiritual endeavor.

Already in Herodotus, and later in Plato and Epictetus, are found such expressions as *to practice truth, wisdom, righteousness* and *virtue*, and even — especially in the tragedians — *to practice wickedness* and *godlessness*. In the popular philosophy the concept is narrowed, so that the principal demand of asceticism is now a negative one — renunciation in respect to enticements and pleasures.[72]

As Greek thought developed, Philo introduced the concept and notion of asceticism into biblically determined ethics, since he prized asceticism as a physical-spiritual exercise for the restraining of the passions and for abstemiousness. The patriarchs and other biblical figures serve as examples and prototypes in his frequently allegorical exegesis. In his own time he finds the ideal represented in the community of the Therapeutics in Egypt and of the Essenes on the Dead Sea. He gives a portrayal of these ascetics in his work *De vita contemplativa*.

It is out of this pre-history that the Christian concept of asceticism as renunciation arises. The word is employed in this sense in the Apostolic Fathers, and afterwards not infrequently in the Fathers of the Church. The Bible uses the word *asceticism* hardly at all. The Greek Old Testament uses it only in 2 Macc. 15:4: "to keep the Sabbath" (ἀσκεῖν τὴν ἑβδομάδα). In the intertestamental texts there is further use of the word as occasion demands.

In the New Testament the word appears only in Acts 24:16. Paul gives assurance: "I take pains (ἀσκῶ) always to have a clear conscience before God and before men." The manner of expression is, especially in view of the two terms ἀσκῶ and συνείδησις, clearly determined by a Hellenistic influence.

A related idea, from a word-group frequently used in Greek ethics to designate ascetical self-control, is expressed in the terms ἐγκράτεια and ἐγκρατής. Even these words occur only infrequently in the New Testament. They are found conveying an ethical sense in 1 Cor. 7:9, and elsewhere in Hellenistically influenced passages such as the catalogs of virtues in Gal. 5:23; Tit. 1:8; 2 Peter 1:6; and similarly in Acts 24:25. Self-control is a virtue of an auto-authoritative ethics, for which reason it will find but little discussion in a morality of faith.

The New Testament is generally reluctant to use words borrowed from philosophical asceticism, for the obvious reason that such terms place an emphasis upon human achievement. Christian asceticism knows well that "it depends not on him who wills, nor on him who runs, but on God, who extends his mercy" (Rom. 9:16). Any meritoriousness of asceticism is problematic.

Far beyond its slight basis in Scripture, the word and term asceticism is very much used in theological and even in exegetical literature. And of course, the thing itself which is indicated today by the term *asceticism* is absolutely essential to the New Testament. Asceticism is to be practiced in the relationship of the Christian to the world. As a creation of God, however, the world is originally good. Insofar as the world is spoiled and can be seductive, an attitude of renunciation toward it can be of necessity (see the present work, Vol. 1, pp. 17–20 and 31–34).

The faith and piety of Israel approve of the world and its fullness as a creation of God. Earthly possessions, marital communion and fruitfulness, long life — all these are gifts and blessings of God. This is the common conviction of both the historical and the didactic books (see below, ch. 23). Nevertheless, the Old Testament is not entirely free of ascetical currents. Basically and positively, the Law commands fulfillment of its legal ordinance; but moral life in accord with the Law often enough demands rigorous renunciation of one's own desires. Sexual continence is required for ritual purity, e.g., for the people who would experience God's apparition on Mount Sinai (Exod. 19:15) and for the soldiers of David who would eat the holy bread (1 Sam. 21:5f.). Sexual contamination excludes from worship (Lev. 15:16-18).

The Law demands ascetical fasting. The levitical commands about food are commands of fasting. On special occasions penitential fasting is imposed on the people, e.g., on the Day of Atonement (Lev. 16:19-31) and on the Feast of Purim (Est. 9:31). The priests refrain, before their service, from the use of wine (Lev. 10:9). The people fast before the Law is read to them (Jer. 36:6). Fasting is observed with a view to quieting God's anger and averting his judgment (1 Sam. 7:6; Jer. 36:9; Joel 1:13f.; 2:12). David practiced fasting in recognition of his guilt (2 Sam. 12:16f.). Fasting makes one a suitable receptacle for divine wisdom and revelation (Dan. 1:16-17; 10:2f.). Both the Old and the New Testaments are acquainted with the renunciatory vow of the Nazirites (Num. 6:1-7; Acts 21:24). In like manner there are other vows mentioned (Num. 30; Jer. 35). From whatever sources these ascetical usages may stem, they were taken up by the religion and spirit of Israel, and interpreted and shaped in conformity thereto (see below, ch. 15).

During the exile and in the period thereafter, Israel had to bear oppression, persecution, and suffering. She tried to understand this as expiation for the guilt of her fathers and for her own guilt; and consequently she practiced penance and abnegation in increasing measure. In the Books of Daniel (1:17), Judith (8:6), Esther (4:16), and Tobit (12:8), prayer and fasting are the well-known means to religious composure and training. Fasting, however, is even a meritorious work which will be rewarded. Even the New Testament makes mention of fasting as an obligatory custom in Israel. Prayer, fasting, and almsgiving are mentioned as dutiful works (Matthew 6:1-18). And the Pharisee fasted twice each week (Luke 18:12).

There was an even more rigorous asceticism practiced in special pious communities. This has come to light most recently in the Qumran scrolls. The members of this community laid claim to no personal ownership (1 QS 9:8). For the most part they did not marry. They shunned sleep, and spent a third of the night in the study of the Torah and in prayer (1 QS 6:7). Throughout the whole year a rigorous order of divine service was followed (1 QS 10:1-15). In clothing and nourishment they observed the utmost simplicity. Their meals were arranged in a ritual and cultic fashion, directed, like everything else, to the stilling of an appetite (1 QS 6:2-5). In the matter of obedience to a superior, the brothers renounced their own wills (1 QS 7; 8:17–9:2). The community of the pious intended in this way to effect reconciliation for each other (1 QS 5:6) as well as for the land (1 QS 9:3f.).

In regard to the New Testament, it must be remembered that even the pagan religious sentiment of late antiquity knew many different ascetical requirements, like commands of fasting and of sexual abstinence. The basis of this may have been, in part, certain age-old notions according to which things (foods) or processes (sexuality and death) belonged to the demons, against whom one had to guard himself by abstinence. New motives, however, entered upon the scene. Late antiquity was the era of a rich and decadent culture. Out of this there arose ascetical demands to refrain from excesses. They manifested themselves as a bucolic enthusiasm for the life of the simple people.

Philosophy, like religion, took up these demands and gave them a new depth. Stoic philosophy recommended asceticism of body as well as of soul, whereby man should attain to external and internal freedom. In Neo-Platonism the soul sought, by mortification of the body, release from the world unto the goal of mystical union with God. An example is Appollonius of Tyana, a contemporary of Jesus. According to his third-century biographer, Philostratus, Apollonius demanded abstinence from meat, wine, and sexual activity in order to attain a nearness to divinity.

In not a few texts the New Testament is a witness to the ascetical currents of its own time. John the Baptist was a product of ascetical

Judaism. He was, no doubt, aware of the community at Qumran, since the place of baptism in the Jordan was in the neighborhood of Qumran. John himself was an example of rigorous asceticism, by his life in the desert, his abnegation in food and clothing, and his celibacy. The demands he made of others were conversion, turning away from injustice, and the fruits of repentance (Matthew 3:4-10).

Between the Baptist and his group of disciples, and Jesus and his followers, the question of asceticism was acute. In word and by the example of his own behavior, Jesus demonstrated to his own followers that there must be some concern for genuine asceticism and even for the disposition of its forms. Jesus speaks with the highest regard for the Baptist as greater than any other born of woman. He is Elijah, who is to come (Matthew 11:7-14). Jesus, however, confronts different ways of living with each other: "John came, he did not eat and drink, and they say, 'He has a demon.' The Son of Man came, and he eats and drinks, and they say, 'Behold, a glutton and a wine-bibber, the friend of tax-collectors and sinners'" (Matthew 11:18-19). Jesus accepts thankfully the good things of creation as the Father's gifts.

The conduct of Jesus' life is free of the more strenuous asceticism. But he calls others into his retinue, and this means being without home and possessions (Matthew 8:20; 19:21). He warns of the dangers of wealth (Matthew 6:19-21, 24; Luke 16:9). He esteems marriage as an arrangement of creation (Matthew 19:3-9), and yet he teaches celibacy for the sake of the kingdom of heaven (Matthew 19:12). To be sure, he speaks reservedly of fasting as a legal achievement (Matthew 6:16; Luke 18:12). But according to the gospel account (Matthew 4:2), Jesus himself fasted for forty days before commencing his mission. This, of course, was done for the sake of complete concentration. He gives to fasting a new dimension. It must be done joyfully, since it is indeed a conversion and return to God (Matthew 6:16-18). Jesus defends his disciples, who, since it now being the high era [*hohe Zeit*] of the Messiah, do not fast. "Can the wedding [*Hochzeit*] guests fast when the bridegroom is with them?" (Mark 2:19).

As a call to renunciation and abnegation, there is a saying of the Lord repeated several times in its tradition: "If anyone would come after me, let him take up his cross and follow me" (Mark 8:34). The sayings in Mark 8:34-36 are found six times in the New Testament, with parallels of Mark found in Matthew 16:24-26 and Luke 9:23-25. Moreover, the sayings in Matthew 10:38f. and in Luke 14:27 and 14:33 are repetitious of parts of this same passage. In a form evolved further, there is the series in John 12:24-26.

This profusion of repetition is scarcely mere chance. What is much more likely, the primitive community already recognized the importance of the saying as citing an absolutely indispensable condition for the following of Christ. It applies to everyone, to the people along with his immediate disciples (Mark 8:34). In the Synoptics it follows upon the first prediction of the Passion (Mark 8:31). The disciples must undergo the Passion along with the Lord. This is quite evidently the import of the saying about taking up the cross. The Church has always understood the saying essentially in regard to the disciple, who follows his Lord on the way of the cross.

Was this saying possible or understandable from the lips of Jesus before his Passion? Exegesis has often posed this same question. The cross and the carrying of the cross was not a sight unknown to the hearers of that saying of the Lord, and the word *cross* was not outside their comprehension. A man condemned to death had to carry the transverse beam of the cross to the place of execution. Accordingly, the cross signifies death and the death penalty. Perhaps the cross and carrying the cross was in this sense a figure of speech common among the people.[73] The saying would then have originally signified: Whoever will follow Jesus must risk everything, putting even his life on the line.

Connection with a messianic movement or with a movement understood as messianic might well, given the conditions of the times, cost one his life. After the way of the cross and Jesus' death on the cross, the saying was seen in a new light. Christ himself led the way with the cross and on the cross, and the disciple must follow him. The saying is transformed and understood in a spiritual sense. When Mark 8:34 says that the disciple must take up *his* cross, the saying is directed toward the personally obligatory. The ascetical significance is clearer still in Luke 9:23: "Let him take up his cross *daily*." Luke 14:27 speaks finally of the "carrying" of the cross.

The import and sense of the admonition is developed further in the

saying of the Lord subjoined to the one under discussion: "Whoever
would save his life will lose it. Whoever loses his life for my sake will
save it" (Mark 8:35).[74] Whoever wants to assure his existence marches
straightway to his downfall. Whoever renounces even the security of
his life will thereby gain the security of his life in an even deeper
sense. The reason and basis for the risk is, in Mark 8:35, "for my sake
and that of the gospel." These words are not found in the other and
probably older form, as in Matthew 10:39 and Luke 17:33. They constitute a later but quite proper interpretation.

Even in the following of Jesus this inversion of the values of life
and death is realized. Christ is at once the prototype and example of
the surrender of life, as well as of the salvation of the life surrendered.
Self-denial (Mark 8:34a) demands similar surrender. To deny oneself
means no longer to know one's own "I," no longer to want to hold
fast to it, but to renounce it and give it up completely. It means to accept one's own death, and in following after Christ, to give oneself
up entirely to Christ and through him to God.

A further saying of the Lord is subjoined to this by way of explanation. "What does it profit a man to gain the whole world, but forfeit his life?" (Mark 8:36). The "world" in this context is not only
the sinful world, with which the disciple has nothing to do, but that
world in which he lives each day, in which he carries on and must
carry on his business, the world which challenges him daily and
which is dear to him and which supports his life. Whoever wants to
gain this world will lose it. Whoever lets it alone and submits his
security to God will come to know this. Better than any care or concern for himself that a man might have, God will care for him. Thus
do these sayings of the Lord decide the conduct of the Christian in
respect to the world and life; and thus are they of fundamental importance for Christian morality.

What it is that is to be surrendered is clarified by the Gospel in a
saying united to the word about carrying the cross: "He that loves
father or mother more than me is not worthy of me; and he that
loves son or daughter more than me is not worthy of me" (Matthew
10:37; and probably expanded, though perhaps in part even more
primitive, in Luke 14:26). The saying is concerned with the younger
members of the congregation, the children, as well as with the older

members, their parents. It does not say that the disciple must shun evil and strive for the good; it does not say that he should devote his life to his household and not dissipate it somewhere else. The disciple must first of all relinquish the most precious of values and realities. Yes, according to Luke 14:26, he is even to hate them. We hate what opposes us, what will damage or endanger our lives. And those values, those good things, can also stand in opposition to us and to our life. The enemy can be in each of them. All of them can be in league against the word and will of God. And if in the hour of decision it is demanded, then the disciple must determine to separate himself from them, abandon them, yes, even hate them.

This attitude of the disciple in respect to the world is delineated also in the parables of the pearl and the treasure hidden in a field (Matthew 13:44-46). The merchant and the farmer have their world in their household and in their farm. These things are their very lives. But in the face of the preciousness of the kingdom, they fade away into the background; they must be surrendered for the sake of what is greater.

There are sayings which make rigid demands, which require that hand, foot, and eye be cast away if they become an enticement and temptation to sin, and a reason for an eternal casting away. This group of sayings is handed on in different forms, more concisely in Matthew 5:29f. and 18:8f., more ample in detail in Mark 9:43-48, which is indicative of the importance ascribed to the warning. The sayings stem from Jewish thought, which localizes a man's sinful impulses in particular members. Thus a Rabbinic maxim states: "The eye sees, the heart covets, and the body completes the sin." No matter what the circumstances, obedience to God is more important than what is nevertheless a very high and extremely important good of man, the members of his body.

There is a saying whose meaning seems uncertain: "Since the days of John the Baptist until now, the kingdom of heaven pushes forward with violence, and violent men snatch it for themselves" (Matthew 11:12). Probably this means that the kingdom of God, first proclaimed in the penitential preaching of the Baptist, even if it is yet hidden, is already present in the person of Jesus, and is marching irresistibly forward. Men who have firmly resolved to take every means necessary, not even stopping short of rigorous personal hardships, snatch up the kingdom for themselves.

Again and again in his preaching, Jesus sounds the warning to be watchful (Mark 13:34; 14:34); and in the primitive Christian preaching this warning never ceases (1 Cor. 16:13; Col. 4:2; 1 Thess. 5:6; 1 Peter 5:8; Apoc. 3:2; 16:15).[75]

Finally we may cite the closing words of the Sermon on the Mount, which require the audience of the sermon to choose for themselves between the broad, easy road to perdition and the narrow, rocky road to life (Matthew 7:13f.), and which add the further warning that life, like a good tree, must bring forth fruits, or, like a useless tree, it will be cut down and thrown into the fire (Matthew 7:16-20). The series of remarks can only be understood as a penetrating catechetical imparting of the teaching that a man's moral efforts and exertions determine his eternal destiny. (In other places, and even in this same Sermon on the Mount, Matthew 6:12f. and 7:7f., the Gospel declares that this determination of man's destiny is effected also and even primarily by the action of God's mercy.)

Like the Gospels, so too the letters of the Apostles demand moral order and endeavor. These Epistles make known their controversial confrontation with the ascetical currents of the time, inasmuch as they protest against false asceticism.

In Rome there was a group of Christians, probably not very numerous, who refrained from the enjoyment of meat and wine (Rom. 14:2, 21); they regarded these foods as unclean (Rom. 14:14). They even observed special feast and fast days (Rom. 14:5). These anxious ascetics — Paul calls them "the weak" (Rom. 14:1f.) — were probably Jewish Christians who had perhaps come under the influence of other abstinential movements. "The strong" (Rom. 15:1) — probably Gentile Christians — scorned the weak, who in turn were scandalized by the freedom exercised by the strong. Paul "knows and is convinced in the Lord that nothing is unclean of itself; it is unclean only for those who think it is unclean" (Rom. 14:14). The prayer of thanksgiving blesses every food (Rom. 14:6). Faith and life are not concerned with eating and drinking but with spiritual things, righteousness, peace and joy in the Holy Spirit (Rom. 14:17). Paul does not permit the strong to hold the weak in contempt. One must not judge; rather, one must be tolerant. Do not give scandal; rather, be considerate of the views of others. It is proper to be interested in others, just as Christ was interested in all (Rom. 15:3-8).

In Corinth there were ascetics who demanded renunciation of marriage by those not already married and by widows; and they demanded continence in marriage by those already married. Paul defends the right of marriage and rejects any enforced asceticism (1 Cor. 7; see below, ch. 20).

The Epistle to the Colossians also has to contend with ascetical movements. The Colossians kept fasts and observed holy days (Col. 2:16). They kept such regulations as: "Do not handle, do not taste, do not touch" (Col. 2:21). The letter explains that the things which the Colossians honor as taboo are in fact profane and not sacred. The Colossians are not following honorable traditions, as they suppose (Col. 2:8), but human regulations, from which the redeemed man is free. They are honoring only elements and powers of the world, while Christ is Lord of the world. With the Colossians everything is turned topsy-turvy. What the Colossians regard as wisdom is not service of God but a cult they have devised for themselves; what is ostensibly a relentless mortification of the body is really only "indulgence of the flesh," because this asceticism is a prideful thing, seeking only its own will (Col. 2:20-23).

Even the Pastoral Epistles are obliged to combat erroneous doctrines, probably gnostic in origin, which forbid marriage and demand abstinence from certain foods (1 Tim. 4:3). The letters draw upon the biblical belief in creation to confirm that all creation is good, and that in any case the foods are made holy by prayer of thanksgiving said over it (1 Tim. 4:4f.). Against every detraction, the letters defend marriage as a work productive of salvation (1 Tim. 2:15).

The Apostle knows and states in his preaching that there is such a thing as misguided piety and false asceticism. His preaching is all the more emphatic in demanding genuine and true asceticism. According to Paul, man is confronted by flesh and by spirit (see the present work, Vol. 1, pp. 133–137). The Christian must, with all his moral determination, make up his mind between the works of the flesh and the works of the spirit.

In contrast to the drunken abandon with which the pagans devote themselves to pleasure, Paul admonishes sobriety and discipline (Rom. 13:11-14; Eph. 5:8-13; 1 Thess. 5:5f.). He describes the situation with exciting realism: "I do not do what I want, but I do the very thing I hate. . . . I have the will to accomplish what is good, but I cannot do it. . . . Wretched man that I am! Who will deliver me from this body of death?" (Rom. 7:15-24). Since the time of the Fathers of the Church, exegesis has asked who it is that is meant by "I"—the Jew and the pagan, or the Christian. Probably Paul is speaking of the unredeemed man as he is revealed to the eyes of faith. In Romans 8, the redeemed is described as filled with the Spirit. Nevertheless, the Christian is ever in danger of falling back into the situation of Romans 7. Therefore it also needs to be said: "If you live according to the flesh, you will die. If, however, by the Spirit you put to death the deeds of the body, you will live" (Rom. 8:13). By chastisements must the body be brought into the servitude of the Spirit (1 Cor. 9:27).

Taking up a theme not infrequent in Jewish as well as Hellenistic literature, Paul likes to use the neat figure of the contest in the arena. The contestant keeps his body well-disciplined in order to win the prize. The Christian must do much the same (1 Cor. 9:24-26; Eph. 6:12-17; Phil. 3:13; 1 Thess. 5:8; 2 Tim. 4:7).[76] Paul, more than anyone else, bears witness to both the necessity and the richness of grace; nevertheless, he demands constant individual moral effort and achievement.

Christian asceticism is to be realized in accord with the cross. The Gospels demand imitation even of the cross and death (Mark 8:34). In the Apostolic kerygma the challenge is deepened. It has its basis in baptism, which is symbolic of being crucified with Christ, of dying with Christ, and of rising again with him. What happened in the sacrament must be carried out in life as death in respect to sin and as new life with Christ (Rom. 6:1-11; Col. 2:12).

The sufferings of the Apostle and of Christians are experienced and effected in communion with the Passion of Christ (2 Cor. 1:5). The word of the Synoptics about bearing the cross is repeated: "We bear always the death of Jesus in our body, so that the life of Jesus may also be manifested in our body" (2 Cor. 4:10). The Apostle is "crucified with Christ" (Gal. 2:19). "Those who belong to Christ have crucified their flesh along with its passions and desires" (Gal. 5:24). The Christian must re-execute the merciless historicity of the crucifixion of

Christ in his own body and in his own life. "By the cross of Christ the world is crucified to me and I to the world" (Gal. 6:14).

In the cross every relationship to the world is radically changed. There is a constant mutual tension between the world and individual. In the cross this pernicious reciprocal pressure of opposition is sublimated and given direction. As once by the cross this intimate connection with the world was broken for Christ, so now it is broken for those who are crucified with him. Paul wants finally "to come to know Christ and the power of his resurrection and the communion of his sufferings, so as to be made like him in his death and to become participant in the resurrection of the dead" (Phil. 3:10-11).[77]

The other Apostles demand the same decision as Paul. The Gospel of John formulates the challenge when it says that man finds himself between light and darkness, truth and lies, life and death. The one class of works he must perform, the other he must hate (see the present work, Vol. 1, pp. 141–152). Exhortations warn against the world and against lusting after the world in the demands that proceed from the flesh, from the lust of the eyes and love of ostentation (1 John 2:16).

The Epistle to the Hebrews was written in a time and for a Church in which many were "growing weary and faint-hearted" (Heb. 12:3, 12). It admonishes not to shrink back (Heb. 10:39), but to persevere to the end and "to engage in the prescribed struggle," yes, "to resist in the struggle even to the shedding of your blood" (Heb. 12:4). Suffering should be accepted as a chastisement from God (Heb. 12:5-8). Christians must share in Christ's suffering, in that they must "go forth to him outside the camp, and bear his humiliation" (Heb. 13:13). Renouncing earthly communion, the disciples must endure together their eschatological delivery to the cross. The prototype is always Christ, "the imitator and perfecter of faith, who endured the cross for the sake of the joy set in front of him" (Heb. 12:2). God repays obedience and fidelity with everlasting joy.

Examples of steadfastness are placed before our eyes. First of all there are such as these from the Old Testament: "As an example of suffering and patience, dear brothers, take the prophets who spoke in the name of the Lord. Behold, we call those blessed who have persevered. You have heard of the patience of Job and have seen the purpose which the Lord has devised" (James 5:10-11). Then there is reference to the example of the suffering Christ. He suffered innocently and patiently. The example of Christ is the "footsteps" in which the disciples must walk and in which they must follow (1 Peter 2:21-23). Christ goes on before as the first. The example he leaves behind eases the way for the challenged. To be the second on a path is easier.

In its preaching of asceticism the New Testament came upon related currents in its own time. It outstripped them all. The genuine doctrine of the Church has always endeavored to repulse such viewpoints which denounced creation as something evil or sinful, and defended the authentic order. The history of morality may inquire, nevertheless, whether an undercurrent of dualist conceptions, disavowing the justice of creation, did not occasionally find entry into the Church.

§ 13. HOLINESS

Primarily holiness[78] is predicated of God, as the primordial Holy One.[79] He himself makes his essence known: "I am holy" (Lev. 19:2). His holiness means his superiority to the world: "I am God and not a man, a holy one in your midst" (Hos. 11:9). "They shall praise your great and terrible name, for it is holy" (Ps. 99:3). The primitive meaning of the Hebrew word for "holy," *qadosh*, is "that which is apart"; God, therefore, is characterized as separate from the world and from everything profane. The Creator, then, is juxtaposed to creation. It is in this sense that our philosophy of religion calls God the "Transcendent" and the "Totally Other."

God's holiness is powerfully effective in time and world. What the primordially Holy One performs or draws into his domain is holy. As dwelling-place of God, the heavens are holy (Ps. 20:7). The place where God appears is holy: the site of the burning thornbush (Exod. 3:5); Mount Sinai (Exod. 19); the tabernacle of God's revelation (Exod. 28:43); the Temple (Ps. 5:8; Jon. 2:5); Zion (Is. 27:13); Jerusalem (Is. 52:1). The ark of God is holy; bringing disaster to the Philistines everywhere, it discloses the holy God (1 Sam. 6:20). The angels and the heavenly hosts are holy (Zech. 14:5; Dan. 7:21). As God's congregation, Israel is holy, "a people acquired for myself before all peoples, a royal priesthood and a holy nation" (Exod. 19:5-6).

The code of holiness (Lev. 17–26) establishes the law and ordinance of Israel as of the holy people. Vocation entails obligation: "You shall be holy, as I am holy" (Lev. 19:2). The representatives of Israel, the priests and levites, and more especially the high priest, are holy (Exod. 29:1-35; Num. 8:5-22). Elisha, the man of God, is holy (2 Kings 4:9). And altogether, godly people are holy (Deut. 5:33; Pss. 4:4; 30:5; and many other places).

The theology of the prophets shapes the concept of holiness further and deepens it. Isaiah announces the nature and works of God with the concept of his holiness. The "Holy One of Israel" is, for Isaiah, God's own proper name (e.g., in 1:4; 5:9; 41:14; and in all, 29 times). In the vision in which he receives his call (Is. 6:1-7), the prophet comes to know Yahweh as the overwhelming Holy One. The Seraphim cry out: "Holy, holy! Holy is Yahweh of the hosts!" In contrast to the apparition of the Holy One, the man discovers himself, in a mortal antithesis, as the unholy one. With his unclean lips he cannot announce God. "Woe is me, I am lost! For I am a man of unclean lips and dwell among a people of unclean lips!" Thus the prophet recognizes his guilt both as an individual and as a member of a sinful people. Before God he is subject to death. An angel purifies his lips with a glowing coal from the altar. Isaiah is made aware of God's word: "Behold, this has touched your lips. Your guilt is extinguished, and your sins forgiven."

The holiness of God is understood as moral holiness. As the "one who is apart," God is separated from sin. The impurity of man is not physical and ritual impurity, but impurity of the moral sort; it is guilt and sin. The warnings and admonitions of the prophets state that ritual correctness is worthless if it lacks moral confirmation (Is. 1:10-17; Jer. 7; Hos. 6:6; Micah 6:6-8).

Other prophets detect other areas in this otherness of God. God is other than man in his incomprehensible love, in which he loves Israel always, even though she is an unfaithful spouse. "I will not execute my fierce anger, . . . for I am God and not a man, the Holy One in your midst, and I will not destroy this people" (Hos. 11:8f.). For

Deutero-Isaiah, God is other in his capacity as Redeemer. "Your re-deemer is the Holy One of Israel" (Is. 41:14; 43:3). God's holiness is ever a new beginning for Israel, and ever a new creation.

God's holiness is manifest in history, in judgment and salvation. His holiness is made known as his majesty, to Israel as well as to the Gentiles. "Inasmuch as I execute judgment, I show myself to you as the Holy One" (Ez. 28:22). "I will gather the people, and prove my-self as the Holy One before the eyes of the Gentiles" (Ez. 28:25). In the great judgment God's majesty and holiness is made manifest to the whole world. "I will prove myself great and holy, and I will reveal myself before the eyes of many peoples" (Ez. 38:23). Then will God's holiness penetrate all things: "In that day the bells of the horses will be holy, and the cooking pots will be as holy as the sacrificial bowls" (Zech. 14:20-21). In the face of the holiness of God, which over-whelms and fills up everything, there is no longer anything profane. The concept of holiness has an essentially eschatological scope.[80]

In late Judaism the ritual dimension of holiness retains its force and is developed even further. Everything that God touches is holy. Now it is that those formulas are developed, which retain their validity in the New Testament and, in part, even to the present time. Jerusalem is "the holy city" (2 Macc. 15:4; Apoc. 11:2). Temple and altar are holy (3 Esdras 1:53; 2 Macc. 1:29). In Josephus, Palestine is called "the holy land." The Torah, as God's word, is "holy scripture" (1 Macc. 12:9; more extensive with the Rabbis; Rom. 1:2; 2 Tim. 3:15). God's name (1 Chr. 16:35) and Spirit (Ps. 51:13; Wis. 9:17) are holy.

As those chosen from among the great masses, the godly men of Qumran know themselves as the holy ones. They are "the holy ones of the people" (1 QM 6:6), "God's holy people" (1 QM 14:12), "the men of holiness" (1 QS 5:13). The community is the temple of the last days, "a holy house for Israel and a most holy assembly for Aaron." The earthly holy house forms with "the holy ones" (i.e., the angels) a community (1 QS 8:5f.). Even the Christians of the New Testament call themselves, with some emphasis, "the holy ones," i.e., "the saints."[81]

That God is the Holy One is valid also for the New Testament. Nevertheless, express reference to the holiness of God — at least in comparison to the frequency of Old Testament usage — is rare. In the high priestly prayer, Jesus addresses the Father as "Holy Father" (John 17:11). God's own declaration (Lev. 19:2) is repeated and applied to the Church: "You shall be holy, because I am holy" (1 Peter 1:16). Christians have "the anointing from the Holy One" (1 John 2:20). God is the Holy One in the visions of the Apocalypse. The four creatures call out without cease: "Holy, holy! Holy is the Lord, God of hosts!" (Apoc. 4:8, with Is. 6:3; Apoc. 3:7; 6:10). God's holiness is mighty in power, which is why the Church prays: "Hallowed be thy name" (Matthew 6:9). This can hardly mean that the name of God should be kept holy and will be made holy by men. God's name is his essence. God himself shall show the holiness and majesty of his being to all peoples in grace and in judgment.

In accord with the Old Testament notion and linguistic usage, the ritual holiness of things and persons is predicated also in the New Testament. The temple is called holy (Matthew 24:15; Acts 6:13; 21:18). There are remarks about the holy place, the holy of holies of the temple, and about the holy vessels (Heb. 9:1-3, 8, 24f.). The angels are holy (Mark 8:38; Acts 10:22; Jude 14; Apoc. 14:10). Persons who were holy under the old covenant are holy also under the new: the holy prophets (Luke 1:70; Acts 3:21; 2 Peter 1:21), as well as the holy women of ages past (1 Peter 3:5).

The Spirit is holy, conceived now as the personified dynamic Holiness of God. Through the Spirit, God becomes active as the Holy One. Holiness determines the being of Christ. It is by the Holy Spirit that he is made man (Luke 1:35); and the Holy Spirit effects a revelation at the baptism of Jesus (Luke 3:22). Christ is "the Holy One of God" (Mark 1:24; John 6:69), "the Holy Servant" (Acts 3:13-14; 4:27), "the Holy and Righteous One" (Acts 3:14), "the Holy and Truthful One" (Apoc. 3:7). He is "designated as the Son of God in power according to the Spirit of holiness since the resurrection of the dead" (Rom. 1:4). He is "the High Priest, holy, sinless, without blemish, separated from sinners and exalted above the heavens" (Heb. 7:26). The properties of Christ are predicated in their fullness, and they are in part cultic, in part historico-personal. The congregation is filled with the Holy Spirit (Acts 2:4). The Spirit operates in the sacraments of the Church: in baptism (Mark 1:8; John 3:5), as well as in the Eucharist, which is spiritual food and drink (1 Cor. 10:3f.).

The Spirit effects the sanctification of the faithful. Through the service of the Apostles the world ought to become "a sacrificial gift, sanctified by the Holy Spirit" (Rom. 15:16).

Now the Church is holy. The Christians are simply "the saints" (Rom. 15:26; 1 Cor. 16:1; 2 Cor. 8:4; Eph. 1:18; Col. 1:2; Heb. 3:1; Jude 3; Apoc. 5:8). They are "the elect of God, the saints, the beloved" (Col. 3:12). They are "the chosen saints, those who are sanctified in Christ Jesus" (1 Cor. 1:2). "Christ has been made our wisdom by God, our righteousness and sanctification and our redemption" (1 Cor. 1:30). It is the activity of God in Christ, and not nature of itself and moral endeavor, that is the basis of holiness. The fullness of the gift of salvation, belonging properly to the eschatological era, is, in him, already present. "You were washed, you were sanctified, you were justified in the name of the Lord Jesus Christ" (1 Cor. 6:11).

To be sure, Paul had to remind the congregation of its sinful past. But now God has created a new reality. The justified are the saints. Like justification, sanctification too is the action of God. It takes place in baptism. By the very fact of God's actions having taken place, Christians can and must live their lives as men who have been made holy. "Christ gave himself up for the Church, that he might sanctify her, whom he purifies by the bath of water in the word . . . , so that she might be holy and without blemish" (Eph. 5:25-27). The objective and ritual sense of the concept of holiness clearly remains, since Paul is able to say that in a mixed marriage the Christian partner sanctifies the non-Christian and that even the children of the marriage are made holy (1 Cor. 7:14).

The moral obligation of the sanctified follows from the action of God. Ritual holiness must be displayed as existential. Being summoned out of the world and set apart from it signifies separation from its impurity and sin. The Church is God's structure. "If anyone destroys the temple of God, God will destroy him. For the temple of God, which you are, is holy" (1 Cor. 3:17).

The holiness of the Church is ruined and destroyed by heresy, strife, and disunity (1 Cor. 3), and also by all pagan vices, as is stated in 1 Cor. 5 and 6, as well as in 2 Cor. 6:14–7:1, where the figure of the Church as God's temple is used again. Every communion with darkness and Belial desecrates the temple. "We must make holiness perfect in the fear of God" (2 Cor. 7:1 — in connection with which it is altogether questionable whether this line originates with Paul). At the same time, each body is a temple of the Holy Spirit and is to be kept holy (1 Cor. 6:19). Lechery, therefore, is forbidden. Holiness is a duty: "As you formerly used your members as slaves in the service of impurity and lawlessness in order to be lawless, so now use your members as slaves in the service of righteousness unto holiness (Rom. 6:19, 22).

The life of the Christian must be "a living sacrifice, holy for God" (Rom. 12:1). From the ritual follows the moral, and the moral is made holy by the ritual. Each individual Christian is obligated to holiness as moral integrity: "This is the will of God, your sanctification, that you abstain from immorality; that each of you esteem his wife, that each keep his wife in holiness and honor, not in passionate desire like the pagans, who know not God" (1 Thess. 4:3-5). Sanctification has its beginning in the will of God, and not only its beginning, but also its goal, toward which it is determined ever anew. Individual demands are enumerated. "But immorality and all impurity or covetousness ought not so much as be mentioned among you, as befits the saints; nor any filthiness, and silly talk, and levity, which are not fitting; but let there be thanksgiving" (Eph. 5:3-4). The letter seems to presuppose a catechesis and order that dare not be violated. God carries the work of sanctification forward (1 Thess. 5:23), and he will lead it on to the goal: "Your hearts are able to be made fast in blamelessness, in holiness before God our Father, for the coming of our Lord Jesus Christ with all his saints" (1 Thess. 3:13).

The First Epistle of Peter takes up the Old Testament watchword: "In accord with the holy one who called you, you yourselves shall also be holy in all your conduct. For it is written: 'You shall be holy, because I am holy'" (1 Peter 1:15-16 = Lev. 19:2). The Church is chosen from out of the world and is sanctified by God (1 Peter 1:1f.). The congregation is "the royal priesthood, the holy people" (1 Peter 2:9, depending on Exod. 19:5f.). The old law of holiness, then, is valid still for the Church. Holiness demands renunciation of the ignorance and licentiousness that marked our lives until now (1 Peter 1:14). Christians have "sanctified their souls in obedience to the truth, for an unaffected love of the brethren" (1 Peter 1:22). Christian morality means, above all else: "Hallow the Lord Jesus in your hearts" (1 Peter 3:15). Christ is by nature the spotlessly holy one (1 Peter 1:19). To "hallow" him means to recognize and bear witness to him as the holy one, that is, the one who is exalted. This must take place "in your hearts", i.e., personally and existentially.[82]

The Gospel of John, too, employs the word and concept of holiness. Christ is the holy one, because he pertains to God (John 17:11) and is sanctified by him (John 10:36). Those who are his own, Christ has "sanctified in the truth" (John 17:19). He beseeches the Father: "Sanctify them in the truth" (John 17:17).

The New Testament speaks of the eschatological perfecting of sanctification. "Strive for peace with everyone, and sanctification, without which no one will see the Lord" (Heb. 12:14). In the Apocalypse of John, the saints are the earthly as well as the perfected and heavenly Church. "The prayer of the saints" is presented to God (Apoc. 5:8; 8:3). Satan "wages war against the saints" (Apoc. 13:7). At the end of time God will "reward his servants, the prophets and the saints" (Apoc. 11:18). After the fall of Babylon, "heaven and the saints and the apostles and the prophets" are invited to rejoice (Apoc. 18:20). Holiness will be made manifest in the last days.

In our usual manner of thinking and speaking, the "saints" are the saints in heaven. This tends to bring into prominence the viewpoints of moral proof and eschatological perfection. If this is not the totality of the biblical concept of holiness, these two viewpoints are, nevertheless, biblical. The Old Testament as well as the New emphasizes the moral duty of sanctification in accord with the divine gift of holiness. They indicate the eschatological goal, since the morality and sanctification of man must stand the test of the final judgment. The concept of the ritual holiness of the Church has not entirely disappeared. We are able to speak even yet of "the holy Church," although the designation of individuals as holy has for the most part been narrowed down to a rather small group of persons. But we still use such titles as "Holy Father," "Sacred College," "Sacred Congregation." In his preaching, St. Augustine addressed the whole Church as "Your Holiness" (*sanctitas vestra*). In a similar manner, other comparable spiritual terms which were applied originally to the whole Church have, in the course of time, become more restricted in their application. This seems to be an expression of a questionable clericalization of the Church.

§ 14. RIGHTEOUSNESS

When we speak of righteousness,[83] we mean the right ordering of human relationships. The will to this righteousness is a virtue which man can win by his own efforts. This is righteousness according to the more ancient doctrine on virtues.

Even Greek antiquity, to be sure, knew something of the truth that right is something higher than a mere human arrangement. In Hesiod (*Works and Days*, 256f.), Right is a divinity near the throne of Zeus. In this earlier period, righteousness is not just one virtue among the many; rather, it is paramount to all. Thus, in the words of Theognis (V, 147; see E. Diehl, *Anthologia Lyrica Graeca*, Leipzig, 1923, Vol. I, p. 124; cited by Aristotle, *Nicomachean Ethics*, 5, 1, 13): "In righteousness every virtue is comprised."

For the Greeks, the laws of the government were of divine ordinance, just like the laws of nature; and man was obliged to keep them. Righteousness, in this viewpoint, became first of all a social virtue, by which obligations to the community are fulfilled. According to Aristotle (*Art of Rhetoric*, 1, 9; *Nicomachean Ethics*, 5, 5, 17), righteousness is that virtue which in all circumstances renders to each the same or to each his own. Righteousness is conceived within a secular context. This is also its concept in the system of the Scholastics, and especially in the Thomistic doctrine of virtue.

The biblical concept of righteousness has an essentially broader extension and a much deeper content. In this instance righteousness is first of all thoroughly determined by the fact that it belongs entirely to God, i.e., the righteousness which is God's own, which he gives and which must perdure in his sight.

In this sense, righteous is an important concept in the Old Testament. The New Testament concept of righteousness (δικαιοσύνη) is determined by the Greek of the Old Testament Bible. The Septuagint renders several terms by δικαιοσύνη, the most frequent of which is the word *zedaqah*, meaning "justness," but also conveying such other notions as "legal precept," "favor," and "contrition." The word *righteousness*, this being its origin, does not represent a narrowly confined juridic concept. Historically, it is a concept embracing the correctness of life's relationships.

Righteousness is in particular the characteristic of the covenantal relationship of Yahweh to Israel. Perhaps the oldest example of this is Judges 5:11, "They praise the righteousnesses of Yahweh." These "righteousnesses" are the salvational deeds of Yahweh in behalf of his people. The petitions of the Psalms anticipate redemption, assistance, and salvation (e.g., Pss. 22:32; 31:2; 119:40; 143:11) in token of God's righteousness. Righteousness and salvation are interchangeable concepts: "My mouth will tell of your righteousness, of your salvation, all the day" (Ps. 70:15 in the Septuagint).

The perfect realization of God's salvation is expected in the last days. Righteousness will be a messianic salvational gift. This is stated already in Is. 9:6; "Great will be his government, and no end of peace for the throne of David and his kingdom, since God establishes it and guards it with justice and righteousness" (cf. Is. 45:8; 60:17).

In the concept of God's righteousness, there is from earliest times a juridical factor to be recognized in respect to the manner in which this concept relates to us. God looks after the welfare of those who are his, guarding and protecting them. He always deals out justice. "You love righteousness and hate wickedness" (Ps. 45:8). In an ancient testimony the Yahwist already places a remark in the mouth of Abraham: "Shall not the Judge of all the earth practice righteousness?" (Gen. 18:25). God creates justice in the people. In Zeph. 3:4f. it is said: The princes, judges, prophets, and priests are deceivers. "In their midst, however, the Lord is just. He does nothing wicked. Every morning he follows his arrangement, his light does not fail. But the unrighteous knows no shame."

This God protects also the rights of each individual. He protects the poor and the weak, assists the oppressed and the miserable. "I cry to you, Yahweh, on account of your righteous rule, and every morning my prayer comes before you" (Ps. 88:13-14). Surely, then, the punishing and the assisting righteousness of God exist side by side. "Yahweh does not allow sin and guilt to go unpunished. But he shows grace and favor to thousands" (Exod. 20:5-6).

If God's righteousness in dealing with Israel is his fidelity to the covenant, Israel must, for her part, respond with a similar fidelity to the covenant. This is Israel's righteousness in the sight of God. It is commanded in the so-called Liturgies of the Gate, Psalms 15 and 24. Only he who practices righteousness before Yahweh can participate in the ritual reception of salvation in the temple.

Since God is righteous, his will and word are expressions of his righteousness. The man who lives in accord with Yahweh's commandment is himself righteous. Righteousness, therefore, is also a human accomplishment. The Old Testament knows men who are models of righteousness: Noah (Gen. 6:9); Abraham, because of his faith (Gen. 15:6); Daniel and Job (Ez. 14:14, 20).

Righteousness is emphasized as a social demand upon the rich and upon those who are powerful in the government. The prophets lament the fact that injustice dominates in the life of public service. "Legal begrudgment instead of just judgment" is the rule (Is. 5:7).

Especially after the exile, when the Law was restored and institutionalized, the righteousness of individual pious persons is extolled and exhibited; thus, in Psalms 1, 73, and 119; further in Job 31; 32:1; Ez. 18:5-9; Prov. 2:1f.; 9. He that follows the Law is righteous. "Thus shall you stand forth as righteous before God, your Lord" (Deut. 24:13). The righteous is worthy of praise. "Hail to the righteous, for it shall be well with him" (Is. 3:10). The righteous expects that God will arrange for public recognition of his (the righteous man's) righteousness and that he will experience justification at God's hands (Job 33:26; Jer. 51:10). The petitioner can appeal to his own righteousness: "Do me justice, O Lord, for I have walked in my integrity. I have trusted in the Lord without wavering" (Ps. 26:1; cf. Ps. 41:13),

In the late Jewish period, good works, especially almsgiving, pass as a proof of righteousness itself. These works have the power to blot out sin and to save. One speaks of "the doing of righteousness" (Dan. 4:24; Sir. 3:30; 7:10; Tob. 1:3; 4:10; 12:8f.; cf. Matthew 6:1f.). Righteousness is a virtue.

Nevertheless, Israel does know that all human righteousness is very questionable. "In comparison to God, no man living is righteous" (Ps.

143:2). The petitioner does not trust in his own righteousness, but he hopes in the mercy of God (Dan. 9:18). The true and complete righteousness is expected, however, only as a messianic salvational gift (see above, p. 179).

The idea is widely accepted in Judaism at the time of Jesus that by the zealous fulfillment of the commandments the righteousness of God can be earned, indeed, that it can be laid claim to. This is especially the case with Pharisaism. If such views were shared even by many a pious individual, such an attitude, nevertheless, cannot be attributed to Judaism in its collectivity. In Midrash 136b to Psalm 46:1, David says: "Many men trust in their good works, many in the merits of their fathers; but I trust in you, seeing that I have no good works."

A deep consciousness of universal guilt finds expression in the Fourth Book of Esdras, for example, in 8:31f.: "We and our fathers lived in the works of death. But even though we are sinners, you will be merciful. Besides we have no works of righteousness, you will be called the Gracious One, if you will show us your mercy." The Fourth Book of Esdras was completed at about the end of the first century A.D. It is influenced, therefore, by the fall of Jerusalem and the destruction of the temple in the year 70 A.D., the national catastrophe of Israel. Perhaps it is in this that the consciousness of guilt finds its origin. Be that as it may, there are similar expressions even in older Jewish books, from before the time of Christ, like *Jubilees* 1:6 and the *Psalms of Solomon* 3:5-7.

The Qumran scrolls are older than the New Testament or, at the latest, contemporary with it. These texts, too, are important for light which they can shed on the New Testament concept of righteousness. The godly men of Qumran strive in deepest earnest after righteousness. Among the obligations of the members of the covenant is "service of righteousness," that is, the practice of duty, truth, righteousness, and justice (1 QS 1:5; 8:2). The pious, therefore, are called "sons of righteousness" (1 QS 3:20, 22). The great teacher of Qumran is the "teacher of righteousness." [84]

Like Paul (see below, pp. 184-185), Qumran too finds a declaration of its legal teaching in Hab. 2:4, "The righteous shall live by his fidelity." The statement is interpreted thus: "This is said in reference to all the actions of law in the house of Judah, which God will save from the house of judgment on account of their assiduity and their fidelity to the teacher of righteousness" (1 QpHab 7:17-8:1). Paul, however, understands the saying in the sense that it is faith that justifies, and not assiduity for works of the law. In Qumran, too, faith is a requirement. In this instance, fidelity to the teacher of righteousness means the acceptance of his legal teaching and the preparedness to devote oneself to new efforts for the fulfillment of the law. The pious of Qumran realize, nevertheless, that, in spite of the most rigid demands of legal righteousness, man cannot, with all his efforts, attain to righteousness in the sight of God, but remains a sinner and is, therefore, dependent upon the divine gift of righteousness: "When I waver, then are God's proofs of favor my assistance forever. And when I stumble because of the wickedness of my flesh, then my justification stands with the righteousness of God in eternity" (1 QS 9:12).

The Judaism of the time of the New Testament cannot be charged straightforwardly with a gross doctrine of righteousness through works. Nevertheless, in the question of their hope in God's grace, there remains this essential difference between Judaism and the New Testament, Paul especially: Pious Judaism hopes in God's righteousness for the pious man, who expends himself for the Law, even though he knows he cannot fullfill it sufficiently. The lawless sinner, especially the pagan, has no hope. The New Testament contention, however, is that salvation is promised to the sinner.

The New Testament is very close to the tradition of the Old Testament and of Judaism of the intertestamental period. It bestows the title of "righteous" on pious persons of antiquity as well as of the present: thus with Abel (Matthew 23:35); Noah (Heb. 11:7); Melchizedek (Heb. 7:2; and note the relationship of this name, meaning "king of righteousness," with the very term under discussion, *zedaqah*); Lot (2 Peter 2:7); the prophets (Matthew 13:17); and of its own time, Joseph, the foster-father of Jesus (Matthew 1:19); Zechariah and Elizabeth (Luke 1:6); Simeon (Luke 2:25). It acknowledges that there are both righteous men and sinners (Luke 15:7). The Father "sends rain upon the just and the unjust" (Mathew 5:45). The measuring stick of this righteousness is "walking blameless in all the commandments and ordinances of the Lord" (Luke 1:6). Because of their fidelity to the commandments, the righteous will be persecuted (Matthew 5:10; 2 Peter 2:7). And there are righteous people among the Jews as well as among the Gentiles (Acts 10:35).

In the Synoptics, nevertheless, there are remarks expressive of reservation and rejection in regard to the accustomed practice of righteousness. An example is the righteousness practiced by the Pharisees. They were sincere and pious men who expended themselves for the law and honor of God. But a saying of the Lord in the Synoptics challenges them: "If your righteousness is not better than that of the Scribes and Pharisees, you will not enter into the kingdom of heaven" (Matthew 5:20).

Severe reproofs are leveled against the righteousness of the Pharisees in the seven reproaches of Matthew 23:2-39. This righteousness is but the hypocrisy of those who would appear just (Matthew 23:5, 28). These just are convinced of their own righteousness, hold others in contempt, and are nevertheless the worst of all (Matthew 23:29-32). God knows hearts. This righteousness before men is an abomination before God (Luke 16:15). The questionableness of the righteousness of the Pharisees is unveiled in the parable of the Pharisee and the publican (Luke 18:9-14). The publican, or tax-collector, is justified without works, made just by God's forgiveness, as a gift.

To the exegete there is the question of whether the attribution to Jesus of such pugnacious words against the Pharisees is not the result of later altercations between synagogue and Church. This may be the case especially with Matthew 23; but Luke 18:9-14 will be maintained as Jesus' own original judgment. Jesus assails the Pharisee of this parable, not because the man is untruthful or immoral, not because he is inconsistent, but precisely because he is consistently a Pharisee.

Here we see the contrast between Jesus and Judaism. The Father of Jesus gives himself to the sinner. The God of rigid Pharisaism is the God of the Law; the Father of Jesus is the God of love. Rigid Judaism received the doctrine of Jesus as a mortal threat to the faith and teaching of Israel. The criticism which Matthew 23 makes of Pharisaism could be misunderstood in such a way that it would be demanding that the requirements which the Pharisees had not fulfilled must now be fulfilled. This would be the true religion; and Christianity would then be a Pharisaism purified of its imperfections, and it would be in fact an ordinary religion of works.

The gospel, however, is the message of grace. Now a new and real righteousness is promised and given. "Those who hunger and thirst after righteousness will be filled" (Matthew 5:6). Righteousness is still promised. To those who yearn for it, it is said: "Seek first the kingdom of God and his righteousness" (Matthew 6:33). True righteousness is not the work of men, but the gift of God, just as the kingdom itself is God's work.

Paul too shares in the supposed traditions of Israel. The Qumran texts in particular make it apparent that the quest for righteousness was essential to the Judaism of his time, and that justification by God was hopefully awaited. To this expectation Paul can promise fulfillment and realization in the salvation prepared by Christ. And in so doing Paul unbinds and realizes again the old significance and power of the concept of righteousness, insofar as this focuses its sights on God's creative justification of man.

As for every other Jew, it is for Paul, too, a firm principle that God is just. Paul says this over and over again, and with special force in Rom. 3:5-8. In the belief of Israel, God is judge of the world. God, therefore, is just. To impugn this would be blasphemy. Such an assertion would put an end to all discussion, and one could only answer it with an impartial judgment, "Well, at least your condemnation will be just!"

With this as his point of departure, Paul finds the concept of God's righteousness one of juridic import. For man it is a question of supreme interest whether or not he will be found just before a just God. In Rom. 1:17 it is stated: "He who through faith is righteous shall live." [85] Paul is quoting Hab. 2:4: "The righteous will, through his fidelity [to God], have a long life." Paul gives the saying a content which is far beyond the significance originally invested in it by Habakkuk, but which is consistent, nevertheless, with the tendency and mentality of the Old Testament, which regularly recognizes that it is not works which make for man's salvation, but the gift of God.

In a lengthy chain of argumentation in Rom. 1:18-3:20, Paul came to the conclusion that in the sight of God there was not formerly, nor is there now, such a thing as righteousness in man. In respect to salva-

tion history, all of mankind can be divided into two parts: Jews and
Gentiles. Both are under sin. "Therefore no human being will be
justified in his sight by works of the Law" (Rom. 3:20). Man knows
that he must respond to God's demand and fulfill his ordinance; but
he knows also that he does not and cannot do this successfully. Consequently, man finds himself a sinner in the sight of the just God. In
the judgment God's righteousness will become man's condemnation.
Man exists under the anger of God. His situation is desperate. Is
there no other possibility for man? Paul is in a position to proclaim
it: "Now is the righteousness of God revealed in the gospel" (Rom.
1:17; 3:21). This revelation is not only an instructional proclamation,
but a powerfully effective event in the world.

As the Righteous One, Paul reasons, God must ever practice righteousness. He can neither approve nor ignore injustice and sin. God's
justice demands atonement. God laid our sins on Christ and "for our
sake made him to be sin, so that in him we might become the righteousness of God" (2 Cor. 5:21). The cross of Christ reveals the righteousness of God as much as it does God's will to save. For Paul, the
concept of God's righteousness has a double proper significance: "He
is righteous; and he justifies him who believes in Jesus" (Rom. 3:26).
The genitive in "God's righteousness" is a subjective genitive as well
as an objective genitive. God's properties are other than those of man.
His properties can, however, in some way pertain to man, because
they are creative. His life becomes the life of the world, his excellence
the excellence of creation. Thus his righteousness becomes the righteousness of the sinner.

Accordingly, dogmatic theology distinguishes between the *iustitia
Dei passiva* (the righteousness which God possesses) and the *iustitia Dei activa* (the righteousness which God gives). Accepting the
saving will of God, the sinner is now righteous. The righteousness of
man never comes as his own righteousness, as his own work, as the
state of his own virtue, but only as a gift of, and a sharing in, the
righteousness of God through forgiveness and redemption for the sake
of Christ. "I have not a righteousness of my own, based on the law,
but that which is through faith in Christ, the righteousness from
God which depends on faith" (Phil. 3:9).[86]

Paul maintains repeatedly: "We hold that a man is justified by faith apart from works of the Law" (Rom. 3:28; cf. 3:20; 4:5; Gal. 2:16). To be sure, Paul is speaking primarily of the works commanded by the Law in the Old Testament. But his perspective takes in also works in general, by the help of which a man might be attempting to assure his salvation. Protestant theology has clarified the statement of Paul in Rom. 3:28 by making an addition to the phrase, "by faith *alone*" (*fides sola*). In point of fact, this elucidation had already been made by the Fathers; and the word "alone" is found already in Origen's *Commentaries on Romans* (Migne, PG 14, 952–953, 955).[87]

Faith is not itself justification, but it is the acceptance of the gift of God, after admission of its lack and renunciation of any self-sufficiency. This is "obedience unto righteousness" (Rom. 6:16). Faith is not a work which wins righteousness, but a prerequisite for the reception of justification. Righteousness is never the work of man; it is always a gift of God. Indeed, Paul speaks of "righteousness by or from faith" (δικαιοσύνη ἐκ πίστεως, Rom. 1:17; 5:1), or "righteousness through faith" (δικαιοσύνη διὰ πίστεως, Rom. 3:22; Gal. 2:16), but never of "righteousness owing to or for faith" (δικαιοσύνη διὰ πίστιν). In the latter instance, faith would be a meritorious work.

Paul carries on the expectation of the Old Testament that God's righteousness is revealed as the salvation which he effects and the assistance which he gives to the oppressed. Nowhere else in the New Testament is the word and concept of justification so essentially important as in the letters of Paul. Paul develops his concept in the struggle against the Jewish counterposition of justification by works, a fact which is perhaps clearer in the Epistle to the Galatians (2:16; 3:1-3; 5:4) than anywhere else.

Nevertheless, Paul's doctrine of justification does not originate in any internal dialectic of the Law. Its foundation is not in a doubt of some sort as to whether or not the fulfillment of the Law is possible. As a Pharisee (Phil. 3:5), Paul was convinced of the righteousness of the Law. The beginning and foundation of his criticism of the Law is the external event of the cross. Gal. 3:13 is a clear enough example of this. Paul has to spotlight the cross of the Messiah. He undertakes to do so in quoting Deut. 21:23: "Cursed be everyone who hangs on the tree." Christ is the sinless Holy One (2 Cor. 5:21). He bears the curse, not for himself, but for the guilt of others, for the sins of all.

The congregation of Christ can no longer abide by the Law, which its Lord has condemned. The Law is abolished, even in view of the salvation of the cross. The theology of the new justification is the meaning of the cross.

For many generations Israel endeavored to acquire righteousness before God. To that end she took upon herself indescribable burdens. Paul says that now at last these efforts have reached their goal. God's righteousness is now attainable, even if otherwise than Israel envisioned it. Paul recognizes an astounding fact: in attempting to establish her own righteousness, Israel failed of her aim; and at the same time, the Gentiles, who never made the effort, have come to know righteousness (Rom. 9:30-33). Christ took sins upon himself in order to intercede for the sinners and to create righteousness for them. He who accepts this righteousness is justified.

The altercation of Paul with Israel about the truth of the righteousness of God can have the appearance of a dead quarrel between a rabbi and his earlier companions in faith. Nevertheless, Paul would probably have said that the question of how a man is able to be righteous in the sight of God is in fact a question of his existence or nonexistence. The concept of the righteousness of God supposes the message of salvation.

Righteousness is bestowed and is not the proper product of moral endeavor. If righteousness were to be acquired otherwise, it would thereby become the starting-point for a new morality. As it is, this new life-situation conquers unrighteousness and sin. Paul speaks repeatedly of "the weapons of righteousness" (Rom. 6:13; 2 Cor. 6:7). The bestowal of righteousness puts a weapon in one's hands with which to effect goodness. Righteousness must bring forth its fruits (Phil. 1:11). Now the "just requirement of the law" can and must be fulfilled (Rom. 8:4).

In moral trial the reality of righteousness is manifested and proved. It must, however, undergo the test over and over again. The genuineness of righteousness will first be revealed in the judgment. By the "power of faith we await, in the Spirit, the outcome of our hope of righteousness" (Gal. 5:5). "For it is not the hearers of the law who are righteous before God but the doers of the law who will be justified" (Rom. 2:13). The final justifying decree of God, which conducts one to the state of righteousness in the new life, must still be awaited. Even this righteousness is not of one's own doing. It is true of all righteousness: "We are justified by his grace as a gift" (Rom. 3:24). Righteousness is always a gift, given in view of the salvational work of Christ. ". . . so that you may be pure and without offense on the day of Christ, filled with the fruits of righteousness through Jesus Christ" (Phil. 1:10-11). Indeed, it is now true: "Now the righteousness of God has been manifested apart from law" (Rom. 3:21).

The righteousness received by faith is already effective in the present. But at the same time, righteousness is also a future good, in that it is promised at the final judgment. Paul's proclamation of righteousness comprises both together. He found no contradiction therein. His preaching is an invitation to a continual encounter with God's judgment as well as with God's grace. This assigns direction to the goal and provides a stimulus for that goal.

Paul does not disavow a judgment according to works. For him there is no question whatever but that in the judgment the doing of good will be critical for man. To be serious about the doing of good, therefore, is genuinely Pauline. What is un-Pauline is the self-deception of the man who supposes that he can create his own redemption by his own efforts.

If the righteousness of God is a concept of central importance for Paul, he has not thereby introduced anything that is foreign to the gospel. He is entirely at one with the Synoptics, inasmuch as he certainly carries their treatment forward in accord with the revelation in the cross and in the resurrection. If Matthew (6:33) says: "Seek first the kingdom and righteousness of God," then the kingdom and righteousness has now arrived in the work of Christ, and is to be accepted with it. And now it is clear, too, how the pledge of righteousness without works in Luke 18:14 is effectual.

In post-Pauline writings, the concept of a righteousness created by Christ appears a few times. The First Epistle of Peter, written under a very strong Pauline influence, is reminiscent of Paul: "He bore our sins in his body on the cross, that we might die to sin and live to righteousness" (2:24). Righteousness is now possible by virtue of Christ's grace of salvation: "Since you know that he is righteous, be assured that everyone who acts in righteousness is born of him" (1 John 2:29).

The relationship between Paul and the Epistle of James [88] is much discussed. Both appeal to the example of Abraham, but they appear to draw entirely opposite conclusions therefrom. James says: "By works is a man justified, and not by faith alone" (2:24). Paul, on the contrary, says: "By faith is a man justified, without works of the Law" (Rom. 3:28). Exegesis inquiries as to the connections which unite Paul and James. If one is regarded as a direct polemic against the other, then the relationship will be determined in accord with the probable time of origin of the two letters. It is probable that Paul would be regarded as the earlier, and therefore James would be contending against Paul.

It is questionable, however, whether James ever knew the Epistles of Paul. It is a more likely possibility that James is polemicizing against false Paulinism. It would appear, from his having made reference to such a false conclusion, that there was already in the time of Paul an opinion current to the effect that the greater one's sins, the greater would be the graces given him (Rom. 3:8; 6:1). Perhaps it is to such a misunderstanding and to such a moral laxity that James turns his attention.

And it must, nevertheless, remain a possibility also that, without any mutual reference whatever, Paul and James each depend upon current Jewish midrash on Abraham, and arrive at opposite conclusions on the basis of their having different purposes in mind and probably having also different emphases in their understanding of the faith.

The theological controversies over the interpretation of the apparent contradiction between Paul and James which have occasionally arisen since the time of Luther have been gradually defused. To be sure, according to Paul, faith alone (without works) justifies. But this faith never is alone; and whenever it is true faith, it is effective in love (Gal. 5:6). According to James (2:22), "faith is effective together with works, and faith is perfected through works." James never reaches the depths of the radical Pauline theology of faith, as it is perhaps expressed in Rom. 4:5: "For the one who has no works, but who has faith in him who justifies the godless, his faith will be reck oned as righteousness." For James, justification is not simply the creative action of God on behalf of the sinner; rather, it takes place in the acknowledgment of faith and of the works performed, this acknowledgment made by the justifying God. For James there is neither faith alone nor works alone.

The preceding attempt to explain the New Testament concepts, especially the Pauline concepts, of righteousness and justification is largely common to modern exegesis. Indeed, it has its basis essentially in the theology of the Reformation. Exegetically it is defended in exemplary fashion by R. Bultmann (*Theologie des Neuen Testaments*, 6th ed., 1968, pp. 271–285). Most recently, however, this understanding has been sharply criticized by E. Käsemann and others of his school.[89] According to this criticism, the previously expounded interpretation of the Pauline concept of righteousness is individualistically limited. It is applicable to a man only insofar as he is able to experience God's grace. On the contrary, Käsemann explains, "anthropology is not the proper concern of justification. Paul was aware of and saw his duty in the apocalyptic urgency of the world-mission."

The theses of Käsemann are further developed in his school. The latter would have it that the Pauline concept of justification signifies the fidelity of God to all creation, and signifies what is revealed in Christ, the dominion of God over the whole world, for which God creates salvation. This is taking place now in the proclamation of the word. Paul is to be understood in a horizontal plane with contemporaneous late Jewish apocalyptists, for whom the concept of the righteousness of God has cosmic breadth. God's justification brings a new and holy claim of God before the world; but ultimately there is to be a new creation of the world for the sake of its salvation. Justification takes the justified into its service for a witness in the world and for service to the world.

What is to be said of this exposition? According to Romans 1–3, justification is directed to the whole of mankind. This may not be considered sufficient; but nevertheless it affects each individual, sinner and believer (Rom. 3:26). It is certain that the goal of God's salvational dealings is new creation (Rom. 8). But is it stated that what this new creation creates is the *righteousness* of God? If Paul does not state this expressly, then he must, says the new understanding, be interpreted from the viewpoint of late Judaism, in which apocalyptic was an all-embracing and all-pervading spiritual impulse. In any case, this much must be said, that apocalyptic was in fact a powerful and often insufficiently appreciated spiritual impulse in late Judaism. It reveals God's might and holiness, his righteousness in judging. But is apocalyptic revelation also creative justification? And is Paul an apocalyptist in the accepted sense of the term? To be sure, he uses an apocalyptic presentation. But how far is this mere form, and how far content? In the broad apocalyptic portrayal in 1 Thess. 4:13–5:11, the Christological testimony in 4:17-18 is decisive by itself.

The biblical concept of righteousness stands in opposition to the profane juridic concept of righteousness. The "higher quality righteousness" (Matthew 5:20) which Jesus demanded renounces any kind of claims or "rights" of its own. It does not merely satisfy the just claim of another, but wants to give in such a way as to far surpass even what the other has coming "by right." It proceeds not according to the rules of law, but according to the example of God, who gives all (Matthew 5:45). The righteousness of God of which Paul speaks is not the righteousness which rewards or punishes in accord with merits, but the dealing of God, which operates "apart from the law" (Rom. 3:21) and in contrast to guilt and merit, as the forgiving and bestowing love of God. God's manner of dealing can, as indicated in Jesus' parable about the workers in the vineyard (Matthew 20:1-15), be in complete opposition to the secular concept of right. This is the right and order of God's kingdom; and through it God's saving will establishes order and right among men and in the world of men. To the extent that it is effectively established, the primeval idea of justice, both as it was conceived in the Old Testament and even as the ancient Greeks conceived it, is thereby fulfilled. There is now, in the new era, a state of righteousness; and it is something other than a relationship to the earthy and secular.

Jesus himself refused to settle any disputes over worldly rights (Matthew 22:15-23; Luke 12:14). His "kingdom is not of this world" (John 18:36). The Church of the Apostles, nevertheless, has to contend with earthly arrangements and to become involved in such. This happens with the tables of duties to one's neighbor, which cannot be otherwise conceived than as profane ordinance and legislation (see below, ch. 17). It happens too with instructions, like those of Rom. 3:1-7 and 1 Peter 2:13-17, on conduct to be observed in relation to the government (see below, ch. 26). On the whole, however, the New Testament is but little occupied with such questions. The Christian community was, in New Testament times, but a small minority, and it had no influence on the shaping of public order. Besides, it regarded the order of the kingdom of God as being incomparably more important.

Here the New Testament is quite different from the Old. In Israel, religion and government was a unified entity. The religious law was the law of the people and of the state. Even the secular ordinance was proclaimed as God's statute and was rigorously enforced.

§ 15. PURITY

Clean and *unclean*, *pure* and *impure* are important words and concepts for the religious and moral thought of all religions, and are found on every level of the history of religion.[90] The questions raised by religious history are very extensive. Our reflections must be confined, for the most part, to the more important religions of our cultural milieu, the ancient Greek and biblical.

In primitive religion as well as in later sophisticated forms, the divine being is experienced as almighty and supreme. His power can operate, in respect to man, either in an inimical or in a friendly fashion. Man must not open relations with the divinity haphazardly. He must be apprehensive lest, because of his unconcern and unworthiness, he receive, not assistance and grace, but punishment. He must prepare himself for the divinity. He must divest himself of all impurity.

In the early Greek religion, as well as in the religion of Israel, occurrences of sexuality, birth, and death render one unclean. Primitive man regards these occurrences, which he himself can neither effect nor control but which overwhelm him, as the operations of supernatural forces. Perhaps at death they are operative even in effecting a timidity before the soul of the one who is dead. In these occurrences man comes into contact with demons. Possessed by them, he can no longer enter into communication with his God.

Cleanness is required primarily of the man who is about to participate in the ritual worship of his God. Even the means of attaining purity are ritualistic in kind and ritually prescribed. The actual performance of such rites cannot be fully described because the light of history has not fully illuminated them. On the other hand, this same light has effectively clarified the development and refinement of the concept of purity. "Pure" changes from a cultic and ritual concept to a moral concept. Divinity is conceived as moral quantity, which puts a moral requirement upon the worshiper. Whoever would approach the Divinity must comply with his moral requirements.

This development is observable in the religious spirit of Greece as well as in that of Israel. According to laws of the greatest antiquity, only one who is ritually pure may draw close to the Divinity for prayer and sacrifice. In the early form of the Agamemnon story, which was reworked by Aeschylus, the murderer requires absolution, not in consequence of his moral outrage, but in consequence of the ghastly weight of spilled blood.

However, in the further history of Greek religion, purity became a spiritual concept. In the mystery religions, to be sure, traditional ritual consecratory usages were practiced more widely; but they were understood in a spiritual and ethical sense. Over the Temple of Asclepius in Epidaurus there is an inscription reading: "He only who is pure may cross the threshold of the perfumed temple. And none is pure save he that thinks on holy things." The communities of Orphics and Pythagoreans strove, under a long tradition of ancient ritual ordinances, for purity of life. The philosophical schools demanded this deliberately and explicitly. Epictetus (*Diss.*, 3, 22, 93) teaches that God is present in man, and that he is insulted and profaned by covetous looks and impure thoughts. Therefore, "the higher capacity of the soul must be purer than the sun." Purity, then, is ethically conceived. It is, however, an affair of man himself. There is no doubt that he can attain to it, if only he will.

Even the Old Testament religion reflects such a religious development. The viewpoint that sexual functions, birth, and death render men unclean (Leviticus and Numbers) originates in primitive thought.

Animals which are consecrated to some other Divinity and are filled with it are contaminating. The swine is an old Canaanite sacrificial beast, for which reason it can neither be offered nor eaten in Israel (Lev. 11:7; Deut. 14:8). The hare is, in the lore of the magician, the bearer of demoniacal powers. For Israel it is unclean (Lev. 11:6; Deut. 14:7).

Uncleanness is an external and ritual fault, not a moral fault. According to Lev. 21:1-3 and Tob. 2:1-9; 12:12, burying the dead is commanded as a work of piety; yet the same pious work makes the one who performs it unclean. As the uncleanness is ritual, so too the purification. The law evolves many regulations of washings, cleansings, purifications, and reconciliations (Lev. 7:20f.; 11–15; 21:7-9). The priesthood develops the notions of ritual purity, while the incumbents of the prophetic office intensify the religio-ethical aspect. The trappings of ritual and ethical purity are contrasted one with another: "I have had enough of burnt offerings of rams and the fat of fatted calves. The blood of bulls, lambs and goats I do not want. Who has commanded you to trample down my forecourts? Wash, and you will be clean! Take away your evil deeds from before my eyes! Cease doing evil!" (Is. 1:11-12, 16). A distinct line of preference of the ethical over the cultic and ritual is to be pursued (Pss. 15:2-5; 18:21-27; 24:4; 51:4; Job 15:14-16; 17:9; Prov. 15:26).

Accordingly, the requirement of ritual purity has meaning only when it becomes an indication and reminder about inner, spiritual purity. After her return from exile, it was necessary for Israel to separate and purify herself from the influences she had come to know in a foreign land. Likewise, in the Maccabean era it was necessary for the people to be protected against the mighty forces of Hellenism, not only in the political arena but also in the cultural and ethical areas. Hence there arose another danger, that the severing of connections and the maintenance of purity might be misunderstood as externally applicable. The Gentiles were unclean, one and all; and association with them contaminated the Jews, so that they had again to be purified of such influences.

Even for the pious people of Qumran, cleanness was of utmost importance. Excavations there have brought to light a huge system of bathing installations. The Qumran scrolls have made available prescriptions for these purifications. The pious ones know, however, that it is not external purification that is essential: "The sinner cannot be made clean in the waters of atonement, nor can he be made holy in seas and rivers; neither can he in any way be made clean by washing in water. He will remain utterly unclean so long as he contemns the laws of God and refuses to discipline himself in the community of his counsel" (1 QS 3:4-6). The Rabbis, too, knew the requirement of inner purity. Rabbi Meir (*ca.* 150 A.D.) cautions: "Keep your mouth from every sin. Then I, the Lord, will be with you always."

As representatives of Hellenistic Judaism, Philo and Josephus are aware of the ancient legal requirements of purity. But personally they are convinced that the requirement intended by God is inner moral purity. It may be regarded, however, as the deficiency and misfortune of the official religious spirit of late Judaism that it overstressed ritual purity and occupied itself with the minutiae thereof, while it remained incapable of setting aside what was primitive and of recognizing and aspiring to the ethical.

In the New Testament the conception of purity as an external cultic and ritual property is conquered. The cultic and ritual commandments are no longer binding. What is required now is moral and religious purity. In principle this is the demand already of Jesus. The purity he requires is always purity of heart, which means purity in the inner man. Cultic ritual purity is unavailing, since it remains external: "You cleanse the outside of the cup and dish, but the inside is swollen with plunder and filth. Blind Pharisees! Cleanse first the inside of cup and dish, and then the outside will also be clean!" (Matthew 23:25-26).

When the Pharisees and Scribes from Jerusalem saw Jesus and his disciples eating without first washing their hands, Jesus quotes Is. 29:13 by way of defense: "This people honors me with its lips, but its heart is far from me. In vain do they worship me, teaching as doctrines the precepts of men. Nothing that goes into a man can make him unclean. In the inner recesses of the heart are the wicked thoughts which debase a man" (Mark 7:2-23).

It is not commerce with Gentiles and sinners that makes a man unclean. Purity is not a matter of occupation. Jesus, therefore, is the friend of tax-collectors and sinners. Another and new kind of purity, then, is required: "Blessed are they who are pure of heart, for they shall see God" (Matthew 5:8). The reward of purity is to see God. This is the perfection of that which purity even now initiates, since the pure are always in the presence of God. As existence in the presence of God, purity is resignation to the will of God, simplicity and integrity in a man's obedience to God. For the sake of purity, extreme sacrifice can be required of a man. If eye, hand, or foot is a scandal to him, in the extremest case he must cast it away (Mark 9:43-45).

Purity, however, does not lie within the capabilities of a man's own efforts. (Here the philosophical and the New Testament understanding of man part company!) God gives purity: "She is forgiven her many sins, because she has loved much" (Luke 7:47). It is not that man's love makes pure of itself; God makes a man pure when that man is united with God in love. Now, however, the presence of God is real in Christ Jesus. The sick and the sinner are made clean by the healing cures of Jesus (Matthew 8:3; 9:12). The disciples are clean in the communion of Jesus (John 13:10; 15:3).

The preaching of the Apostles carries out the word of Jesus. In the primitive congregations there was a long altercation carried on about the validity of the old commandments, especially about the laws concerning foods. The accounts appear to be somewhat at cross-purposes. In the Acts of the Apostles (10:15; 11:9), the recognition of the purity of foods is represented as a revelation given to Peter. God himself explains to the Apostle in a vision that the animals formerly unclean are now clean, and invites him to enjoy them. In this significant question, then, it is God himself who has instructed the Church. This is to be taken as a representation in retrospect of a long and collective evaluation. According to the narrative of the Acts of the Apostles (15:3-21), a decision was first reached later, after the debating of contrary positions at Jerusalem in a general congress of the Church, to require of the Gentiles only that they abstain from the service of idols, from unchastity, and from the enjoyment of animals not ritually slaughtered.

Paul tells again of an incident in the congregation at Antioch, caused by the fact that for Peter the question of eating at table with pagans was not yet settled (Gal. 2:11-14). Paul more than anyone else led the fight for a new understanding of purity. He recognized that the root of the prohibitions was the anxiety over the ostensible demoniacal possession of the "elements of the world." He perceived in this the remnants of a primitive fear of demons. And if this is true in respect to the pagan deities, it is true also for the Torah (Gal. 4:3-9).

On the other hand, then, it is a fact that the Christian faith is by its nature a radically ethical religion and a religion of the conscience. Paul calls to mind that the whole world, as God's creation, is pure and belongs to the faith (Rom. 14:20; 1 Cor. 10:26). The Apostle likewise makes reference to the salvational and redemptive work of Christ: "I know and am convinced in the Lord Jesus that nothing is in itself unclean; only for those who regard it as unclean is it unclean" (Rom. 14:14). He asks the Galatians whether they want to be subjected again to the old commandments: "How can you turn back again to the weak and beggarly elements, in order to be enslaved to them anew?" (Gal. 4:9). The Epistle to the Colossians has much the same admonition: "With Christ you have died to the elements of the world. Why then do you submit yourselves to regulations, as if you still lived in the world?" (Col. 2:20). The only gauge now is the obligation of love: "Do not, for the sake of food, destroy the work of God! . . . It is better to eat no meat and to drink no wine, nor to do anything else at which your brother is scandalized" (Rom. 14:20-21).

Paul seldom uses words like *pure* and *purification* (καθαρὸς and καθαρισμός). He speaks of the intended things with other words, such as *holy, sanctify,* and *sanctification* (ἅγιος, ἁγιάξω, and ἁγιασμός). Linguistic usage makes the essentials of the Christian understanding of purity apparent. God, the primordially Holy One, is pure. Only in relation to God, as the Holy One who sanctifies, can there be any human purity. To be sure, Paul uses the word *impurity* (ἀκαθαρσία) more frequently in describing anything adverse to God (Rom. 6:19; 2 Cor. 12:21; Gal. 5:19; 1 Thess. 2:3). Impurity is, of course, an achievement of man.

The expressions *pure* and *purify* are more frequent in the Pastoral Epistles, the Epistle to the Hebrews, and in the Johannine literature, which, therefore, at least in their use of words and in their conceptualizations, again come closer to the Old Testament Jewish presentations. They share, however, in the New Testament knowledge that God creates purity. The death of Jesus is an efficacious sacrifice which takes away sin by atonement and thereby effects a new purity for him who is united with Jesus. "The Savior gave himself up for us, so that he might redeem us from all lawlessness and purify for himself a people that will belong to him and will be zealous for good works" (Titus 2:14). Another text says: "I thank God, whom I serve with a clean conscience, as did my fathers before me" (2 Tim. 1:3). Here is a Christian who talks like a Jew, who is thankful that he belongs to the chosen people, that he has held fast to the law of God. Nevertheless, his purity is not ritual and legal purity, but purity of conscience. The new purity is contrasted to the old ritual cultic purity as the true and perfect purity: "If the blood of goats and bulls and the strewing of the ashes of a heifer sanctifies the unclean unto the purification of the flesh, how much more shall the blood of Christ, who through the eternal Spirit presented himself without blemish to God, purify our consciences from dead works, so that we might serve the living God" (Heb. 9:13-14).

A basic declaration of John's Gospel is that the disciples are pure. "I am the vine, and my Father is the vinedresser. He takes away each tendril that bears no fruit, and purifies each that does bear fruit, that it may bear even more fruit. You are already purified by the word which I have spoken to you" (John 15:1-3). The purity of the disciples is effected through union with Christ (John 13:10). If the Old Testament Jewish words and concepts are in use again, it is because, so to speak, the old words of hope and promise are now fulfilled. The whole of Israel's endeavor for the Law was directed to presenting man as pure before God. This was also the goal of all man's moral efforts. All these hopes have now arrived at their goal and are fulfilled.

§ 16. PERFECTION

The goal of the moral life is designated in the Bible as "perfection" (τελειότης).[91] The disciples ought to become "perfect" (τέλειος). The nearest source for the origins of New Testament usage is the Old Testament. The concept of perfection is a living one in the Old Testament and in the Jewish range of ideas and literature. Perfection in these sources is to be understood entirely in a context of divine law. God's word and directive is the norm, and that which corresponds thereto is perfect. A purely ritual usage is closely definable. The sacrificial beast that is free of every blemish is "perfect" (thus forty-one times in the Psalms, eleven times in Ezechiel). In the moral sense, he who follows the commandments and requirements of God is perfect. God himself, as the one who is absolutely holy, is at the same time the one who is absolutely perfect. "With the Holy One you are holy, with the Perfect One you are perfect, with the Pure One you are pure" (2 Sam. 22:26-27).

Human perfection, then, is ordered to God. The reality of God challenges man. The ritual and the ethical viewpoints are not difficult to separate. It is commanded: "You shall be perfect before the Lord your God" (Deut. 18:13). The desire of the pious man is in utter conformity with the commandment of God. He says in praise: "May my heart be perfect in your ordinances" (Ps. 119:20). From the consciousness of imperfection, nevertheless, there comes the petition: "Who can say how often he errs? Absolve me of my hidden faults! Let not your servant be numbered with the presumptuous. Then I shall be perfect and free of transgression" (Ps. 19:13-14).

Even the pathway and conduct of the righteous is called perfect (Ps. 15:2; 18:33; Job 4:6; Prov. 11:20). The men of antiquity are examples of perfection. "Noah was a righteous man, perfect in his generation; Noah pleased God" (Gen. 6:9). Blameless and perfect were Abraham (Gen. 17:1) and Job (Job 1:1, 8). The pious man is "perfect and undivided of heart" (1 Kings 8:61; 15:3, 14; 1 Chr. 28:9). Perfection is complete and undivided obedience to God. The divine pleasure rests thereon.

The concept of perfection is of considerable significance in Qumran. The members of the community call themselves "those who conduct their lives in perfection" (1 QH 1:36), "the perfect ones of the way" (1 QS 4:22), "perfect men of holiness" (*Damascus Document*, 20:2-7). The community is "a house of perfection and truth in Israel" (1 QS 8:9). Perfection consists in the total fulfillment of the will of God, concretely in the observance of the prescriptions and ordinances in the community of Qumran. Nevertheless, in the final analysis, perfection is a gift of God. For "perfection comes only from the hand of

God" (1 QS 11:10f.). The pious man knows: "My justification is with God, and in his hand is the perfection of my way" (1 QS 11:2).

In Greek antiquity the concept of perfection is encountered in philosophical ethics as well as in more solemnly religious contexts. The wise man is perfect when he has won a correct understanding and puts it into virtuous practice. This is taught by Plato and Aristotle, and the Stoa as well.

The word *perfection* is important also in the mystery religions. The great consecrations are called "the perfect mysteries," and the consecrated ones are termed "the perfect." The gnosis took up these concepts and ideas, extended them and gave them new depth. This is clear enough in the witness of the Fathers of the Church, as well as in the gnostic texts themselves, e.g., *Corpus Hermeticum*, 4, 4: "Now they accepted the announcement and were baptized in the spirit (*nous*), became sharers in understanding and perfect men, who have received the spirit (*nous*)." Even in Mandaean literature there is frequent talk of the perfect ones and the perfected ones. According to the Neo-Platonist Jamblichus (*De mysteriis*, 3, 7), he is perfect who knows and has experienced "what enthusiasm is, and how it arises."

Philo attempts to unite Jewish and Greek thought. The perfect ones are, for Philo, the righteous of the old covenant. They are wise men also, however, since they fulfill the ideal of human ethics; thus with Abraham, Isaac, and Jacob.[92]

The linguistic usages of the New Testament are associated primarily with Jewish literature. In the Gospels the concept of perfection is sometimes used in a ritual sense: thus with Christ, when he says, "and on the third day I must be perfected" (Luke 13:22); and with the group of disciples, "that they may be perfected unto unity" (John 17:23). The Gospel of John also employs the term "to sanctify" with this same meaning. Christ himself says: "I sanctify myself" (John 17:19). Even the disciples are to be sanctified (John 17:17, 19). The equating of "to sanctify" with "to perfect" has its roots in the Old Testament; cf. Exod. 29:33; Lev. 4:5 (LXX); 16:32.

On the other hand, Matthew employs the term "being perfect" in the ethical sense. Thus in the invitation of the Sermon on the Mount: "You shall be perfect even as your heavenly Father is perfect" (Matthew 5:48). The form is predetermined through similar Old Testament passages: "You shall be holy, because I am holy" (Lev. 19:2); and "you shall be perfect before the Lord" (Deut. 18:13). If it is principally ritual and sacral holiness that the Old Testament has in mind, the gospel, nevertheless, is concerned with the holiness of moral living.

In all Scripture, it is only in the saying in Matthew 5:48 that the concept of perfection is applied to God. It is through this concept that there is both a formal and a contextual relationship between Matthew 5:48 and Matthew 5:45; ". . . so that you may become sons of your Father in heaven." In both instances there is representation of God as an example, and in both there is a lauding of the goodness of God. In the Synoptic parallel in Luke 6:36, God's mercy is named in place of his perfection. God's perfection, accordingly, is his boundless love.

In Matthew 5:45, 48, discipleship is portrayed in the highest terms conceivable. God's perfection is the measure and prototype of human morality. The statement in Matthew 5:48 is possible only if it is taken as a directive in the manner of a promise. Since God's love is bestowed upon man and sets him free, it is possible also for man to be set loose from himself and to surrender himself in love. Such action and conduct, however, is not to be understood as an achievement of human virtue and a reason for self-adulation; rather, the praise belongs to the Father in heaven, whose gift it is (Matthew 5:16). This is the exceeding righteousness (Matthew 5:20) that is of such great worth. This righteousness, since it is God's work, transcends the work of man.

The gospel uses the term *perfection* once again in the narrative of the rich young man (Matthew 19:16-22). The rich young man inquires about what is good. Jesus enumerates the commandments. The young man indicates that he has kept them all, and inquiries further: "What do I still lack?" Jesus answers (according to Matthew): "If you would be perfect, go, sell your possessions and give it to the poor, and you will have a treasure in heaven; and then follow me." The formulation probably originates with Matthew. According to Mark 10:21 and Luke 18:22, Jesus answers: "One thing you lack." It is essentially the same. When the one thing lacking is supplied for, then the questioner will be perfect. However, the young man goes away sorrowful. He does not understand Jesus — and scarcely could he understand him, seeing that he was raised in what until then were regarded as valid presuppositions. According to Israel's conviction, possessions and goods are a blessing from God.

Probably what is commanded is to give alms generously, but not as yet a total surrendering of everything (see below, ch. 24). The saying of the Lord does not speak of two kinds or degrees of morality, an imperfect and a perfect. According to Matthew 5:48, perfection is the goal of all discipleship. In Matthew 19:21, entry into life is already promised in return for keeping the commandments. This is the greatest promise that can be given. Perfection doubled could not win anything more.

Nevertheless, for this man, in addition to keeping the commandments and in consequence of his riches and the dangers which his riches hold for him, there is a special obligation of renunciation. The imitation requested of him cannot be of the narrower sort within the circle of the Twelve, but can only mean discipleship in a broader sense. From this particular instance it is possible to arrive at knowledge, based on principle, of what perfection is. What is required is the fulfillment of God's commandment apprehended in its totality. This requires the complete renunciation of oneself as total surrender in the imitation of the Master.[93]

The Letters of the Apostles make frequent reference to the concept *perfection*. Paul calls all Christians "perfect" (1 Cor. 2:6), just as he calls all "spiritual" (1 Cor. 2:13). They are perfect through the gift of the Spirit. The Spirit imparts the love of God (Rom. 5:5), a love that perfects. Love belongs to him who is perfect. Faith and hope pass away, but love abides (1 Cor. 13:10). The Spirit is even now an imparted sharing in the futurity of God (2 Cor. 1:22; 5:5), who is the fulfillment. The Apostle can announce wisdom to the perfect (1 Cor. 2:6). Faith and existence in faith win their consummation through this true divine wisdom.

The gift is given continuously; but it also involves an obligation. "Do not be children in your thinking. In evil, be naive; but in thinking, be perfect" (1 Cor. 14:20). Human planning and perfection effected by the Spirit are in no way contradictory. On the contrary, the former penetrates and sheds light on the latter. Perfection is to be realized in the consummation of the Christian life. The measure of perfection is "the will of God" (Rom. 12:2). This is the Old Testament doctrine to the core (see above, pp. 198–199). Paul distinguishes between "being perfect" and "being perfected." "Not as if I had already attained to Christ or were already perfected. . . . All of us, we who are perfect, ought to be so minded" (Phil. 3:12-15). Paul acknowledges the perfection that is bestowed, but it is not yet the consummation thereof. This will first be apparent as an eschatological work of God. It must first be won in obedience to the call.

Christian perfection always knows itself as not yet completed. It cannot be confused, then, with any kind of self-righteousness, nor with an enthusiastic belief in a union with the Godhead, such as the mystic might hope for and strive after. Its consummation is always a still future gift of God. In 1 Thess. 5:23 Paul is speaking of perfection as an eschatological gift, even if, in this instance, instead of τέλειος, he uses other terms: "May the God of peace sanctify you completely; and may your spirit with soul and body be kept intact and spotless for the coming of our Lord Jesus Christ."

The Epistle to the Colossians likewise speaks of Christians as those who are perfect. The Apostle wants "to present every man perfect in Christ" (Col. 1:28). Perhaps some communities in Colossae, in accord with their own peculiar teaching, have designated themselves as perfect in wisdom and powers (Col. 2:8-23). The Apostle wants to emphasize that the Christian is indeed perfect, insofar as he is in Christ, but that this perfection is not his own achievement nor the product of his own wisdom. Perfection has its foundation in Christ, wherein also it is hidden (Col. 3:3). For that reason, perfection is yet to be realized through fulfillment of God's will. Prayer and solicitude have, for the Church, the goal: "that you may be perfect and filled up with all that is God's will" (Col. 4:12). "Love is the bond of perfection" (Col. 3:14). Love effects this perfection, in that it unites and binds the members of the congregation to the one body of Christ (Col. 2:19). It can also be said that love is the form and essence of Christian perfection, since, as love of God and neighbor, it is the great commandment in which all other commandments are comprised.

The First Epistle of John also unites love and perfection.[94] The consummation of love is gift of God and activity of man. "Whoever keeps his word, in him is the love of God perfected" (1 John 2:5). The creative love of God, which is his reality, begets love in man, which, in obedience to God, comes at last to eschatological consummation. "In love there is no fear. Perfect love casts fear out. Fear is apprehensive of [divine] punishment. Whoever is afraid is not perfected in love" (1 John 4:18). In the continuity of this passage it is stated that love is not first man's love, but God's love for man, which takes away from him his fear of punishment. When man becomes recipient of God's love, he is freed of fear and filled with confidence.

The Epistle of James uses the word *perfection* repeatedly: "Steadfastness will possess a perfect work, that you may be perfect and complete, having no lack in you" (James 1:4). This "perfect work," no doubt, is the Christians themselves, who attain to eternal life. One's own efforts are emphasized in respect to the achievement of consummate perfection. "The faith [of Abraham] was perfected by the work [the sacrifice of Isaac]" (James 2:22). Faith is first. It perfects itself in the work of obedience to God. Ultimately, of course, there is no perfection with men. "We all fail in many things. Whoever fails not in speech, the same is a perfect man" (James 3:2). Perfection on the part of man is seen as an impossibility. Only God can give perfection: "Every good gift of God and every perfect endowment comes from the Father of lights" (James 1:17). Light is always a precious gift. Since God is the creator of light, there come from him only good gifts, in particular the perfection envisioned by man.

The word *perfect* and its derivatives ($\tau \acute{\epsilon} \lambda \epsilon \iota o \varsigma$, $\tau \epsilon \lambda \epsilon \iota o \tilde{\upsilon} \nu$, and $\tau \epsilon \lambda \epsilon \acute{\iota} \omega \sigma \iota \varsigma$) are of considerable importance in the Epistle to the Hebrews,[95] wherein these terms carry with them a ritual as well as a moral connotation, thereby continuing the line of the Old Testament. God perfects the person and work of Christ. He perfected the author of salvation through suffering (Heb. 2:10). Christ is perfected, in that he is appointed High Priest (Heb. 5:9; 7:28). Himself made perfect, he becomes the author of eternal salvation for all who are submissive to him (Heb. 5:9-10). The consecrated consecrates others, the perfected perfects others. The Old Testament sacrifices were not able to consecrate in perfection; but this is done through the one sacrifice of Christ, which calls forth a new covenant (Heb. 9:9-14). "By a single sacrifice he has perfected for all time those who are sanctified" (Heb. 10:14; cf. 2:10).

Ritual consecration is to be consummated in subsequent personal activity. This activity is primarily the acceptance of faith. Christ is the "leader and perfector of faith" (Heb. 12:2). He is the example and source, the beginning and consummation of faith. Here the concept "faith" changes from the maintenance of faith to the goal of faith, which is salvation. The required activity is "the purification of our conscience from wicked works to the service of the living God" (Heb. 9:14). A true heart (Heb. 10:22) and a good conscience (Heb. 13:18) are the content of Christian perfection. This is the new covenant, now consummated (8:7f.). The citizens of the eternal city are "the blessed spirits of righteous men made perfect" (Heb. 12:23). The true consummate perfection is God's gift in the eschatological future. Only then can there be *total* perfection.

The term and notion of perfection in the Epistle to the Hebrews can be explained only in part by the (Greek) Old Testament. Over and above this, the letter seems to have some dependence upon late Jewish-Hellenistic tradition (O. Michel), as well as upon gnostic terminology and ideas (E. Käsemann).

In the New Testament, and especially in the letters of the Apostles, the term and concept of perfection is, as compared to the Old Testament, of relatively frequent occurrence. This may have its basis in the simple fact that in the Jewish milieu of the New Testament the concept had come into more frequent use, a fact to which the Qumran scrolls can bear witness. It must also be asked whether in the Greek world contemporary to the New Testament the terms were not used more frequently even in consideration of the language of secular hopes. It might be that in this way a contact with earlier gnosticism took place. Whatever the case, in the New Testament the concepts are interpreted in biblical-historical fashion, in reference to the word and will of God.

IV. VARIOUS AREAS FOR CONSIDERATION

§ 17. VIRTUE AND VIRTUES

From basic moral attitudes a certain line of conduct must follow. These attitudes must show themselves and stand the test in the particular areas of life and in the basic arrangements of society.[96] Conduct and attitude in accord with moral duty is designated as "virtue," whereas wickedness grown to habit is called "vice."

The word and term ἀρετή, meaning "virtue," is a Greek gift to the Bible. Etymologically the word signifies "goodness, excellence, strength"; and it can be used, accordingly, in respect to gods, men, and things. From the time of Socrates and Plato onward, it is an important word in philosophy.

The Old Testament knows numerous virtues, but it is utterly lacking in a word or term for the general concept of virtue. The Greek version of the Old Testament, under the influence of Greek ethics, first employs the term and concept "virtue" (ἀρετή). According to its basic significance, and just as in profane Greek literature, the word indicates divine power (Is. 42:8; Zech. 6:13; Hab. 3:3); but it is also significant of the religious-moral conduct of the pious (Wis. 4:1; 5:13; 8:7). In the period of the New Testament, the concept of virtue is of considerable importance in Judaeo-Hellenistic writings, e.g., Philo, and 2 and 4 Maccabees.

The New Testament, too, makes use of the familiar word ἀρετή, and here too it can designate the various properties of God, his majesty and power (1 Peter 2:9; 2 Peter 1:3). The word is also characteristic, however, of moral probity. Paul's admonition is significant: "Whatever is true, whatever is honorable, whatever is just, whatever is pure, whatever is agreeable, whatever is praiseworthy, whatever there is of virtue and praise, think about these things!" (Phil. 4:8).

This is the single instance in which Paul uses the word "virtue," and it is surrounded by ethical conceptualizations of Greek and especially of Stoic origin. The list is distinct from other such so-called catalogs of virtues. To begin with, the neuter adjectives are peculiarly unbiblical. Virtue and praise appear elsewhere as broad concepts from the Greek political arena. Paul encourages the Church at Philippi to recognize the moral endeavor and reality of the world, in which the Church lives, and not to be inferior to this morality but to assimilate it into the Christian life and into the community. The heritage of Greece, however, is given a Christian determination through the context of the Epistle to the Philippians. This is the case, for example, in the preceding sentence, in which Paul expresses the wish: "May the peace of God protect you in Christ Jesus" (Phil. 4:7). Pursuant to Phil. 4:8, with its philosophical ethics, there is Apostolic admonition and Christian morality: "What you have learned and received and heard and seen in me, that shall you do!" (Phil. 4:9). Paul draws attention to ecclesiastical tradition, catechesis, and preaching. That which is Apostolic is already canonically authoritative.[97]

The word *virtue* appears once more in the Second Epistle of Peter: "So make every effort to supplement your faith with virtue, your virtue with probity, your probity with knowledge, your knowledge with self-control, your self-control with steadfastness, your steadfastness with piety, your piety with brotherly affection, your brotherly affection with love" (2 Peter 1:5-7).

The Second Epistle of Peter is determined very strongly by Greek conceptualization and intellectuality; this is evident in the foregoing catalog of virtues. Most of these terms are to be found also in popular philosophical ethics and in profane catalogs of virtues. The series, however, is enveloped by the biblical concepts *faith* and *love*, and is modified thereby in its entirety. Then too, the terms *probity* and *brotherly love* are as Christian as their biblical-eschatological observance. Faith is seen as the basic attitude of Christian morality, love as

its fulfillment. The "virtue" referred to in the series is not virtuous-
ness in general, but one virtue among others, perhaps moral strength.
According to the context, virtue is not only personal achievement, but
gift of God as well. The end in view is to be fruitful in the knowledge of Jesus Christ (1:8).

Although the concept of virtue as moral conduct and probity is certainly important in the New Testament, the word "virtue" rarely
occurs therein. There must be a reason for this. Perhaps it found the
word too anthropocentric and too prone to the suggestion of human
achievement and human merit. The New Testament allows no pride
or self-glorying in virtue.

The Bible already attempts a simple and systematic ordering of
morality. This is evident in the catalogs of virtues and vices, as well
as in the tables of duties to one's neighbor.

The oldest biblical catalogs of virtues and vices are listings which
are extant in various settings. For the decalogue there is Exod. 20:2-17
and Deut. 5:6-21; and further catalogs are adduced in Exod. 23:1-19;
Lev. 19:2-37; Deut. 27:15-26. The primitive character of these catalogs,
and especially of the decalogue, shows itself in the fact that they adduce concrete lapses and individual deeds. A long path of ethical reflection still lay ahead before such lists could be so constructed as to
deal directly with dispositions. Even a penetrating criticism of society, its activities and its vices, is to be found in later catalogs.

There is a very early and highly exalted catalog of virtues in Is. 11:2:
"There rests on him the spirit of God, the spirit of wisdom and understanding, the spirit of counsel and of might, the spirit of knowledge
and of the fear of God." The spiritual powers are closely distinguished, and all are described as gifts of God. The Wisdom literature
provides further catalogs. It knows the four cardinal virtues, first set
down in order by Plato and afterwards frequently enumerated by the
Stoics: prudence, temperance, justice, and fortitude. They are not,
however, to be understood as virtues self-acquired, but as gifts of God
(Wis. 8:4-7). A list of vices is adduced in Wis. 14:22-29. The insights
of Greek ethics are collected in such catalogs. They are the common
property of paraenetic tradition. In addition, the Qumran scrolls (1
QS 4:2-11) furnish a grand double catalog of virtues and vices, which

are attributed to good and bad spirits. Here we have a distillate of Jewish tradition.

The numerous New Testament catalogs of virtues (Gal. 5:22f.; Eph. 4:32–5:2; Col. 3:12-14; Phil. 4; 1 Tim. 4:12; 6:11; 2 Tim. 3:10; 1 Peter 3:8; 2 Peter 1:5-7) and vices (Rom. 1:29-31; 1 Cor. 6:9f.; 2 Cor. 12:20f.; Gal. 5:19-21; Eph. 5:3-5; Col. 3:5-8; 1 Tim. 1:9f.; 2 Tim. 3:2) are a product of the collectivity of these past collections. These New Testament catalogs are continued in the writings of the Fathers (*Didache*, 2 and 3; 5:1f.; Hermas' *Shepherd*, Mandate 8). The New Testament catalogs are in accord, in their general tenor and largely even in their particular terms, with prior traditions. In the older catalogs the Jewish influence seems to be stronger, whereas in the catalogs of the Pastoral Epistles it is the Greek influence which is dominant.

Since prior schemata are employed and set formulas are repeated in such catalogs, one cannot conclude from the texts themselves to concrete relationships in the community. The catalog of vices in Rom. 1:29-31 is certainly directed toward the pagans, whereas other fiercely censorious catalogs, like that in Gal. 5:19-21, are intended for Christians. In neither instance does Paul make a direct reflection upon particular siutations.

The New Testament is able to place a new emphasis upon the traditions it borrows. In the catalog of vices in Rom. 1:31, the pagans are called "loveless, merciless." [98] In pagan catalogs, nothing like this can be found. According to the Stoa, sympathy is a disease of the soul which man must conquer. The consideration that the worship of idols is the foundation of vices is biblical, Judaic (Wis. 14:27) as well as Christian (Rom. 1:25). In the catalog of Gal. 5:22f., virtues are designated as "fruits of the Spirit," and in Eph. 5:9, "fruits of the light." They are, therefore, not the product of human endeavor, but in either case they are ultimately effected by the Spirit and are a gift of God. Renewed according to the image of Christ, as "the elect of God, holy and beloved ones," Christians can and must have virtues as their own (Eph. 4:1f.; Col. 3:10-13).

In the New Testament catalogs of virtues there is emphasis, often through positioning them at the beginning or at the end, upon the Christians attitudes of faith (1 Tim. 4:12; 6:11; 2 Tim. 3:10; 2 Peter 1:5) and love (Gal. 5:22; Col. 3:14; 1 Tim. 4:12; 6:11; 2 Tim. 2:22;

3:10; 2 Peter 1:7). Concepts such as righteousness, joy, and peace, which can be found in Greek lists as well as in the New Testament catalogs, are given a new interpretation in the latter (see above, chs. 11 and 14).

Other listings are presented in the tables of duties to one's neighbor [99] (Eph. 5:22–6:9; Col. 3:18–4:1; 1 Tim. 2:8-15; 6:1f.; Titus 2:1-10; 1 Peter 2:13–3:7). And again these tables are continued in the Apostolic Fathers and other very early writings (*Epistle of Clement to the Corinthians*, 1:3; 21:6-9; Ignatius of Antioch, *Letter to Polycarp*, chs. 4 and 5; *Didache*, 4:9-11; *Letter of Barnabas*, 19:5-7). Inasmuch as these tables of duties to neighbor are descriptive of the ordering of domestic life and of one's familial relationship to the world around, they represent an attempt of the most basic sort toward a moral codification of the body of social duties.

The Old Testament provides no texts comparable to the tables of social duties, except perhaps Tob. 4:3-21 and Sir. 7:18-35. These Scriptures, however, belong to Hellenistic Judaism, a fact which points out the origin of the schematizing of duties to neighbor, namely, in the Greco-Roman ethics popular at that time. Examples are found in Epictetus (*Diss.*, 2, 14, 8; 2, 17, 31), Seneca (*Letters*, 94, 1), and others. It is after such examples that the serial form of admonitions is shaped. With some modifications and variations, duties are set down in respect to gods, country, parents, brothers, wife and children, relatives, household, and slaves. The sphere of obligations is at first related quite broadly, and later becomes somewhat narrower.

The New Testament borrows this sort of schema, probably through the intermediary of Hellenistic-Judaism. Examples indicative of this are Philo, *Decalog*, 165–167, and Josephus, *Against Apion*, 198–210. But what the New Testament borrowed it also changed. The cult of the gods, which stands at the head of the pagan tables, is lacking in the Christian catalogs. Divine worship is not a citizen's civil duty but a grace. Probably the oldest catalog of the New Testament is Col. 3:18–4:1. The Christian character of the table of duties is recognizable only by the observation repeatedly interjected, "in the Lord" (Col. 3:18, 20, 22-25; 4:1). In the Letter to the Ephesians (5:22–6:9) dependent thereupon, the relationship of the marriage partners is presented as a relationship of Christ with his Church. An allusion to Scripture is also subjoined (Eph. 5:31; 6:2f.). In the Pastoral Epistles, and to some extent in the Apostolic Fathers, the tables of duties to neighbor become intimately ecclesiastical, being directed toward the ordering of the congregation.

As with the catalogs of virtues and vices, so too with the tables of duties, it must be remembered that they are stylized literary products, and it is therefore a question as to how far concrete relationships and needs of the congregation are actually expressed therein. The tables of duties make it clear that in his social activities and relationships the Christian has to preserve his obedience to Christ the Lord. With that in mind, certainly the individual social relationships are not to be regarded as valid irrespective of time (for example, obviously not the establishment of slavery, and not even the subservience of a wife to her husband). With a changing milieu, obligations also change. But the command to live a Christian existence in one's relationship to the world remains always the same.

§ 18. DIVINE WORSHIP AND PRAYER

If the concrete reality of the New Testament morality is to be applied to individual moral subjects and areas of life, then it is only with some reservations that the worship of God can be so described and treated as first in a series with the other areas.[100] In other instances it is a question of human behavior in an area which pertains to this present life, such as property or marriage or government. These are relationships in which man is placed, in which it is unalterably necessary that he live, and with which he must come to terms. They are subjects or areas of which it is incontestably and indisputably necessary that they be set in order, and the rationality of which can be shown and made perceptible.

It is otherwise with the subject of the worship of God, understood as the way in which faithfulness is expressed externally and especially in association with others. The tangible substance of its arrangements — this, of course, belongs to the present life, in the same way that prayer and cult pertain to this life. At the same time, however, its existence in this present life receives its rationality only from God's existence beyond this life, which cannot itself be demonstrated but can only be believed. Probably, then, one can speak of the obligation of divine service, just as one speaks of the obligation of righteousness and truthfulness. On the other hand, is the service of God an obligation, or is it, at least as the Bible conceives it, a vocation and a grace? According to the New Testament, the worship of God is not a virtue dependent simply upon the good will of man; rather, it in fact becomes possible only when access to the Father has been opened by Christ.

For Israel there is basically no question of the possibility and law of prayer. The community of the people places itself in the presence of God in ritual worship with sacrifice and prayer. The pious person always has access to God in prayer. Cult is praise and acknowledgement, thanksgiving and petition, sorrow and repentance. Prayer frequently takes also the form of petition, as with the prophets on behalf of the people (Exod. 32:20-32; Amos 7:2-6; Is. 63:7–64:12; Jer. 14:7-9; 42:1-4), as well as of the individual petitioner (Pss. 60; 79; 85).

The petition for forgiveness is deepened and intensified by late Judaism's oppressive consciousness of guilt (Esdr. 9:6-15; Neh. 9:1-37; *Psalms of Solomon*, 9; *Eighteen Benedictions*, 5f.). Israel's petition for messianic salvation grows ever more earnest (*Psalms of Solomon*, 11; 17; 18; *Eighteen Benedictions*, 10f.). The Qumran scrolls contain, especially in the *Hodayoth* (1 QH), a grand treasury of meditation and prayer.[101]

The influences surrounding Israel were many and varied. Any earnest sense of prayer was long since lost to Greek culture. The old religion had become merely a mythology. Pantheistic and Skeptic philosophy contested the possibility of prayer and dissolved it in analysis. Prayer was ridiculed in literature.[102] In the mystery religions there were still some small communities that assembled in quest of union with the godhead. If this should be attained, prayer would no longer be necessary. Often, however, magical practices were substituted for prayer.

Something of the service of pagan gods can be seen also in the mirror of the New Testament. A remark of the Lord relates: "They make use of an empty babble and multiply words" (Matthew 6:7). The lengthy prayers of the pagans are well-known through texts and formularies, litanies and hymns. They attempt to "tire out the gods" (Horace, *Odes*, 1, 2, 26). The worship of pagan deities is known in Israel not only from the narrative of the Old Testament (1 Kings 18:21-29), but also from actual contact with it. Throughout the Jewish countryside there were grand pagan temples with their own priest-hoods, rituals, and feasts (as in Samaria and Caesarea). Beside these, Israel's prayer is comparatively free of feigned pathos, pomposity, and even intellectual mysticism.

The New Testament presupposes the order and demeanor of the Old Testament, and for the most part it lives basically within the framework thereof. This is true even of Jesus. He belongs to a people who prayed earnestly and much. Jesus will have observed the daily periods of prayer, with the confession: "Hear, O Israel . . ." (Mark 12:29f.). As a pious Israelite, he blessed his food with a prayer of thanksgiving (Mark 6:41; 14:22); and he taught his disciples to pray for their daily bread (Matthew 6:11). He requires of his disciples that they pray always (Luke 18:1). Jesus participates in the celebration of ritual regulations (Luke 4:15f.), and he speaks of the temple in terms of great reverence (Matthew 5:23f.; 23:17f.). As the Son, Jesus lingers in prayer with the Father (Mark 1:35; 6:46-48; 14:32-43), and testifies to this unity in an acclamation of joy (Matthew 11:25f.). If Luke (3:21; 5:16; 6:12; 9:18, 28; 22:32), in the manner of redactional notes, constantly inserts the motif of the praying Lord, the community of disciples too is constantly mindful of the praying of Jesus.

Jesus penetrates to the inner and true sense of divine service and prayer. The Sabbath ought to be a joy and blessing for man. It must, therefore, be permissible for the hungry disciples to pluck the ears of grain on the Sabbath (Mark 2:27); and it must be permitted to heal on the Sabbath (Mark 3:4). Sacrifice is offered to God, who is merciful and kind. But he wants mercy and not sacrifice (Hos. 6:6 = Matthew 9:13; 12:7). A sacrificial offering to God is not possible if love of neighbor is not practiced. Whoever lives at odds with his brother cannot be at peace with God (Matthew 5:23f.). Without the sacrifices demanded by love of neighbor there can be no sacrifice to God (Mark 7:11).

Jesus warns about the perversion of prayer. Prayer is conversation with God alone. It is hypocrisy, therefore, if one makes a great display of his prayer before men and in the synagogue and on the streets (Matthew 6:5f.). In the parable of the Pharisee and the publican in the temple (Luke 18:9-14), the Pharisee prays in vain, while the publican experiences justification. The Pharisee's wrong consists in his belief that he lacks nothing. The situation of the publican, or tax-collector, however, is truly desperate. His occupation is at once his life and his guilt. If he is to repent, he will have to surrender his existence; indeed, more than that, he will have to make good his past injustices. He is truly a sinner, not a righteous man and smug. He knows he has nothing and stands in need of all. It is in view of this insight that the righteousness of God is given him.

The Christ of John's Gospel requires that the Father be worshiped "in Spirit and truth" (John 4:23). Worship of God in the Spirit is not to be understood as some kind of internal, spiritual worship of God, in contrast to religion with material sacrifices or determined modes of ritual; nor is it to be taken in the sense of the spiritual worship of God already announced by the prophets (Is. 66:1; Ps. 50:8) as superior to ritual and cult. Truth does not mean philosophically purified recognition of God or a religion which consists in submission to truth. None of this constitutes the new hour, now definite, of which Christ speaks (John 4:23). The Spirit here named is the operative Spirit of God (John 3:34; 7:39). The truth spoken of is, as generally in John's Gospel, the revelation of God in Christ (John 14:6; 17:17). The "true worshipers" are those who are conceived of Spirit and truth (John 3:5) and are sanctified therein (John 17:19). This worship takes place in the broad communion of the Father. It takes place as prayer "in the name of Jesus" (John 14:13f.; 15:16; 16:23, 26) in the union with the Son.

Jesus teaches his disciples to pray. In a manifold tradition (Matthew 6:9-13; Luke 11:2-4; *Didache*, 8:3) the ancient Church traces the formal prayer, "Our Father . . ." to the direct instruction of Jesus. The differences in its tradition point to the fact that this prayer was a formal prayer of the community, but not at the same time a prayer solidified into mere formula. The shorter Lucan form is the earlier, although some of the individual words of the prayer may find their original form in Matthew. In the prayer as given in Matthew, we can distinguish seven petitions, among which the first three and perhaps also the last two are in reference to the coming of the kingdom of God. God's majesty is an area of great concern to the petitioner. In the fourth petition, asking for bread, the very life of the disciple is confided each day to God. The bread for which man labors is, at the same time, a gift of God. Man's concerns and needs find expression in the prayer through the repetition of the words *us* and *our*. The whole prayer revolves about its opening address, "Our Father," which expression, being Jesus' concept of God, sums up the gospel. Time and eternity are in the hand of God.

Certainly the gospel is aware of the notion and the possibility of the prayer of petition. Jesus teaches us to pray for "good gifts" (Matthew 7:11). Prayer conquers demons (Mark 9:29). The prayer that "the Lord of the harvest might send laborers into his harvest" (Luke 10:2) is concerned with the future of the disciples as a group. The disciples are to pray "that they might not enter into temptation" (Luke 22:40). But prayer may even be offered in respect to such commonplace matters as that our flight from the enemy "might not take place in the wintertime, or on the Sabbath" (Matthew 24:20).

In fact, the promise is made in respect to prayer: "All that you ask for, believe that you have received it, and it will be done for you" (Mark 11:24). Faith alone, then, suffices for a favorable response to prayer if the petitioner prays with such a certainty as if he had already received his request. The saying of Mark 11:24 appears in the ecclesial arrangements of Matthew's Gospel (18:19f.), where it is related to the community. What the disciples ask for in communion with each other, the Father will grant. The center of this communion, however, is Christ. Does all this perhaps suggest that the communion of prayer excludes any self-seeking in its petitions?

Imaginative examples (Matthew 7:9-11) and parables (of the friend who listens, Luke 11:5-8; of the unjust judge, Luke 18:2-8) state that if even men respond to a petition, how much more will the heavenly Father grant the requests of his petitioning children! While, according to Matthew 7:11, God gives "good things" to those who ask, Luke 11:13 says that God gives the "Holy Spirit." Is it possible that Luke formulates it in this fashion to indicate that prayer does not receive external good things, but the internal gift of salvation? In the explanatory saying concluding the parable of the unjust judge, the answering of prayer seems to be transferred from the area of present experience to the eschatological day.[103]

At the transition from the Gospels to the Church and theology of the Apostles, we must consider that basically there was no longer any autonomous ritual in the Church. The Church was aware of herself as the true Israel, and she possessed a hope and a confidence that all Israel would recognize Jesus as the Christ. The community of disciples at first participated in the temple service of Israel (Acts 2:46). The separation was soon forced, however, by Israel's rejection of the gospel. The Church separated herself from the divine service of Israel, into her own proper conventicles (Acts 2:42, 46).

And soon enough the separation was given a theological basis. The theology of the Passion announced Jesus as the true sacrifice, abrogating the continual sacrifice in the temple. Christ is himself the paschal Lamb (1 Cor. 5:7) and the one sacrificial Lamb who takes away the sins of the world (John 1:29). Christ is the world's atonement (2 Cor. 5:19); therefore all expiatory rites and sacrifices are abrogated. Christ is the true High Priest. His priesthood abrogates every former priesthood and sacrifice, and suffices for all time (Heb. 9:11-28). In the Church, there can continue to be ritual worship only as a representation of the salvational work and ritual worship of Christ, in accord with the commission of the Lord: "Do this for a remembrance of me" (1 Cor. 11:25). It is in this sense that all the declarations on the Church's ritual worship are to be understood.

The Acts of the Apostles speaks often of the prayer and worship of the New Testament Church. Divine service is undertaken with the preaching of the Apostles (Acts 2:42; 5:42; 20:7), the celebration of baptism (Acts 2:41; 10:47f.) and of the Eucharistic Meal (Acts 2:46; 20:11), and even with the laying on of hands calling one to an official status (Acts 8:17; 13:3; 14:23). Divine service is always accompanied by prayer (Acts 4:24-31; 12:12). The leading of the congregation in prayer is a part of the special service of the Apostles, who are to persevere "in prayer and in the service of the world" (Acts 6:4). Like Jesus himself in the Gospel of Luke (see above), so too the Church of the Acts of the Apostles make its every decision in prayer (1:14, 24f.; 6:6; 9:11; 10:9; 12:5; 13:3; 27:35; 28:15).

And again like the Gospels (see above), Acts too tells of the collision with pagan ways. The pagans have a superficial belief in the appearance and interjection of divine powers among men, which, for the Christians, is idolatry (Acts 14:12-18; 28:6). The cult of Artemis in Ephesus is an example of the operation of pagan religion, with pilgrimage, pomp, and publicity (Acts 19:24-40). In contrast to this is Paul's sermon on the Areopagus, wherein he posits that God is not confined in holy places and temples, nor does he have any need for the services of men. It is he who imparts life and breath to all (Acts 17:24f.).

Other witnesses to the prayer and worship of the most ancient Church are the hymns to Christ which are found in the letters of the Apostles (Phil. 2:6-11; Col. 1:15-20; 1 Tim. 3:16). The liturgy depicted in the Apocalypse (4:8-11; 5:8-14; 7:9-12; 11:15-17; 15:3f.; 19:1-8) is presented by John probably while calling to mind that liturgy in which he himself had participated in the Jewish or Christian community.

The letters of Paul contain a great deal of further information and testimony about prayer and divine service. Paul too has to contend with perverted religious sentiments. The true worship of God has nothing in common with the orgy. In issuing his warnings, Paul calls Old Testament history to mind. At one time Israel participated in the orgiastic cult of Baal with her pagan neighbors. "They ate and drank and then rose up to play. And there fell in one day twenty-three thousand" (1 Cor. 10:7-9). Paul presses forward toward an understanding of ritual festivities. The Epistle to the Galatians (4:10), as well as that to the Colossians (2:16), confutes false teachers, who demand of Christians that they observe the Jewish feastdays. This, Paul says, would mean being bowed beneath the elements of the world. Modern methods of investigating the history of religion confirm this, inasmuch as they affirm that certain days are holy (taboo) and must be accompanied by awesome rites, because they are regarded as being in close union with cosmic processes.

Divine worship must be conducted in sobriety, purity, and truth. Paul holds visions and enraptured speech in esteem. But he knows too that these phenomena can be experienced outside the community (1 Cor. 12:2), and for that reason he warns about overestimating them. "I would rather speak five words in the Church with understanding than a thousand words in rapture" (1 Cor. 14:19). The criterion of the genuineness of enthusiasm is the edification of the community (1 Cor. 12:7) in the service of love (1 Cor. 13:1). Atonement and sacrifice have a new basis, a new reason. It is not their function, like that of idolatry, to appease an angry God or to win his favor. God's mercy has already been dispensed. The Church has experienced it abundantly. God has himself established atonement and its service; it but remains for faith to accept it (2 Cor. 5:18-21).

Worship takes on a deeper significance in respect to morality when we recall that its reason and import is to be achieved in the personal and moral life. If baptism means dying and rising again with Christ, then it is true, too, that to realize the sacrament in one's moral life is to die to sin and to live to God (Rom. 6:11). The one Spirit effects the one baptism. The one community must not be torn asunder by schism (1 Cor. 12:13). The communion of the Lord's Supper is a pledge to keep oneself apart from strange gods and to belong exclusively to the Lord (1 Cor. 10:16-22). The sacramental Body of the Lord signifies also the one body of the Church. The communion of brotherly love must not be damaged or destroyed by factionalism (1 Cor. 11:17-34).[104]

Divine service, then, like cult, is word and confession. These things, however, are enjoined upon all. All are obligated thereby, and all must assist in mutual edification of each other. "When you come together, each one has a psalm, a lesson, a revelation, a tongue, an interpretation. Let all be done for edification" (1 Cor. 14:26). Each one must serve the mission and the proclamation: "If all speak in prophecy, and an unbeliever or an unsanctified person come in, he will be convicted by all, by all will he be called to account. The secrets of his heart will be disclosed. He will fall on his face, worship God, and acknowledge that truly God is in your midst" (1 Cor. 14:24-25). The whole priestly community has the right and duty of proclamation. For the Church, divine worship is of fundamental importance. The Epistle to the Hebrews has an admonition in this regard, as if zeal for divine worship is already flagging: "We would that our assemblies were not neglected, as is the habit of many, but that they should be much more an encouragement to each other" (Heb. 10:25).

Such admonitions are continued in the subsequent writings of the era of the ancient Church. Among the traditions and testimonies of the primitive Church, there is Ignatius' description of the importance and power of worship: "Be zealous, and gather together more frequently for God's Eucharist and for giving praise. For when you assemble together frequently, the powers of Satan are brought to nought, and his destructive force is itself destroyed in the unity of your faith" (*To the Ephesians*, 13:1).

Ultimately the whole life of the Christian is cult. "I appeal to you, brethren, by the mercy of God, to present your bodies as a living sacrifice, holy and pleasing to God, as your logical worship of God" (Rom. 12:1). In every religion, *sacrifice* is primeval — both the term and the fact. The gospel does not release; rather, it fulfills. No relationship with God can be entered into without sacrifice as an earnest to make it binding. But the sacrifice has become something new, since the sacrifical object is new. It is not an item of his possession that man gives, but his own body, his life, his very self, in an action determined by obedience. Sacrifice means and demands that one's whole life be an existence for God. "The body is for the Lord and the Lord for the body" (1 Cor. 6:13).[105]

For the Apostle Paul, prayer is an ever-enduring reality. He himself prays always (Rom. 1:9; 1 Thess. 1:2). He admonishes the Church to pray likewise: "Be constant in prayer" (Rom. 12:12). "Pray without cease. Give thanks for everything. Such is the will of God in Christ Jesus, in your regard" (1 Thess. 5:17-18; Col. 4:2). Christian living must be constant prayer and thanksgiving. Paul begins each of his letters by shaping the traditional formula of greeting into a prayer for the grace and peace of the Father and of the Lord, and he concludes each letter with a prayerful blessing. His letters are interwoven with prayer throughout. His prayers are frequently a few words in praise and thanksgiving for the call (Rom. 6:17; 1 Cor. 1:4); for God's grace working in the community (Phil. 1:3-6); for the success of the work in the mission (2 Cor. 2:15); and for practical, active love in the community (2 Cor. 9:8-15).

Paul's prayer is in the manner of a petition on behalf of the community (Rom. 15:5f.; 2 Cor. 13:7; Eph. 1:17; Col. 1:9-12; 1 Thess. 3:12), and at the same time he asks the community to pray for him and for his service to the gospel (Rom. 15:30; 2 Cor. 1:11; Eph. 6:18f.; Col. 4:3; 1 Thess. 5:25; 2 Thess. 3:1). The Church must offer prayers of intercession for kings and all in authority, and in fact, for all men (1 Tim. 2:1f.). Indeed, the petitioner must "with thanksgiving, let all his cares and desires be known to God" (Phil. 4:6). If it is to be done "with thanksgiving," it is because from the very outset there is confidence of being heard.

In 2 Cor. 12:6-10, Paul speaks of a special prayer. He bears a thorn in his flesh. An angel of Satan beats him with his fists. Three times he besought the Lord that this might be taken away from him. The Apostle's prayerful request would seem to have been that the inadequacy of his corporal constitution might not weigh upon him too heavily and hinder his missionary activities. He recalls distinctly that he besought the Lord three times for his release. The answer he received: "My grace is sufficient for you." And Paul accepted it: "Now I will boast much more of my weaknesses. . . . For when I am weak, then am I strong."

The New Testament too must occupy itself with the problems to which reflection on prayer always give rise. There are problems about the possibility of prayer and of prayer's being answered. Perhaps there are intimations of this already in the later telling of the gospel (Luke 11:13; 18:8; see above, in the present chapter). In a manner comparable to that of John (4:23), Paul says that prayer must be offered in the Spirit. Christians are sons of God. God has sent the Spirit of sonship into their hearts, so that now they can address God as sons address a father, with the cry: "Abba! Father!" (Gal 4:6).

Of ourselves we do not know what we should pray for, nor what is fitting, in consideration of God's holiness, power, and love. Man cannot of himself either find or set out upon his pathway to the other world. Nevertheless, man's praying is not a senseless undertaking which never arrives at a goal. Prayer is a mysterious activity taking place between God and man. For God is himself considerate of man's incapacities. The divine Spirit given to us, who comes from that other world to which all our praying and sighing is directed, takes up our petition and pleads its cause before God. He purifies it, so that it will be a seemly and worshipful prayer. In this way, what is presented to God is not a foolish human wish, but a true and ardent supplication, such as we ourselves cannot understand. This is true prayer, which the Spirit utters in words inexpressible (Rom. 8:26).

Further Apostolic admonitions return again and again to this true prayer in the Spirit (Eph. 6:18; 1 Peter 2:5; Jude 20). Ultimately, faith has the certainty that God, "in virtue of the power at work within us, is able to do far more abundantly than all that we ask or think" (Eph. 3:20). The immeasurable grandeur and majesty of God is effective, in those who believe, "in accord with his power and might" (Eph. 1:19). This actively present redemption which God effects is the fulfillment of prayer beyond our wildest imagination.

Other later texts of the New Testament seem to reflect experiences of prayer. The enthusiastic assurance that every prayer is answered (Matthew 7:7; Mark 11:24; see above, in the present chapter) no longer finds expression. The Church has the privilege and possibility of "frank and open speech (παρρησία) before God, if our hearts do not condemn us"; and we will receive everything that we ask for "because we keep his commandments and do what is pleasing to him" (1 John 3:21-22). Sin upsets prayer. Obedience to God's commandments is prerequisite for the effectiveness of prayer. To be sure, 1 John 5:14f. is comparable to Mark 11:24, inasmuch as it says that we know that the Son of God hears us, whatever be our prayer, and that knowing this, when the petitioner prays, his requests are even then as good as granted; nevertheless, favorable response is in this place made contingent upon our asking "in accord with his will."

The Epistle of James treats over and over again of prayer. First of all, it says: "God gives to all men generously and without reservation." Therefore, whoever asks will receive (James 1:5f.). This text is reminiscent of a saying of the Lord (Matthew 7:7; Mark 11:24). As in similar cases in the Epistle of James, exegesis is divided on the question of whether the Epistle is itself dependent upon the saying of the Lord, or whether both are derived independently of each other from Jewish-Christian epigrammatic Wisdom literature. Nevertheless, if God gives graciously, it must be the fault of the petitioner when prayer is not answered. Some qualifications are indicated already in James 1:5: "If anyone lacks wisdom, then he should ask." Prayer ought to be offered in reference to spiritual goods. And prayer must be offered "in faith and without the slightest doubt" (just as also in the Synoptic logia, faith is certainly demanded as a prerequisite for effective prayer, e.g., Matthew 21:21f.; Luke 17:5f.).

There is a severe reproach in James 4:2-3; "You do not have, because you do not pray; you pray, but you do not receive, because you pray with a wicked end in view, so that you might squander it on your passions." The first declaration, that Christians are not praying, is very harsh. But then the letter itself tempers this somewhat, and freely admits that they do pray, and that it is addressed to those who pray in vain, because they pray badly and unworthily, asking for things which would but serve their selfish desires. These are bitter words for a primitive Christian congregation. In such passages of the Epistle of James we can probably assume that the letter simply repeats customary admonitory reproaches and does not base its condemnatory remarks upon the actual condition of the community.

A further instruction on prayer is given in James 5:14-17. The prayer of the "elders of the Church," and of anyone for anyone, effects health of body and remission of sins — the welfare, therefore, of the whole man. There would seem to be an intimation of reservations in such phrases as "the prayer of faith" and "the powerful prayer of the righteous." An example is given — the prayer of the prophet Elijah. No promise of being heard attaches to the mere recitation of words, nor to the prayer offered by a man in sin.

Prayer is a practice of every religion. Nevertheless, in the name of philosophical reflection and even in the name of ostensibly genuine religion, questions are asked of the religions and of prayer which are certainly not easy to answer. It will be recognized that a prayer of praise is significant, provided that God is, for man, a personal "thou." Nevertheless, questions such as these are asked: Is man able to influence the decisions of God with his prayer? Is it not incredibly egotistical to want God to decide in our petty personal interests? Is it not obvious that experience itself often militates against the effectiveness of intercessory prayer.

It will not be enough simply to counter this with the insistence that faith is aware that it has a right to pray, which right it dare not relinquish. Indeed, man's religious will can err. It is this will that has built for itself systems of idolatry. Prayer of petition has its biblical and Christian justification in the example and words of Jesus and the

Apostles. This, in fact, is the solitary basis of its justification. The fact
that the prayer of the Christian community has its basis and justification in Christ finds profound and beautiful expression in its reception
of the word with which Jesus addressed God, and the use of which he
imparts to his disciples and enjoins upon them: "Abba Father!" (Matthew 6:9; Rom. 8:15; Gal. 4:6; 1 Peter 1:17).[106] Ultimately the same
thing is stated when it is said that prayer is to be offered "in the name
of the Lord Jesus Christ" (John 14:13f.; Eph. 5:20; James 5:14).

In the whole Bible, Old and New Testament, faith makes its presence known in prayer and in the visible worship of God. Not until
their later periods, however, does either the Old or the New Testament have at its disposal a term to characterize the practice and special virtue of piety. We refer to the word εὐσέβεια [107] and its various
forms. It may be taken as indicative that in the whole of the Scriptures the service of God is not just a particular obligation among
others, but it is a basic attitude of man which must be operative in
every aspect of life.

The word and concept εὐσέβεια are found in Greek literature from
earliest times. In the Hellenistic period the word is frequently found
in inscriptions detailing the virtues of a personage to be publicly honored. It indicates as much the fulfillment of particular ritual obligations as a general attitude of pious and reverential awe in respect to
the gods and the divine order. The word εὐσέβεια appears also though
sparingly, in the Greek translation of the Old Testament (Is. 11:2;
33:6; Sir. 49:3; Prov. 1:7), usually in the form εὐσεβής. In the Fourth
Book of Maccabees, written in the New Testament era, the form
εὐσέβεια occurs forty-seven times; and it is used frequently in Josephus
and in Judaeo-Greek literature.

In the New Testament the word εὐσεβής appears (except for Acts
3:12), strictly speaking, only in relation to the Greek world, as in
Acts 10:2, 7, where it describes the Roman centurion, and Acts 17:33,
describing the people of Athens; or in those later books of the New
Testament which are related in a special manner to Greek culture,
occurring ten times in the Pastoral Epistles and four times in 2 Peter.
Perhaps the emphasis which the word places upon human effort and
human morality is too much for biblical morality. Instead of piety, the
New Testament, and Paul especially, speaks of election and holiness as

the deed of God on man's behalf, to which man responds in faith and love.

What εὐσέβεια means in the Pastoral Epistles is expressed most clearly perhaps in 1 Tim. 3:16: "Great is the mystery of piety." The content of this mystery is disclosed dialectically in a hymn, probably pre-dating the Epistle itself. It is the revelation of God in Christ's becoming man and in his exaltation above peoples and angels. Here εὐσέβεια does not mean subjective piety but the salvation-history event. The words might perhaps be restated more clearly: "Great is the mystery of the Christian religion."

The concept of piety embraces faith and life collectively. The letters admonish Christians to "depend upon sound doctrine, which is in accord with piety" (1 Tim. 6:3). The "knowledge of truth is grounded in piety" (Titus 1:1). False teachers "have only the appearance of piety, while denying its power" (2 Tim. 3:5). Such enemies "make of piety a means of gain" (1 Tim. 6:5). Christians ought to be able "to lead a quiet and peaceful life in perfect piety and respectability" (1 Tim. 2:2). Piety is the life which is pleasing to God and man. Timothy is admonished: "Train yourself in piety" (1 Tim. 4:7). "Strive after righteousness, piety, faith . . ." (1 Tim. 6:11). Although piety is originally a Greek concept, here it is determined by the two biblical terms, "righteousness and faith." Children and grandchildren of widows should learn first of all to be "pious" toward their families (1 Tim. 5:4).

Christianity can be described thus: "God's saving grace has appeared and guides us onward, to renounce godlessness and worldly passions, and to live sober, upright, pious lives" (Titus 2:12). Virtue is not the work of one's own strength, but is made possible by the grace of God. To be sure, piety must expect to suffer: "All who desire to lead a pious life in Christ Jesus will be persecuted" (2 Tim. 3:12). But still the letter is firm in the conviction that "corporal training [which probably means bodily chastisement such as a dualistic gnostic philosophy might demand] is of lesser value. Piety, however, is of value in every way. It holds promise for the present life and for the life to come" (1 Tim. 4:8).

In the Pastoral Epistles, then, piety, or εὐσέβεια, means the doctrine of faith, and a manner of living proceeding from faith and determined by faith. If the term still has something of an old ring of the

Hellenistic teaching on virtue, it now has at the same time its measure and basis in the commandment and grace of God, the Creator and Redeemer. The false piety which is rejected (2 Tim. 3:5) is probably a form of gnosticism, an enthusiastic morality exposed as indifferent, and, in the judgment of the letter, orderliness set to nought.

In 2 Peter the word εὐσέβεια and its forms occur four times. All things that pertain "to life and piety" have been bestowed by God (2 Peter 1:3). A catalog of virtues enumerates "knowledge, self-control, patience, piety, brotherliness, love" (2 Peter 1:6-7). The series mentions terms and concepts familiar to popular Greek philosophical ethics, just as they are found in profane catalogs; and along with them there are also biblical Christian terms, such as *patience, brotherliness,* and *love.* In eschatological expectation, Christians must "live in a holy manner and in piety" (2 Peter 3:11). The history of the rescuing of righteous persons in the Old Testament teaches us that God "knows how to rescue the pious from their trials" (2 Peter 2:9). In the total context of 2 Peter, piety is the hallmark of the Christian life, as compared to the lawlessness and erroneous teachings of the gnosticism which the letter opposes.

According to the visions of the Apocalypse of John, there is no temple to be found in the heavenly city: "I saw no temple in it; for the Lord, God the Almighty, is its temple, and the Lamb" (Apoc. 21:22). In the eschatological fulfillment, when all creation will have returned to God's love, special edifices for the worship of God will be unnecessary. But until then, special times and places for the worshiping of God are necessary. They are not an expression of God's nearness, but of the estrangement of the world from God.

§ 19. LIFE

1. THE GIFT OF LIFE

It is perfectly clear to man, and beyond question, that he cannot give life to himself.[108] Life is imparted to him; and in the understanding of religion, it is termed a divine gift. The proposition can be taken either mythically or, at the same time, historically, in the sense that the Godhead imparts life to man in an act of creation; or it can be taken philosophically, in the sense that world and man participate in the divine life which abides in everything.

The Greek, in accord with his mentality, encounters and grasps life spontaneously in the reality and fullness of nature. The occasion and conveyor of life is a vital power, often termed ψυχὴ = soul. Later the principle of life is frequently differentiated, life with its natural processes on the one hand, and its spiritual capabilities (νοῦς or λόγος) on the other. The latter in turn undergoes a development, deep and far-reaching, until at last in Platonic philosophy it is understood as a divine element in man. It is indestructible and immortal. The religious awareness of late antiquity regards the divine life, in which man participates through a sharing in immortality, as the true life. Gnosticism seeks to teach and make known the way by which the soul may be admitted to the eternal life from which it came forth.

His own impotence is, for the biblical man, evidence enough that God is the One who lives, he who lives forever (Deut. 32:40; Josh. 3:10; Dan. 12:7; Sir. 18:1). Himself being the fullness of life, it is he that gives life. In the Yahwist creation narrative, God's breath makes man a living being, like unto God (Gen. 2:7). Nor is this simply the historical recital of a single, solitary act of creating. It purports that God is ever the source of all life (see the present work, Vol. 1, pp. 83–89). He is Lord over life and death (Num. 27:16; Deut. 32:39; Ps. 104:29f.; Job 12:10). Man's life is dependent upon him (Deut. 8:3). God is the fountain of life (Ps. 36:10; Jer. 2:13; 17:13). Should God take back the breath of life, man would collapse into dust (Ps. 104:29f.; Job 24:14f.). God grants life to his people (Deut. 30:19f.; 32:6, 47). To those who obey God, there is the promise of blessing, fortune, and life; but to the disobedient, a curse, misfortune, and death (Deut. 30:15, 19).

The present life is promised to the righteous (Ez. 18:5-9, 21-25). Fidelity to God's commandment and ordinance is a guarantee of a long and prosperous life (Gen. 15:15; Lev. 18:5; Deut. 5:16; Amos 5:6-14; Jer. 21:8; Prov. 3:1-2). To the Israelite, life, with all its good things, is a treasure (1 Kings 3:14; Job 2:4; Prov. 3:16). It is synonymous with health, well-being, and fortune (Ps. 56:14; Mal. 2:5; Eccl. 9:9). Sin diminishes and destroys life. Man, originally created immortal, loses life in consequence of sin (Gen. 2:17). Surely reality must often militate against the conviction that the pious man is here and now assured of life and good fortune.

A more perceptive interpretation recognizes that life, properly speaking, is in the association with God. "Your favor is better than life" (Ps. 63:3). Out of the ruination of death there arises the hope for an imperishable life with God (Pss. 16:10f.; 23; 26:8f.; 29:16; 73:24-28). This hope continues to become clearer and firmer right up to the expiration of the old covenant (Is. 25:8; 26:19-21; Dan. 12:2; 2 Macc. 7:9-29; Wis. 4:14; 5:15). The conviction is still more certain in the writings of Qumran. "The way to all life" proceeds from God (1 QH 15:22). The pious man gives thanks because even now "God has redeemed his life out of the pit and has caused him to be raised up from the hell of damnation unto the heights of eternity" (1 QH 3:19f.). The transition from death to life is already taking place (cf. John 5:24).

In Hellenistic Judaism the hope in eternal life comes under the influence of Greek philosophy and accepts the belief in the immortality of the soul (Wis. 8:19f.; *Psalms of Solomon*, 3:16; 4 Macc. 15:3).

The New Testament, too, says that man's life is vulnerable, not at his own disposal (Luke 12:20; 2 Cor. 1:9), and perishable (James 4:14). It is God only who, in the proper sense, is living (Matthew 16:16; 26:63; Acts 14:15; Rom. 9:26). "God alones possesses immortality and dwells in unapproachable light" (1 Tim. 6:16). All life comes from God (Acts 17:25, 28). He is Lord over life and death (Matthew 10:28f.). He causes things either to live or to die (Rom. 4:17). It is her that imparts life to all (1 Tim. 6:13). He is the judge of the living and the dead (1 Peter 4:5).

Present earthly life can be designated as a singular and priceless good (Mark 8:37). The messianic service of Jesus is devoted in large part to the restoration of healthy life. The power of the Christ is called upon to save the life that is threatened (Mark 5:25f.), and to restore it when lost (Luke 7:12; John 11:3). At the same time, the present earthly life is understood as but a preliminary. The natural man, in spite of all his evidences of life, is to be characterized as dead (Matthew 8:22; Luke 15:24; Eph. 5:14; Col. 2:13). The true life is dependent upon the word of God (Matthew 4:4 = Deut. 8:3). It is only that future life after death that can be termed, purely and simply, "life" (Matthew 7:14; Mark 9:43; 1 Peter 3:7). This is eternal life (Matthew 19:16; Rom. 1:17). If man cannot create even his natural life for himself, how much more, then, is it evident that he cannot create for himself this future life! But neither does man possess this life, as Greek philosophy teaches, as an immortality of the soul. Eternal life is an "inheritance," and as such it is never merited, but is always a gift (Mark 10:17). There is the gift of a future world (Mark 10:30). It will be realized in the resurrection of the dead (Mark 12:26f.). It is obedience to God's will that decides one's participation in that future life (Matthew 25:46). Whoever surrenders his life now will win eternal life (Matthew 16:25; John 12:25). This can take place in a bloody martyrdom or even in a daily bloodless martyrdom. God determines in advance who shall live (Acts 13:48).

The gospel, however, is now; it is now that future life is promised and is assured, in the death and resurrection of Christ. The paschal message about the life of Christ (Luke 24:5) is the proper message of salvation (Rom. 6:10; 14:9). In Christ is life (Rom. 8:2), and through his life we will be saved (Rom. 5:10). Like a new Adam, Christ has become the beginning of a new life of mankind (Rom. 5:12-17; 1 Cor. 15:20-22). He is the leader of life (Acts 3:15), and has brought to light the life which is imperishable (2 Tim. 1:10). The future life operates inwardly in the present. For the faithful it is present reality. We live in Christ (Rom. 6:11), as we will one day live with him (Rom. 2:7; 2 Cor. 13:4). If earthly life can be a daily dying, even in this the life of Christ is manifested (2 Cor. 4:11). "As dying, we live" (2 Cor. 6:9).

Present death and future life are inextricably interwoven (Rom. 8:2-11). Eternal life is still hidden in Christ (Col. 3:3), and yet it is already present (Eph. 2:5f.). Present and future life can be conceived of as a unit. Faith possesses "the promise of the present life and of the life to come" (1 Tim. 4:8). If the present life is already Christian living, then it must not be derogated or contemned as wicked or worthless, as is likely to be done in a dualist philosophy. Certainly it can be a source of temptation; nevertheless, "neither death nor life, neither angels nor powers, neither things present nor things yet to come, neither height nor depth, nor anything else in all creation can separate us from the love of God in Jesus Christ" (Rom. 8:38). Life can be a powerful force controverting what is divine, and the superior strength of the biologic can kill the spirit. The risk is such that Paul is able to say, in effect: "We live in the flesh. But life in the flesh must not become life according to the flesh" (2 Cor. 10:3).

The hope which is founded in Christ is the determining force of the present life. Now man must no longer live for himself; he must live for Christ, who died and rose again for all (2 Cor. 5:15). They who are redeemed by Christ must live for God (Rom. 6:11-13; 14:7f.; Gal. 2:19). They who have received the Spirit must walk in the Spirit (Gal. 5:25). He who, by faith, is just, will live (Rom. 1:17). Whoever believes, shares in the life of Christ, which knows no termination (Rom. 6:23).

Life is a promise made not merely to the individual; it aims at the conquest of death in general. Certainly death will prevail as the enemy up to the very end. But then it will finally be conquered (Rom. 6:22; 1 Cor. 15:26-28; Gal. 6:8).

The concept of life is important in Johannine theology. The Father possesses life, and gives it to the Son (John 5:26; 6:57). The pre-existing Christ was and is eternal life, with God and for men (John 1:4; 1 John 1:1f.; 5:11). Christ has a commission from the Father to dispense eternal life (John 12:50). He too, like the Father, gives life (John 5:21). His words are spirit and life (John 6:63, 69). He is "the light of life" (John 8:12), "the way, the truth, and the life" (John 14:6). He is the resurrection and the life (John 11:25). He is, and imparts, the Bread of life (John 6:35, 58). This true life is begotten of God (John 1:13; 1 John 2:29). Even now the transition from death to life already exists as the gift of God (John 5:24, 29). Whoever believes, possesses eternal life as the gift of God's love (John 3:16, 36; 20:31; 1 John 5:12). Life from God bears an "eternal future" within itself (John 4:14; 6:27).

2. Protection of Life

It is universal among men that human life is protected. Murder is a crime. This ordinance of natural law is found also in the decalogue: "Thou shalt do no murder" (Exod. 20:13; Lev. 24:17; Deut. 17:8-13).

Biblical morality draws forth from the belief in creation a precise and deeper basis for the prohibition against murder: "Whoever spills the blood of a man, the blood of such a one shall be spilled by man. For it is in God's image that man is made" (Gen. 9:6). Whoever raises his hand against a man, raises it against a work of God, — yes, against the image of God and therefore against God himself, who is the author of life and who, continuing as Lord and Father, exercises his control over all life. The first murder is experienced and portrayed as a horrible and sinister deed. The earth, the maternal basis of life, the most elementary foundation of existence, has drunk up a brother's blood. The earth denies to the murderer both home and fruitfulness. He becomes a homeless wanderer (Gen. 4:8-14).

The New Testament repeats several times the commandment of the decalogue: "Thou shalt do no murder" (Matthew 5:21; Mark 10:19; Rom. 13:9; James 2:11). The New Testament bears witness to its judgment in respect to murder when it speaks repeatedly of the assassination of Abel. Upon the generation which murders the Messiah and persecutes his congregation will come "all the righteous blood which has been shed upon the earth, from the blood of Abel the innocent, to the blood of Zechariah the son of Barachiah" (Matthew 23:35).

With Abel and Zechariah (2 Chr. 24:20f.), the gospel names the first and the last of those just men named in the writings of the Old Testament who were martyrs. Something of the horror over the first murder is re-echoed here. The blood that was spilled ravishes the earth. Blood and guilt accumulated and continued to accumulate. They remained and continued to remain unforgiven. The word of God in Gen. 4:10: "The voice of your brother's blood cries to me from the earth," is taken up again in Heb. 11:4: "Abel is still speaking, even though he died." From the blood of Abel a call issues forth to God's justice, until, in the consummated kingdom of God, Abel will be fully indemnified for his innocent death. Murder remains unforgiven on earth until the judgment; nevertheless, "the blood of the mediator of the new covenant, Jesus, speaks better than the blood of Abel" (Heb. 12:24), since it does not cry out for vengeance but flows unto forgiveness and effects purification.

Murder and its perpetrator are excluded from the community of disciples. Though this need hardly have been said, it is in fact several times expressly affirmed. The pagans, filled with every kind of wickedness, are full of murders as well (Rom. 1:29). Christians are warned that none of their number should ever have to appear in court and suffer punishment as a murderer (1 Peter 4:15). At the last judgment murderers will be excluded from the eternal kingdom of perfection and will be condemned to hell (Apoc. 21:8; 22:15).

If such a self-evident proposition has but little need of formal expresssion, it is nonetheless essential to New Testament morality; and an authoritative saying of the Lord now interprets the old prohibition of murder in the context of expectation of the kingdom: "You have heard that it was said to the men of old, 'Thou shalt not kill! And whoever kills shall be liable to judgment.' But I say to you, everyone who is angry with his brother shall be liable to judgment. Whoever says to his brother, 'You blockhead!' shall be liable to the Sanhedrin. And whoever says, 'You fool!' shall be liable to hellfire" (Matthew 5:21-22).

It is not only the ghastly deed of murder itself, then, that brings guilt upon a man, but even wicked intent and anger, which are at the root of the wicked deed. This pinpointing of the law extends the guilt even to the curses and imprecations that are uttered so frequently and so thoughtlessly. To call another man a "blockhead" is an impeachment of his rights in human society. To call him a fool (i.e., a godless person) is as much as to pronounce him excluded from the companionship of God. Wicked intent is no less subject to divine judgment than is murder consummated.

In conformity with the divine commandment, Paul warns his congregations against indulging in envy, strife, anger, and hatred. The pagans are full "of envy, murder, strife, deceit, and malice" (Rom. 1:29). These are "works of the flesh" (Gal. 5:19f.). The Christian community must be far removed from such sins as these: "Let every kind of bitterness, wrath, anger, unruliness, and slander be put away from you, with every wickedness. Be kind to one another, tenderhearted, and forgive each other, even as God has forgiven you in Christ" (Eph. 4:31; cf. Col. 3:8).

According to 1 Tim. 6:5, "envy, quarreling, slander, distrust, and especially contentiousness" are the product of false teaching; and according to 2 Tim. 3:1-5, hatred, calumny, and slander pertain to the disorders of the last days. In such admonitory passages as these, the Apostolic preaching on morality makes use of common catalogs of vices; and this being the case, it is not possible to conclude from such admonitions to the actual conditions prevailing in the congregation (see above, ch. 17). The old admonitions are given a new basis in reference to the Christ — who surrendered himself for the sake of all, whose example excludes all strife and exhorts to the service of others (Phil. 2:4f.) — as when they are turned to an affirmation of the unity of the Church, which can neither be interrupted nor destroyed (Eph. 4:31), and are summed up in general in the Christian commandment of love (Rom. 13:9f.).

The First Epistle of John attaches certain reflections and deductions to the history of the first murder. "We must not be like Cain, who was of the evil one and who slew his brother. And why did he slay him? Because his deeds were wicked, while those of his brother were righteous" (1 John 3:12). Murder and the murderer originate with the evil one (ὁ πονηρός), which, in 1 John 2:13f.; 5:18, being in the masculine singular, is a personification, and is to be understood as the devil. The murderer is of satanic descent. Murder is an inhuman act. In murder the depth of man's wickedness is plumbed. He kills because his deeds are wicked. The very core of the murderer's being is wickedness, pure and simple. The Epistle considers that love and hate portend the two spheres of life and death. Whoever loves has passed from the sphere of death to the sphere of life. "Whoever does not love remains in death. Everyone who hates his brother is a murderer of men" (1 John 3:14-15). Hatred is no different than murder. Just as in the saying of the Lord in Matthew 5:21, the intent and the consummated deed are equivalent. "No murderer of men possesses eternal life" (1 John 3:15). The axiom that the murderer forfeits his own life (Gen. 9:6) is effectively carried over to the spiritual, supernatural life.

3. QUALIFYING CIRCUMSTANCES

It must be considered whether there are apparent in the Bible, Old Testament and New, any qualifying circumstances which have a bear-

ing upon our modern ethics in regard to the ancient commandment
"Thou shalt do no murder."

a) Capital punishment.[109]

The Old Testament law decrees the death penalty for murder:
"Whoever spills the blood of a man, the blood of such a one shall be
spilled by men" (Gen. 9:6f.; Exod. 21:12; Lev. 24:17, 21; Num. 35:16-
21; Deut. 19:11f.). Even for certain other crimes the law attaches the
death penalty (idolatry, Sabbath-breaking, insulting of parents, sexual
transgressions). And probably in more ancient times the penalties
were actually carried out.

Capital punishment is no easy problem for our society. Certainly
the Old Testament law does not resolve the problem. It but demonstrates the breach of God's word in the cultural and temporal-historical context of the Old Testament. Neither will the New Testament
resources provide an immediate resolution of the problem; but still,
the New Testament must be heard. The narrative about Jesus and the
adulteress is of quite ancient tradition (John 7:53–8:11).[110] The Scribes
and Pharisees demand the stoning of a woman taken in adultery. Certainly at the time of the New Testament such a penalty was rarely,
if ever, exacted. Jesus confounds the zeal for punishment exhibited by
those men with an appeal to the individual conscience of each (John
8:7).[111]

In regard to the right of the civil government to legislate punishments, Paul says: "If you do wrong, then be afraid; for it is not in
vain that governmental authority bears the sword. Indeed, that authority is God's servant, the avenger of his wrath against the evildoer"
(Rom. 13:4). Paul's words are amazingly free of any reservation (see
below, ch. 26). Has the Apostle forgotten the unfairness and injustices
which he was obliged to bear, from the Jewish as well as from the
Roman authorities? (Acts 16:22; 2 Cor. 11:24). Does Paul not know
what Christ was made to suffer by the Roman government under
Pontius Pilate? Previously the Apostle had said: "Who will separate
us from the love of Christ? Shall tribulation or distress or persecution
or hunger or nakedness or peril or sword? Indeed, it is written, 'For
your sake we are struck down like sheep to be slaughtered'" (Rom.
8:35-36). The "sword" mentioned by Paul is the civil government's

sword of judgment. Does Paul have a premonition of what he can expect at the hands of the government?

The Apocalypse of John beholds a Babylon "drunk with the blood of the saints and with the blood of the martyrs of Jesus" (Apoc. 17:6). Already there are many in Rome and throughout the Empire who have become martyrs in the Church. Perhaps the Apocalypse is referring to the persecutions under Nero, or possibly even to those under Domitian. The New Testament recognizes that the civil government has a right to administer punishment. But what does the government make of this right? The cross of Christ, which presides over the New Testament, and the sword, which strikes the Church.

b) War.[112]

The problem of war does not allow of a direct solution from the Bible. The Old Testament, especially in its more ancient parts, reports unhesitatingly of many wars — indeed, it even extols them. Often it is Yahweh himself who commands wars. There is a *Book of the Wars of Yahweh* (Num. 21:14). Wars are holy wars. Israel does not shrink from the horrible customs of war common to its time. If, in the name of Yahweh, the Old Testament demands fulfillment of proscription on its conquered enemies (Num. 21:1-3; Josh. 6; Judg. 1:17; 1 Sam. 15), and if the law demands the extermination of the idolatrous peoples of Canaan (Deut. 7:1-5; 20:16-18) — well, these are accounts whose severity must be endured.

Prophecy expects that in the final days there will take place one last great war with the enemies of Israel (Is. 8:9f.; 17:12f.; 29:7f.; Micah 4:11f.; Ez. 38f.; Joel 4). The *War of the Sons of Light with the Sons of Darkness*, contained in the scrolls found at Qumran, describes the apocalyptic battle in detail. The prophets, however, laud the messianic era of salvation, because it is then that swords will be re-forged into plowshares; and justice, righteousness, and peace will reign on earth (Is. 2:4; 9:1-7; 11:6-9; 65:17-25; Jer. 23:5; Hos. 2:18; Joel 3:18; Zech. 9:9-10). The background attitude of the New Testament is such that it seems to regard war as something which is, from time to time, an inevitable and fateful reality. Nevertheless, when war is mentioned, it is neither accepted nor approved. Moreover, it must not be forgotten that a war in those times was not like the modern war, with its horrible destruction and mechanized murder such as we know it today. But certainly in investigating this problem the question must be asked: Does the New Testament have anything to say about our modern problem of war?

Many of the texts customarily adduced in respect to this question have scarcely any bearing on the matter. That John the Baptist did not denounce the profession of those soldiers who came to him at the Jordan (Luke 3:14) is certainly no approval of war. Much less can it be construed as approval when Jesus praises the faith of the Roman officer, without demanding of him that he renounce his career (Matthew 8:5-10). Neither does Peter demand such of the centurion Cornelius (Acts 10).

Paul frequently uses images drawn from the affairs of war (2 Cor. 6:7; Eph. 6:11-17; 1 Thess. 5:8). Such metaphors may suggest a certain appreciation of military virtue. One must not conclude therefrom, however, that Paul took any pleasure in the contemplation of war.

At the time of Jesus, the Zealots, a powerful political party, anticipated and prepared for a violent armed conflict with Rome. Jesus was in no way allied with the Zealots. He warns of the disaster which their policies will bring upon Jerusalem (Mark 13:1f.; Luke 13:34; 23:28-31). The Christian community did not allow itself to become involved in war with Rome; rather, in its refusal to become so involved, it followed the example of its leaders (Mark 13:24-34).

In the gospel there are the invitations of Jesus not to resist one who is evil (Matthew 5:39) and to love one's enemies (Matthew 5:44). These words are not spoken directly about war. They refer to the personal relationships of the disciples; but the pursuit of war is, nevertheless, in diametric opposition to discipleship. There is the threat that all who take up the sword will perish by the sword (Matthew 26:52). Even this is said primarily of private conflicts and is not referred to wars between nations. However, the warning has about it something of the ring of an adage. It sums up universal experience, and reflects also the experience gained in the waging of war. In actual fact, the experience of many wars shows that their end result is not victory but disaster.

In regard to the establishment of peace, however, there is the beatitude: "Blessed are the peacemakers, for they shall be called sons of

God" (Matthew 5:9). God is the God of peace (Rom. 15:33). The purpose and goal of Christ's incarnation is peace between God and men (Luke 2:14), and even between men who previously were inimical to each other (Eph. 2:14). Whoever makes peace does God's work of salvation; that is why they are called his sons. To be sure, messianic peace is divinely effected salvation far beyond any human expectation. Even peace among men on the new earth pertains thereto. The beatitude (Matthew 5:9), then, has also a social and political significance. "Pacifism" derives its name from the Latin translation of Matthew 5:9, *Beati pacifici*. It would be valid for a peace movement to appeal to the Sermon on the Mount.

In the problems which confront him as a citizen, the Christian cannot hold himself dispensed from the morality of the New Testament. If the political sphere is justified in its own independence, the citizen is, nevertheless, whether in his personal and private affairs or in matters of public record, one and the same man; and he must endeavor to comport himself in all areas as a Christian. The condemnation of every kind of war might, then, be the attitude which a Christian, in faith and conscience, derives from the word and spirit of the Sermon on the Mount. This must not be construed to mean the total rejection of military service, even in peacetime. Military service can have for its rationale the preservation of peace. But the conditions and developments which thrust Christianity again and again into the nightmare conflicts of wars must not on this account be presumed to be unalterable.

The New Testament attempts to understand wars as eschatological signs. They are the apocalyptic miseries out of which the new world is to be born (Mark 13:7). In the Apocalypse (ch. 20), the last days are filled with terrifying wars. John portrays victory and war as apocalyptic riders (Apoc. 6:1-8). They take the field in successive order: victory, then war; and often enough this is actually the case — a victory but constitutes the causes for another war. And in its entourage are famine and death. Even if, in accord with the biblical expectation, wars are to continue until the end of time, and indeed, will be the characteristic by which the last days may be recognized, the disciple must nevertheless struggle to bring about peace. Sin and wickedness

too will remain, but the Christian must not on that account be tolerant of them.

c.) Reverence for life.

The commandment "Thou shalt not kill!" is in reference to man. It
is not mere sentimentality, however, to extend its interpretation to the
taking of life in general. According to Albert Schweitzer, reverence
for life is the foundation of all morality. "Good is to preserve and
benefit life; evil is to destroy and obstruct life"[113] We might think
also of St. Francis of Assisi, the great admirer and protector of
animals.

With what nonchalance do we assume disposition of divinely created life, whether of plants or of animals! The creation narrative
(Gen. 1:26, 28) awards man the dominion over all the beasts. This
however, is no more than a permission and directive to domesticate
and train them to useful tasks, not to kill them. The account further
states: "Behold, I give you every plant that bears seed on the whole
earth, and every tree on which there is a seed-bearing fruit. These
shall be your food" (Gen. 1:29). Even for the beasts, vegetable nourishment — and that only — is provided (Gen. 1:30). To maintain
life, man and beast are to make use of the fruitfulness of the plant
world. Such was the original and undisturbed order of peace in
paradise. The first mention of any strife and killing between man and
beast is found only after the expulsion from paradise (thus in Gen.
3:15, the mortal enmity between man and serpent; 3:21, the making
of garments from skins; 4:4 and 8:20, the slaughter and sacrifice of
beasts). In deliberate contrast to Gen. 1:29, the later commandment
says: "All that moves and lives, that shall be your food" (Gen. 9:3).
Such are the conditions of the world, now that it has been disordered
by sin.

Psalm 8, a song of creation (the date of composition is uncertain,
since it can be seen as influencing Gen. 1 as easily as it can be regarded as presupposing Gen. 1), understands man's dominion over the
beasts — hunting, capturing, and slaughtering them — as a sovereign
right proceeding from God, whereby man's being given a position of
superintendence over creation is made apparent. "You have given him
dominion over the work of your hands; you have laid all things at his

feet: sheep and cattle and beasts of the field, birds of the air and fish of the sea, whatever passes through the watery paths" (Ps. 8:7-9). Man must not suppose that his dominion over creation is his inherent and brutal right; rather, it is given to him by God, and before God he must answer for his exercise of that dominion.

The Pauline Epistles bear the testimony of the history of religion to the reverence for life. Being a pious man, the Oriental knows that God is the Creator and Lord of all life. Man, therefore, cannot make disposition of life; he must not kill any living thing without bringing it to God, to whom it belongs, as a sacrifice. Even the butcher observes this with at least a desultory ritual; and thus it is a fact that, properly speaking, every piece of fleshmeat that is sold in the market is really meat offered in sacrifice. This is the background of the problem of the Corinthians: whether or not the Christian might buy and make use of such meat. Paul answers, to be sure, with grandiose freedom, that "the idols have no real existence at all, and there is no God save the One" (1 Cor. 8:4). "The earth is the Lord's, and everything in it" (1 Cor. 10:26 = Ps. 50:12). The world is the gift of God to men, they have but to use it properly.

Paul looks upon the anxiousness and longing for salvation as a phenomenon common to all earthly life. In accord with ancient biblical expectation (Is. 65:17), he perceives in this an agonizing cry for messianic redemption. Because of the guilt of the first man, all creation was subjected, along with man, to instability and transitoriness. Along with man, it is impatient; and it utters its sighs from the depths of its misery while it awaits its salvation (Rom. 8:19-22). Such expressions and ideas as these to which Paul gives utterance — ought not man be mindful of these words and ideas even while he exercises his dominion over the creatures, when he exercises that dominion even to the extremes of his title thereto, and takes their lives for his own advantageous use? Even then he must hear the shrieks and groans of the creature.

From time immemorial, care and attention in respect to life and limb have been a part of human culture. This attention has achieved its most notable results in our own time. Diseases have been repressed and conquered; the span of human life expecctancy has been considerably lengthened. The generation of new life is responsibly planned. Occasionally the frontier to the manipulation of life appears to be reached. For the Bible and the New Testament, the saving of life is a matter of deep concern. According to later Christological reflections (John 11:25; 14:6; Rom. 14:9; 2 Cor. 13:4), life is given in Christ, just as with the miraculous cures in the Gospels. The Fathers speak of Christ as the Physician. There are biblical texts pointing in that direction, such as Mark 2:17: "Those who are well have no need of a physician, but those who are sick"; Luke 4:23: "You will say to me, 'Physician, heal yourself' "; 1 Peter 2:24: "By his wounds you have been healed." Ignatius of Antioch, in his *Letter to the Ephesians* (7:2), refers to Christ as "the Physician who, in death, is life." Christ's title, the Physician, appears in the older Acts of Apostles (*Acts of Philip*, 40; *Acts of Thomas*, 10, and *passim*), as well as in the *Letter to Diognetus*, 9:6; in Clement of Alexandria (*Paidagogos*, 1, 2, 6); and Origen (*Against Celsus*, 2, 67 and elsewhere).

No other period of history can compare to our own in its profligate and sinful squandering of life. To this period must be delivered the message of life as the higher good of creation and of new creation.

§ 20. MARRIAGE AND CELIBACY • UNCHASTITY

I. MARRIAGE AND CELIBACY

Today weighty questions about the ordering and realization of Christian marriage are being discussed.[114] There are questions about the legal form of marriage and about responsible parenthood. To such questions there is no answer to be found in the New Testament — or in any case, no direct answer. These questions are the result of a historically lengthy development, or they have their basis in the relationships of modern society, which are quite different from those which existed at the time of the New Testament. At the same time, it is not merely the world as society that has changed around us, but even the world as experience within us.

For our modern educational and pastoral elucidation and solution of the problems of marriage, it seems to us that it is essential to understand the relationship between sexual love and marriage to regulate them as forces which mutually support, create, and fulfill each other. Indeed, even from antiquity there is a heritage of beautiful and profound words about marriage and matrimonial fidelity. But properly speaking, it is only since the period of Romanticism that the poetry and philosophy of our society speak emphatically and reflectively of the experience of love and of marriage as the fulfillment of the personality as well as of human communion. It is not to be expected, then, that the New Testament should speak expressly or in detail about this. Nevertheless, the New Testament Church does know about the critical significance of marriage for the individual person, for the Church itself, and for all society; and of this the New Testament does speak.

For many centuries the narratives about the creation of mankind as man and woman in Genesis 1–2 — which narratives are not alike in form, nor are they of precisely the same mentality — belonged to the written body of Israel's sacred tradition (see Vol. 1 of the present work, pp. 83–97). According to this tradition, man and woman were created separately and successively (Gen. 2:21f.), both however in a similar fashion, in the image of God (Gen. 1:27). Passionate longing draws man and woman together (Gen. 2:24), and they have carnal knowledge in their mutual embrace (Gen. 2:23; 4:1). It is out of their companionship that new life is to arise (Gen. 1:28; 3:16). Both of the ends of marriage that are generally enumerated today, then, are in accord with God's will in creation: the loving companionship of the spouses, as well as the begetting of new life. Marriage is not only a law of nature but an establishment made by God. This is, especially in view of the relationships then prevailing in Eastern lands, an extraordinarily exalted view of marriage. The knowledge of sexuality and the experience of shame, however, are the consequences of sin (Gen. 2:25; 3:7). Does this perhaps indicate a conflict in regard to sexuality from the very beginning?

Even if the reality of marriage in Israel was somehow encumbered with prejudices and guilt, Israel never forgot that sacred history. To the young Tobit and his bride, marriage is a commandment of the highest order (Tob. 8:6-8). The prophet Malachi (2:14-16) warns and reproves, declaring that God is not pleased with the sacrifice. "Why is he not pleased? Because God was witness for you and the wife of your youth, to whom you have behaved so faithlessly. She was your companion. . . . Take heed to yourselves, therefore, and let no one break faith with the wife of his youth. For I hate divorce, says the Lord, the God of Israel." Here, in an economy of words so much the more impressive since it belongs to a period which rarely spoke thus, there is an intimation of the happiness of a first love. God was and continues to be witness thereto. Marriage demands indissoluble fidelity.

In Israel's Wisdom literature of the proverbial sort, which dates mainly from (and therefore testifies to) the period after the return from the Babylonian exile (when the principles of social life had to be ordered and shaped anew), the wife who was a capable and careful manager is praised. A poem arranged in accord with the twenty-two letters of the alphabet presents an elevated notion of the ideal wife. Domestic prudence and industry, solicitude for husband and servants, purity and nobility of soul, generosity and reverence for God — these are the qualities which distinguish her and make her the precious treasure that she is (Prov. 31:10-31). To this same period, perhaps, belongs the Song of Songs, a collection of songs about love and marriage, which, with a genuine understanding and even in highly artistic forms, celebrate the joy and happiness of the spouses. Bridal and marital love are exalted and extolled when they become for Israel the figure of God's love for his chosen people.

The prophet Hosea furthered this idea in word and example. At the command of God he embarked upon a marriage with a woman who knew no fidelity. And as he, the prophet, continues to love his adulterous spouse, so too God continues to love Israel, in spite of her disloyalty. Then God declares to Israel: "I will betroth you to me forever; I will betroth you to me in justice and righteousness, in goodness and mercy; I will betroth you to me in fidelity, so that you may know the Lord" (Hos. 2:19-20). Later prophets re-announce the security of this promise as a comfort to Israel in times of disaster. As the youthful beloved, they say, is desired ever anew by her lover, so too God receives Israel ever anew in mercy and in love (Jer. 31:3;

Is. 54:4-8). With the acceptance of the Song of Songs into the canon of Sacred Scripture, what originally were secular love songs are interpreted as an exposition of the intimate relationship between God and Israel.

The rigid demand which the New Testament makes in regard to marital fidelity is not without precedent in Israel. Jesus condemns wicked desires: "Everyone who looks at a woman lustfully has already committed adultery with her in his heart" (Matthew 5:28). The decalogue itself had already voiced the prohibition: "Thou shalt not covet thy neighbor's wife" (Exod. 20:17). Job too knows that a custody of the eyes must be practiced: "With my eyes I have made a covenant not to look upon a virgin" (Job 31:1). There is mention of "eyes of wantonness" in Num. 15:39; Ez. 6:9, as well as in the Qumran scrolls (1 QS 1:6; 1 QpHab 5:7). One of the Rabbis declares: "Thou shalt not commit adultery, not with thy hand, not with thy foot, nor with thine eye nor thy heart."

The Mosaic Law recognized and regulated divorce. "If anyone takes a woman home and marries her, but discovers in her something shameful, he writes her a bill of divorce and dismisses her out of his house. And she can marry another" (Deut. 24:1-2).

The bill of divorce was an arrangement for the protection of the wife. A husband could no longer send his wife away in a moment of whimsy. He was obliged to draw up a written document and arrange for witnesses to its being served. He was obliged to have and to specify serious grounds (in point of fact, to discover something shameful about the wife). Discharge of the document took time, and perhaps the husband's anger might be appeased. And by means of the bill of divorce the woman could prove to another that she was free and could marry again.

Certainly it was possible for that which ought to have been an instrument for the protection of the wife to become no more than a handle to a husband's despotism. The Law of Moses was vague in its expression: "If he discovers in her something shameful . . . ." Certainly it meant a conspicuous physical deformity. At the time of the New Testament, Rabbinic exegesis busied itself with the explanation of each word. A more rigorous tendency understood "something shameful" as meaning unchaste conduct, and permitted the divorcing of a wife only on those grounds (for consummated adultery the death penalty was prescribed in Deut. 22:22).

Many teachers disapproved entirely of divorce. One of them remarks: "When someone repudiates his first wife, the altar itself sheds tears because of him." At the same time, however, there was also a laxer interpretation which recognized every pretended grounds as sufficient for divorce, ultimately even the spoiling of a meal, or even for the sake of the pleasure of another woman. And it was possible to marry a woman for one day and send her away the next, which was no more than the legalizing of prostitution.

Against the divorce law of Deuteronomy, Jesus appeals to Gen. 1:27 and 2:24 (Mark 10:6f.). Even the pious men of Qumran appealed to Genesis, when they accused their opponents: "They live in unchastity, inasmuch as they take two wives into their life, although the principle of creation is, 'As man and woman he created them'" (Gen. 1:27). And those who entered into the ark went in in pairs (Gen. 7:2f.; *Damascus Document*, 4:20f.). Jesus and Qumran both see in Gen. 1:27 an expression of monogamous marriage as the ideal, a thing which the words themselves do not state directly. Jesus sees therein a condemnation of divorce; Qumran, a condemnation of (simultaneous or successive?) bigamy. Since these were unquestionably permitted according to the Law of Moses, it is evident that at Qumran, just as with Jesus in the Synoptics, Jewish marriage law was criticized from the viewpoint of Genesis, which was accepted as the original order of God's creation.

It is not to be supposed, however, that in Israel at the time of the New Testament, marriage was either entered upon thoughtlessly or frivolously disdained. Not without reason was Judaism proud of her marital chastity, and especially so when she beheld the disorder prevalent among the pagans (1 Thess. 4:5).[115]

In the Gospels (Matthew 19:12), and in the Epistles of Paul (1 Cor. 7:29) as well, marriage is affected by the pressures of eschatological hope. Here the New Testament shares in the apocalyptic expectation of its time. Excited by this expectation, the *Syriac Apocalypse of Baruch* (10:13) cries out: "Bridal couples, enter not the bridal chamber! Maidens, forget your garlands and adornments! Wives, pray not for the blessing of children!" The members of the Qumran community — at least the majority of them — were celibate (1 QS 2; 1 QSa 1:9f.). Up to the present time the scrolls discovered there have shed no light on the rationale of their celibacy. Possibly one reason for it was the fear of ritual impurity. According to Lev. 15:18, an emission of semen made one unclean. In the *Damascus Document* (12:1f.), marital intercourse was prohibited on the Sabbath and in the holy city of Jerusalem.

The position of woman and esteem for marriage must not be painted as an entirely gloomy picture even in the pagan surroundings of the New Testament. One must not forget the great feminine characterizations of the poets (Andromache, Penelope, Antigone, Iphigenia, Phaedra). Stoic philosophy had a high esteem for marriage. According to Musonius Rufus (68, 5f.; 69, 15), marriage is the most intimate companionship conceivable. It is a common life of mutual assistance and sympathetic understanding. Even Plutarch is capable of saying much the same. The Stoa purposes to lead men to freedom, even freedom from sexual passion (Epictetus, *Diss.* 4, 1, 21). Philosophy, therefore, condemns divorce (Epictetus, *Diss.*, 4, 2), as well, of course, as any extramarital sexual intercourse. The latter violates the law and is disgraceful (Musonius Rufus, 64, 1-9). With any impure act one defiles the God residing within one's own breast (Epictetus, *Diss.*, 2, 8, 13).

From the Gospels it is evident that, just as in the contemporaneous Judaism, so too in the Church questions about the legal and moral aspects of marriage were posited. Tradition has preserved in four places in the Gospels a saying of Jesus about divorce. The saying appears as a more or less isolated remark in Matthew 5:32 and in Luke 16:18, and in the context of dialogic disputation in Mark 10:2-12 and Matthew 19:3-9.[116] This saying of the Lord was known also to Paul (1 Cor. 7:10). It is a saying of critical importance to the community, for the regulation of marriage as a foundation of the community.

According to Mark 10:2, Pharisees, men zealous for the Law, submitted to Jesus a question on the legality of divorce, much as one might question a Rabbi. The question — whether it is permitted for a man to dismiss his wife — is certainly a remarkable one, since the Law plainly permitted divorce. Is it to be understood from the question that this law and its operation were regarded as doubtful by those who asked the question? Doubtful to a portion of the Rabbinate? Led to it by Jesus through his counter-question, the questioners defend the practice of divorce with an appeal to Deuteronomy, in which Moses permitted divorce (Mark 10:4). They speak of that which is permitted, and support it. They are interested in the formal law, according to which a marriage is to be entered upon with formal validity, and is to be broken with formal validity. Whatever is in proper order in the presence of the notary is thereby in proper order also in the presence of conscience and in the presence of God.

Jesus answers them. He offers a comment on the word of Moses. "Because of your hardness of heart did Moses write this commandment for you" (Mark 10:5f.). The will and ordinance of God are not set forth in their ideal purity in the law of Moses, but are only haltingly rendered. The bill of divorce is permitted in view of the wickedness of men. It is, therefore, an infringement on the ideal of fidelity.

Indeed, the bill of divorce is itself an indictment for malice and a revelatory judgment on the callousness of those who have anything to do with it. The pristine will of God is not set forth in later laws but is found in the beginning itself, as established by God. On the morning of creation the world was not yet spoiled. At that time it still had its ideal majesty and grandeur. Jesus recalls: "In the beginning of creation God made them man and woman" (Mark 10:6). Jesus appeals to the concept of their creation and to the word of the Creator, according to Gen. 1 and 2. The union of the sexes in marriage is the work of God, his establishment. Jesus quotes additionally as the word of God spoken at that time: "For the sake of his wife a man will leave father and mother, and they will become two [117] together in one flesh" (Mark 10:7f.). The order of marriage, therefore, is superior to the relationship to parents. And if a man cannot dissolve that relationship, how much less can he sunder the union of marriage!

The saying of the Lord speaks of the physical unity of the spouses. But in the linguistic usage of the Bible, both Old and New Testaments, *flesh* signifies not only the body in distinction to the soul, but the whole man; thus, in Luke 3:6: "All flesh will behold the salvation of God." In marriage, husband and wife become one flesh, which is to say one human being, one personal unity, one person. A person is not portionable. The words of Genesis, however, are not the mere account of an isolated deed of God; rather, it is God even today who binds in matrimony. It is by his will that each marriage is solemnized. Divorce is a violation of the present will of God. It is true of every marriage: "What God has joined together, let no man put asunder." All morality must realize the totality of God's arrangements.

Constant examination must be made lest the legal ordinances of men become too lax. Man can make use of the merely legal in order to gainsay the truth and to conceal injustice. Life and society can hide their deep disorders behind a façade of perfect order. The gospel allows man no excuse, no artifice. It does not gloss over sin, but exposes it as that which brings man before the judgment seat, where all will be revealed.

The establishment of ordinance and law is absolutely necessary in human society. The insufficiency thereof is perhaps nowhere so evident as in the law on marriage, whether profane or sacred. Hence the conclusion: "Whoever dismisses his wife and marries another commits adultery, and whoever marries a woman who has been dismissed commits adultery (Matthew 5:32; Mark 10:11; Luke 16:18). This may be regarded as the shortest and most primitive formulation of the saying. Whoever dismisses his wife still remains really married to her, and the one who was dismissed remains as she was before, still in her hitherto existing marriage. This marriage which continues to exist is sinned against when the one who dismisses and the one who is dismissed marry again. Whoever dismisses his wife is guilty of the adultery that takes place when she marries again. New guilt is piled on old. The dismissal itself already makes one guilty of adultery if it is effected with a view to the remarriage of either partner. Every divorce is itself adultery. A marriage cannot be dissolved, but is only sinned against, and that with the greatest of culpability. With this doctrine Jesus placed himself in the sharpest opposition to the rabbinate and to Jewish law.

One of the canons of ecclesiastical law derives from the saying of the Lord that the marriage which has been joined together by God must not be parted asunder by man. The indissolubility of marriage is regarded as a point of divine law, from which no human dispensation is possible. There are important questions involved therein.

The declaration about the indissolubility of marriage appears in Matthew 5:31f., in the series of antitheses in the Sermon on the Mount. These antitheses are lofty moral demands and obligations. Are they also juridically tenable paragraphs of a lawbook? Another antithesis says that anyone who is angry with his brother or who insults him is liable to judgment (Matthew 5:22f.). No one has ever attempted to see these antitheses as legal principles. Did not Jesus, after all, when engaged in argumentation with Jewish law, simply withdraw marriage from the area of controversial human law and base it upon the simple primeval order established by God?

Only Matthew (5:32; 19:9) subjoins to the prohibition of divorce the phrase "except on ground of unchastity" (= adultery).[118] The clause is probably an addition of later tradition or of the Evangelist, in accord with prevailing Jewish marriage law, which required a husband to dismiss an adulterous wife. With this, then, even the Christian community desires to take into account the hard necessity of life, when it acknowledges a dissolution of marriage in the event of adultery. Even Paul (although for him the word of Jesus on the indissolubility of marriage is perfectly valid) admits an exception in allowing that a Christian spouse may separate from a partner who remains pagan when it develops that there is no peace in the marriage (1 Cor. 7:10-15).

The clause in the Gospel of Matthew has not been maintained in the Church, but certainly the concession made by Paul was recognized from then on (as the "Pauline privilege").[119] Nevertheless, even in the Catholic Church, there was for a long time no uniformity of judgment in this matter until the Council of Trent shaped a definitive law according to which Christian marriage is indissoluble. Even to the present day the Greek Orthodox and the Protestant Churches recognize adultery as grounds for divorce. The principle remains that man dare not put asunder the marriage that God has joined together. Nevertheless, by human guilt it is sundered in adultery. It is, therefore, according to the doctrine and law of the Greek Orthodox and Protestant Churches, an open and difficult question whether, under the word of God, a new wedding with a different spouse may be entered upon and blessed before the Church, or whether it must perhaps be entered upon in another and simpler manner.[120]

If one calls to mind all the remarks of Jesus about marriage, one will remember also that the Rabbis were accustomed to refer to the wedding feast for an image of the messianic joy and fulfillment; and Jesus too liked to apply the image of the wedding feast to himself and to his messianic work. When someone reproached him because his disciples did not fast, he replied that, since he was now tarrying with them, it was for them a wedding feast and they could not fast (Mark 2:19f.). Jesus compares the kingdom of God to the celebration of a wedding feast (Matthew 22:1-14). Or, in the parable of the five wise and five foolish virgins, he compares himself, the Messiah, to the bridegroom who comes to the wedding (Matthew 25:1-13). Marriage, therefore, is an image of joy and festivity of which Christ thoroughly approves and elevates to the status of messianic symbol.

In the gospel, which speaks so highly of marriage, there are, nevertheless, other remarks indicative of some reservation. In the Gospel of Matthew, the saying of the Lord about the indissolubility of marriage has another saying about celibacy attached to it: "There are celibates who are born such from their mother's womb, and celibates who are made such by men, and celibates who have made themselves such for the sake of the kingdom of heaven" (Matthew 19:10-12).[121] The saying deals with the various possibilities of celibacy as they are found. There is a celibacy which is physiologically occasioned — the celibates who are born such from their mother's womb; a celibacy brought about by human force and violence — the celibates who are made such by men; and a celibacy that is freely embraced for the sake of the kingdom of heaven.

This dominion of God is at all times pressing onward, forcing itself nearer; indeed, in Christ it is, though hidden, already present (Luke 11:20). If Christ himself is the beginning of God's dominion, then "for the sake of the kingdom of God" means the same thing as "for the sake of Christ." There are men who order and direct their whole energy, their whole life, toward the advancing kingdom of God and to its presence in Christ, so that they allow themselves to be occupied with nothing else; indeed, they are neither able nor desirous of being occupied with anything else. Much the same is remarked in such a saying of the Lord as this: "Everyone who has left houses or brothers or sisters or father or mother or children or lands for my name's sake will receive in turn a hundredfold, and will win eternal life" (Matthew 19:29). The proviso is both eschatological and Christological.

Jesus speaks of those who are, by human agency, compelled to remain celibate (Matthew 19:12). Probably the saying referred originally to such as were, by surgery, made unfit for marriage. We will be justified in understanding the words in our time as applying to those many persons who are forced by the pressure of social and economic conditions, by political catastrophes and wars, or by whatever fateful event, to remain unmarried all their lives. Present statistics indicate that in many European countries one third of the women must, against their will, remain unmarried. The defenseless woman often becomes the victim of the unnatural conditions of life in our society. The saying of the Lord might well be applied to cases such as these, where celibacy is compelled by men and is by no means willingly accepted. But certainly even a celibacy that is not initially the result of free choice can be approved, perhaps at first as a painful sacrifice, and afterwards in willing correspondence with all the potentialities and duties which can bring fulfillment even to celibacy.

The gospel reports other sayings, too, which are indicative of certain reservations about marriage. The Sadducees approached Jesus with a bizarre problem: At the resurrection, to whom will a wife who was married to seven brothers, one after another, belong? Jesus answered: "When they arise from the dead they neither marry nor give in marriage, but they are like the angels in heaven" (Mark 12:18-27). There is a new era of the world in the offing, in which there will no longer be any marrying. Marriage pertains to a world fallen victim to death. It ceases, therefore, with the new and glorified world of the resurrected. The risen will possess the spiritual form of angels.

This saying of Jesus runs counter to the usual Jewish notion of the future, which expected the joy of marriage and the joy of children in the highest degree even in the new age. Jesus says that marriage will be at an end. Perhaps his statement is meant to indicate that the end is already operative in the present age, and that marriage too, like everything else, is limited in view of the end. This does not rob marriage of its significance now nor of its present riches. After all, Jesus speaks also of the majesty of the tender blossom which tomorrow must perish.

There is a further word of caution in the parable of the great feast, as recounted by Luke (14:15-24). The feast is ready. The king sends his messengers out to invite his guests. They will not come. In the parable as found in Matthew (22:1-10), it says only: "They paid no heed. One went off to his farm, another to his business." In Luke, however, the excuses they make are recounted individually. "I have bought a farm. I have bought five yoke of oxen. I have married a wife." In the parable the feast signifies the kingdom of God which is at hand. Luke's Gospel points out that business, work, and livelihood keep one back from entry into the kingdom. Even this much must have been difficult to understand, since pious Israelites shared the conviction that work, livelihood, and riches were a blessing from God. It must have been still more astonishing that marriage should hamper one's entry into the kingdom. Was this not utterly foreign to the doctrine and faith of Israel, according to which marriage was of God's founding? The passage in Luke seems to be so completely un-Jewish that it has been asked whether or not we may already discern here the Christian conclusion drawn from a saying of the Lord.

Another saying of Christ draws a warning from the example of the people at the time of the deluge: "They ate and drank, married and let themselves be given in marriage, until Noah went into the ark. Then the flood came and all perished." (Luke 17:26f.). Judgment is imminent — a fact which the world, in the midst of its secular concerns, is inclined to forget. Marrying and being married belong to such a one as is characterized by this worldliness. It is not as if eating and drinking and marrying were something evil in themselves and therefore forbidden. One can, however, through the use and enjoyment of natural benefits, neglect the approach of God and thereby become liable to judgment.

There are other sayings of similar import which can be added to these texts from Luke's Gospel which speak of the questionableness of marriage. Matthew 10:37 says, in regard to the renunciation that is required of the disciple: "Whoever loves father or mother or son or daughter more than he loves me is not worthy of me." And Matthew 19:29: "Everyone who leaves houses or brother or sister or father or mother or children or lands for my name's sake will receive in turn a hundredfold and will win eternal life."

These sayings of the Lord are significantly different in Luke's re-
porting of them. Thus, in Luke 14:26: "Whoever comes to me and
does not hate father, mother, wife, children, brothers, and sisters . . .
cannot be my disciple." And Luke 18:29: "No one leaves house or
wife or brother or children or parents for the sake of the kingdom
of God who does not receive them back, and in the age to come
eternal life." Luke has introduced into both of the sayings of the Lord
(Matthew 10:37 and 19:29) the renunciation of wife, and therefore of
marriage. His Gospel has a tendency to emphasize in a special way
the critical importance of marriage in relation to the impending kingdom of God. Is it perhaps but an individual evangelist who speaks
here, whereas in fact the whole fullness of the New Testament also
includes other themes and declarations?

The gospel approves of the world and announces that it is the order
of God's creation; and marriage is a part of it. But there is also another order, by which the order of creation can be surpassed and sus-
pended — the order of that which is for the sake of the impending
kingdom of God.

The writings of the Apostles too must occupy themselves with the
order of marriage. Paul treats of this in detail in 1 Cor. 7. In this chapter there are such statements as: "It is good for a man not to touch
a woman" (7:1). "Because of unchastity, let each man have his own
wife, and each wife her own husband" (7:2). "It is better to marry
than to burn" (7:9). "In view of the present distress it is good for a
person to remain unmarried" (7:26). "If you marry, you do not sin"
(7:28). "The unmarried man, the unmarried woman, are anxious
about the things of the Lord, how they shall please the Lord. Married
people, however, are anxious about the things of the world; the husband, how he may please his wife, and the wife, how she may please
her husband" (7:32-34). Paul counsels the betrothed who are not certain whether they ought to marry or whether it would not be better
to remain single, "if it must be so," and if they "cannot hold their
desires in control," to marry. "They do not sin." If, however, they do
not marry, "they do better" (7:36-38).[122] In so speaking, does not Paul
effectively disparage matrimony? The question has been asked not
only by Paul's opponents but even by his friends.

The text requires explanation. The first thing to be considered is the occasion and purpose of 1 Cor. 7. Paul does not mean to present a complete treatise on Christian marriage. He is simply answering the questions sent to him by letter from Corinth while he was sojourning in Ephesus (1 Cor. 7:1; 16:17).

When Paul begins: "In regard to what you wrote about: It is good for a man not to touch a woman" (7:1), it becomes exegetically questionable whether this verse contains an expression of Paul's own conviction. It is possible that the passage is a quotation from the letter from Corinth, of which Paul makes direct use. In any case, however, Paul replies to a Corinthian asceticism which was inimical to marriage.

In late antiquity there were ascetical movements which required abstinence of every sort (see above, ch. 12). Even abstinence from marriage was demanded. Philosophical considerations were contributing to these movements in the Greek world. In accord with Platonic philosophy, the body was considered as evil, the spirit as good. According to Aristotle and in the Stoa, sexuality was rejected because its effects disturbed the dispassionateness of the sage. Stobaios (*Ecl.*, 4, 22, 28) declares in a straightforward manner: "It is not good to marry." Weariness and pessimism over marriage were well on the way to becoming the fashion. Divorces increased in a menacing manner.

Perhaps the questions of the Corinthians were determined also by gnostic considerations. In accord with its dualist view of the world, gnosticism disavowed the world, and, for the sake of the true knowledge (gnosis), demanded abstinence from food and from sexual traffic.

Besides these possible origins, such themes might also have derived from a genuine though untempered Christian enthusiasm. To be sure, there were Christians who feared sexuality and regarded it as a stain against holiness and as a hindrance to spiritual progress, as can be gathered from Paul's reply in 1 Cor. 7:14. Thus are the Corinthian movements inimical to marriage to be explained. Paul, however, defends the right and order of marriage against false asceticism. From the very outset he stands on the side of marriage and not of a recommendation of celibacy.

For Paul, the Jew, the Law of Moses is God's unimpeachable revelation. The same is true of the Paul who writes 1 Cor. 7. Even now

Gen. 1 and 2, wherein it is recounted that God established marriage in paradise and blessed it, are valid for him. In other places Paul repeatedly adduces decisive statements from Gen. 2. (1 Cor. 6:16; 11:7-9; 15:45, 47), whereby it is evident that for him the biblical account of creation is ever present. This reality of creation is acknowledged by Paul when he speaks with perfect certainty about marriage.

To ward off the danger of unchastity, every man ought to have his wife, and every woman her husband (1 Cor. 7:2). This is a very dismal outlook, almost insultingly so. But do not psychology and sociology say the same thing, that sexuality in marriage has a stabilizing purpose which protects society against aberrations? Paul counsels the spouses not to draw apart from each other. He acknowledges the marital obligation which is binding upon both (1 Cor. 7:3-5). At most the partners may, for the sake of prayer, renounce the marriage bed for a short time. This should by no means become a permanent arrangement, so as to suspend the marriage on ascetical grounds. Paul counsels the unmarried and the widows that it is better to marry than to burn (1 Cor. 7:9). He warns about experiments and every sort of coercion, which only end in catastrophe. In all humility the Church must be prepared to listen to these words of Paul and to take them earnestly.

Paul was aware of the problem of divorce, both from the contemporaneous Jewish discussion of the problem and from the ordinary experience of living. For him as well as for the congregation, it was settled by the saying of the Lord handed down in the Synoptics. "To the married, not I but the Lord gives charge that the wife shall not separate from her husband, and the husband shall not dismiss his wife" (1 Cor. 7:10-11). Here Paul confirms the principle which distinguished the Church from Israel and from the general practice of all antiquity.

The actual circumstances of life, however, open up many questions. Paul is aware, it would seem, of particular instances of *de facto* divorce in the congregation which had taken place previously and perhaps in ignorance. In such a case the only possibilities are that the divorced spouses remain unmarried or that they be reconciled to each other (1 Cor. 7:11).

Mixed marriage was frequent, even normal, in the community. Marriages were mostly between a Christian and a Jewish or pagan spouse. Can a Christian, in life's most intimate relationship, remain with an infidel? Indeed, Christianity was obliged to separate itself with all its might from an already too powerful paganism. But Paul's counsel is that the spouses should remain in such marriages. The Corinthian Christians feared, perhaps, that the ritual demonism of the pagan spouse might make the Christian spouse unclean. Paul assures them: "The unbelieving husband is made holy by his wife, and the un- believing wife is sanctified by the brother. Otherwise your children would in fact be unclean — but as it is, they are holy" (1 Cor. 7:14).[123]

Here, and elsewhere quite generally in the Bible, whether Old or New Testament, the term *holy* is not used in the moral sense com- mon to our language, in which a holy life is a sinless life. Holiness in its primitive meaning is consecration by God and acceptance into the communion of God, who is the primordial Holy One (Is. 6:3; see above, ch. 13). The communion of marriage is of such force that the one spouse is made holy by the other, and the children of the marriage are sanctified. The salvational power of Christ is greater than the dis- ruptive power of the world with its demoniacal trappings. This is the basis of Christian freedom (1 Cor. 8:4-6). Paul would have it be known that, on the grounds of this freedom, every kind of coercion is to be ignored. If a peaceful life together is not possible, then the Christian spouse is no longer bound (1 Cor. 7:12-16); the marriage may then be dissolved. Paul does not say whether, in such a case, remarriage is to be regarded as permissible. This is taken for granted. Marriage is possible only upon the freely willed acceptance of its partnership. It cannot be forced. Peace and freedom is the broad im- port of God's will (1 Cor. 7:15). Nor can any deadly casuistry of law annul that will.

For Paul, marriage is part of creation, part of the redemption thereof, and therefore a divinely established arrangement. It is also a fact, nevertheless, that Paul knows and speaks of another possi- bility as a way of life. "I would that all men were even as I am. But each man has his own particular gift of God's grace, one in this way, another in that" (1 Cor. 7:7). Paul lives a celibate life, and he terms celibacy a particular gift of grace. It is possible as a vocation, but cer- tainly only as a vocation. Although Paul treasures this calling so highly, he nevertheless assigns it to its proper place in the Church. Celibacy must not become proud, as if it were something special. There are also many other gifts of grace, such as the Apostle enumerates in Rom. 12:6-21 and 1 Cor. 12-14. He mentions service, doctrine, wisdom, knowledge, faith, power to heal, and other capabilities — prophecy, interpretation, and above all, love (1 Cor. 13) and the availing word (1 Cor. 14).

Paul offers a further basis for celibacy: "The time has grown short. Therefore, those who have wives ought to live as if they had not; those who weep, as if they wept not; those who buy, as if they owned not; those who deal with the world, as if they dealt with it not. For the form of this world is passing away. I only want you to be without anxieties" (1 Cor. 7:29-32). Paul rather anticipates that Christ's return and the end of time are close at hand, but he does not teach this as certain knowledge. He says, therefore, that in relation to Christ and Gospel blessings, all life's values are secondary and are to be weighed in the balance. He takes into account marriage and possessions, and even such spiritual matters as sorrow and joy. And Paul considers that in the short time that possibly is left it would be better not to marry. Whoever lives in the married state will, in this time of eschatological urgency, "be distressed for the external man."

Paul may have deceived himself over the actual calendar day of the end of the world; nevertheless, it does not invalidate what he says in 1 Cor. 7. When that day will be is uncertain and unimportant. What is important is that faith in the approaching advent of God stand firm and that the arrival of God and of Christ in judgment and grace take place continually in time and in the world. The Church lives ever in the hope of the parousia of its Lord, and ever in expectation and presence alike of this parousia. Celibacy is that position of the Church which, in order to express its constant preparedness, wants to remain free of every other bond. The saying of the Lord in Matthew 19:12 about celibacy for the sake of the kingdom of heaven expresses the same idea. Celibacy is the eschatological sign of the Church.

Paul gives expression to this again when he designates the Church as a betrothed virgin who goes out to meet the Lord Jesus Christ: "I am jealous for you with a divine jealousy. I have betrothed you to one husband, in order to present you to Christ as a pure bride" (2 Cor.

11:2). In respect to the Church of Corinth, the Apostle is like the father of the bride, who zealously watches over the bride in order to keep her unsullied for the bridegroom until the wedding. For the Church, the wedding day, the day of union with her Lord, is the day of Christ's return at the end of the ages.

The Apocalypse (14:4; 19:2, 7; 21:2, 9) already beholds in its visions the marriage taking place at the consummation of the ages, the marriage of the Lamb with the Church, which is majestically adorned like a bride. In such New Testament declarations, the unmarried state is equated with Christian virginity, approved, and achieved in faith.

Paul describes celibacy as the possibility of belonging entirely to the Lord. The man who is not married thinks on the things of the Lord, how he shall please him. The married person thinks on the things of the world: the husband, how he shall please his wife, and the wife, how she shall please her husband (1 Cor. 7:32-34). Do Christian spouses have questions for Paul in this matter? They will admit that every marriage has its problems which can encumber a man and make a prisoner of him. Does not, however, the marital union, with its mutual love, care, and fidelity of the spouses, fulfill God's commandments, the commandment of love in particular? Do not married people, too, have in this way a mind for the things of God?

Shortly after the year 200 A.D., Clement of Alexandria (*Stromateis*, 3, 88, 2), one of the earliest expositors of Paul's saying, asks: "Is it not possible to live in harmony with God while seeking to please a wife, and to give thanks to God conjointly? Is it not permitted also to the married person, conjointly with his partner, to keep in mind the things of the Lord?" And on the other hand, is celibacy always and of its very nature an undistracted freedom for the Lord?

But Paul, at least in the present context, says nothing of all this. Is one obliged to concede that his statement is incomplete? Is he perhaps speaking in consideration of the vocation of the Apostle and Prophet, who must ride on restlessly through the land, in order to announce the gospel in these last days and to establish the Church, and who would certainly find marriage a hindrance? And then too, Rom. 16:13 must be taken into account, where Paul says: "Greet Rufus, the elect in the Lord, and his mother, who is also mine." Is this not a moving indication of the fact that Paul knew something of what the care of a wife for a husband can mean?

Some further passages of Paul's letters make it possible to complete, to broaden, and to deepen what has already been said. Thus, in 1 Thess. 4:3-5, there is the admonition: "This is the will of God, your salvation: that you abstain from unchastity; that each of you take care to win your wife in holiness and honor, not in the passion of lust like the heathen, who know not God." Through these words there shows very clearly the self-consciousness of the Jew, who takes pride in chaste sexuality and in the order of marriage, things which are valued in Israel; and who takes special pride therein when he is faced daily with the pagan immorality of his surroundings.

The passage states further about Christian marriage (similar to 1 Cor. 7:14) that marriage is a sanctifying companionship. Perhaps it also states that it is a personal communion. Paul seems to be hinting that the common life of marriage must be a husband's permanently new courting of his wife's love, in order to "win" her. In none other of his letters does Paul echo so forcefully the common expectation of the Lord's speedy return as he does in the First Epistle to the Thessalonians (4:13-18). Nevertheless, contrary to the First Epistle to the Corinthians, here Paul says nothing which might seem to make the great blessing of matrimony questionable. It is even more in expectation of the Lord's return that the Christian can and must live a holy life in marriage.

Turning to the critics of his ministry, Paul asks: "Do we not have the right to be accompanied by a sister (i.e., a Christian woman) as wife, as even the other Apostles and brothers of the Lord and Cephas?" (1 Cor. 9:4-5). Paul, too, would have the right, as did the other Apostles, to allow himself, as a missionary, to be accompanied by his spouse, and to receive from the congregation support for himself and for his wife. All this Paul renounces because he wants to announce the gospel gratuitously, so as not to be encumbered in his journey, and so as to give his opponents no occasion to charge him with enriching himself by his being an Apostle. Marriage, however — and Paul states it clearly — is by no means something which is incompatible with the ministry of the Apostle. The spouses Aquila and Prisca were highly esteemed co-workers of Paul on the mission in Ephesus and Rome, and according to the Apostle's own words, the whole Church owed them a debt of gratitude (Rom. 16:3-5; Acts 18:2f.). The married couple Philemon and Apphia harbored the congregation in their house at Colossae (Philemon 1f.).

The New Testament Church had no thought of making celibacy into a law, at least for particular select groups or classes. This it could not do so long as it held fast, on the one hand, to the conviction that marriage is an establishment of God which could in no way be accounted a thing of evil, and so long as it held fast, on the other hand, to the conviction that celibacy is a vocation and a gift.[124]

On account of the depth of its understanding, Eph. 5:22-33 is very significant and has had a great effect on ecclesiastical doctrine: "As the Church is obedient to Christ, so too should wives be obedient to their husbands in all things. Husbands, love your wives, as Christ loved the Church and gave himself up for her in order to sanctify her." The letter then calls upon Gen. 2:24: "For this reason a man shall leave father and mother and cleave to his wife, and they will be two in one flesh. The mystery [of this saying] is great. I apply it to Christ and the Church."

The Epistle to the Ephesians clarifies the concept and nature of marriage in the Church, inasmuch as it compares it to the relationship of Christ with his Church. As Christ loves his Church, so should a husband love his wife. The letter sees in the word which God pronounced in the beginning about the unity of the human couple a prophetic forecasting of the unity of Christ with his Church. The unity of man and wife intended at the creation is verified in the union of Christ and the Church. Marriage, which in the old covenant is the order of creation, is accepted in the new covenant in the redemptive, salvational work of Christ. Every marriage in the Church calls to mind that unity of Christ and the Church, and this unity is demonstrated in the companionship and love of the spouses, realized and made visible. If celibacy is the eschatological sign of the Church's expectation of her Lord, then one can and must say of marriage that it is the sign already present of the already realized union of Christ and the Church.

Even the New Testament tables of neighborly duties, since they describe Christian social conduct, must necessarily treat of marriage (see above, ch. 17). To be sure, wives are admonished above all "to be subject" to their husbands (Col. 3:18; Eph. 5:22). Here there is something of an influence of the marital arrangement of the ancient world, whereby the wife was subordinate to the husband. The admonition is taken up in the Epistles, however, in the universal Christian order of mutual service: "Be filled with the spirit, . . . subject to one another in the fear of Christ" (Eph. 5:18, 21). In the tables of neighborly and domestic duties borrowed from profane ethics, an entirely new and essentially Christian statement is added: "Husbands, love your wives" (Col. 3:19; Eph. 5:25, 28, 33).

Thus it is that in Christian marriage that word comes to be spoken and that power comes to be recognized which appear to us to be essential to the communion of marriage. It is not *eros* that is spoken of, however — not that love which lives by need and longing and which becomes rich at the expense of the beloved; rather, it is *agápe*, the love which bestows itself on another out of its own wealth, which very wealth is given for love (see above, ch. 9). The love which, according to the gospel, is always and in every way to be practiced among men, among Christians, must also and above all be realized in the communion of marriage. If it is valid for the whole Church, it is valid also for the Church which shows itself even in the individual household: "Bear with one another and forgive one another! Above all else, practice love, which is the bond of perfection" (Col. 3:13f.).

The Pastoral Epistles, too, exhibit important texts on Christian marriage. First of all, there is one which is directed quite strongly against "people who have fallen away from the faith. They prohibit marriage and enjoin abstinence from foods, although such foods were created by God to be received with thanksgiving" (1 Tim. 4:3). The false teachers who prohibit marriage and foods are additional representatives of that ascetical current of late antiquity which Paul was obliged to combat in First Corinthians (see above). The Pastoral Epistles too make a forceful rejection of these excessive demands; they see therein a derogation and disavowal of God's creation.

There are clever feats of asceticism which must not be represented as a higher morality. Accordingly, there are further admonitions which require explanation. "Women should pray in a becoming manner, chaste and modest. . . . Woman will be saved by bearing children, if she hold fast to faith, love, and holiness, in modesty" (1 Tim. 2:9-15). Again, the remarks are directed against certain sectaries who disavow marriage.

In the second century, some time after the Pastoral Epistles, the apocryphal Acts of Apostles appear, bringing with them another demand for sexual abstinence and the dissolution of marriage. Irenaeus (*Adv. haer.*, 1, 23, 2) tells of false teachers who maintain that "marriage and procreation are spawn of the devil." Against such doctrine the Pastoral Epistles defend the right of marriage. 1 Tim. 2:15 does not mean that a woman ought to exhaust herself in childbearing as a means of gaining entry to heaven. Probably what the letter is saying is that the works of marriage and procreation, performed in faith and love, are holy and productive of salvation. This is reinforced: "I would have young widows marry, bear children, rule their household, and give the enemy [i.e., the devil] no occasion to revile us" (1 Tim. 5:14).

The Pastoral Epistles belong to the later writings of the New Testament. They make it clear that there were at that time dangerous and false ascetical currents attempting to work their influence on the faith and life of the Church. The New Testament Church perceived the danger and the adulteration, and repulsed it in the full confidence of its forceful rebuttal.[125]

In their descriptions of the requirements of official positions, the Pastoral Epistles demand that bishop, presbyter, and deacon be "a man of one wife" (1 Tim. 3:2, 12; Titus 1:6). Only a woman who was "the wife of one husband" may be admitted to the ecclesiastical status of widowhood (1 Tim. 5:9). The texts can be understood as meaning that those who hold office must not be guilty of adultery or of illicit relationships; or they may mean that only men who have been married but once are to be admitted to ecclesiastical office. What is excluded might be remarriage after civil divorce, or even after the death of the first spouse. The Fathers of the Church already interpreted the texts in the latter fashion, and Catholic exegesis invariably follows this view of the matter. In this view, we would have here, in regard to marriage, an ascetical demand made on those who hold office, which could be understood as a first step toward the later law of perfect priestly celibacy.

Nevertheless, exegesis is not entirely in agreement on this matter. The commentaries contradict each other, even to the present time. Indeed, it might be a cause of surprise that bishops and other office-holders were able to be suspect of such grievous lapses as adultery. At the same time, however, other serious faults are mentioned as possible. The bishop must not be addicted to wine, must not be violent nor greedy for money (1 Tim. 3:3). The catalogs of vices are but representative of the usual lists, so it must not be concluded that the list is drawn from concrete cases. In 1 Tim. 3:4, 12, the only express demand made of bishop and deacon is that they govern their household well and raise their children in an orderly manner. The Pastoral Epistles reject the excessive demands of heretical asceticism. Ought they at the same time require special ascetical achievements of those who hold official positions?

Again, there is an ordinance about Christian marriage in First Peter; and in this instance it is found in a table of neighborly and domestic duties. "Women should be submissive to their husbands so that if some do not heed the word, they may be won without a word, by the behavior of their wives, when they see your reverent and chaste behavior. . . . Likewise, in living with their wives, husbands should be considerate of the female sex as the weaker vessel, honoring their wives as the joint heirs of the grace of life, so that your prayers will not remain fruitless" (1 Peter 3:1-7).

The letter reminds women of their subordinate position. This arrangement, nevertheless, is not of human institution but of divine creation (1 Peter 2:13). It is from the order of creation that the husband is the head of the family.

The text discusses the problems of mixed marriage. A woman is Christian, but her husband does not heed the word (i.e., the preaching of the gospel). If the husband refuses to have anything to do with the word, he should not be harassed any further with talk. The truth of the gospel, as exhibited in the behavior of the wife, ought to win the man. He ought to be able to surmise and accept as true the fact that there is a higher power governing the life of his spouse which she fears to offend and which she endeavors to please. It is by the pure and noble conduct of his wife that the husband will come to acknowledge the reality of God.

Husbands too are admonished in this First Epistle of Peter. They also must heed the order of creation. If, in this order, the wife is subject to the husband, she is not, however, surrendered to his whim. The husband must remember that his wife is the weaker vessel, and he must on that account make understanding and discretion the rule. He must not see malice where there is perhaps only another way of doing things and perhaps only physiological weakness. And the husband, too, must find in the Christian faith his motivation to loving conduct. The wife participates and will participate in the same grace of life. Being called alike to salvation, husband and wife are of equal rank and value; and the wife can lay claim to honorable treatment on the part of her husband.

The letter's final admonition to married couples is: "Your prayers must not remain fruitless." The most precious fruit of marriage is the companionship of the spouses in prayer. Disruption of this is the deepest and most severe damage that a marriage might suffer. Fruitful prayer, however, would not be possible if the marital union of the spouses were to be disturbed or destroyed through a lack of loving kindness — and the letter refers expressly to such a lack on the part of the husband. Only where peace and love are present among men is the love and service of God possible (Matthew 5:23).

The New Testament had already in its own time to defend the dignity and holiness of marriage against an ever-threatening disparagement of its values. It is inconceivable that this depreciatory concept of marriage could have infiltrated the New Testament itself. To be sure, Apoc. 14:3f. is often understood in such a way. The hundred and forty-four thousand who abide with the Lamb on Mount Zion are designated as those "who are redeemed from the earth, who have not defiled themselves with women. For they are virgins." But this cannot mean virgins in the sense of virginal men and women who, by renunciation of marriage, consecrated themselves to Christ in a special way. Were this the case, then it would be saying that marriage means being defiled with women. John beholds these hundred and forty-four thousand also in the grand vision of Apoc. 7:2. Here they represent the totality of the redeemed Church. But certainly it cannot be said of this multitude, as if of all Christians, that they lived celibate lives. So the virginity of the hundred and forty-four thousand probably means only their union of love with Christ, much after the fashion of Paul's designating the Church as the pure bride of Christ who has been betrothed to Christ (1 Cor. 11:2).

The later history of the Church is witness to the fact that the conflict surrounding marriage, a conflict which began already in the New Testament, continued on afterwards. It cannot be disputed that representations of marriage as something wicked and defiling occasionally encumbered the doctrinal perspective of theology.

The danger becomes clear in view of the history of the New Testament text. Here and there readings found their way into the manuscripts which are clearly detrimental to a correct understanding and which, if allowed to remain, would change the New Testament teaching on marriage. In Luke 2:36, for example, it is told of the pious widow Anna, who greeted the Infant Jesus in the temple, that after her virginity she lived *seven years* with her husband, and had now lived to a great age as a widow. Some texts would have it that she lived *seven days* with her husband. Apparently it is an attempt to shorten as much as possible the duration of the pious widow's marriage.[126]

In 1 Cor. 7:3f., Paul says: "The husband should give to his wife her conjugal rights, and likewise the wife to her husband." Some texts read that husband and wife should render comfort to each other.

In 1 Cor. 9:5, Paul asks if it is only he among the Apostles who has not the right to have with him a sister (i.e., a Christian woman) as his wife. Not a few texts read: "Did I not have the right to have with me a woman as a sister?" This would imply that the Apostle might live with the woman not in marital companionship but only in a brotherly relationship.

In 1 Peter 3:7 the text says that husbands should be considerate in *living with* their wives. The Greek term could be understood in regard to marital companionship and could be translated "cohabit." It is undoubtedly for this reason that some texts are changed, employing a term which excludes such meaning, saying only that husbands should *dwell* with their wives.

In conclusion, there are two passages which perhaps ought to be mentioned. The opposition between these two passages is particularly worthy of reflection. In the fourth century of the Christian era, Jamblichus wrote his biography of Pythagoras, the great Greek philosopher who lived in the sixth/fifth centuries before Christ. He recounts as a word of Pythagoras' advice to women: "If you come from your marital consort, it is a divine privilege even on that very day to visit the holy shrines; but by no means, of course, if you are coming from forbidden intercourse." The Council of Trent called for the publication of a comprehensive book of religious doctrine which even to the present day, as the *Catechismus Romanus*, or *Catechism of the Council of Trent*, constitutes the authoritative norm of faith and life, and ought to be accepted everywhere as the basis for the proclamation of the gospel. In the chapter on the Eucharist it says: "The dignity of so great a Sacrament demands that before the reception of the Eucharist married persons abstain some days from marital intercourse." It can scarcely be denied that this advice but continues the unbiblical, disparaging attitude toward marriage which was shared by many of the Fathers of the Church (see translator's note, #127).

II. UNCHASTITY

If the New Testament is at one with the more serious ethical notions of its time in its rejection of adultery, it surpasses them in its unequivocal condemnation of unchastity, whether prostitution or any other kind of extramarital or unnatural sexual activity. Here the New Testament is of one mind with Judaism, which is rigidly intent on the sexual orderliness and chastity of the people. Unchastity is the sin of the Gentiles (Lev. 18:24f.). Because the Gentiles know no God, they also know no law — hence, unchastity and all their other vices (Wis. 14:24-26; Rom. 1:18-32).

From the Gospels it is clear that even in Israel there was public prostitution. Naturally, the pious and the righteous kept themselves away from harlots. Jesus, however, upon encountering such a woman, leads her to an admission of her sinfulness and makes her a partaker in forgiveness in advance of the righteous. "Tax-collectors and harlots go into the kingdom of God before you" (Matthew 21:31). In the narrative of the sinful woman with the ointment (Luke 7:36-50), the guilt that was forgiven her is generally understood as proceeding from sins of unchastity. Still, it is not expressly so stated. Be that as it may, Jesus pronounced the woman taken in adultery free, because no one is without sin. Nothing is mentioned of her doing penance; and she experiences forgiveness entirely as a gift (John 7:53–8:1).[128]

There were burning issues occasioned by the entry of Christianity into the Greek world. In the Apostolic decree which set such minimal requirements as would make it possible for Jews and Gentiles to live together in one congregation, abstinence from unchastity is demanded of Gentile Christians (Acts 15:20, 29; 21:25). The primary import of this demand is certainly in reference to marriages within forbidden relationships, which, in accord with Lev. 18:6-18, the Rabbis designated as unchastity.

In the tradition of the catalogs of vices, unchastity is also mentioned and condemned in Rom. 1:24-27; 13:13; 1 Cor. 5:10f.; 6:9; 2 Cor. 12:21; Gal. 5:19; Eph. 5:3f.; Col. 3:5; 1 Tim. 1:10; 2 Tim. 3:4. Paul paints dismal pictures of pagan immorality (Rom. 1:24-32; 1 Cor. 5:1, 9-11). In these vices the Apostle sees the judgment of God working its effect on paganism. "God gave them up to shameful passions" (Rom. 1:24). In such judgments as these, even the New Testament bespeaks the Jew's consciousness of the moral superiority of his people (1 Thess. 4:5; Eph. 4:18f.). If the Church of the Gentiles can spring from such desolation, now it is sanctified in Christ and in the Spirit of God (1 Cor. 6:11; Col. 3:7). Paul warns the congregation against backsliding (2 Cor. 12:21). Its holiness demands abstinence from unchastity (1 Thess. 4:3). Unchastity is a work of the flesh (Gal. 5:19). Unchastity and impurity of whatever sort should not even be named among

Christians (Eph. 5:3). The unchaste will have no part in the kingdom of God (1 Cor. 6:9; Eph. 5:5).

The conditions prevailing in such a sophisticated city as Corinth
impelled Paul to warn its Christians in an especially penetrating manner against unchastity. Paul is indignant because the community there
has tolerated an instance of unchastity "such as is found not even
among the pagans" (1 Cor. 5:1-13). A Christian had, so it would
appear, after the death of his father, married his father's wife, his own
stepmother. Paul demands: "Purge the evil from the midst of you!"
(Deut. 17:7). He severely condemns all prostitution (1 Cor. 6:12-20).
He refutes a frivolous argument of the Corinthians: "'Food is for the
belly, and the belly for food'; but God will destroy them both." Paul
counters that the body is not for immorality but for the Lord. God
will raise the body. The bodies of Christians are members of Christ.
They must not be made members of a prostitute. The body is the
temple of the Holy Spirit. It belongs to God, and is not at the arbi-
trary disposal of the Christian.

The Apocalypse too reprimands unchastity as a vice of the pagans.
This vice can, however, penetrate even into a Christian community
(Apoc. 2:14, 20). The reproof probably is in regard to certain
libertine Gnostics who reckoned their own loose living as freedom and
superiority. In the Apocalypse, Rome — understood both as the historical city and as a symbol of Satanic hostility to God — is portrayed
as a great whore, the mother of prostitutes, the great seductress of the
world (Apoc. 17:1-5). What is meant thereby is primarily the vicious
unchastity of the city whereby it corrupts the earth (Apoc. 19:2).
Whoredom also signifies, however, its unprincipled politics, in that it
allies its political power with others according to expediency and
profit (Apoc. 18:3, 9).

Finally, the idolatry of the capital city is stigmatized; it seduces the
people to a whoreson apostasy from God to the idols and to the persecution of the saints and the righteous (Apoc. 18:24). The final judgment will destroy the idolaters and murderers and the unchaste as
well (Apoc. 21:8; 22:15). Standing in opposition to the whore is the
Bride of the Lamb. She is united to the pure and sober Logos of God
(Apoc. 19:13). She is the holy city of Jerusalem, to which nothing unclean gains entry (Apoc. 21:10, 27).

§ 21. TRUTH AND FALSEHOOD · OATHS

I. TRUTH

The biblical and the Greek concepts of truth [129] (the latter is the more usual for us) are different. The word used in the Hebrew text, *'emeth = truth*, has the same root as the word *'amen = firm, durable; entrusted*, in the sense of what is authentic or binding. Accordingly, *'emeth* signifies "truth" in the sense of that which endures, that which has continuance and duration, in fine, that which is unchangeable and remains forever. Truth is something that is, something that is realized in actuality.

The etymological significance of the Greek word ἀλήθεια is something that is not hidden; rather, it is something that is of public knowledge. Its existence, however, is disclosed through recognition. In the Greek (and therefore Western) concept, truth is something that is recognized, known, contemplated, and finally stated. A word is true if it expresses a circumstance correctly and validly.

In the Greek translation of the Old Testament, the Old Testament import of truth goes into the Greek concept of truth. God is truth, purely and simply; and, as the ultimate reality, God is true. His revelation is the disclosure and communication of truth. In God's revelation the realities are disclosed to man. In accord with the Old Testament import, the word *fidelity* can also be used to translate *truth*. God's truth is his fidelity to his covenant. "Your truth [fidelity] is firm as the heavens" (Ps. 89:3). "Grace and truth [fidelity] stand before your face" (Ps. 89:15). "My truth [fidelity]and grace shall accompany him" (Ps. 89:25; likewise Pss. 40:12; 61:8).

If in these places God's truth is united with his grace, there are other passages where it is associated with his holiness (Ps. 71:22) and righteousness (Ps. 111:8; Zech. 8:8; Neh. 9:33). The truth of God is protection (Ps. 41:4), light (Ps. 43:3), assistance in the face of the enemy (Ps. 54:7). As a promise, God's word is true, as in the promise of everlasting continuance to the House of David (2 Sam. 7:28-29). God's law is true and it is truth, since, like God, it endures forever

(Pss. 19:10; 119:68). The priest should "teach the instruction of truth" (Mal. 2:6). God's whole truth will be revealed at the end of time. Then will the righteous "acknowledge the truth" (Wis. 3:9). God's truth places an obligation on man; he must heed it and follow it. That is the import of the phrase "to walk in the truth" (Pss. 26:3; 86:11; 1 Kings 2:4; 2 Kings 20:3). The pious man prays: "Lead me in your truth and teach me" (Ps. 25:5).

Recognition and possession of truth is an essentially human attitude or endeavor, like intelligence and wisdom. Thus it is mentioned along with other virtues of social living: "Justice is turned back, and right-eousness is far away; truth stumbles in the streets, and uprightness finds no entry" (Is. 59:14); or, "Buy truth, and do not sell it; buy wisdom, breeding, and intelligence" (Prov. 23:23). There is an admonition, "Fight even to the death for truth" (Sir. 4:28). Truth having been recognized, one must follow it. The dying Jacob bids his son Joseph: "Show me your love and truth [fidelity]" (Gen. 47:29). The judge must "judge the poor in truth" (Prov. 29:14). Truth and truthfulness continue to exist. "Truthful lips endure forever, but a lying tongue for only a moment" (Prov. 12:19).

The word and concept *truth* are encountered not infrequently in the Qumran scrolls. The truth is hidden from the natural man, and is not attainable by his own unaided efforts. It is revealed and granted by God. God "is the truth" (1 QH 4:40). He discloses the truth of the just way (1 QH 4:25). He cleanses of guilt, so that "all deeds are done in truth" (1 QH 6:8f.). "God purifies the works of men by his truth . . . and purifies them by his holy spirit" (1 QS 4:20f.). Truth and holy spirit are one gift of God (as in John 4:23). Truth, as op-posed to error) is not only in the intellect, but it is realized in activity and deed. "Abomination to truth are deeds of wickedness, and abomi-nation to wickedness are the ways of truth" (1 QS 4:17). Like the New Testament (John 3:21; 1 John 1:6), the Qumran texts too say that "truth is for doing" (1 QS 1:5; 5:3; 8:2; 1 QpH 7:10-12).

In the later period of antiquity, an existential and religious signifi-cance enters into the concept of truth. The true is that which truly exists, the eternal, that which alone is real, the divine. The under-standable conviction of the Greeks to the effect that truth is accessible to reflection is rendered dubious and is in fact abandoned. Man comes to share in truth when the limits of the human are surpassed, be it by ecstasy, be it by divine revelation. The kingdom of truth is distinguished from the earthly and human. Truth becomes a concept of a dualist understanding of the world. The divine truth possesses its own peculiar reality. The human world of waxing and waning is but appearance, and, in fact, a lie. Such is the representation and conceptualization of Gnosticism, which seems to come into close contact with the New Testament.[130]

In the New Testament the word *truth* comprises both the Old Testament Jewish sense and the Greek philosophical sense. Truth designates the divine reality. It stands opposed to human existence, but discloses itself in revelation. If God's essence and word remain ever a mystery to man, man must nevertheless continue to apply himself in seeking a knowledge of divine truth. Undoubtedly the New Testament demands the morality of truthfulness. The word of Jesus demands that in speech the "yes" and "no" of the disciples be pure truth. Anything else is of the evil one (Matthew 5:36).

The metaphor in the Sermon on the Mount speaks again of this simple truthfulness: "The eye is the lamp of your body. If your eye is sound (ἁπλοῦς = simple, unclouded, honest), your whole body is in the light. But if your eye is sick, your whole body is in the darkness" (Matthew 6:22f. = Luke 11:34f.). Late Judaism prizes simplicity (ἁπλότης) as the simple, honest uprightness of thought and deed (1 Chr. 29:17; Wis. 1:1; and in the *Testaments of the Twelve Patriarchs*, Reuben 4:5; Simeon 4:5; Levi 13:1; Issachar 4:1). Matthew 6:22 belongs to this ethical tradition. The eye, which receives the light, here signifies metaphorically the receptiveness of man for God. The healthy eye, i.e., the honest man, can take in God. When this happens, the whole man is in the light. Faith makes man honest and truthful. If a man is in the dark in respect to God, he is totally in the dark.[131]

In the doctrine of the Apostle Paul, the God who was formerly revealed in Israel just as now he is revealed in the Church, is the God of truth, as opposed to the falsehood of the idols (Rom. 1:25). The true God is he who lives and produces, he who gives the life of salvation. Truth is also an attribute of God. As a just Judge, he judges according to truth (Rom. 2:2). God's truth becomes tangible in his

fidelity to his promises (Rom. 15:8). This truth of God is now revealed in Christ, who is the simple "yes" of God, because in him are
all God's promises fulfilled (2 Cor. 1:19f.; Eph. 4:21). Just as formerly the Law was truth (Rom. 2:20), now the gospel (Gal. 2:5, 14;
Col. 1:5) and its preaching (Eph. 1:13) are truth. Christian existence
is simply this: to live "in belief in the truth" (2 Thess. 2:12f.).

In the Pastoral Epistles the Apostle Paul is "the teacher of the Gentiles in faith and truth" (1 Tim. 2:7). The Church is the "pillar and
bulwark of the truth" (1 Tim. 3:15). Christians are they who are
obligated "to the belief and to the knowledge of the truth" (1 Tim.
4:3; 2 Tim. 2:25; Heb. 10:26). False teachers however, are "depraved
of mind and bereft of truth" (1 Tim. 6:5). They whom they lead
astray "will turn away their ear from truth, and lend it unto myths"
(2 Tim. 4:4). The truth is the "sound teaching" now brought forward
by the Church (1 Tim. 1:10).

The Catholic Epistles employ similar expressions. God's truth is
made available by the Church. "He begot us by the word of truth"
(James 1:18). Christians "sanctified their souls through obedience to
the truth" (1 Peter 1:22). They are "confirmed in the present truth,"
i.e., in the truth present in the Church (2 Peter 1:12). Disbelief and
sin are "lapse from the truth" (James 5:19). Orderly life in the Church
is the "way of truth." This way is defamed on account of the licentiousness of those who have been led astray (2 Peter 2:2). In this late
biblical and early Christian understanding, truth is comprised and
exhibited in the Church's already magisterial proclamation thereof,
and in the fixed rule of faith then developing (see above, ch. 6).

The divine gift of truth imposes an obligation of moral conduct
ordered to truth and truthfulness. The Church must be true, just as
God is true, since the "yes" of God to creation and history is vitalized
in Christ. "That is why we sound the 'Amen' through him, to the
glory of God" (2 Cor. 1:20). Paul's congregation already responded to
the liturgical songs and prayers with the shout of assent "Amen!",
which signifies: "Yes, so it is!" With its "Amen," the Church expresses its faithful response and attestation to the fact that God's
words are true and always come to pass.

The whole of the Apostolic ministry pertains necessarily to the truth. "For we cannot do anything against the truth, but only for the truth" (2 Cor. 13:8). The truth here referred to is the all-embracing right order, and salvation in the Church and in all creation. The one and only purpose of Paul is to make known and to demonstrate this truth in his preaching. "For the truth of the gospel must be preserved for you" (Gal. 2:5). When Paul saw that Peter and several others "were not behaving straightforwardly according to the truth of the gospel . . . he withstood him to his face" (Gal. 2:11, 14).

When the Apostles were announcing the word of truth, their own lives and conduct had to be in harmony with their preaching. Paul asserts that his own word and that of his co-workers is honest and clear, and was not yes and no at the same time (2 Cor. 1:19). When his word was subsequently corroborated, it was a source of great satisfaction to him (2 Cor. 7:14).

Each Christian must make a personal effort to live in accord with the truth. In the face of God's truth, it becomes perfectly clear that every man is a liar (Rom. 3:4, 7). Nevertheless, there is now a new possibility of truth in the new creation. Christ is the exemplar of truth. Paul assures himself that "the truth of Christ" is in him (2 Cor. 11:10; similarly, Rom. 9:1). The Apostle admonishes the Church in Ephesus: "You have been taught that in Jesus is the truth" (Eph. 4:21). The admonition to truthfulness is repeated again and again.

By a typological explanation, Paul finds such an admonition by using the ritual observance of the paschal feast as an example. "We do not want to celebrate the festival with the old leaven, not with the leaven of malice and wickedness, but with the unleavened bread of sincerity and truth" (1 Cor. 5:7-8). Here Paul is using an allegory occasionally employed even by Jewish teachers. Christians are the unleavened, as those who are sanctified by the work of Christ. They must exhibit the fact of salvation in their lives. Sin has to have ceased. The new morality is designated as sincerity and truth. In this application of the word *truth*, there may be still at work an influence of the Old Testament usage, in which truth, predicated of man, can signify much the same as righteousness (see above). Truth and injustice are opposites. "Love does not rejoice at injustice, but rejoices in the truth" (1 Cor. 13:6). Godlessness suppresses the truth in injustice

(Rom. 1:18). They must expect judgment who "attend not unto truth but unto injustice" (Rom. 2:8).

The lack of accord between the sanctifying action of God and un-holiness in the life of a Christian would be falsehood in one's very being. Christian morality is true and truth when there is harmony between God's operations and the life of the Christian. The Epistle to the Ephesians says much the same: "Put on the new man who is created according to God in the righteousness and holiness of truth" (Eph. 4:24). The image of God, after which man is created (Gen. 1:26f.), is now raised up again out of sin. The righteousness and holi-ness of his primordial state are created anew. Man again corresponds to the design of creation. In his original, divinely willed form, man is again in truth. The state of existence of the new man is, purely and simply, being true.

A challenge follows therefrom: "Inasmuch as you have put away falsehood, let every man speak the truth to his neighbor, for we are members of each other" (Eph. 4:25). This moral rule is quoted in a fashion very similar to that which is found in the Old Testament (Zech. 8:16). But now it is given a new and more profound basis. The lie, which is put away, is the untrue life, lived in vain. The new, true life demands truthfulness in speech. The Epistle makes further refer-ence to the unity of the Body of Christ, which must not be disturbed nor destroyed by a lie. "Walk as children of the light. The fruit of light is found in all that is good and righteous and true" (Eph. 5:9). To exist in the light means being light and being a source of light to others. The light that has been received streams out into the world in holiness, in being good and righteous and true.

The Church is admonished further: "Let us effect the truth in love" (Eph. 4:15). Truth exists not merely as a property of the intellect; it must become apparent in love, and love must demonstrate truth. "Stand firm, then, your loins girded with truth, having put on the armor of righteousness" (Eph. 6:14). Again an Old Testament say-ing is used (Is. 11:5). In Old Testament understanding as well as New, truth and righteousness are the salvational activity of God, with which man is fitted out and which, throughout his life, he must defend.

Paul has a penchant also for the concept of integrity (ἁπλότης; see above). The *Testament of Levi* (13:1) admonishes to walk "in integrity according to the Law." Total submission is explained anew by Paul as "sincerity toward Christ" (2 Cor. 11:3), the quality which must attend the Church's belonging to her Lord. Sincerity must also be the mark of Christians' relations with each other. Alms should be given "in simple (disinterested) kindness" (Rom. 12:8). Paul praises the wealth of liberality" (ἁπλότης) with which the congregations of Macedonia have helped the Church of Jerusalem (2 Cor. 8:2). The wealth of a congregation is bestowed "in the utter simplicity of the joy of giving" (2 Cor. 9:11, 13). Slaves are especially admonished "to do the will of God wholeheartedly, to be obedient in singleness of heart, as to Christ" (Eph. 6:5). Simplicity orders man toward God.

Such exhortation is continued in the later Epistles of the New Testament; and so, too, in the Epistle of James. If strife and division prevail in the congregation, Christians cannot suppose that they possess wisdom, nor can they pride themselves in it. They "lie in the face of the truth" (James 3:14). Another admonition declares: "Since you have sanctified your souls in obedience to the truth unto an unfeigned love of the brethren, love one another earnestly from the heart" (1 Peter 1:22). God's word is an operating, sanctifying power. Out of the truth of God brotherly love has now been made possible. Truth and holiness must bring forth love if they are in any respect genuine.

True and *truth* are important terms in the Johannine writings. Truth is the revelation of God in Christ. This event sets the present sharply apart from the past. "The Law was given through Moses; grace and truth have come through Christ Jesus" (John 1:17). The old covenant could only lead up to salvation and promise it. Christ is the gift of divine favor, and the revelation of the divine reality. Hope has now come true. To this truth, which is Christ, John the Baptist bore witness (John 5:33). Christ now reveals the truth, in that he proclaims the word he heard from the Father (John 8:26, 40, 45f.). He bears witness to the truth (John 18:37). As the Word of the Father, he is the Truth disclosed (John 17:17). He is "the Way, the Truth, and the Life" (John 14:6).

This revelation, however, is certainly not an item of knowledge obtainable from the teacher and then once and for all available. The truth makes itself available only to one who is on the way with Christ, on the way to Christ — it is a historical acquisition. Christ bequeathes to the Church "the Spirit of truth" (John 14:17; 15:26). This Spirit will lead the disciples to the fullness of truth (John 16:13). That Christ is revelation is practically concealed from the world, most especially by Christ's death on the cross. He is more scandal and vexation than revelation. The Spirit permits the disciples to recognize the truth, and convinces the world thereof. The Spirit can be straightway called "the Truth" (1 John 5:6), because he makes the truth evident and real. In the Church, therefore, as also in the world, Truth and Spirit are identical.

Life must be determined by truth. Christ imparts the truth vocally. The disciples recognize the truth and believe in it (John 8:45f.). The true disciple is "of the truth" (John 18:37; 1 John 3:19). He is sanctified in the truth (John 17:17-19). The truth renders free (John 8:32). What is meant is not the human freedom of spirit in the rationalist sense, but the actual becoming free of oneself through faith, and freedom from that which is opposed to the divine reality, i.e., freedom from sin (John 8:34). Since truth means the reality of God, the concept is equivalent in significance to several other figurative expressions of that reality: life (John 17:3); light (John 3:21); and love (1 John 4:16).

The Church knows and practices worship "in spirit and truth" (John 4:23f.). These often repeated words must not be understood in the light of such concepts in a philosophy then current; rather, they can be understood only in the light of the gospel itself. Spirit and truth do not refer to a philosophical worship of God, some sort of pretended cultic religion. The Spirit is much more the divine Holy Spirit. The Truth is the revelation of God present in Christ. True worship takes place in Christ's community of salvation. It is the knowledge of Truth that structures the congregation; and this Truth remains in it (2 John 1f.). The disciple must do what is true (John 3:21; 1 John 1:6). Certainly this means keeping the commandments, and good moral conduct in general (John 15:10); and in a more profound way, the carrying out of the genuine and permanent, in which regard it is truth that is essential. The disciple can and must be the "co-worker of the Truth," inasmuch as he serves the mission of the Word (3 John 8).

II. FALSEHOOD

In the primitive history in the Bible it is recounted that in the matter of primordial guilt the lie was disastrously prominent — the lie of
the serpent and man's lie as well (Gen. 3). Cain deceived his brother
and lied to God. And when the lie ended in murder the crime was
great beyond measure, quite unforgivable (Gen. 4).

In the decalogue there is the commandment: "Thou shalt not give
evidence against thy neighbor as a lying witness" (Exod. 20:16).
What is forbidden is the making of an untrue declaration before the
court, with the purpose and end in view of doing damage to the possessions, reputation, or life of another. And only false witness against
one's neighbor (a fellow national) is forbidden; nothing is said of
one's behavior toward the stranger. Nor does it forbid falsehood and
lying in general.[132]

By the letter of the law, the use of a lie is not plainly condemned in
the Old Testament. In the form of the text that has come down to us,
the mostly harmless use of a lie may occasionally be criticized in the
light of later considerations. The theme of the ancestral woman saved
from unusual demands by a lie (told by Abraham and Isaac respec-
tively) occurs repeatedly (Gen. 12:10-20; 20:1-8; 26:7-11). Our exegesis
is not unanimous. The narrative can hardly be understood, however,
as unhesitatingly justifying the white lie as a kind of prudence. Besides, the woman is only placed in even greater danger because of
the lie. It is not human cleverness that saves her, but God's interven-
tion. The liar is finally put to shame by the one deceived. The collective sense of the narrative is that God's plan of salvation remains in
effect in spite of the unholiness of the human performer.

Nor does the narrative about the deception practiced against poor
blind Isaac approve of the transaction. The lie and fraud on the part
of Rebecca and Jacob are given no sympathy, while the tragedy of
Isaac and Esau is portrayed with deep insight and understanding
(Gen. 27:1-29). Israel's traditions condemned Jacob's action as a fraud
of profound and far-reaching consequences (Ps. 12:4f.; Jer. 9:3).

When the Hebrew midwives deceive Pharaoh, their artifice is justified in view of the wicked command to kill the newborn boys, which

it circumvents. It is out of the fear of God that they so act, and *that* is why they are blessed (Exod. 1:15-21).

The narration of the artifices and lies with which Michol, Jonathan, and David sought their own advantage (1 Sam. 19–21) makes no moral evaluation of their actions at all. In the matter of his atrocities against the Philistines, David unhesitatingly managed the deception of the Philistine prince who had shown him hospitality (1 Sam. 27).

The moral conscience becomes more refined, and ethical judgment becomes sharper. The prophets demand uprightness and truthfulness in word as well as in the heart, and condemn all lies, calumnies, and deceptions. Speech and intent must be in accord with each other. A lie is a crime which God will avenge (Hos. 7:1; Jer. 9:3-9; Nahum 3:1). The righteous men of the Psalms bewail the prevalence of lies everywhere (Ps. 59:13f.; 62:5; 109:2f.). The condemnatory judgment of the lie is repeated frequently in the Wisdom literature. The prohibition against false witness in a formal court setting is enjoined again and again (Is. 59:4; Job 15:35; Prov. 6:19; 14:5; 19:5, 9; 21:28). It is discovered that a lie is destructive of society and life. "Like hammer, sword, and arrow does false witness kill" (Prov. 25:18). The truthful man saves lives (Prov. 14:25).

The direct lie is condemned (Prov. 12:19; Sir. 20:24-26; 41:17); and condemned likewise is calumny, double-dealing, and dissimulation (Prov. 4:24; 26:23-28; Sir. 5:14; 28:13-26). God, to whom all untruth is alien, abominates every lying device (Prov. 12:22; Eccl. 7:30). God, whom man cannot deceive, demands truth (Job 13:9).

The aphoristic literature, particularly the Psalms, recognizes godlessness as the cause of lying. Whoever denies God, who is Truth, is a servant of Falsehood, in whose power he is. Godlessness puts its trust in lies (Hos. 10:13); and out of the mouths of the godless come only lies (Ps. 58:4). Particularly grievous are falsehood and lies in one's dealings with God (Ps. 78:36f.; Hos. 7:13). Essentially, falsehood and deceit are idolatry (Is. 57:4f.; Jer. 13:25; 16:19f.; Hab. 2:18). Before God all men are, in the last analysis, liars (Ps. 116:11). He intends to destroy the lie and the liar alike (Ps. 5:6f.). In the eschatological era of salvation all lying will be at an end (Zeph. 3:13).

In the New Testament the unqualified prohibition of falsehood

meets the demand for truth. In this matter there is scarcely any room
for haggling. Jesus repeats the prohibition of false witness according
to the decalogue: "You know the commandments . . . 'Thou shalt
not bear false witness' " (Mark 10:19).

As godlessness in the Old Testament, so is disbelief a lie in the
New, and a constant source of untruth. Already in the Greek Old
Testament it is possible for the godless man to be designated as a
hypocrite (Job 34:30; 36:13). Hypocrisy, which in the New Testament
is charged especially to the Pharisees, is found also in the discrepancy
between thinking and speaking, between the actuality and the appearance (Matthew 6:2; 23:15; Luke 13:15; also Gal. 2:13). But discord plumbs its depth in the refusal to believe in the present messianic
salvation and in Christ. "You hypocrites! You know how to interpret
the appearance of earth and sky! Why, then, do you not know how to
interpret the present hour?" (Luke 12:56).[133]

Hereafter disbelief will be proclaimed by lying prophets (Matthew
7:15) and false messiahs (Matthew 24:11, 24). Clearly the idea here
is of the hypocrisy of a later time. Since correct and false religious
avowals go their separate ways, false doctrine is designated as "the
hypocrisy of those who speak lies" (1 Tim. 4:2). It is in this sense that
in the *Didache* (8:1), the Jews are termed simply "hypocrites."

The letters of the Apostles repeat the warnings against falsehood.
Paul, in fact, makes his own the deeply pessimistic judgment of the
Old Testament: "God is truthful; but every man is a liar" (Rom.
3:4 = Ps. 116:11). The moral life is constantly endangered by the
temptation to falsehood. Now, however, there is a new opportunity
for truth. If man's very being did formerly become falsehood, now
the true image of man has been set up anew; in this true image falsehood can have no part. The knowledge of new creation and of one's
calling must constantly deepen and renew truthfulness. "Do not lie
to one another! Put off the old man and his deeds, and put on the
new man, who is being renewed in the increase of knowledge, after
the image of his creator" (Col. 3:9-10).

Truthfulness is an obligation, in view of the unity and society of
the Church. "Put away falsehood, and let each one speak the truth
with his neighbor, because we are members one with another in one
body" (Eph. 4:25). Membership in the Body of Christ is union with

Christ as of cells one with another. A lie is an injustice to one's neighbor, to the whole Body of Christ, and to Christ himself.

Christ is the exemplar of truthfulness; imitation of him is of obligation to the Christian. "He did no sin, nor was any deceit found on his lips" (1 Peter 2:22). Christians must do likewise. "Put away all malice and all deception, hypocrisy, envy, and all slander" (1 Peter 2:1). The lie dissolves fraternal companionship and destroys love (1 Peter 2:22). To lie to the community is to lie to God and to the Holy Spirit, who fills up the Church (Acts 5:3f.).

If, according to John's Gospel, the truth is order and salvation, then the opposite of truth is something other than a mere untrue word. Ultimately a lie is the antithesis of God, and as such diabolical. "The devil has nothing to do with the truth, and the truth is not in him" (John 8:44). If truth is life (John 17:3), its counterpart, as lie, is death. As the denial of the divine reality, the lie is nothingness; and it destroys the proper existence of any who pursue it. The lie kills, and the devil is a liar (John 8:44); his lie is a concrete statement of what is not true, by reason of the simple fact that he denies the revelation. Thus, the devil is "a murderer from the very beginning" (John 8:44). Just as there are men who are of truth (John 8:47), so too there are men who are of the devil (John 8:44).

The First Epistle of John, so it appears, is combating a kind of Gnosticism which was disseminating a false teaching about Christ, a teaching which constituted a denial of the true humanity and historicity of Jesus. In the sense in which the Epistle uses it, the term *lie* means heretical falsehood, which detaches one from the reality of God. If the revelation in Christ is truth, the denial of this truth is a lie. He who denies it is the anti-Christ (1 John 2:22). He is "prophet of falsehood" (1 John 4:1). If it is required to live the truth (John 3:21; 1 John 1:6), he who behaves contrary to the truth is a liar: "Whoever says, 'I have known him' and does not keep his commandments, is a liar and the truth is not in him" (1 John 2:4). Whoever maintains that he loves God but hates his brother is a liar (1 John 4:20).

The Apocalypse of John is quite sharp in its condemnation of every sort of lie. A lie is untruthfulness, such as disbelief and idolatry. In the mouths of the blessed who follow the Lamb no lie was found

(Apoc. 14:5; 21:27). Those who belong to the community of Christ
are "virginally" untainted by any kind of lie (Apoc. 4:4). Satan and
his helpers go about with lies, which the recipient of the vision portrays in mythical imagery as demons. The prophet of lies is actively
associated in his works with the apocalyptic beast (Apoc. 16:13; 19:20;
20:10). The lie is a sin which is punished with eternal damnation; it
is the embodiment of all vices. "Its lot is in the lake that burns with
fire and brimstone, and this is the second death" (Apoc. 21:8; 22:15).

III. OATHS

Since truth is an absolute necessity for the existence of human society, and since the latter is all too frequently endangered by lies,
society seeks for some way to assure truth. In general, such assurance
is sought through a protestation of a special kind — the oath. An oath
calls God to witness. As the omniscient One, he knows the truth of
what is declared; and as the holy and almighty One, he will punish
the act of perjury. Or else, the oath pledges as security the most valuable possession of the one swearing, his very life, in fact, which is to
be forfeited if what he swears to is false. Often in connection with
the oath is a curse.

If in antiquity the oath was in general use, the questionability of
the practice did not go unnoticed. Many of the Greek authors treating of ethical practice disallowed the oath. The Pythagoreans were
required "never to swear by the gods. Each man must strive always
to be worthy of belief" (Diogenes Laertius, 8, 22; Jamblichus, *Life of
Pythagoras*, 47). Epictetus (*Enchiridion*, 33, 5) commanded his students: "Avoid the taking of an oath in all such cases as it can be
avoided; otherwise, only so far as is permissible."

In Israel, too, the practice of swearing an oath was known in every
period of her history. It can be effected by and between individuals.
Esau swears at the demand of his brother (Gen. 25:33); Joseph, at
the demand of his father (Gen. 47:31); the scouts, on the demand of
Rahab (Josh. 2:12-14); Joab before King David (2 Sam. 19:8). Kings

require oaths of princes and peoples (1 Sam. 14:28; 1 Kings 18:10; 1 Esdr. 10:5; Eccl. 8:2). Agreements are sworn to in such a way as to make God the judge between the causes of the parties (Gen. 31:49-53). The law requires of the accused an oath both in regard to his sworn testimony and in his oath of purgation (Gen. 14:22; Exod. 22:8, 11; Num. 5:21; Job 31). Marriage itself is a covenant concluded with an oath (Ruth 4:7-12).

Naturally, the only oath permitted in Israel is one sworn by Yahweh (Deut. 6:13; 10:20). To swear by any other god is idolatry (Jer. 5:7; 12:16; Hos. 4:15; Amos 8:14; Zeph. 1:5). If the oath is a ceremonial confession of belief in God (Is. 19:18; 48:1; Jer. 12:16), to swear falsely is a misuse of the name of God (Exod. 20:7; Lev. 19:12). The one who swears curses himself in the event of breaking his oath (Num. 5:21; Is. 65:15; Jer. 28:22; Job 31). Divine punishment will reach out to him (1 Kings 8:31).

Even Yahweh swears; and since there is none greater than he, when he swears he can swear only by himself (Gen. 22:16; Exod. 32:13; Amos 6:8; 8:7; Is. 45:23; Jer. 11:5). God makes pledge of himself with his oath, for the truth and endurance of his word (Ps. 110:4).

In Israel, too, the oath and the practice of taking an oath began to be abused. The later prophets bewail the decline (Zech. 5:13; Mal. 3:5). The Psalms (15:4; 24:4) demand fidelity to one's oaths. Jesus Sirach (23:9-11) warns of frivolous oath-taking, as being a common practice. One is somewhat hesitant about oath-taking, too, in consequence of human unreliability (Eccl. 9:2). Since frequent swearing was regarded as a questionable practice, one could at least try to avoid the misuse of the name of God by substitution of another name. This could easily give rise to a certain casuistry whereby one might attempt to elude the obligation of his given word. A pious Jew, seeing through such a subterfuge, will have rejected such an evasion as disgraceful. This is clear enough from the reprimand spoken by Jesus (Matthew 5:34-36; 23:16-22), and from Rabbinic sources as well.[134]

The Mishna tries to check the abuse of swearing, and punishes the false oath with scourging. According to Philo (*Decalogue*, 84-93), the best way is not to swear at all; next best is to swear rightly; worst of all is perjury. Whoever swears should first ask himself whether he is "pure in soul, body, and tongue. For it is sinful for offensive speech to proceed from the same mouth which speaks the most holy name." The Essenes required of those entering the order a most serious oath; and other than this, they proscribed oath-taking entirely (Philo, *Quod omnis probus liber sit*, 84; Josephus, *Jewish War*, 2, 135–142). Even the Qumran community required at entrance an oath on the Law of Moses (1 QS 2:1-18; 5:8; *Damascus Document*, 15:6, 8). The *Damascus Document* permits an oath before the court, but not private swearing. The name of God, however, and the Torah are not to be mentioned in swearing (*Damascus Document*, 9:8-10; 15:1-4).

The criticism of swearing in the New Testament is still more stringent than the reservations expressed by Judaism. This criticism is externalized in one of the antitheses of the Sermon on the Mount (Matthew 5:33-37). The law of Israel tried to protect the sanctity of the oath and to guarantee the keeping of vows. But more is required in the New Testament community of disciples, which is in expectation of the kingdom of God. In this community Christ is recognized as the messianic Lawgiver, and his command is heeded: "I say to you, do not swear!" In the new order, the oath no longer has any reason to exist. Its only reason for existence, its only necessity, is where one must reckon with the possibility of a lie, or where the lie is a commonplace. The saying of the Lord proscribes swearing entirely. Should the use of the name of God be avoided in swearing only by the use of substitute words, it is no more than a game of words. To swear by heaven and earth is certainly equivalent to swearing by their Creator; and to swear by Jerusalem, God's city, is to swear by God himself. Neither can a man offer his own life as the pledge of his oath, since it is not properly in his possession.

An oath is of its very nature an attempt to put God at one's disposal, to involve him in what is earthly and human, and ultimately to entangle his truth in man's lie. How, then, is man to conduct himself? He must remain in his own sphere, the sphere to which he is obligated. The simple words "yes" and "no" must suffice, and they must mean fully what they say. An oath added thereto would be "from evil" (Matthew 5:37); or it might also be understood "from the evil one." In any case, the "evil" is referred to the devil, who tempts men to swear. And the devil is "a liar and the father of lies" (John 8:44).[135]

The casuistry of the oath is discussed also in an indictment of Pharisaic conduct (Matthew 23:16-22). An oath or a vow by the temple, so say the Scribes, counts for nothing; but an oath by the gold of the temple is binding. In naming the temple, one might have in mind only the great edifice itself, while giving no thought to its determination as God's house. In this event, God is not being summoned and called upon as witness. But the gold ornaments and vessels served only one end — the honor of God. In any case, to swear by the gold of the temple means to swear by God, at least by way of inclusion. Jesus' criticism answers that the temple nevertheless is more than the gold therein. The temple sanctifies the gold that adorns it. Of similar futility is the distinction between the altar and the gift on the altar, or between heaven and God, whose throne nevertheless is in heaven.

In Matthew 5:33-37, oaths are condemned in general; but in Matthew 23:16-22, it is only the misuse of the oath that is condemned. The relation between the two passages, however, is scarcely such that Matthew 23:16f. expresses a tradition of which Matthew 5:33f. is unaware or that Matthew 23:16f. views the matter merely from a Jewish viewpoint. Much more likely, Matthew 23:16f. is simply an altercation with Pharisaism. Here a total prohibition of the oath would be meaningless. This can be accomplished only in the new community.[136]

Among the exhortations of the Epistle of James, mention is made of swearing (5:12): "Do not swear, neither by heaven nor by earth, nor by any other kind of oath. Rather, let your yes be yes and your no be no, so that you may not fall under judgment." Like the saying of the Lord in Matthew 5:33f., therefore, the Epistle also forbids the taking of an oath and demands absolute truthfulness. Every yes should be a real yes; every no a real no.

The letter does not cite the saying as a word of the Lord. Thus it is an open question, as also in regard to other statements in the Epistle, whether James is in fact quoting a saying of the Lord, or whether the words of Jesus and those of James are derived independently of each other from the treasury of Jewish aphoristic wisdom. If in fact James is quoting a saying of the Lord from the tradition that has come down to him, its brevity is such as to suggest that it was perhaps more primitive than the later and somewhat expanded form in Matthew 5:33f. The difference between James 5:12 and Matthew 5:37 would hardly justify the distinction proposing that the saying in Matthew

5:37 enjoins simply a formula of protestation (*yes, yes*; or, as the case may be, *no, no*), while James requires absolute truthfulness. Much more to the point, both demand such truthfulness of speech that every falsehood is excluded. The life of the disciple must be conducted in the full light of the truth.

In his letters, though he never formulates an express oath, Paul does frequently and unhesitatingly make use of protestations similar to an oath. He calls upon God as witness to his truthworthiness: "Faithful God! Our word to you is not yes and no" (2 Cor. 1:18). In similar fashion Paul calls upon God as his witness in Rom. 1:9; Gal. 1:20; Phil. 1:8; 1 Thess. 2:4, 10. Possibly Paul is following certain Old Testament formulas in which God is called upon as witness between two partners (Gen. 31:50; Judg. 11:10; Josh. 22:22; 1 Sam. 12:5; 20:23).

Besides his appealing to God, Paul calls also upon Christ (2 Cor. 2:17; 11:10; 12:19) and upon the Spirit (Rom. 9:1). Paul pledges even his very life: "I call God to witness against my life" (2 Cor. 1:23). According to Matthew 5:36, to swear by one's head is certainly prohibited, because man has not the disposition thereof. In these adjurations there is a manifestation of the Apostle Paul's consciousness of his being in every way bound and obligated to the service of God. In accord with his vocation, the Apostle must always account for everything. The passages mentioned certainly are in but ill accord with the gospel's prohibition of oath-taking. Such sayings of the Lord as in Matthew 5:33-37 probably were unknown to Paul. In his protestations it is only natural that Jewish customs find their way into his speech.

Accepting the Old Testament declarations, the New Testament speaks unhesitatingly of the oath-taking with which God promised his mercy to the fathers (Luke 1:73; Acts 2:30; Heb. 2:11, 18; 4:3). The Epistle to the Hebrews offers an explanation of some texts, e.g., Gen. 22:16: "God made a promise to Abraham, in which he swore by himself, since he could swear by none greater" (Heb. 6:13).[137] God gives his guarantee with his oath in order to verify the inviolability of his will (Heb. 6:17). The oath which God swears is, accordingly, a reminder of God's condescension and a pledge of his fidelity. Again, it is with the swearing of an oath (Ps. 110:4) that God established the priesthood of Jesus. The Levitical priesthood, because it was set up without the swearing of an oath, is inferior to the priesthood of Jesus

(Heb. 7:20f.). The oath both manifests and provides a basis for the incomparable dignity of the High Priest, Christ. This too is why the new covenant is superior to the old (Heb. 7:22).

The Epistle to the Hebrews proceeds from the Old Testament statements about God's oath to the significance of the oath in general: "Men swear by him that is greater than themselves; and their oath serves to confirm, thus putting an end to their every objection" (Heb. 6:16).[138]

With men, then, it is otherwise than with God. He swears by himself. Men, however, appeal in their oaths to the great God and call upon him as guarantor. Such an oath is, in human society, of undisputed value; indeed, it is necessary in order to confirm the validity of the word. The use of an oath presents no problem for the Epistle to the Hebrews. It can hardly be disputed that Hebrews and Matthew 5:33-37 stand in opposition to each other.

Nor will the use of an oath be offensive to the Apocalypse of John. There an angels appears and swears a solemn oath by the eternal, living God, the Creator of all things. The oath asserts and guarantees that the eschatological redemption is both certain and close at hand (Apoc. 10:6).

Not only in the Bible in its totality, which extends over a lengthy period of time, but even in the New Testament itself there is a lack of complete accord in the condemnation of oath-taking. The basic prohibition of the oath in the saying of the Lord in Matthew 5:33f. is not of universal renown.

Even the Church of Jesus has not, in its history, been able to fulfill the ideal word of its Lord. Certainly it has, in response to the word of Jesus, always condemned frivolous, private swearing. At the same time, however, it has always recognized the oath in the secular sphere, even after state and society had become Christian. Considering the demand for oath-taking even in unimportant matters, the number of perjuries punished, and the immense number of perjuries remaining unpunished, any evident necessity for an oath presents a truly urgent demand for assistance.

Nevertheless, even in the Church itself, oaths have been and are constantly required. Churches of every confession justify the necessity of oaths and reject the refusal to take an oath as sectarian fanaticism. That an oath is to be taken in the Church on that very Gospel book in which it says, "Thou shalt not swear at all," is a thing difficult to sustain. Such a state of affairs certifies that the Church is not the kingdom of God, but that it too is in the world, in which evil holds sway. And she does therefore pray without cease: "Deliver us from evil!" (Matthew 6:13).

§ 22. WORK

Not the least among the factors which determine the moral character of one's life is one's personal involvement with work.[139] If the concept of work has, in our modern industrial society, a range and importance of which the Bible could not in its time have had an awareness, the Bible has, nevertheless, made a powerful contribution to the morality of work.

According to Greek mythology, in the beginning, in the golden age, the earth dispensed its fruits of itself, and man was spared any labor. "And they lived like the gods, still without human cares, free of labor and distress. . . . The nutriment-dispensing earth bore fruit entirely of itself alone" (Hesiod, *Works*, 112–118). Work is "the most oppressive misfortune that Zeus imposes upon men from their very birth" (Homer, *Iliad*, 10, 71).

Historical reality, however, seems not to have disdained work so thoroughly. In Homer, the oldest parts of whose poetry are a mirror of life in the aristocratic Greek world of the eighth century before Christ, every kind of useful labor is held in esteem. The god Hephaestos (Vulcan) himself labors as a skillful smith. Kings and heroes are occasionally portrayed as putting their own muscles to the task at hand (Homer, *Iliad*, 6, 313; 21, 37). The princess performs womanly tasks along with her maids (Homer, *Odyssey*, 1, 358). To be sure, such esteem for labor vanishes later. The fashionable and the rich withdraw more and more from personal labor. Farm work and manual labor are relegated to hired hands and slaves. Only the muse of science, of poetry and art, or participation in civil government are worthy of the free man.

Philosophy attempts to establish a theoretical basis for these social relationships. Plato and Aristotle believe that the confining manner of life of the manual laborer is damaging to virtue and soul. The ranks of philosophers, soldiers, and rulers must be free of labor. The Stoa, however, came more to a positive estimation of work. Marcus Aurelius (5, 1; 9, 12) explains that man, who is by nature an energetic being, may advance the harmony of the world through his labor. In Roman antiquity, in which free farmers fashioned the state, labor was respected. The writings of the elder Cato provide ample evidence thereof. But even here the esteem for work deteriorated. Cicero (*De officiis*, 1, 42) expresses the judgment of the Roman aristocracy: "All manual laborers are engaged in a shabby business, and there is nothing noble in a workshop."

According to the primitive history of the Yahwist's account, work pertains to the original order of creation and to man's condition in paradise. "God took man and put him in the garden of Eden to cultivate and preserve it" (Gen. 2:15). The work morality of the Old Testament is determined fundamentally through the creation narrative of the Priestly text (Gen. 1:1–2:4). Through the alternation of day and night and the sequence of six workdays and a day of rest, there is established a rhythm of work and rest. This arrangement has its foundation in God's own creating and resting, and in his express command (Gen. 2:3; Exod. 20:11). Human labor is a reflection of God's work. This arrangement holds good for all men, even for alien peoples (Exod. 20:10; Deut. 5:14). Even to the beast is a breather granted on the day of rest (Exod. 20:10; 23:12).

Nowhere outside of the Bible can a similar social order be found. Elsewhere it is the freeman's privilege to be at leisure, while those in bondage are obliged to work day after day. The common weekly day of rest is a social establishment of incalculably great importance.

In Psalm 104, a hymn constituting a further account of creation, free labor is allotted to man, who is distinct in this from all other creatures and who enjoys a pre-eminence over them. It is God's ordinance that with the new day man goes forth to his labors (Ps. 104:23). For this reason is the Creator to be praised: "You make the sun to rise. . . . Now does man go forth to his work, to his daily labor until the evening. How manifold are your works! In wisdom you have made them all!" (Ps. 104:22-24).

According to the understanding of this world and this life, to work is a universal commandment, a universal obligation. It is the same for everyone: "By the labor of your hands shall you eat. You shall be happy, and it shall be well with you" (Ps. 128:2). The Old Testament Wisdom literature reproves the lazy and praises the industrious laborer (Prov. 6:6-11; 14:23) as well as the capable housewife (Prov. 31:13-27). Whoever does no work, rightly starves (Prov. 10:4; 12:11; 19:15; 21:25).

Certainly work is not in itself divine service; for indeed, it is prohibited on the Sabbath day of rest, which day is dedicated entirely to God. The divine service of the Sabbath was later expressly prescribed (Lev. 23:3; Is. 1:13).

The necessity of labor is not a curse in consequence of the fall of our first parents. Man readily perceives the toil and frequent fruitlessness of labor, and he reckons it as a curse. But it is not labor itself that is cursed, but the fields: i.e., it is the condition of labor that is cursed (Gen. 3:17-19). In consequence of Cain's crime, the ground no longer produces a yield (Gen. 4:12).

Among the people of Israel, everyone who is righteous and pious performs some labor. God teaches men their work. God instructed the farmer how to plow, sow, and harvest properly (Is. 28:26-29). God fills artists with his spirit, for all their labor as goldsmiths, workers in bronze, joiners, and weavers (Exod. 35:30-35). The pious trust that God will send his blessing upon their labors. "May the favor of the Lord our God be upon us You will promote the work of our hands, yea, promote it, the work of our hands!" (Ps. 90:17). The blessing of their work is God's reward to the righteous (Deut. 15:10; 16:15; Job 1:10). Physical and mental labors alike are held in esteem. Israel's teachers, the Rabbis, invariably took care to pursue a profession calling for the labor of their hands. The trade of more than one hundred of the learned persons mentioned in the Talmud is known.

In Israel in the Hellenistic period there were new tones audible, echoes of the Greek evaluation of labor. Work is viewed pessimistically. After the fashion of Greek discussions of the problem, the vanity and transitoriness of labor are bewailed (Eccl. 1:17; 2:11, 17-23). The labor which God imposed upon the children of men is a painful business (Eccl. 1:13). The Greek viewpoint is manifest, too, when physical labor is disparaged in comparison to the leisure of scriptural study. Husbandman, carpenter, smith, and potter devote their every thought and prayer to the work of their hands. In the council and assembly of the people they do not sit. They do not strengthen the condition of the world (Sir. 38:24-34, adding the negative with Sinaiticus).

Quite clearly, such a passage presupposes Greek attitudes and concepts, and constitutes an acceptance of Greek morality. Nevertheless, it is apparent from later books of the Old Testament, as well as from non-canonical writings and from sayings of the Rabbis, that the genuine Jewish morality of labor was not lost; cf. Sir. 10:27; Prov. 28:19. A poem of Pseudo-Phocylides, pertaining to this period and probably of Jewish origin, praises husbandry, manual labor, and commerce, much in the older fashion. The Essenes applied themselves daily to hard physical labor from morning till night (Josephus, *Jewish War*, 2, 8, 5). They kept no slaves. "All are free, and they work with each other" (Philo, *Quod omnis probus liber sit*, 76 and 79). In Qumran, probably also an Essene community, there was a maxim: "When my hands and my feet engage in their labor, I will praise your name" (1 QS 10:13). The fruits of labor were held in common. "In labor and in property all shall prove their obedience" (1 QS 6:2).

At last, however, in late Judaism there were sporadic breaches of this morality, proceeding from another consideration. This is a period marked by the conviction that the very being of man is spoiled by sin. Even his works are of questionable value. "Unjust are all the works of man" (3 Esdras 4:37). "Of what use is it to us if we are promised the immortal world, when we have done mortal works?" (4 Esdras 7:119).

The Old Testament Jewish esteem for labor is valid also for the New Testament. The Gospels portray the life of Jesus as a life in which, as in a Jewish milieu, labor is simply to be taken for granted. Jesus is born to the laboring class, and does his share of the work (Mark 6:3; Matthew 13:55).[140] If he is respected at the same time as Rabbi (Mark 9:5; 10:51; 11:21), this double profession but bespeaks the tradition of his people. The immediate disciples of Jesus come mostly from the laboring class; indeed, they are called away in the midst of their work (Mark 10:28f; Matthew 4:18-22; 19:27-29; Luke 5:11, 28f.).

The sayings and discourses of Jesus, and above all his parables, show him as a man who viewed the daily labor of various callings with great attention and sympathy. He speaks of all professions: the farmer, how he sows and reaps; the faithful and unfaithful shepherd, the fisherman, the hired hand in the vineyard, the tax-collector, the soldier, the merchant, the judge, and the physician. He portrays every walk of life: servants and domestic slaves, who are outside the pale of law; steward and tenant; the slave-girl at the mill, the woman about her housework, the solicitous head of a household and the brutal master, the minister, the ruler, the king.

The parables demand industry and fidelity in labor and service (Matthew 20:1-16, the workers in the vineyard; Matthew 21:28-32, the two sons; Matthew 24:45-51, the faithful servant and the unfaithful; Luke 16:1-10, the unprofitable servant; Luke 19:12-27, the administrators of the minas). Everyday affairs and the commonplace labors thereof are quite sufficient for illustrating the conditions of the future kingdom of God. A direct statement on work is heard, perhaps, in the parable of the talents (Matthew 25:14-30). The servant who buried his talent in the ground is punished as a lazy and wicked servant. The industrious servants, who worked with their capital, are praised; and they are rewarded by being granted entrance into the joy of their lord. Ultimately, the parable says that labor does not have its purpose and goal in this life, but in the future world.

The New Testament delineates the Sabbath arrangement. The holiness of that day dare not be profaned by labor of any sort. This would happen through plucking ears of grain, which would constitute harvesting (Mark 2:23f.); through helping the sick when there was no urgency (Mark 3:1); and through transgression of the Sabbath journey (Acts 1:12). In order that the Sabbath might not be violated, the body of Jesus had to be interred on the evening before the Sabbath (Mark 15:42-47). In accordance with custom, Jesus and his disciples went to the synagogue on the Sabbath in order to participate in divine worship (Mark 1:21; 6:2). The primitive Christian missionaries likewise preached and taught on the Sabbath at the divine service (Acts 13:14f., *et passim*).

To be sure, the Gospels tell also of conflicts in regard to the Sabbath. Poles apart from the teaching of the Rabbis, which admitted that unavoidable necessities might be attended on the Sabbath, there is the saying of the Lord: "The Sabbath is there for the sake of man, and not man for the Sabbath" (Mark 2:27). Just as Jesus loosed other commandments of the decalogue from their legalistic torpor and required that they be fulfilled in the totality of their intent, so too he interpreted the Sabbath commandment anew. The Gospels, however, with their narratives of Sabbath conflicts, tell not only of former concrete events; no, the congregation is attempting thereby to provide a basis for its disengagement from a Sabbath commandment statutorily understood.

The New Testament recognizes and promotes the eschatological conception of the Sabbath as a prefiguring of the heavenly rest. Possibly there is a hint of this already in the Old Testament (Ps. 95:11; Is. 32:18; Jer. 6:16; 31:2). The idea is expressed and developed in the Epistle to the Hebrews (3:7–4:11). The Sabbath rest after the work of creation constitutes God's promise to his people. Man's work is not endless restlessness; like the work of the Creator, it will partake of a crowning rest. The ultimate end of man is not work but rest.[141]

Nevertheless, the morality of work is not entirely unbroken even in the New Testament. The determination to work must not be the service of mammon (Matthew 6:24). In the saying of the Lord, "Do not be anxious about your life. . . . Look at the birds of the air" (Matthew 6:25f.), beasts do not become an example for unconcern and indolence; rather, they are witnesses to God's solicitude (see the present work, Vol. I, pp. 15–16). Depending on this solicitude, the disciple can do his work in security. It is here that the gospel is proclaimed for the working man. The narrative about the visit of Jesus in the home of Mary and Martha also warns about being anxious after too many things (Luke 10:38-42). His remark, "You are anxious and troubled about many things; one only is needful," means that concern for work must not cause us to forget what is more important — our being open and ready for the word of God, which makes eternal life available. The parable of the great banquet in its Lucan form (Luke

14:15-24) contains a warning against losing oneself in industry and profit, to the neglect of God's eternal banquet.[142]

In accord with Israel's esteem for labor and with Rabbinic practice, Paul learned and practiced a trade (Acts 18:3; 20:34). Paul speaks repeatedly of it in his letters. It is the missionary's right to receive his support from the congregation. The Old Testament as well as common usage provide the basis for this right, and Christ himself has so arranged it (1 Cor. 4:12; 9:4-18; 2 Cor. 11:7-14; 12:14; 1 Thess. 2:9; 2 Thess. 3:7f.). In the Pastoral Epistles, this rule of conduct is repeated (1 Tim. 5:17f.; 2 Tim. 2:4-6). Paul, however, and Barnabas too, renounced this right (1 Cor. 9:6). Paul conducted himself in this manner so that his opponents, Jewish and Judaistic, could find no pretext for accusing him of enriching himself by his preaching of the gospel (1 Cor. 9:3; 2 Cor. 11:12). It was also, however, by his own personal resolve; for Paul did not want anyone to be burdened with the necessity of supporting him (2 Cor. 11:9; 1 Thess. 2:9). Nor did he want the gospel to be in any way retarded (1 Cor. 9:12). In any case, he did accept assistance from the congregation in Philippi, which was especially close to him, and on whose part there was nothing to be feared by way of any misunderstanding (2 Cor. 11:9; Phil. 4:10, 15).

But it remains to the glory of the Apostle that he makes the gospel available with no request for remuneration (1 Cor. 9:15; 2 Cor. 11:10). He is convinced that this carries with it its own special reward (1 Cor. 9:17-18). Whereas the wandering Greek scholars, the like of which Paul might have met on the streets, thought it but owing to the dignity of themselves and their wisdom to shrink away from working with their hands, Paul considered that he was, for the sake of his mission, obliged to the labor of a trade.

Even in his congregations Paul requires quiet and steady daily labor. It is no mere coincidence that only in such New Testament writings as pertain to a Greek milieu is the shunning of work reprimanded. In Jewish congregations a morality of work was taken for granted. From the very beginning Paul encouraged the congregation in Thessalonica to work (1 Thess. 4:11; 2 Thess. 3:6, 10). In this regard the expectation of the imminent return of the Lord (2 Thess. 2:2) may have misled many to abandon any sort of fixed labor, which would no longer have seemed necessary. Therefore

Paul's warning: "We admonish you to live quietly, to attend to your own affairs, and to work with your hands, so that you may walk honorably before the outsiders and be dependent on nobody" (1 Thess. 4:11-12). Christians have an obligation in regard to the reputation of the congregation, in a milieu that was frequently enough envious. Furthermore, labor guarantees one's personal freedom. Anyone who does not work is unworthily dependent upon others.

The Second Epistle to the Thessalonians repeats: "Whoever will not work, neither shall he eat. Indeed, we hear that some among you are living in idleness, gadding about and doing no work. Such persons we direct and exhort in the Lord Jesus to do their work quietly and to earn their own living" (2 Thess. 3:10-12). Labor is an arrangement incumbent upon all. Idleness is "disorderly living" (1 Thess. 5:14; 2 Thess. 3:6, 11). Whoever wants to eat without working shirks the common obligation. Work is the ordinance of creation. It is also an obligation of justice. A man must not allow himself to become a burden to others (2 Thess. 3:8). If Paul admonishes the community again and again in the name of God (1 Thess. 4:9) and in the name of Christ (2 Thess. 3:6) to lead an orderly manner of life, then, in the last analysis, idleness is not an indication and consequence of a false eschatology, but of the absence of an eschatology. The shirker of labor forgets the accounting which he one day must make.

The exhortation to labor has still another basis: "Let the thief no longer steal; rather, let him work, earning a wage with his hands, so that he can share with the needy" (Eph. 4:28). Labor provides an outlet for the exercise of beneficience, and makes it possible to interest oneself in common ideal enterprises. There is a hint of this in the remark of Paul in Acts 20:35. Under the challenge of his own example, the Apostle issues a summons to work. Labor is to be performed even for the reason that a man may thus be in a position to assist his neighbor. "To give is more blessed than to receive."

The biblical admonition to work keeps itself free of any exaggerations. It does not pretend that work is nothing but joy, or that it carries within itself its own rationale as a life-fulfilling factor. Even the Old Testament knows that the substance of life is oppressive labor and toil (Ps. 90:10). Man is born to affliction (Job. 5:7). The gospel speaks realistically of the hard labor of the slave working in the fields (Luke 17:7). The joy of the eschatological period is the true reward of one's labors (Matthew 25:21).

It is to Paul's credit that he earned his own living by the labor of his hands, and he says truthfully: "We labor, working with our own hands" (1 Cor. 4:12). In the catalogs of his trials he lists: "in beatings, in imprisonments, in tumults, in labor, in watching, in hunger" (2 Cor. 6:5). The Apostle carries out his ministry "in toil and hardship, often through sleepless nights, in hunger and thirst, in cold and nakedness" (2 Cor. 11:27). Paul's labors are more difficult than those born by the other Apostles (2 Cor. 11:23). These sufferings are not additional and self-imposed chastisements, but often enough the privations resulting from poverty.

The gospel uses the same term κόπος [143] to mean both physical labor and the ministry in the community of disciples (Matthew 9:37f.; 10:10; Luke 10:2, 7). Jesus calls his life's work the "labors" which the Father assigned to him (John 5:36; 9:4). Paul, too, describes the ministry of the missionary as tiring and difficult labor. Under a single term he includes both manual labor and Apostolic ministry: "Certainly you remember our labor and toil. Day and night we worked, that we might not be a burden to any of you while we proclaimed the gospel of God" (1 Thess. 2:9). Paul speaks not only of the work of others in mission and community, as a labor involving considerable personal exertion (Rom. 16:12; 1 Cor. 15:58; 2 Cor. 10:15). The superiors of the community expend themselves in toil (1 Thess. 5:12f.).

The linguistic usage that can use the term *labor* both for manual toil and for ministry, probably invented by Paul, is continued in the Acts of the Apostles (20:35), as also in the Pastoral Epistles (1 Tim. 4:10; 5:17). The work, labor, and patience of the Christian have their basis and motivation in faith, hope, and love (1 Thess. 1:3). Work and toil are carried out for the Lord and for the community, "in the Lord" (Rom. 16:12).

If finally Paul exhorts to "good work" (Rom. 2:7; 2 Thess. 2:17) and to the "work of faith" (2 Thess 1:11), the orderly arrangement of labor and toil also pertains to the good work of Christian living.

In the saying, "Whatever you do, in word or work, do all in the name of the Lord Jesus" (Col. 3:17), the term *work* is used in a comprehensive sense. It includes, in a special way, the work of labor. Labor and toil are sustained, however, by the grace of God: "I worked harder than anyone else; yet, it was not I, but the grace of God which is with me" (1 Cor. 15:10). Apostles are "co-laborers of God" (1 Cor. 3:9; 1 Thess. 3:2). Paul says confidently: "Always be rich in the work of the Lord, because you know that your labor in the Lord is not in vain" (1 Cor. 15:58).

There are sayings and parables of Jesus which presume the reality of slavery (Matthew 18:23-35; 25:14-30; Mark 12:2-5; 13:34; Luke 12:42-48; 16:3). Servitude can be a hard life (Luke 17:7-10). But the gospel knows also the "good and faithful slave" (Matthew 25:21). In the parables the life of the slave serves to portray service in the kingdom of God. And thereby slavery itself is elevated. The otherwise despised title of slave becomes a title of honor in the brotherhood. "Whoever would be first, let him be slave to all" (Mark 10:44). Paul often calls himself "slave of Jesus Christ" (Rom. 1:1, *et passim*), and slave too of the congregation (2 Cor. 4:5). In the Christian congregation the distinction between free man and slave is surmounted, if not legally and socially, at least in the ways that befit a human being and a Christian. In Christ "there is no longer slave nor free" (Gal. 3:28). The slave is freedman of Christ, just as freedman is slave of Christ (1 Cor. 7:22).

Paul sends the slave Onesimus, whom he converted to the faith, back to his master. The Apostle respects the existing legal order. Nevertheless, the Christian slave is now "brother in the flesh and in the Lord" both in respect to his master and to the communion — brother both as man and as Christian (Philemon 16). In view of the imminently expected fulfillment of the ages, Paul is inclined to advise the slave who might obtain his freedom to remain in his present condition (1 Cor. 7:21), which is no small demand. Even slaves should become, as it were, an ornament of Christian teaching (1 Tim. 6:2f.; Titus 2:9f.). The suffering of the slaves, about which hardly anyone concerned themselves, is brought by faith into a relationship with the greatest suffering it knows — the Passion of Christ, which effected salvation (1 Peter 2:18-25).

The New Testament tables of duties to one's neighbor (see above, ch. 17) all speak in detail of the slaves, an indication of how deep was the concern of the communities in these problems. New factors, derived of Christian faith, are introduced into the traditional themes of these tables of domestic duties. Slaves are to perform their tasks "as slaves of Christ, who do the will of God with all their heart" (Eph. 6:6). They are to render their service "with a good will, as serving the Lord and not men" (Eph. 6:7; Col. 3:23-25). At the same time, however, masters are admonished to vouchsafe their slaves "what is just and right" (Col. 4:1). Slaves and masters have one and the same Master in heaven (Eph. 6:9).

The New Testament preaches no social revolution, nor does it demand any emancipation of slaves. The living conditions of slaves in antiquity were for the most part thoroughly bearable, and indeed, often enough quite favorable. Not a few obtained manumission. The master was at once the provider and protector for his slaves. A general emancipation would have meant social chaos. It must needs be yet a long time before slavery would be abolished, at least legally, in the Christian world and at last in all lands. And today contrary social systems level the mutual accusation against each other that it is in every respect but slavery in another guise that continues to deprive the workingman of his freedom. It would be unjust to charge the New Testament with having been unable to solve this problem in only a few years.[144]

In conclusion we may make mention of a remark from the Epistle of James. The letter is concerned with pleading the rights of the poor against the rich. Thus it warns: "The wages of the laborers who mowed your fields, which you have kept back from them, cry out; and the cries of the harvesters have penetrated to the ears of the Lord Sabaoth" (James 5:4).

The rich (perhaps not within the community, but in general) are accused of having acquired their riches by withholding the just reward of labor. Like the greater part of the Epistle of James, this passage too is full of traditional themes. Injustice cries to heaven (Gen. 4:10; Deut. 24:15; *Ethiopian Henoch*, 47:1). The Law and the prophets warn again and again against the sin of withholding wages (Lev. 19:13; Deut. 24:14f.; Mal. 3:5; Tobit 4:14; Sir. 31[34]:26f.).

More commonly expressed is the theme in Hermas (*The Shepherd,* Vision 3, 9, 6): "You that pride yourselves in your wealth, take care lest the needy be obliged to groan, and their groans mount up to the Lord."

The history following from the New Testament has shown what is comprised in the biblical morality of work. It has produced an immense cultural work. The New Testament does not treat of the meaning that work has for the advancement of culture; this lies beyond the mandate of its preaching. One can, however, find the cultural mandate already hinted at in the Old Testament account of creation (Gen. 1:28; 2:15). Culture is a gift which was contributed to the gospel.

§ 23. PROPERTY · POVERTY AND WEALTH

I. PROPERTY

Work has for its goal the making of goods and the winning of possessions and property.[145] Like theology, law and ethics too have expended considerable efforts in establishing the doctrine of property and in developing it in all areas. The Old Testament contains numerous legal determinations, both sacred and profane, on property, as well as many ethical reflections and admonitions on the attitude toward possessions. The New Testament has no interest in juridical questions on property; but certainly it is interested in the right appreciation and in the moral use of possessions.

That a man owns property is for both the Old and the New Testaments a valid and basically self-evident proposition. Property is protected by the prohibition of thievery. The decalogue contains a double commandment in this regard: first of all the prohibition of stealing, then the prohibition of covetous schemes of preying upon another's property (Exod. 20:15, 17; Deut. 5:19, 21). Additional texts repeat the prohibition (Lev. 19:11) and develop it casuistically

(Exod. 22:1-15; Prov. 6:31). Theft of articles devoted to sacred use
(Josh. 7:1, 25) and the kidnapping of a man with the intention of
enslaving him (Deut. 24:7) are especially grievous cases and are
punished with the death penalty. In the reprimands voiced by the
prophets, theft is placed next to murder, adultery, and perjury (Jer.
7:9), and the prevalence of theft and robbery is deplored (Hos. 7:1).
The Wisdom literature stigmatizes the machinations of thievery
(Job 24:14, 16; Prov. 6:30f.; Sir. 5:14; 20:25). The special case of
false weights is mentioned (Prov. 11:1). While in other bodies of
Oriental law the death penalty is often imposed for crimes against
property, the law of Israel judges otherwise. Life is more precious
than possessions.

After Israel had been obliged to live in Egypt as a people enslaved and without legal rights, about the year 1250 B.C. she entered
into the land of Canaan, conquered it, and took it into possession. It
was the conviction of the nation that it was God who had bestowed
upon her the victory and the land. The land, therefore, was the
property of Yahweh, and was given by him for tenure. "The land
belongs to me, you are guests and sojourners with me" (Lev. 25:23).
Every tribe and every member of the nation is to have the same
rights and an equal share in the land. No one can appropriate vast
tracts of land. In spite of the recognition and protection of property,
therefore, the possession of land and soil, which is always the most
valuable of possessions, is restricted or even made questionable.

In every seventh year, the sabbath year, the fields, the olive groves,
and the vineyards are to lie fallow so that the poor among the people may eat thereof (Exod. 23:10f.). One who has been taken into
slavery through purchase is to be set free in this sabbath year (Exod.
21:2; Deut. 15:12). In the same way a loan to a fellow-countryman
is to be remitted (Deut. 15:2). Every fifty years, in the jubilee year,
the land is to rest; and any real estate that has been alienated during
this period, and in special cases even the house that has been alienated, is to revert to the original owner or to his heirs (Lev. 25;
Num. 36:4). The laws of land tenure in Israelite society were quite
extraordinary.

The prohibition of interest taking, which is enjoined repeatedly, limits ownership in money. In the lands bordering on Israel the usual interest rate was from twenty to thirty percent. In Israel it is forbidden to take interest on the loan of money or commodities (Exod. 22:25; Lev. 25:36f.; Deut. 23:19f.; Ps. 15:5; Ez. 18:8; Neh. 5:7). The taking of interest is accounted as usury; and it is a breach of the solidarity between fellow nationals. In any case, interest may be taken from foreigners, who also charge interest (Deut. 23:20). Whoever increases his wealth through charging interest will surely lose it again, if not sooner, then certainly when he dies. God will make the settlement (Prov. 28:8).

These laws, the like of which cannot be found elsewhere among the legal ordinances of the ancient East, act as a preventative against the amassing of enormous holdings of land and money, and against the acquiring of colossal power by any individual in the nation, while guarding the less affluent against the extremes of utter poverty and protecting the freedom and security of each and every member of the nation. If it also appears that these laws, especially in the area of land tenure, were essentially idealistic projections which, in any case, were rarely if ever enforced in the New Testament era, such regulations were, nevertheless, so interwoven in the daily circumstances of life that the concept of property and ownership could not grow dull.

Property was encumbered by the temple tithes (Lev. 27:30-33) and by the tithes for the poor (Deut. 26:12-15). The firstborn of man and beast (Exod. 13:2; Num. 3:13; Deut. 15:19-23) as well as the firstfruits of the harvest (Lev. 23:9-14) belong to God and must be redeemed. Despotic and reckless control over properties was further hindered in Israel by the fact that compassionate help and almsgiving to the needy were regarded as a strict obligation in view of the divine command. "Willingly shall you open your hand to your poor and needy brother in your land" (Deut. 15:8, 11). In Israel a great deal of charity and philanthropy was practiced, both on a private and individual basis, as well as through the organized benefactions of the community.[146] This obligation to deeds of beneficience was deeply implanted in the moral consciousness. Charity remains even to the present time Israel's claim to honor.

First of all, the New Testament presupposes the continued validity of the ownership arrangement as it found it in its own time. Even Jesus [147] recognized the existing relationships and circumstances of everyday living, assuredly, however, without intending thereby to render any juridical decisions or to draft any popular economic programs for his own time or for the future. None of this was his task, none of this his intention. "Who made me a judge or divider of inheritances over you?" (Luke 12:14). Jesus had about him nothing of the fanatical wrath of the ascetic, of the hatred of the disinherited, of the zeal of the social reformer, nor even of the primitive and self-satisfied cynic. He accepts the invitations of the rich and powerful (Mark 14:3-9; Luke 7:36-50; 14:1; 19:1-10). He allows himself to be served by certain women, in so far as they were able (Luke 8:2). There were councillors among his disciples (Mark 15:43; John 19:39).

Jesus speaks of social affairs of the rich and prominent in his parables in such a way that it may be concluded that he regarded such matters as right and proper. The festive banquet (Matthew 22:1-14; Luke 14:15-24) serves him as a figure of the heavenly banquet. In the parable of the good Samaritan, Jesus sketches the portrait of a wealthy and high-minded man (Luke 10:29-37); in the parable of the prodigal son (Luke 15:11-32), we see the picture of a wealthy home and at its head a genteel father who, at the return of his son, clothes him in a festive garment and gives him a gold ring for his finger. It is worth recalling, too, that even Luke, who entertains certain critical reservations in regard to possessions, passes on so many of these accounts.

Certainly, however, Jesus is not impressed in any naive way by wealth. He himself is poor (Matthew 8:20); and his heralds too are to be poor. They are not to carry anything with them, "neither gold nor silver nor copper in your belts, no bag for your journey, nor two tunics, nor sandals, nor a staff. Without pay you have received, without pay shall you give" (Matthew 10:8-10; somewhat different in Mark 6:8ff.). Without provision and concern for himself, the disciple depends entirely upon the conviction that his needs will be provided for. The disciples in Jesus' immediate following abandoned their possessions. It is not simply the very lack of possessions, however, that is the ideal. Poverty has meaning only in the light of the imitation of Christ: "Behold, we have left all and have followed you" (Mark 10:28).

After the fashion of Israel, the gospel demands charitable beneficence as regards the communion of faith. Jesus admonishes that those suffering need are to be assisted by our goods and possessions (Matthew 25:40; Mark 12:41-44; Luke 6:34). "When you give alms, sound no trumpet before you" (Matthew 6:2). The admonition calls to mind the manner in which help was sometimes extended. Benefactors were publicly honored, and they desired this publicity. Even the teachers of Israel warned that almsgiving should be practiced in secret. One Rabbi said: "He who gives alms in secret is greater than Moses." Jesus, too, requires of his disciples that there be no public show of their good works. What is hidden from men, however, is evident to God; and he will reward their good deeds (Matthew 6:4). This rewarding may take place in the present time (Matthew 6:33); but primarily it will take place at the final judgment (Matthew 25:31-46).

The New Testament confirms the Old Testament prohibition of thievery, as in the decalogue (Mark 10:19; Luke 18:20; Rom. 13:9). Thieves, robbers, and the covetous are mentioned in one breath with lechers, adulterers, idolaters and murderers. They will not attain to the kingdom (1 Cor. 6:10). They spoil the reputation of the community (1 Peter 4:15). But now it is not merely demanded of the thief that he abandon his former deeds; he is to live by his labor, and from his surplus he will be able to give to the needy. In this way he will become a useful member of the congregation (Eph. 4:28).

The Old Testament prohibition of coveting the goods of another is continued in the New Testament admonition against greed ($\pi\lambda\epsilon\text{ov}\epsilon\xi\text{ía}$). A catalog of vices in the form of a saying of the Lord includes greed as one of the evil things which come forth from the heart (Mark 7:22). To the parable of the foolish grain farmer there is an admonition attached: "Take heed and beware of all greed! Even if a man has an abundance, his life does not depend upon his possessions" (Luke 12:15).

The admonition is accentuated and confirmed when it is said that a man must not defraud another, his brother, in business (1 Thess. 4:6). The gift to the collection in the congregation should be a gift unto blessing, in no way marked by a spirit of greed (2 Cor. 9:5). As the gift brings the blessing of God upon the donor, so too the donor dispenses good fortune, abundance, and prosperity to the recipient. Therefore the gift must be given joyfully and richly; it must not betray a wretched avariciousness.

Greed is mentioned also in the catalogs of vices in the Apostolic preaching. Along with other sins, greed belongs to the manner of life to which God surrendered the pagans as a punishment (Rom. 1:29). Among Christian people, as befits the saints, immorality and covetousness ought not so much as be mentioned (Eph. 5:3). The covetous man is an idolater (Eph. 5:5). Does this mean, as is said in Matthew 6:24, that with avarice a man becomes subject to a power opposed to God? Paul demands of the congregation that it should have no traffic "with a brother who is immoral, or covetous, or an idolater or a robber" (1 Cor. 5:11; similar catalogs in 1 Cor. 6:9f.; 2 Tim. 3:2). The Epistle to the Hebrews (13:5f.) advises: "Keep your life free from love of money and be content with what you have at hand." Surely even profane rules of conduct could say as much. Still, it is a new formulation, because it is given a basis in the word of God: "Indeed, he has himself said, 'I will never abandon you nor forsake you'" (probably after Deut. 31:6).

In a detailed exhortation, 1 Tim. 6:5b-10 speaks about possessions. Its themes are of a profane sort, transmitted through Hellenistic ethics and Jewish wisdom, and supplemented only a little from the experience of the congregation. Primarily it is a warning to those who suppose that godliness is a means of gain. Probably it has in mind those false teachers who gain entry and win followers through propaganda (and thus in Tit. 1:11; Jude 11f.; 2 Peter 2:13-14). To counteract such as these, it admonishes contentedness. We brought nothing with us upon coming into the world, and can take nothing with us when we leave. "The root of all evils is greed." Striving after riches easily leads to destruction. Some have, on account of greed, fallen away from the faith.

II. POVERTY AND WEALTH

1. POVERTY

The social contrast between poor and rich gradually became visibly apparent in Israel during the period of the kings and thereafter, when the court, with its level of pre-eminence, possessions, and power, raised itself above the rest, who settled down more and more to the position of a citizenry destitute and without legal recourse. The unity of the one nation was destroyed (Amos 2:6-8; Is. 10:1f.; Ez. 22:6-13, 24-29; Micah 2:1f.; Ps. 37:14). The prophets took the poor under their protection and interceded for them in the name of Yahweh. They recall that Yahweh once led the whole people, poor as they were, out of Egypt (Amos 2:10; 4:1; 5:11; Is. 3:15). The poor beseech God and trust in him. They are God's people in a special way (Is. 10:2; Zeph. 3:12). In the Psalms God allows the poor to experience his special protection (Ps. 9:19; 18:28; 40:18; 72:4, 12; 140:13). The poor and the godly are the same (Ps. 86:1; 132:15f.). The enemy of the poor is likewise the enemy of God (Ps. 109:31).

After the destruction of Jerusalem in 586 B.C., Israel lived for fifty years in exile in Babylon. In the urgency of this period Israel was drawn together again as a unified community of the poor (Is. 54:11; 61:1-11). As soon as Israel returned to her own country, however, the old social inequalities began again.

There is ample witness to this in the Wisdom literature, which was at that time a literature of the genteel. The actual conditions are portrayed. The poor man is oppressed (Sir. 13:3), isolated from society (Prov. 14:20; 19:4, 7), and discontented (Sir. 31:1). The beggar is held in utter contempt (Sir. 25:2; 40:28; 41:1-4). Possibly he is deserving of his lot through laziness (Prov. 6:6-11) and frivolity (Prov. 23:21). It is clearly recognized, nevertheless, that it is God who gives poverty as well as wealth (Prov. 22:2; Sir. 11:14). The pious man must not hold the poor man in contempt. God will be merciful to him who shows mercy to the poor (Sir. 4:1-10).

An ancient and genuine spirit of piety as regards the poor finds expression again in the Qumran writings. The poor man is the humble one who, acknowledging his sinfulness, expects salvation from the grace of God. The poor are God's elect (1 QpHab 5:4). The poor are persecuted by evildoers (1 QpHab 12:3). God rescues the soul of the poor man from the hands of the violent (1 QH 2:32-35; 4:18; 1 QM 13:13f.). He is with the wretched and with the "poor of grace" (1 QH 5:21f.). In the eschatological conflict the hosts of Belial will be brought low "by the poor of God's deliverance" (1 QM 11:8f.). "The communion of the poor will possess the high mountain of Israel, while the godless will be purged and blotted out forever" (4 QpPs37, sec. III, 10-12).

In the *Damascus Document* (4:17; 8:7) possessions, wealth, and material gain are severely censured. The poor of the flock, however, will be saved (*Damascus Document*, 19:19). Solicitude for the poor and destitute is incumbent upon the community. Two day's wages each month are to be put at the disposal of the community. "The orphans are to be sustained thereby; and thereby are the poor and wretched to be supported. And it shall be used also for the aged man, when he dies; and for the man who is homeless, and for such ever as have been led away captive among an alien people, and for the virgin who has none to protect her" (*Damascus Document*, 14:14-16).

The poverty of the pious people of Qumran is conspicuously evident, since they renounce all personal ownership. Only the community has property (1 QS 6:22-25; 9:7). Both Philo (*Quod omnis probus liber sit*, 84-86) and Josephus (*Jewish War*, 122-127) speak of the community of possessions observed by the Essenes. Nevertheless, ownership in common provides material security, however modest, for the members of the community. When the Gospels, on the other hand, demand the complete renunciation of property, the disciple is placed in total insecurity, in total dependence upon God.

In the New Testament the warnings against the dangers of wealth are in accord with its treasuring of poverty. The Old Testament piety toward the poor is producing an after-effect. Jesus himself is poor, and his followers are to be poor. When John the Baptist was in prison, he sent his disciples to Jesus to ask him whether or not he was the expected Messiah; and Jesus answered: "The sick are healed, the dead rise, and the poor have the gospel preached to them" (Matthew 11:5). The beatitudes in the Sermon on the Mount (Matthew 5:3-10) begin with an emphasis upon the first: "Blessed are the poor in spirit." The poor are synonymous with those afterwards particularized: those who mourn, the meek, those who hunger for justice, the merciful, the pure.

The Gospel of Luke makes a further addition to these texts. "The poor, the crippled, the lame, and the blind" will participate in the eschatological banquet (Luke 14:21). In the sense of the gospel, these guests are not only the poor of society but certainly the Gentiles as well, in contrast to those Jews who regard themselves as rich. In another parable about the rich man, it is Lazarus, the beggar, who receives eternal happiness (Luke 16:22).

In a quick survey of his congregation, Paul sees that "not many are called who are wise according to the flesh, not many who are powerful, not many who are of noble birth" (1 Cor. 1:26). But he praises the congregation of Macedonia, because "in a severe test of affliction their abundance of joy and their extreme poverty overflowed in a wealth of liberality on their part" (2 Cor. 8:2). This will always be the image of the Church, that it unites the contrasting elements of external poverty and internal wealth. What the Apostle achieves by way of example is ever true of the Christian way of life: "poor, yet enriching many; having nothing, and yet possessing all things" (2 Cor. 6:10). The world, whose wisdom fails to recognize what is essential, sees only the external poverty of the Church and knows nothing of her true riches (1 Cor. 1:23-25).

The Epistle of James[148] is a witness to piety in regard to the poor as well as a powerful polemic against the rich. The poor man is the exalted one, the rich the humiliated. The latter will pass away like the flower of the grass (James 1:9-11). God has chosen the poor, as being rich in faith, to inherit the kingdom. The rich, however, oppress the poor and defame the name of Christ. It is unjust if, in the congregation, a rich man with gold rings and fine garments is honored and given privileges denied the poor (James 2:1-7). Misery will fall upon the rich who gathered treasure for themselves, who luxuriated, who held back the wages of the laborer, who have killed the righteous man (James 5:1-6).

James's letter portrays the rich quite realistically and censures them severely, even bitterly, but includes in other respects the traditional themes of Old Testament Jewish piety in respect to the poor. Since it makes use of standard examples, it is difficult to say how far the letter draws upon personal experiences and actual circumstances and events in the community. The presumptive historical background of the letter's polemic is that more and more rich and prominent people are joining the congregation. And the longer this development goes on, the more frequent are the instances; and the tide will not be stemmed. Many a difficulty might be occasioned thereby. Perhaps, then, from this and other indications, the letter is to be dated in the late Apostolic age, the circumstances and conditions of which it presupposes.

2. Wealth

As the prophets interceded for the poor in the face of social inequalities, so too they warned and admonished the rich (Amos 3:10; 5:7, 10-12; Jer. 5:26-31; Ez. 22:6-13). The rich, along with the pomp and grandeur of Jerusalem, will go down into the underworld (Is. 5:14). The rich city will be waste and empty (Is. 32:12f.).

The post-exilic Wisdom literature, nevertheless, gives unhesitating approval to the possession of riches. Wealth is won by industry (Sir. 31:3) and diligence (Prov. 10:4; 11:16; 24:4). Wealth means a full and happy life (Sir. 44:1-8; Prov. 10:15; 14:20). Wealth makes it possible to do good works (Sir. 31:8; Tob. 12:8). Even if the very striving after riches can lead one on paths of perversity (Sir. 31:5-8; Prov. 28:6), nevertheless, wealth and piety can be connected (Sir. 13:24; Prov. 3:16; 10:15; 15:16). Wealth is God's gift and blessing for the righteous (Sir. 11:15f.; Prov. 10:22; 22:4; Job. 1:10). The good fortune of the godless is only in appearance, and soon it vanishes. God will bring about the proper arrangement (Ps. 37; 113:7f.).

In a later period leading up to the New Testament era, the apocalyptic literature takes a stance of strong opposition to the situation of the rich and powerful. Passion and hatred mount against them (*Eth. Henoch*, 94:6-10; 96:5; 97:8-10; *Psalms of Solomon*, 1:4). The rich will be punished and destroyed along with all other sinners. Then will the poor be extolled as the righteous ones (*Eth. Henoch*, 103f.). They will be wealthy and filled with joy in the world beyond (*Syriac Apoc. of Baruch*, 29:6, 73:2; 78:6).

In the New Testament the question of wealth is consistently colored by eschatological considerations. Among the Synoptics, in Mark 10:17-31, the remarks of Jesus concerning possessions are set down thematically, in an order which possibly pre-dates Mark's Gospel. (The material is ordered in essentially the same fashion in Matthew 19:16-30 and Luke 18:18-30). A rich man asks Jesus how he can win eternal life. Jesus reminds him about the commandments of the decalogue, which place certain obligations upon the man in respect to his neighbor; and finally he says to the questioner: "One thing only is lacking to you. Go, sell what you own and give it to the poor, and you will have treasure in heaven. Then come and follow me." But the rich man went away saddened because he could not bring himself to give up his possessions (Mark 10:17-22).

The narrative must not be understood as meaning that the surrender of possessions is an additional obligation over and above the commandments; rather, the authenticity and integrity of the fulfilling of the commandments shows itself in the surrender of possessions. Besides which, almsgiving amasses heavenly treasures (so too in Matthew 6:2-4). Willingly to become poor is the beginning of the imitation of Jesus.

An additional saying of the Lord states that it is difficult for those who have many possessions to gain entry to the kingdom of God (Mark 10:23); and a further one, that is just as impossible as it is for a camel to pass through the eye of a needle (Mark 10:25). But what is impossible in human estimation can be done by divine grace (Mark 10:27). Wealth is a great danger to salvation.

In the course of the conversation Peter finally points out that the disciples following Jesus have abandoned all else; and Jesus promises those who have given up family and home for his sake and for the sake of the gospel that they will be recompensed a hundredfold now and in the age to come (Mark 10:28-30).

This saying of the Lord bears the hallmark of a formulation of the community. It speaks already of the gospel, as also of the future age, which term is not otherwise employed by Jesus. When the disciple is promised houses, brothers, and sisters even now, it is probably an allusion to the community, which adopts the one who has left his kinsmen or has been turned away by them. The pericope contains an abundance of themes and aspects directed toward the Christian community's judgment of ownership. In accord therewith it might be said that the ideal community is a community of the poor.

In two sayings of the Lord (Matthew 6:24; Luke 16:9) property is designated as "mammon." The term *mammon* is found also in Rabbinic writings where property is spoken of disparagingly; and so too in 1 QS 6:2 and in the *Damascus Document* (14:20). *Mammon* appears in Hebrew as a loan word, probably of Punic, and in any case of pagan, origin. In Israel, money, like mammon, is something alien and heathen. The term *mammon* betokens money and property as something dishonest and unjust. Mammon is a master, like a slave-owner; and indeed, he is opposed to God. "You cannot serve God and mammon" (Matthew 6:24). This warning is found in the Sermon on the Mount, in the midst of remarks about the dangers of wealth. A man collects earthly treasures for himself and sets his heart on them, even though such possessions are fickle (Matthew 6:19-21). Inasmuch as he will lose God in the process, the man is obliged to choose between the two masters, God or mammon.

Striving after possessions is at bottom an expression of the pagan anxiety which seeks to make oneself secure in life through material goods. The disciple trusts in the solicitude of the Father (Matthew 6:25-34).

The parable of the unjust steward (Luke 16:1-13) ends with the admonition: "Make friends for yourselves with the mammon of iniquity." One is not to surrender possession because a thing is iniquitous; rather, possession itself, purely and simply, is iniquitous mammon. In the face of the approaching judgment the possessor must free himself thereof by surrendering it for the benefit of the poor. It is in this way, and in this way only, that participation in eternal life can be won through earthly possessions.

An additional saying of the Lord is subjoined (Luke 16:11) which has a somewhat different implication. Even with the iniquitous

mammon, worthless as it is, the disciple must conduct his stewardship conscientiously and faithfully. Only then can he hope, in truth,
to share in eternal goods.

In the explanation of the parable of the sower, the thorns which
suffocate the seed of God's word signify "the cares of this world and
the deceitfulness of riches" (Mark 4:19; Matthew 13:22), or "the
cares and riches and joys of life" (Luke 8:14). The explanation of
the parable is a very old allegory and homily. The texts contain,
therefore, at least a critical judgment of the New Testament Church
on ownership. It is deceptive and alluring, and impedes the acceptance of the word of God.

The Gospel of Luke[149] contains more numerous and more emphatic passages on poverty and riches than do the other Gospels.
The relationship of the Christian to possessions was, for this evangelist, a pressing problem. Therefore he collected such particularized
traditions as were available to him, probably even sharpened criticism which he came upon in the sources he utilized, as is indicated
by Synoptic comparison with Matthew and Mark.

Among the passages peculiar to Luke there are four pertinent
parables which set forth how disastrous for man the striving after
possessions and the ownership of possessions can become: the parable of the foolish grain farmer (Luke 12:13-21); of the prodigal son
(Luke 15:11-32); of the unjust steward (Luke 16:1-13); and of the
beggar Lazarus and the rich man (Luke 16:19-31). The import of
the parables is that it is utter foolishness for a man to suppose that
he can assure his life through wealth (Luke 12:20f.).

In the discourse of Luke corresponding to Matthew's Sermon
on the Mount, Jesus literally glorifies the poor and hungry, while
he threatens the rich with his "woe-betide-thee's" (Luke 6:20-26).
The imitation of Jesus is the fulfillment of the requirement of poverty. Luke emphasizes (5:11, 28; 18:22): "They left *everything*"
(while Mark 1:18, 20; 2:14; 10:21 consistently says only that those
who were called followed him). Only in Luke is the disciple bidden
to dispose of his possessions in alms:[150] "Sell what you have and
give alms" (Luke 12:33; otherwise in the parallel passage in Matthew 6:19). While Matthew 23:26 warns the Pharisees to cleanse
the inside of the dish (i.e., to be intent upon an untainted liveli-

hood), Luke 11:41 admonishes that if the content of the dish be given in alms, all will be clean.

In Luke 6:34f., as compared to Matthew 5:47, the admonition to love one's enemy is more expansive: "Love your enemies, and do good, and lend without expecting something in return." In the parable of the great banquet, the ones invited in the second place are, according to Matthew 22:9, all who chanced along; but in Luke 14:21 they are "the poor, the crippled, the blind, and the lame." Luke takes the tradition and accentuates it in accord with his own mentality. Even the Lucan infancy narrative has a special affection for the poor. Mary praises the works of God: "The hungry he fills with good things, the rich he sends empty away" (Luke 1:51-53). In direst poverty Christ is born in a stable, and the poor shepherds are the first to find the child (Luke 2:6-17).

The Acts of the Apostles portrays the Church as a community in which, while private ownership remains a possibility (Acts 5:14), still, in accord with the ideal, everything should be held in common by all (Acts 4:32-44). The poor are provided for from a common purse (Acts 4:34; 6:1-6). In this picture of a primitive Christian community, the evangelical ideal of freedom from possessions is realized as best it can.

Paul has no regard for material wealth; and thus he speaks so much the more of the spiritual riches of the community. God is true and abundant wealth. With God is there wealth of kindness (Rom. 2:4), of glory (Rom. 9:23), of mercy (Eph. 2:4), and of grace (Eph. 1:7), the depth of riches and of wisdom and of knowledge (Rom. 11:33).

Christ, who was rich and for the sake of men became poor (2 Cor. 8:9), is rich for all who call upon him; and he imparts his wealth to the Church (Rom. 10:12). The Church is "rich in every way, in all speech and all knowledge" (1 Cor. 1:5), rich in the word of Christ (Col. 3:16), enriched through the glory of the mystery (Col. 1:27). God makes the Church rich "according to the true wealth of his glory" (Eph. 3:16). It is the task of the Apostle to announce and make accessible to the Church the unfathomable riches of Christ (Eph. 3:8).

In the face of the impending eschatological crisis, all goods, and especially material possessions, become utterly insignificant. "The time has grown short. . . . Therefore, those who buy should forthwith be as if they had no goods; those who deal with the world, as if they had no dealings with it. For the form of this world is passing away" (1 Cor. 7:29-31). The power of the kingdom overcomes the demoniacal urge of possessions.

Like the Gospels, the Apostles issue further admonitions to deeds of beneficence. Especially within the congregation should helpfulness be practiced, just as the gospel says: everyman can be one's neighbor. "So long as there is time, let us do good to all men, and especially to those who are of the household of the faith" (Gal. 6:10; Rom. 12:13). A great concern of Paul, an undertaking for which he encourages and solicits aid again and again, is the collection for the "saints" in Jerusalem (Rom. 15:25-28; 1 Cor. 16:1-4; Gal. 2:10; Acts 24:17; and in special detail in 2 Cor. 8 and 9).

Christ, who was rich and for the sake of men became poor, is the exemplar of giving (2 Cor. 8:9). Works of charity are a proof to the Church of her obedience to the gospel (2 Cor. 8:24). An extensive exchange should take place between material and spiritual goods of the congregations (2 Cor. 8:13-15). The Church should return thanks to God for his abundant graces (2 Cor. 9:11-15).

In the circumstances of the early Church, hospitality was a special command (Rom. 12:13; Heb. 13:2). Missionaries who might be seeking to escape a hostile neighborhood were to be received as brothers in the faith.

To maintain ownership is, nevertheless, thoroughly possible in the community and quite permissible. The rich should know, however, that wealth is precarious, and they should use it in doing good works. In this way they can store up treasure for eternal life (1 Tim. 6:17-19). Whoever has possessions must not withhold them from a brother in need. How could such a one abide in God's love? (1 John 3:17).

It is likely to cause some surprise that, already in the New Testament era, greed threatened to destroy the integrity of the ecclesiastical ministry and office. Paul already defends himself repeatedly and ardently against the accusation or imputation of conducting his ministry for the sake of profit (2 Cor. 8:2; 1 Thess. 2:5), or of ever

taking advantage of anyone thereby (2 Cor. 7:2). In order to pre-
clude any such suspicion, Paul does not even make use of the right
of an Apostle to allow himself to accept support from the community. He earned his own support by the labor of his hands (1 Cor.
9:7-12; 2 Cor. 12:13-18; Acts 20:33f.).

Among the qualities which the bishop must have, the Pastoral
Epistles enumerate that he "must not be a lover of money" (1 Tim.
3:3; Tit. 1:7). The deacon, however, must "not be greedy for base
gain" (1 Tim. 3:8). Already the elders must be admonished: "Tend
the flock of God not for base gain but devotedly" (1 Peter 5:2).
Those who hold office can hardly expect already a fixed compensation. But they can lay claim to support and probably receive also
donations from the congregation. They could be tempted to undertake the office for the sake of personal pecuniary gain.[151]

Polemicism throws greed into the teeth of the false teachers.
Probably it is such teachers who are meant with the reference to
"people who have lost the truth and who suppose that godliness is
a means of gain" (1 Tim. 6:5). The false teachers "abandon themselves, for the sake of gain, to Balaam's error" (Jude 11, 16). According to later tradition (already in Deut. 23:5), Balaam accepted
a bribe to curse Israel. Thus he is the prototype of greedy and blasphemous suborners. False teachers follow after him. No less vehe-
ment are the remonstrances of the Second Epistle of Peter. The ad-
versaries "in their greed, make a profitable transaction of false
words" (2 Peter 2:3, 14). False teachers are like greedy merchants.[152]

§ 24. HONOR AND GLORY

Honor is, if we may so define it, the worth which one has in his
own eyes or in the judgment of another. High esteem in the judgment of someone else is glory.[153] There is internal honor and external honor. It is a personal as well as a social value.

Holy Scripture regards honor as a higher good. The Old Testament says that every man possesses his honor from God's gift and

promise. God made man in the image of his own substance and handed over to him dominion over creation (Gen. 1:26). "You made him a little less than heavenly beings, and with honor and glory you crowned him" (Ps. 8:6). With the clarification of the expectation beyond, even the future honor of a man is vouchsafed. Wisdom summarizes it: "The godless know nothing of God's mysteries. They have no hope in a reward of piety nor any belief in an honorable prize for spotless souls. God created man for incorruptibility and made him to the image of his own substance" (Wis. 2:22-23).

Man, being a creature destined for glorious incorruptibility, has his glory too as a creation of God. The pious man knows, therefore, that ultimately all honor pertains to God and not to man. "Not to us, Yahweh, but to your name give glory, for the sake of your graciousness, for the sake of your fidelity" (Ps. 115:1) Man must not glory in wisdom, in strength, in riches, but in God, who works grace, justice, and righteousness on earth (Jer. 9:22f. = 1 Cor. 1:31; 2 Cor. 10:17). The community, in its ritual celebration, praises this God (Pss. 5:12; 32:11). This praising will continue even in the judgment (Ps. 149:5f.). Self-glory, on the contrary, is not only a singular fault, but it is the basic posture of disbelief, in which a man wishes to stand by himself and not be dependent upon God. It is but the boasting of violent men and godless (Ps. 94:3f.).

It pertains to the ordinances of Israel to pay honor to such men as are deserving of honor and who have a legitimate title thereto. The decalogue already orders that parents are to be honored (Exod. 20:12; Deut. 5:16). The commandment is emphasized anew with the promise of being blessed with peaceful days, consequent upon its keeping (Sir. 3:3-8). The aged man is to be honored (Lev. 19:32), the king (Wis. 14:17), the physician (Sir. 38:1), and even the poor man (Prov. 14:31) and the faithful slave (Prov. 27:18).[154]

From quite early times Greek culture had endeavored to grasp the concept and nature of honor and glory. Classical ethics said that virtue was the true honor. To the Stoic, what is essential is the consciousness of one's own worth as internal honor. The wise man prizes also external marks of esteem, but he does not seek them out and is capable of renouncing them.

Under the influence of Greek ethics, reflection on honor was broadened and deepened in Hellenistic Judaism. Internal as well as external honor is an important value. Man will exert himself after both. He must win his own honor for himself, but he can also lose it. The most stable and most personal honor is godliness and righteousness. "The true glory is the fear of God. Despicable is he who transgresses the commandment" (Sir. 10:19-22). He who is generous is honored by his fellowmen (Prov. 22:9). Of wisdom, which is essentially the fear of God, it is said: "Prize wisdom highly, she will cause you to be honored" (Prov. 4:8).

External honor can be impugned through insults. In the Old Testament there are statements indicating that enmity can be checked in two different ways: by speech or by silence. In one instance it says: "Answer the fool in accord with his folly, that he may not suppose he is wise" (Prov. 26:5). To return insult with insult is, in the last analysis, in the interest of the insulter himself, so that he may desist from his arrogance. But the godly man can also waive his defense, leaving his honor to God: "I became like a man who does not hear, in whose mouth there is no rejoinder. For on you, Yahweh, do I await. You will answer, O Lord my God" (Ps. 38:15-16).

The conduct of Jesus shows no essential antipathy to honors and marks of esteem. He accepted tokens of esteem and defended those who sought to please him thereby. When Simon the Pharisee neglects to honor him as one would, according to custom, honor a respected guest, Jesus points it out to him and defends the sinful woman who, in thankfulness, is anointing his feet (Luke 7:36-50). At his entry into Jerusalem, when a crowd of his followers recognizes him joyfully as the Messiah-King and some Pharisees demand that he reprove them, he justifies his disciples: "I tell you, were these to remain silent, the very stones would cry out" (Luke 19:37-40). Similarly, when the children in the temple were greeting him as the Son of David, he defended them against the chief priests and Scribes: "Have you never read, 'Out of the mouths of babes and sucklings you have prepared praise for yourself'?" (Matthew 21:15f.).[155]

According to the Gospels, Jesus defended himself against insults.

Noting that he was not given to ascetical practices, his opponents throw it up to him that he is a carouser, a wine-bibber, and a friend of tax-collectors and sinners. In a mysterious remark, Jesus declares that wisdom has its own justification within itself (Matthew 11:19). When the Pharisees maintain that he works his wonders in league with the devil, he characterizes this charge in the sharpest of terms as blasphemy against the Holy Spirit, which is forgiven neither in this world nor in the next (Matthew 12:24-37).

Jesus recognizes the traditional order, and in accord with the decalogue he requires that honor be shown to father and mother (Mark 7:10; 10:19). Human ordinances cannot abrogate the commandments of God (Mark 7:9-13; see below, ch. 25).

The Johannine Christ is exalted beyond any honoring or dishonoring of himself on the part of men. In the world men accept honors from each other and try to find security therein. The honor that God gives they do not seek (John 5:44). Christ "accepts no glory from men" (John 5:41). He does not allow them to make him king (John 6:15). Nevertheless, he will not let the charge that he is a Samaritan, i.e., a heretic and one possessed of demons, pass unchallenged. Were he concerned only with his own honor, he might allow it to pass; but he is concerned with the honor of his Father, since whoever blasphemes the Son dishonors the Father (John 8:48-54). The Christ of the Passion is free before the tribunal of the world, which cannot condemn him. The question put by the high priest is as unjust as the abuse administered by the high priest's servant (John 18:19-23).

The same Christ warns again and again against seeking after honors and preferments from men. He warns against practicing righteousness, giving alms, and praying and fasting when these things are done in order to be seen by men (Matthew 6:1-18). He warns about seeking honors after the fashion of the Scribes and Pharisees: "They do all their works in order to be seen by men. They lengthen their prayer straps and the tassels of their cloaks. They love the places of honor at banquets, the best seats in the synagogue, and salutations in the public market" (Matthew 23:5-7).

With a profane rule of prudence, a saying of the Lord admon-

ishes that at a banquet it is not the fisrt but the last place that
should be taken. An invitation to go up higher will honor a man
before all who are present (Luke 14:7-10). The false attempt at
glory by which one exalts himself unjustly is condemned: "Everyone who exalts himself will be humbled, and whoever humbles
himself will be exalted" (Luke 14:11; 18:14). These sayings of the
Lord start with commonplace, everyday affairs; but they provide a
glimpse of God's manner of action in eschatological matters. Jesus
cries woe upon those who are held in honor by men: "Woe to you
when all men speak well of you; for so their fathers did to the false
prophets" (Luke 6:26). It ends, not in the flattering praise of men,
but at the judgment seat of God. And this is of special concern to
the follower of Christ. If his conduct answers to the earnestness of
the challenge, he will prefer to be recipient of annoyance than recipient of proper praise.

The Sermon on the Mount goes far beyond the censuring of the
false quest for honors when it requires that insults be taken while
making no defense: "If someone strikes you on the right cheek,
turn to him the other also" (Matthew 5:39). Jesus serves notice on
his disciples that they will experience disdain and persecution. In
imitation of their Lord they must take up the cross, i.e., they must
become like honorless criminals who, cast out by society, are on
their way to death (Matthew 10:25; 16:24; see above, ch. 12).

Jesus warns the disciples against ruining their companionship
through a greed for honors. To the question of who will be the greatest
in the kingdom of God, he answers that it is he who esteems himself no more than a child (Matthew 18:1-4). In the communion of
disciples it must not be like it is in the world, where kings and
lords strive after might and power. "Whoever would be great
among you must be the slave of all. For even the Son of Man came
not to be served but to serve" (Mark 10:42-45). Even in the community of disciples there is striving after honor and glory, and
there is personal and social honor. We mean the honor of being a
child of God, which is demonstrated by way of example in a child;
this, however, is accomplished by service in the brotherhood.

In a remark exhibiting a paucity of words, and which has about
it an Old Testament ring (Dan. 12:3), the gospel points to a hope

of future honor and abiding glory: "Then the righteous will shine like the sun in the kingdom of their Father" (Matthew 13:43).

The divided judgment on honor which is found in the gospel is encountered also in other parts of the New Testament. The congregation of disciples in Jerusalem is pictured as enjoying the favor of the people (Acts 2:47; 5:13, 26). At the same time, the congregation experienced also opposition and rejection from Jews and pagans, and bore it joyfully. For the Apostles it was an honor to be dishonored for the sake of Jesus' name. What the world regards as shame is, in truth and before God, honor (Acts 5:41).

The dialectics of the history of Paul exhibits much the same state of affairs. In Philippi the Apostle was publicly dishonored by being whipped and imprisoned. He appeals to the rights of his Roman citizenship and demands that the civil authority come and exculpate him (Acts 16:37). When false apostles impugned the honor of his person and of his office before the congregation, Paul repels the attack vehemently and with a passion (thus in Philippians, in Galatians, and in both Epistles to the Corinthians). Paul says of himself that he is intent upon his good name. "We have given no kind of scandal to anyone, lest fault might be found with our office" (2 Cor. 6:3). "We aim at what is right not only in the Lord's sight, but also in the sight of men" (2 Cor. 8:21).

The congregations which Paul founded are his joy and honor: "My dear brothers, my joy and my crown, stand firm in the Lord" (Phil. 4:1). The Church in Corinth is the Apostle's letter of introduction to all men: "A letter from Christ, delivered by us, written with the Spirit of the living God" (2 Cor. 3:2f.). In the end these communities will be the hope, joy, and glory of the Apostle at the coming of Christ (1 Thess. 2:19). Paul warns his congregations, too, to have a regard for their public image. "Make it a point of honor to live peaceably, minding your own affairs and working with your hands, as we have charged you, so that you may be well thought of by the outsiders with whom you deal" (1 Thess. 4:11f.; Col. 4:5). He who seeks righteousness is striving after genuine honor and will win true honor — now and in the future: "To those who are tenacious in the performance of good works and who strive after glory, honor, and incorruptibility, God will grant eternal life" (Rom. 2:7).

The Christian must pay every honor to him to whom honor is due. "Pay all of them their due, . . . honor to whom honor is due" (Rom. 13:7; 1 Peter 2:17). Even in the New Testament, the old commandment of honoring father and mother is still valid. A new depth is given the commandment in the New Testament, however, with the admonition that this is to be done "in the Lord" (Eph. 6:1-2).

Within the family, man and wife must live together "in holiness and honor" (1 Thess. 4:4). Men must treat their wives, as the weaker sex, with a certain deference, and they must "honor them as co-heirs of the grace of life" (1 Peter 3:7). It holds good even for the community of disciples: "Love one another with brotherly love; outdo one another in showing honor" (Rom. 12:10). Even that Christian whose natural and spiritual endowment is less is to be shown special honor, and in that way harmony in the community will be established (1 Cor. 12:23f.). In a great household there are various vessels, some precious, some of lesser worth, "some for honorable purpose, some for ignoble purpose." There are false teachers, and there are godly persons. "A holy vessel of honorable purpose, useful to the householders and suited to every good work" — such a one is the Christian who keeps false teachers at a distance (2 Tim. 2:20f.).

Magistrates and kings have, by reason of their office, a claim to honor: "Honor all men, love the brotherhood, fear God, honor the king" (1 Peter 2:17). This holds good in spite of the fact that First Peter was written on the eve of the persecution, when what the Church had to expect from the State could no longer be hidden from the epistle. The office of king (emperor) has its honor. Slaves should regard their masters as worthy of honor (1 Tim. 6:1). Even slaves themselves are to be regarded as co-members of the congregation. They are free in Christ (1 Cor. 7:22; Gal. 3:28), in whose one Spirit they participate (1 Cor. 12:13). A slave is a brother "as a man and as a Christian" (Philemon 16).

The New Testament says already that honor is due those who hold office in the Church. Paul's admonition is that recognition and obedience are to be accorded to those who expend themselves for the congregation (1 Cor. 16:16, 18). Epaphroditus, who did his work well, should be received by the community in Philippi "with all joy in the Lord. Such men are to be held in honor" (Phil. 2:29).

The Pastoral Epistles speak even more clearly about the constitution of the official position. "Let the elders who were proficient in their management be accorded a double share of honor,[156] those especially who labor in preaching and teaching" (1 Tim. 5:17). Those who belong in the ecclesiastical rank of widows are to be honored (1 Tim. 5:3). The Epistle to the Hebrews (13:7) admonishes that official position is to be respected. "Remember your leaders, who have announced to you the word of God." Proclamation of the word lends authority. "Obey your leaders and submit to them; for they are keeping watch over your souls as men who will have to render an account" (Heb. 13:17). As with Judaism and ancient morality in general, Christianity prescribes reverence for the teacher. The teacher, however, will be answerable to the coming judgment, just as will be the one who is taught.

External honor is a great good; but it is not an absolute good. Paul does not seek honor from and in the sight of men (1 Thess. 2:6). In the long run, human judgment is of little worth: "It means nothing to me that I am judged by you or by any human court. . . . It is the Lord who judges me" (1 Cor. 4:3-4). The Apostle finds his honor in his service. "Our glory is this: the testimony of our conscience that we behaved in the world in holiness and godly sincerity, . . . by the grace of God" (2 Cor. 1:12). True glory is not won by human effort, for it is a gift of God. "By God's grace I am what I am" (1 Cor. 15:10).

God's power, however, is manifested even in the weakness of man, and therefore the Apostle glories in oppression (Rom. 5:3) and in weakness (2 Cor. 11:30; 12:9). This is the glory of the cross, in which the Apostle shares (Gal. 6:14). Genuine honor and glory will turn out to be his on the day of judgment. Therefore "we pride ourselves in the hope of the glory of God" (Rom. 5:2). This holds good for the Apostle as well as for his congregation. "We will be your glory, just as you will be ours, on the day of our Lord Jesus" (2 Cor. 1:14; 1 Thess. 2:19f.). Again and again Paul makes his shattering avowals that the very being of the Apostle embraces an almost unbearable tension between internal honor of the highest order and external dishonor. "We have become, as it were, the refuse of the world, the offscouring of all things, even to the present time" (1 Cor. 4:9-13; 2 Cor. 4:7-12; 6:3-10; 11:23-29).

The moral teaching of the Pastoral Epistles demands that bishops and deacons be blameless and of high repute (1 Tim. 3:2-5, 8, 11). "The bishop must have a good name with those who are outside" (1 Tim. 3:7). The Church and its officials must be regarded as honorable by civil society. Every sort of evil gossip must be avoided (1 Tim. 5:14; 6:1; Titus 2:5). The hard reality becomes evident, nevertheless, when all Christians and especially those in official positions are told: "All who desire to live a godly life in Christ Jesus will suffer persecution" (2 Tim. 3:12).

If Paul calls upon the congregation too to look to the honor of its reputation, he reminds it, nevertheless, that striving after honor can easily lead one astray. In the congregation false striving for honor more than anything else can be unhealthy. Paul warns and admonishes, therefore, "not to strive after what is appropriate, but but to strive after discretion" (Rom. 12:3). "Live in harmony with one another; strive not after loftier things, but content yourself with the more lowly. Regard not yourselves as wise" (Rom. 12:16). "Let us pursue no idle honor, nor provoke one another, nor be envious of one another" (Gal. 5:26). The Apostle's word calls to mind the gospel's admonition about being of service to everyone: "Do nothing for the sake of self-seeking or in an idle quest for glory, but let each one humbly regard the other as better than himself" (Phil. 2:3).

Paul warns of false glory and false self-glory. Jews as well as Gentiles are sinners, guilty in the sight of God (Rom. 1:18–3:20). "No man dare boast in the sight of God" (1 Cor. 1:29). "All boasting is excluded" (Rom. 3:27). Every good thing is indeed a gift of God. "If you have received it as a gift, how dare you to boast, as if it were not something given you" (1 Cor. 4:7). If in the foolishness of the cross and in the weakness of Christ all self-glory is brought to nothing, and salvation itself is a gift (1 Cor. 1:25-31), there remains but one legitimate boast: "We pride ourselves in God through our Lord Jesus through whom we have been granted reconciliation" (Rom. 5:11). This basic theme is repeated in later writings. "In virtue of grace have you been saved by faith, and not by your own doing — it is God's gift — not because of works, lest any man should boast" (Eph. 2:8-9). "We are Christ's house, if we hold fast our confidence and pride in our hope to the end" (Heb. 3:6).

False doctrine and false glory easily go hand in hand. "These have indeed the appearance of truth in their self-chosen worship and abasement and severity against the body. But these things are done not unto honor, but unto gratification of the flesh" (Col. 2:23). The passage, uncertain as to its interpretation, probably borrows, for polemical purpose, concepts from the teachings of special groups who prided themselves on the godliness of their own rigidly ascetical manner of life whereby they attempted to prepare themselves for the reception of a fulfillment ostensibly divine. They made this their claim to special honor. This, however, the Apostle contests. All things considered, what is being promoted there is only the gratification of one's own will and a false glorying in self. This is not mortification, nor is it of the spirit; rather, it is cult of the flesh.

The true and precious honor of the Christian, even if it is as yet inconspicuous, is his calling and his pardon. Just as when the potter makes vessels for honorable and for ignoble purpose, there is a difference introduced at the outset. God endured the vessels of wrath, which were prepared for destruction, and he wanted "to make known the riches of his glory to the vessels of mercy which he has prepared for glory" (Rom. 9:21-23). The manner of expression is carefully chosen. God intended beforehand the glorification of the elect. But Paul does not say that God intended from the very beginning creatures who were destined for his anger and for destruction. Within the mystery, it remains clear enough who bears the guilt for this. And perfect glory is an eschatological good. Those "who are tireless in good works . . . will experience glory, honor, and peace, in eternal life" (Rom. 2:7, 10). Glory comes not of one's own deserts, but is in truth always a gift (Rom. 3:20, 24). The gift of salvation is always salvation through Christ.

The disciples must be ready and willing to endure dishonor and insult. The suffering Christ is his model in this (1 Cor. 4:10; Heb. 12:2; 1 Peter 2:23; and many others). After the Passion, Christians are to share in the glory of the resurrection: "If we suffer with him, we will be glorified with him" (Rom. 8:17). "When Christ, our life, is revealed, then will you also be revealed with him in glory" (Col. 3:4; Phil. 3:21). Christ is "the hope of glory" (Col. 1:27).

The First Epistle of Peter likewise speaks of the present and future glory of the Christian calling. Christ is the cornerstone and foundation, precious and elect (after Is. 28:16). He carries the Church. Those who are united with him in faith share in his glory; and in the judgment they will not be put to shame (1 Peter 2:6f.). Then "the genuinity of your faith will redound to your praise, glory, and honor, at the revelation of Jesus Christ" (1 Peter 1:7). God is his own glory and honor for ever and ever (1 Tim. 1:17; Apoc. 4:9). He gives a share therein.

The final, all-embracing end and goal is God's glory. "Let your light shine before men, so that they may see your good works and give praise to your Father in heaven" (Matthew 5:16). Disbelief seeks honor before men, not before God. To have faith means to seek God's honor, and to seek God's honor is faith (John 5:44; 12:43). Paul concludes his summation of the course of all history: "From him and through him and unto him are all things. To him be glory in all ages. Amen" (Rom. 11:36). The glory of God is the ultimate goal of every moral endeavor in God's congregation: "Maintain good conduct in the presence of the pagans, so that if they speak against you as wrongdoers, persuaded by your visible good works, they may glorify God on the day of visitation" (1 Peter 2:12).

§ 25. FAMILY

The most basic and closest society in which a man lives is the family.[157] And the Bible must necessarily treat of the family situation. In the old covenant the family arrangement finds its basis in the commandment of the decalogue: "Honor your father and your mother so that you may live long in the land which God will give you" (Exod. 20:12; Deut. 5:16). As a primitive codification of law, the decalogue prohibits particular severe lapses which destroy society through their external performance: murder, adultery, theft. The commandment to honor parents, however, is of quite another sort and goes far beyond these other commandments. It bids and requires an internal attitude of reverence which is never at an end and which must give rise consistently to its external manifestation. Mere formal legality will never suffice for this commandment.

In this commandment father and mother are mentioned together, without distinction. In the customs and legal arrangements of early times there is a superiority of rights accorded either to the father or to the mother. As with other peoples, Israel too appears, at least in individual nomadic groups, to have maintained the maternal arrangement at first, which finally, however, with the acceptance of the cult of Yahweh and with her own development into a nation, gave way to the paternally orientated arrangement. In this latter arrangement, however, the wife is easily pressed into a position in the family in which she enjoys little by way of legal rights. This is a particularly inevitable consequence of polygamy. This was the case in Israel just as in other nations of the ancient world.

Nevertheless, in the commandment of the decalogue, father and mother are placed side by side. Both have equal claim to being honored in the family. In the decalogue this commandment stands before the others that concern the social order, and to this commandment alone does the sanctioning promise attach: "so that you may live long" (a fact to which the New Testament [Eph. 6:2] rightly calls attention). This commandment binds unconditionally. Whether father and mother in any particular instance are worthy and can demand to be honored does not enter into the question. In every instance the requirement is the same: Honor your father, honor your mother. Nor is it that the very concept of fatherhood and motherhood is worthy of honor; rather, parents are to be honored because they are there.

The book of the covenant sharpens the commandment of the decalogue when it establishes the death penalty for anyone who would curse or strike his father or mother (Exod. 21:15, 17). Later

Judaism repeats the demand of the book of the covenant. The commandment of honoring parents is an important point of instruction (Sir. 7:27; 23:14; Tob. 4:3-5; *Letter of Aristeas*, 238).

The synagogue brings a set of exact rules to the prescription of reverence toward parents; but it also debates the limits of the commandment. It considers which is to take precedence, the honoring of God or of parents; and its answer, naturally, is that the honoring of God comes first. The Rabbis also affirm, however, that the duty of studying the Torah weighs as heavily as that of reverencing parents, and that teacher precedes father. This casuistry comes into play also in the gospel (Mark 7:9-13).

In the New Testament the old order has further validity. Jesus himself confirms the commandment of the decalogue. When a man comes to him and asks him what he must do to inherit eternal life, Jesus answers: "Thou shalt not kill, thou shalt not commit adultery, thou shalt not steal, thou shalt not bear false witness, thou shalt not defraud. Honor thy father and thy mother" (Mark 10:19). The unusual order of the commandments seems to proceed from the prohibitions to the positive commandment of honoring one's parents. The latter commandment is given a special emphasis by placing it at the end. Jesus repeats even that form of the commandment which prescribes the death penalty for the abusing of parents (Mark 7:10), through it is not to be expected that the penalty would be carried out in his day. This penalty, attached in antiquity to not a few lapses, had long since passed into disuse.

Just as with his new interpretation of the Old Testament law in the Sermon on the Mount, so here too Jesus demands adherence to the original spirit of the ordinance, as opposed to a casuistry which provided for outrageous breach of the law: "How wonderfully do you bring God's law to naught so that you can observe your traditions! . . . If someone says to his father or mother, 'What you might have received from me is *corban*, a consecrated gift,' then you consent to his doing nothing for his father or mother. Thus do you make void the word of God by your tradition which you hand down" (Mark 7:9-13). The case adduced is that of a son who — perhaps in a hypocritical piety, or perhaps in a moment of pique — devotes that which he owes his parents to the temple as a consecrated gift. The promise was in fact a purely illusionary vow, since the one making the vow retained, at any rate, the usufruct of what he vowed.

According to the Gospels, Jesus gave expression to the fact that he knew and assented to the joy and blessedness which a child portends for adults. For this is indeed a blessedness pertaining principally to the family, the society in which the child matures. This is stated once in the account of Jesus' blessing the children (Mark 10:13-16). In Mark (and afterwards also in Matthew 19:13-15), the passage follows immediately after the remarks of Jesus about marriage and divorce (Mark 10:1-12; Matthew 19:3-12).

This correlation is by no means fortuitous. In its context the passage in question is a comment on the riches of marriage. Children are brought to Jesus so that he might lay his hands on them and pray over them. It takes for granted a beautiful Jewish custom. On the Sabbath, parents took care to bless their children, and on festival days they took their children to be blessed by a Scribe. Just as a Rabbi, out of a pious respect for his person, is asked to bless one's children, so too is a blessing sought of Jesus, the great and godly Master. In Israel a child is treasured as a gift of God, because it preserves the race (Gen. 33:5; Ps. 127:3); it is treasured, then, as of value for the future. Its own personality is less regarded. Be that as it may, the psalmist is profoundly moved at the sight of childlike piety (Ps. 8:3).

The child stands in need of rigid rearing, divine as well as human (Prov. 3:11f.; Sir. 30:1-13). Certainly the child is not yet bound by the Law, and it may well be guiltless; but by the same token, it is also without merit, and since it is merit alone that counts, the child is of no consequence. Such, no doubt, was the thought of the disciples when they kept the children back from the Master. To come to the Master — that is not an affair for children but only for adults, who can and must decide to follow him. But now a word from the Lord says that it is precisely for children that the kingdom is intended. Nor is it on account of their presumed innocence and purity that they are called. That is no biblical way of thinking, since according to biblical judgment every human being has a heritage of evil (Gen. 8:21; Ps. 51:7).

The gospel alludes to the reason: "Whoever receives the kingdom like a child" (Mark 10:15). The child is prepared to receive, it is able to receive, and it allows itself to be a recipient. It does not yet propose to accomplish anything of itself, and does not boast of its own works. It expects nothing of itself, everything from those who are older and richer. The child is an example of confident expectation and of faith. The kingdom can be received only as a gift. The child in a family is perennial frankness and confidence in relation to the kingdom and all its gifts. And since the kingdom comes where it will be accepted, the child portends the continuing advent of the kingdom.

At the entry of Jesus into Jerusalem the children recognize in him the Messiah; and in the temple they pay homage to him as the Son of David, in spite of the indignation of the chief priests and Scribes (Matthew 21:15f.). While the congregation of the temple stands aloof, the children receive salvation; and it is they who are the true members of the messianic kingdom.

A narrative in the Gospel of Matthew (18:1-14),[158] in which various logia are brought together, takes as its starting point that Jesus called a child and put him in the midst of the disciples. Several sayings about children and "little ones" are then subjoined. A child can gain entry to the kingdom of God, because its estimate of itself is humble indeed. "Who therefore humbles himself is the greatest in the kingdom of heaven" (Matthew 18:4). In its littleness before God, the child demonstrates the kind of faith that expects everything from God. Whoever receives a child in Jesus' name, receives Jesus himself (Matthew 18:5). Jesus is the protector of the defenselessness of the child. He makes the care of the child the duty and obligation of the community. Probably the Church already exists as an institution. Probably it is the Lord of the community's enhancement that is speaking here. He identifies himself with the child and is even present in the community through the child.

The narrative concludes with the further remark: "See that you do not scorn one of these little ones. . . . In heaven their angels look always upon the face of my Father in heaven" (Matthew 18:10). According to the notion of the Rabbis, there are among the invisible heavenly hosts various ranks. The "angels of the visage" comprise the innermost circle; they are next to God and may look upon him. The Qumran texts also speak of these angels. The priests are to serve God "like angels of the visage in the holy dwelling to the honor of the God of hosts" (1 QSb 4:25f.). The most majestic duties are confided to these highest angels. Perhaps it is they who are the princes of the nations (Deut. 32:8; Dan. 10:13).

Yet, this saying of the Lord states that the angels of the little ones can behold the face of the Father. The protection of the little ones is confided to the highest angels. No greater duty can be given them. The honor of the guardian angels is the honor of children. Children may seem to be powerless and without recourse, but whoever would touch them must answer for it to the holy power of God. Judaism cherished a great awe toward heavenly beings. One had to revere them in order, by their help, to approach God. But here the mightiest beings of heaven are at the disposal of little children, who belong to Christ. A child in the family signifies that God's presence, his protection, and his fidelity are watching over that family.

Because the condition of the child makes him so well-adapted to being used as an example, the Gospels seem to have taken up quite readily the designation "the little ones, who believe in Jesus" (Matthew 18:6), making it into a title for the disciple. In Jesus' cry of praise, however, those still in their minority are the recipients of the revelation which remains hidden from the wise (Matthew 11:25).

The messianic era of salvation which has now begun will bring salvation also to the family in need. The angel proclaims of John, the precursor of the Messiah: "He will turn the hearts of the fathers again to the children" (Luke 1:17). The prophetic hope and promise is fulfilled: "He will turn the hearts of fathers to their sons and the hearts of sons to their fathers" (Mal. 4:6). In the account of the childhood of Jesus, he is an example of childlike obedience, and the family in Nazareth is a model of the faithful family (Luke 2:40, 51-52).

If marriage can be entered into in the face of the crisis of the eschatological time (see above, ch. 20), it is for the sake of the greater good of the family that this is so. Jesus indicates as much by his own conduct. One day some of those who were close to him came "to seize him. For they said, 'He has lost his senses'" (Mark 3:21). "And his mother and his brothers came, and standing outside they sent to him and called him. . . . But he looked at those sitting around him and said: 'Behold, my mother and my brothers! Whoever does the will of God is my brother and sister and mother'" (Mark 3:31-35).

Jesus is a riddle and a scandal. They are indignant because he does not come on time for his meals (Mark 3:20). They cannot abandon their narrow provincialism, and he does not fit. His very being soars to spiritual heights; but they can only judge it insanity. They are concerned over the call of family and kinfolk, and want to take him home. Something of this relationship between Jesus and his family is indicated elsewhere. "Not once did his relatives believe in him" (John 7:5).

Jesus replies to such demands of the family that he must be loosed from every merely human and natural relationship. A new society is forming around his person. It is as inviolable as that which comes forth from a mother's womb. Spiritual brotherhood is taking the place of the natural one, and a new family of faith is replacing the old natural family.[159]

Just as with Christ himself, so too can the disciple come into conflict with his family. Then there must be no wavering as to the decision to be made. "Whoever loves father or mother more than me is not worthy of me; and whoever loves son or daughter more than me is not worthy of me" (Matthew 10:37). In order to be a faithful follower among the disciples, it may be demanded that one sever the bonds of family. The obligation of discipleship is greater than the obligation of filial or paternal devotion. The demand is made still firmer and clearer: "Whoever comes to me and does not hate father, mother, wife, children, brothers, sisters, and indeed, his very life cannot be my disciple" (Luke 14:26). "Hate" may be a figure of speech, traceable to the Hebraic idiom, which means "to put in a secondary position, to relegate to the rear"; but it is still forceful enough.

At the same time, it is not possible to loose or renounce family ties on the pretext of religion, but really to serve one's own ends.

This is precluded by the demand of hating one's own life. This renunciation must not be made for the sake of one's own advantage, but only in order to attain the higher good. A sly, pseudo-religiosity, such as that exhibited in the misuse of *corban* (Mark 7:13), is repulsed.

The possible necessity of a separation from family is expressed in a biographical notice: "Another said to him, 'Let me first go and bury my father.' Jesus, however, answered him: 'Follow me, and let the dead bury their dead'" (Luke 9:59). Care for the dead is a highly regarded work in Israel. This is portrayed in exemplary fashion in the Book of Tobit (1:17f.; 2:7).

Solicitude about the burial of his father quite obviously pertains to the duties of a good son. That the possibility of such an extraordinary demand is now a reality is announced: Let the dead bury their dead! It is not a question of the special case of a son's obligation to a dead father, not a question of whether or not piety is to be practiced; rather, it concerns life and death in general. The dead who are to bury the dead are those not ready for discipleship, not ready to follow the Master, those not yet awakened to life. They can take care of the burial; for they belong to the past, yes, to death. It is a hard saying, but its purpose is to turn one not yet decided from death to life. All men are naught but corpses until the call of Jesus reaches them: "Now is the hour when the dead are hearing the voice of the Son of God; and those who hear will live" (John 5:24).

A separation may take place in the very midst of the family. "Brother will deliver brother to death, and the father his child; and children will rise up against parents and slay them" (Matthew 10:21). "I have not come to bring peace, but the sword. I have come to set a man against his father, and a daughter against her mother, and a daughter-in-law against her mother-in-law; and a man's enemies will be those of his own household" (Matthew 10:35-36). In both logia prophetic proclamations are fulfilled (Micah 7:6; Zech. 13:3; *Ethiopic Henoch*, 100, 2). The prophecy is an eschatological prediction. The urgency of the eschatological time will cause families to distintegrate (Mark 13:12). Again, according to the *Book of Jubilees* (23:16, 19), in the eschatological period family members will end up in conflict, each reproaching the other with having kept neither covenant with God nor his laws.

The disciple, however, who accepts the way of renunciation has the promise of rich blessings. Whoever leaves family and household "will have in return a hundredfold, houses and brothers and sisters and mother and children and lands, now in this world — and certainly persecutions along with them; and in the future age, eternal life" (Mark 10:30). The promise about the present time cannot mean anything else than the congregation of disciples. Whoever leaves his family finds a new, larger, and better family in the communion of the Church. The natural family is superseded and outdone by the family of the faith. And present renunciation will at last win the future age.

In the letters of the Apostles there are numerous admonitions concerning order in the family. Paul expounds in detail regarding the virtually insignificant question of whether or not a woman should have her head covered at divine service. "The head of every man is Christ, the head of a woman is her husband, the head of Christ is God. . . . Man is the image and glory of God; but woman is the glory of her husband" (1 Cor. 11:3-7). Man is the reflected splendor and likeness of God insofar as, in Adam, he is created immediately by God and therefore refers back immediately to God. Woman is the reflected splendor of man, since in her creation she was formed out of man (Gen. 2:7, 22). Woman refers back to man, and only through man to God. Paul concludes: "Man was not created for the sake of woman, but woman for the sake of man" (1 Cor. 11:9).

Paul follows Rabbinic interpretation of the creation narrative in Genesis, and accepts Hellenistic cosmological speculations and scholarly traditions. In that respect he is limited by temporal philosophical considerations. In no way, however, can a man make these views a justification of his lording it over woman. Man must recognize that he has Christ over him as his head.

In respect to the here-and-now relationships between man and wife, the ordering that counts is "in the Lord." "In the Lord there is neither woman without man, nor is there man without woman." In the Lord neither is independent of the other, but each points to the other. It is a simple historical reality: "As woman came from man, so now does man come from woman (in the natural course of birth). Everything, however, is from God" (1 Cor. 11:12). Ultimately, both man and woman come in the same way from God. They have, therefore, the same rights and the same worth. Man must concur with his wife in love (Eph. 5:25; Col. 3:19).

About divine and human fatherhood, it is said: "I bow my knees before the Father, from whom every family (πατριὰ) in heaven and on earth takes its name" (Eph. 3:4-15). Everything that bears the name father, bears it in analogy to God, the true Father. Were it not for him, one could not speak at all of fatherhood; and everything that bears this name refers back to God as its origin, and looks ahead to him as its goal. God's being Father is manifest and evident in the family gathered together about its father (as also in a united fatherland). "There is something divine in fatherhood, because there is something fatherly in God" (G. Schrenk).

In the tables of duties to others (see above, ch. 17), the obligations binding within the social unit of the family are described (Eph. 5:22f.; 6:1-3; Col. 3:18-20; 1 Peter 3:1, 7). If the obligations of children to their parents are spelled out, so too are those of parents toward their children; and the limits of paternal authority are shown. It must not be used capriciously. "You fathers, do not embitter your children, lest they despair" (Eph. 6:4; Col. 3:21). The Epistle to the Hebrews (12:5-11) employs Old Testament terms (Prov. 3:11-12) in speaking of the severe punishment of a child by its father. It is easily admitted, however, that the earthly disciplinarian is discretionary in dealing with men, and is subject to error and misconception. All the ancient recognition of paternal authority notwithstanding, criticism and liberty will have their say.

The individuality of Jesus in his esteem for the child is especially clear when contrasted with the attitude of Paul. For Paul, what is childlike means that which is unfinished, indeed, childish. In contrasting child with adult, Paul conforms to the mode of expression familiar to his own time. Thus he says: "I had to speak with you as with men bound to the flesh, as with children in Christ." The Apostle had to offer them milk, not solid food (1 Cor. 3:1f.). "Children in Christ" are, accordingly, mere beginners as to understanding. "When I was a child, I spoke like a child, thought like a child, reasoned like a child. When I became a man, I gave up childish ways" (1 Cor. 13:11). Children are not yet ripe for a deeper understanding. "Brethren, do not be children in your thinking; rather, be childlike in respect to evil, but mature in your thinking" (1 Cor. 14:20). Here, side by side, are disparagement of childish thinking and the notion of childlike innocence. Nevertheless, Paul says elsewhere (Gal. 4:1-5) that the status of a child is one of imperfection, which has now been overcome through fully enfranchised sonship. We must put aside childhood as a minority subject to every kind of error, and grow up to the manhood which is the fullness of Christ (Eph. 4:13-15).

Again, the Epistle to the Hebrews (5:12-14) reproaches Christians as being still immature, in need of milk and not solid food. The First Epistle of Peter (2:2) recognizes the positive importance of childlike innocence, even if what is said is primarily in reference to baptism: "Like newborn babes, long for the pure spiritual milk."

The discrepancy between the Synoptics and Paul in their judgment on childhood can perhaps be largely explained away in view of the fact that Paul also says that the wisdom of the world is conquered by the foolishness of God (1 Cor. 1:19f.) — human wisdom, so to speak, put to naught by God's revelation. In the Synoptics, childhood means not being dependent upon one's own ability; and Paul too says that salvation is a gift, and all glorying in one's own abilities is precluded (Rom. 3:27).

If the gospel designates the community as a new family (Mark 3:34), it may well be that other appropriate titles similarly derived were used in the community. In relation to the community, Paul knows that he himself is the father (1 Cor. 4:15; 1 Thess. 2:11), and indeed, a nursing mother (Gal. 4:19; 1 Thess. 2:7). Just as Jesus addresses his disciples as children (Mark 10:24; John 13:33; 21:5), so too the Apostles and teachers speak to Christians as children (1 Cor. 4:17; 2 Tim. 1:2; Tit. 1:4; 1 Peter 5:13; 1 John 2:12, 18; 2 John 1; 3 John 4). Interwoven here is the old Oriental usage of calling the teacher and spiritual leader "father." The Rabbis speak of the begetting of a scholar by the teacher. They collect the instructions of the teachers as "sayings of the fathers."

At the same time there is perhaps a clash between this manner of speaking and the influence of the Mithraic mysteries, in which the *mystes* honored the initiating priest as father. The development did not come into Christian communities without disagreement. Christ says: "Call no man your father on earth. One only is your Father, he that is in heaven" (Matthew 23:9). The logion presupposes that there are already in existence congregations with some claim to formalized instruction; and for that reason the saying is not to be regarded as a primitive word of the Lord, but as a word of the community.

§ 26. CIVIL GOVERNMENT

While from the earliest times the Greek and Latin languages and cultures formed terms and concepts for civil government [160] and used them with understandable frequency, the Bible, both Old and New Testaments, uses such expressions very sparingly. In the New Testament, πόλις occasionally comes close to the meaning "(urban) commonwealth." Occurring only twice is πολιτεία (Acts 22:28 = *citizenship*; Eph. 2:12 = *commonwealth [of Israel]*); and once, πολίτευμα (Phil. 3:20 = *commonwealth, home land*). Political theory and abstract teaching on law and government, such as was produced by ancient learning, is utterly foreign to the (Old and) New Testament. The New Testament, however, speaks not infrequently of Jewish and non-Jewish, civic and governmental authorities and governing bodies. It is in these that the government becomes visible and confronts the Christian and the Church. In their concrete historical relevance, however, certain fundamental conceptions and judgments must be discussed.

In the New Testament, Judaism hardly seems to be a political power. The Jewish state had forfeited its sovereignty completely. The altercations that take place, at any rate, are between the community of disciples on the one hand, and the synagogue and Jewish hierarchy on the other. For the most part it is a question of the validity and binding force of the Old Testament law. When the Church began to free itself from Jerusalem and its Jewish matrix, however, these relations and altercations, no longer having any relevance, were at an end.

It was in the world of the Roman Empire that the gospel was preached — one of the proudest and most powerful governmental creations that has ever existed. Any utterances of the New Testament about the State are never to be taken as purely theoretical and about government in general, but always in relation to this particular governmental organization.

The judgment on Rome and its Empire was divided even in the world of its own time.[161] Rome's power was known and recognized. Roman efficiency was celebrated, as also Roman piety toward the gods and Roman justice toward her peoples. The Hellenistic historian Polybius (1, 4) calls the Roman Empire "the most glorious and most useful creation of history" (*ca.* 120 B.C.).

The City of Rome itself is a copy of the world-ruling Empire. The City is the Empire's center and essence. It channels together the currents of the Empire's destiny. Without its power of organization the world could not exist. When Christianity came to Rome, the latter was already called "the eternal city" (by Cicero, Tibullus, and Vergil). Stoic philosophy understood the Empire as an expression of the unity of a world pantheistically conceived. This unity was visible and was authenticated in the person of Caesar Augustus, the "illustrious Emperor."

Political philosophy, the example of the Oriental cult of the ruler, ancient religious currents in general, which were well-prepared to worship the manifestation of the divine in prodigious happenings and in men of immense power — all these things combine to promote the religious worship of the imperial genius already in the first Augustus and in increasing degree with his successors, until finally the worship of the Emperor was demanded of every citizen as a token of his fidelity to the nation and State. This Rome-ideology, however, encountered not a little contradiction and opposition, and first of all, of course, among the conquered peoples. The Greeks and Orientals accuse the Romans of materialism, false dealing, cruelty, greed, and lust for power. And there were Romans themselves who warned the nation to take counsel of itself. Cicero (*De prov. consul.*, 3, 6) speaks once of the "well-nigh righteous hatred against our Empire."

Even in Israel the attitude toward Rome and relations with her was divided. A current of tradition, reaching far back into antiquity and having its ultimate source in the earlier prophets, gained new breadth and depth in late Judaism — the traditions of a theology of creation and of history which recognized and taught that God, as Lord of all, is Lord also of kings and nations (Is. 24:21; Jer. 10:7-16; Ps. 22:29), and that he leads the powers of the pagan world ahead, only to let them sink back again.

Assyria is regarded as a scourge in the hand of Yahweh (Is. 1:20; 5:25-29). Cyrus is the anointed one of God (Is. 45:1). Nebuchadnezzar executes God's angry judgment (Jer. 5:15-17; 16:13; 21:4-7). It is God who "sets up kings and removes them" (Dan. 2:21; Jer. 27:5-11). God bestows power and rule, and judges how they are used (Wis. 6:3f.).

Now the Romans pass before the horizon of the Bible; and it is admitted that, while they are strong and powerful, they are also faithful toward their friends. A Rabbi (in the New Testament era and before the destruction of Jerusalem) requires that there be "prayer for the welfare of the (Roman) government. For if it were not for the fear of her, each one would devour the other." Thus the conquest of Jerusalem by Pompey (in the year 63 B.C.) was interpreted as a punishment and as a warning to make expiation (*Psalms of Solomon*, 2). Philo (*Legat. ad Gaium*, 152f.; 355f.) and Josephus (*Jewish War*, 2, 10, 4; *Against Apion*, 2, 6) tell of sacrifices offered in the temple at Jerusalem for the Emperor and for the the Empire.

Nevertheless, Judaism has also a hearty voice in the anti-Roman chorus of antiquity. The earliest witnesses of this are the threats presented to us as prophecies in the third and fourth books of the *Sibylline Oracles*, of which the oldest Alexandrian-Jewish manuscripts originate *ca.* 100 B.C. According to these oracles (3:175-193, 520-536; 4:145–148), Rome, the barbarian nation, will indeed succeed at first in overthrowing and plundering the cities of Greece and the East. But the Empire will be filled with injustice, greed, and lechery; and she will be hated by the nations. A king coming from the East will defeat her. Rome, the delicate virgin with the gold-glistening tresses, now so much wooed and feted, will then be naught but a slave girl, whose mistress will shave her hair. Rome will be dragged down from the heavens to the earth.

The indictments from after the fall of Jerusalem, which are preserved in the apocalypses of Esdras (4 Esdras 12:11-31) and Baruch (*Syriac Apoc. of Baruch*, 67:7f.), as well as in the fifth book of *Sibylline Oracles* (5:143-178), become even more violent. The fourth of the beasts beheld by Daniel, which was strong and dreadful and which ground and devoured everything in its iron teeth (in Daniel 7:7 surely it is the Seleucid Empire that is menat) is now understood as meaning Rome (4 Esdras 11:38-46). In writings from the beginning of the second century of the Christian era, Babylon becomes an abusive sobriquet for Rome, considered as the enemy (*Syr. Apoc. of Baruch*, 11:1; *Sibylline Oracles*, 5:143, 159). Even Rabbinic Judaism speaks very critically of Rome. Roman culture and civilization, theaters, cities, business and commerce are an abomination to the pious Jew. The *Eighteen Benedictions* (12) prays: "To the apostate may there be no hope, and may the shameless rule (i.e., Rome) be swiftly extirpated."

The Qumran writings reach into the period of the New Testament. In the *Commentary on Habakkuk*, the *Commentary on Nahum*, and in the scroll on the *War of the Sons of Light with the Sons of Darkness*, the Kittians are frequently named as the enemy of Israel. The Kittians, taking their name originally from the city of Kition on Cyprus, dwell, according to the later parts of the Old Testament, in the lands on the Mediterranean, to the west of Palestine. Probably in Dan. 11:30 Kittians is already a sobriquet for the Romans; and the Septuagint does not hesitate to translate *Kittim* as "Romans." The predominant interpretation today is that *Kittians* in the Qumran scrolls signify the Romans. Of these Kittians it is said: "They are impetuous and strong in battle. They take possession of many lands, and do not believe in the laws of God" (1 QpHab 2:12-15). "Dread and terror come upon all nations in their presence" (1 QpHab 3:4). But when all is said and done, it is these

Kittians who will execute God's judgment upon Israel as well as upon the Gentiles (1 QpHab 4:7f.; 9:4-7).

Jesus expresses no opinion on the all important relation between his nation and Rome. To him it seems to be of no importance who exercises dominion in the land. Political and national ardor are — originally, at least — foreign to the gospel.[162]

The Synoptics preserve a significant saying of the Lord: "Render to Caesar the things that are Caesar's and to God the things that are God's" (Mark 12:13-17). In the gospel narrative, the opponents of Jesus want him to decide the question of whether or not paying to the Emperor the especially hated head tax, the tangible sign of foreign domination, is in accord with Israel's religious law. They wanted to compel him thereby to declare himself for or against Rome, and by that very token for or against his own people.

Jesus broadens and deepens the question about the tax, turning it into the more comprehensive question of duty in general to Emperor and to God. The term usually translated "render" is ἀπόδοτε. It is used twice in the short passage; and both times it conveys the idea of settlement of a debt. Its more precise meaning is "give back." If the word can be interpreted narrowly, it says that the tax is owed as a recompense for the achievements of the Roman government.[163] The duty to the Emperor is joined to that toward God with the simple connective *and*. This does not mean that both obligations stood side by side, separate from each other and of obvious and equal authority, as if Jesus wanted to grant autonomy to the political and religious spheres, so that ultimately the State might emancipate itself from God.

Separation of Church and State is a modern idea. In Judaism, and in antiquity in general, religion and nation are an obvious unity. God, however, is over all. He is Creator, Judge, and Lord of the world, and therefore of men also, assembled as they are in a governmental State. In Jesus' answer, the first part is circumscribed by the second. Emperor and State have their rights. Nevertheless, the rights and demands of the State are bounded by the rights and demands of God.

So far as Jesus replies to the immediate question about the payment of the tax, his solution is not the mutiny which the zealots were inciting and crying out for and which was plunging Jerusalem and the nation into catastrophe; nor is it that renunciation and resignation which abandons to the world of politics its own evil sphere, in order to withdraw into the world of God and to live there undisturbed, as in fact pious Pharisaism was doing; and finally, neither is it idolatrous deification of a tyrannical government. The questioners are in fact informed by his answer, that God's work must take place in and in reference to the world, and that it is to him that faith must ever make an accounting for its performance. For the kingdom of God is always in the midst of the world.

In the saying about paying the tax, the Emperor is mentioned. Other logia treat of rulers in general and thereby make immediately clear the attitude of the gospel toward the imperium. "Those who are supposed to rule over the Gentiles oppress them, and their great men offer violence to them. . . . Whoever would be great among you must be your servant, and whoever would be first among you must be the slave of all. Even the Son of man has not come to be served but to serve" (Mark 10:42-45). According to this saying, the common characteristic of dominion in the world is force and the misuse of traditional power. Of the governmental exercise of power in the framework of service, it knows little.

To be sure, the gospel in no way rejects striving after greatness and the position of one who is first among all. But the greatness of such a one must be in his service. Even the Son of Man himself belongs in the ranks of these great ones and princes, not because he elevated his life by serving his servants, but because he surrendered it totally.

In the face of this saying of the Lord, does not all earthly power and dominion become questionable? Are not power and greatness at bottom a temptation to force and injustice? It would seem to be only one step more to the very summit of temptation, in which Satan points out from the mountain top all the kingdoms of the world and their glitter (Matthew 4:8f.). It is here that Evil proffers world dominion. Is it possible that all dominion proceeds from Evil?

Jesus himself is confronted by Emperor and State when he stands before Pilate, the representative of Rome (John 19:8-15). Pilate informs Jesus that his life is in the hands of the magistrate. In point of fact, a man's life is in the hands of the State. But Jesus' reply reminds Pilate that he can only carry out God's mandate: "You would have no power over me unless it had been given you from above" (John 19:11). The text does not say, "unless that power had been given you from above"; the "it" is simply the impersonal manner of expression, and it does *not* have "power" for its antecedent. Jesus' reply simply states that it is by God's will that he finds himself in Pilate's power; but it does not constitute a statement of principle on the source of the power of the State.

Nevertheless, the Johannine Christ does say that there is an irrevocable opposition between the divine kingdom of truth and the kingdom that is of this world (John 18:36f.). This opposition becomes apparent in the opposition between the Messianic King and the Roman Emperor (John 19:12, 15). The imperium pertains to the world, and, in the mind of John's Gospel, is forfeit, along with the world, to evil. That is the judgment of John's Gospel on the world of politics.[164]

In both his writings, it is Luke's intention to introduce the gospel into the world of Greek culture and Roman government.[165] In numerous passages his presentation is made after the manner of an apology. Among the points of information peculiar to Luke's account, we find the Jews presenting to Pilate what is an expressly political complaint (Luke 23:2). Nevertheless, the representative of Rome three times affirms the innocence of Jesus (Luke 23:4, 14, 22). Pilate does not expressly condemn Jesus to death; but he turns him over to the will of the Jews (Luke 23:25). It is they who kill the prophets (Luke 13:34).

In the Acts of the Apostles the continuing progress of the mission opens a path to Rome.[166] The gospel must be testified to before synagogues, kings, and heads of state (Luke 12:11; 21:12). The first convert from paganism is a Roman centurion (Acts 10:1). The Roman proconsul of Cyprus, "a man of intelligence," summons Paul and Barnabas, in order to be reliably instructed. He is won to the faith (Acts 13:6-12). In vain the Jews prefer political charges against Paul to the magistrate of Thessalonica (Acts 17:6-9). In Corinth the Roman proconsul Gallio, in his capacity as judge, recognizes the political harmlessness of the Apostle. The controversy is entirely an internal affair of the Jews (Acts 18:12-16).

Paul himself is able to maintain that he has offended neither against the Jews nor against the Emperor (Acts 25:8). The Roman court finds Paul innocent (Acts 25:10; 26:32; 28:18). In accord with the divine plan, Paul has to repair to Rome, in order to bear witness there to the gospel (Acts 19:21; 23:11). He himself had had such an intention in mind for a long time (Rom. 1:13). Rome is the center of the world, and whoever would win the world to the gospel must win Rome. Paul is the Apostle of the Gentiles. If he wants to fulfill his commission he must proclaim the gospel in Rome, the chief city of the Empire. When the Acts of the Apostles is able to report the arrival of Paul in Rome, the goal has been reached, and the narrative concludes (Acts 28:30-31).

Paul repeatedly declares himself in regard to the State. The problems involved in how the Christian should relate to the government were both urgent and difficult. The Acts of the Apostles (16:22f.), as well as Paul's own writings (Rom. 8:35f.; 2 Cor. 11:23-26), tells of harassment by civil authorities. Among the more notable statements of Paul: "Let every person be subject to the governing authorities. For there is no authority which is not from God. . . . Whoever resists authority, resists what God has appointed. Rulers are not a terror to good conduct, but to wicked. . . . Authority is the handmaiden of God" (Rom. 13:1-7).[167]

Paul is speaking "of the actual State, as it exists," and therefore of the Roman government and its authorities, not of some abstract, theoretical government. The remarks of the Apostle are notably unreserved. Civil authority is given utmost recognition. The State is God's arrangement. Paul says this of the tribute and tax officials, who are in such ill repute in the Synoptic Gospels. Whoever behaves properly has nothing to fear from the State; indeed, he will be treated by it with consideration. Possibly Paul is remembering public commendations and signs and tokens of honor shown himself. The wicked man, however, has experience of the State's system of justice. The one in authority is "the minister of justice serving God's wrath" (Rom. 13:4).

Has Paul forgotten what he himself experienced at the hands of

Roman officials, and what Christ suffered in the name of imperial justice? How is Paul to be understood? The hypothesis usually advanced, that in rejecting a fanatical and revolution-minded spirit of unrest in the Roman community he emphasizes in a one-sided manner the duty of submission, does not bear investigation. To begin with, Paul's teaching is certainly sympathetic to the esteem for the government which is a part of the Jewish theology of creation and theology of history. Secondly, in providing a basis for the obligation of obedience, Paul refers to conscience, a term and concept which comes to the New Testament ultimately from the Stoa, and which derives, therefore, from natural theology (see the present work, Vol. 1, pp. 137–138).

Here Paul is not arguing from what is properly Christian, but with ordinary, realistic, common-sense considerations. If, however, the State is worthy of esteem and has rights because it is God's minister, by that very fact — or at least in consequence thereof — its limitations are made clear. It is God's servant, not a lord powerful in its own right, so that whatever it found expedient is just; and above all, it is not a false god in God's place. Paul recognizes the relationship of government to law as the work of God. The State is a divine instrument, operative in the area of God's wrath. God, however, does not intend punishment only, but he wills much more the cure. For this part of the divine will the State is not authorized. The State is not God's vicar, purely and simply. The State's commission is circumscribed.

Paul does not consider the possibility of an unjust government. Granted, however, that Paul sees the finger of God in the secular legal ordinance, does not the State destroy its own authority when it breaks faith with the law? Paul speaks only of the obligation of underlings to the State, the only side of the coin which the Roman Empire knew about at the time of the New Testament; it knew nothing of a co-responsibility of the citizen in and for the State, nothing of a commitment resulting therefrom. And finally it must not be forgotten that Paul counted on the speedy arrival of the end of the ages, a notion to which he alludes in Rom. 13:11-14. The State too pertains to the form of this world that is passing away (1 Cor. 7:31). The Christian is not committed to it, since this tem-

porary world is of no importance to him. In this world he has but
to stand the test, so as to serve God (Rom. 12:1f.). Thus does the
text of Rom. 13:1-7 open paths to the solutions of further
problems.[168]

There are other texts not easily reconciled with Rom. 13:1-7. This
seems to be the case whenever Paul bases his argumentation on that
which is peculiarly Christian and eschatological. To the congregation in Corinth he writes that it is quite intolerable that Christians
should bring their litigations before the courts of the unrighteous.
In general, when a controversy arises between Christians — a thing
which should not happen — the matter should be adjusted by Christians. As the saints, Christians will one day judge the world; and
they will, therefore, be the judges also of the unrighteous (1 Cor.
6:1-8).

Paul may be proceeding from the fact that the Jewish congregations in the diaspora set up their own civil courts. The Christian
community must do likewise. Through their being endowed with
grace, Christians are of incomparable worth. As the brotherhood of
the saints, Christians are withdrawn from the State. As the future
judges of the world, they are superior to the world. Paul calls the
officially appointed representatives and custodians of the law purely
and simply the unrighteous. Paul now concludes from this to one
thing only, that Christians must not appeal to the governmental
courts. The consequences of his principles might be drawn much
further. Should not the Church be obliged to secede from the State,
and function as a State unto itself? Rom. 13:1-7 opposed any such
conclusions when it recognized the governmental powers as something established by God. Thus 1 Cor. 6:1-8 signifies: Even if love
can in fact renounce its rights, there will, nevertheless, still be legal
arrangements in the world.[169]

The thought is expressed again and again in the New Testament
letters, that the Christian has his true home not here but in another
world, the heavenly world. This holds good whether in respect to
Jerusalem or in respect to Rome. The Christian is set apart from
both cities and from both reigns. The earthly, present-day Jerusalem, along with her children, has been led into slavery. Our mother
is the Jerusalem above, she that is free. Just as in times past, so too

even now the earthly Jerusalem persecutes the heavenly (Gal. 4:26-31). The many, who are lost, "are minded to earthly things." "Our homeland is in the heavens; from there we await a Savior, our Lord Jesus Christ" (Phil. 3:19f.). The commonwealth of Christians is the kingdom of heaven.

Is this Synoptic declaration intended by Paul to refer to actual expectations in the political sphere? With the words πολίτευμα, σωτήρ, κύριος, Paul seems to be using politico-religious terminology. Does Paul mean to say, in polemical manner, that Christians already belong to the heavenly government and are alien to the earthly one? It is from heaven and not from this world that Christians expect their Lord and Savior.[170] This consciousness of belonging to another kingdom, the eschatological one, finds expression again when the once estranged Gentiles are told that they "are no longer strangers and sojourners, but fellow citizens with the saints and members of the household of God" (Eph. 2:19).

Is Second Thessalonians also of some pertinence to these considerations? According to 2 Thess. 2:6f., a restraining power or some restraining person is as yet delaying the incursion "of the mystery of lawlessness." The Church Fathers (Hippolytus, *Commentary on Daniel*, 4, 21, 3; Tertullian, *The Resurrection of the Dead*, 24) already understood thereby the organizational forces of the Roman Empire and of the Emperor, which counteract the destructive power of the Antichrist.

This interpretation is occasionally defended even today. With this interpretation, the letter would be declarative of a superior appreciation of the Roman imperium. Nevertheless, the application of this obscure text to Rome is uncertain. It is rejected by the majority of modern commentaries. Among the explanations attempted there is one which sees the letter as alluding to the Christian mission. The period of time vouchsafed for the spread of the missions is still delaying the arrival of the Antichrist and the subsequent parousia. Neither is this application entirely conclusive. What seems most probable, surely, is that by a delaying force is meant the divine plan of salvation, the plan of the ages, which has not yet proceeded to its conclusion.[171]

Paul is a Christian, an Apostle, and a Roman citizen. As an Apostle he awaits the heavenly Lord, who will soon make his appearance, and his eternal city. As a Roman citizen, he lives under the arrangement of the Empire, and he appeals to the rights which the State guarantees to every citizen (Acts 16:37; 22:25; 25:10). His teaching on the State concerns both worlds. His relationship to the State is broken, as is his relationship to this world in general, since the Christian possesses what he has as if he did not possess it (1 Cor. 7:29-31).

Like Paul, the Epistle to the Hebrews (13:12-14) also reminds Christians of their heavenly homeland. They must be ever prepared to forsake their earthly city. "Jesus suffered outside the camp, in order to sanctify the people by his own blood. So too let us go outside the camp, bearing abuse for him. For we have here no lasting city, but we aspire to that which is to come." Christ suffered outside the city of Jerusalem, cast out by men and despoiled of honor. Following his example, Christians must be prepared to give up all claim to the security of their civil and political existence, yes, to renounce world and time in general, in order to live with the Lord their society's alien existence of the cross.

The antithetical image of the earthly and the heavenly cities is developed further. "You have come to Mount Zion and to the heavenly city of the living God, to the heavenly Jerusalem, to the myriads of angels, to a festive gathering and to the assembly of those who are the first-born, who are enrolled in heaven" (Heb. 12:22-23). Former holy States like Zion and Jerusalem become figure and sign for the developing and already existing kingdom of God.

Christians already belong to the new heavenly congregation, which is incomparably more majestic than the former community of Israel. As an assembly gathered for the worship of God, it is also called a "festive gathering" (Hos. 2:11; Amos 5:21; Ez. 46:11). Now the Church is in truth this festive gathering. The angels, as companions of God at his very throne, are no longer apart from the assembly; rather, the angels and the assembly together constitute a heavenly community. The earthly Church is already displayed in the union with the "assembly of those who are the first-born," which phrase probably means those of the old and new covenants who are consummated in righteousness. As co-members of the heavenly assembly, the godly are "strangers and pilgrims here on earth" (Heb. 11:13).[172]

When the earthly and the heavenly cities are contrasted one with the other in the New Testament passages, and the Christian is admonished to surrender the former in order to win the latter, it must be remembered how much the man of antiquity counted on the city as a guarantor of freedom and order. In the commonwealth a man's life and existence expands in material and spiritual culture. The history and laws of cities are regarded as having been established by gods and heroic figures, and are grounded in myth and religion. A city extols itself in its cult. The man of antiquity prays for the preservation of his city. Jewish Gnosticism busied itself with a doctrine about the eternal Jerusalem, and after the destruction of the temporal city it awaits the new, divinely directed construction of an earthly, messianic Jerusalem (*Syr. Apoc. of Baruch*, 6:9; 32:4). In Italy, the particular area of reference of the Epistle to the Hebrews (13:24), Rome is monarch, the eternal city. The intentions of the New Testament become clear in the antithesis which speaks of the ephemeral nature of the earthly city as compared to the durability of the heavenly.

In many respects the morality of the Pastoral Epistles is well-balanced — and so too their attitude toward co-operation with the State. The Church is encouraged to prayerful intercession for the State. "First of all, I urge you to make supplication, prayer, intercession, and thanksgiving for all men, for kings [emperor] and all in high positions, so that we may be able to lead a quiet and peaceful life in all godliness and respectability" (1 Tim. 2:1-2).

Just as it is likely the practice of every praying community in the world to pray for the regime and the government, so this was done also in Greek and Roman temples and in the synagogue as well. The Christian Church too will adhere to this practice. For the public orderliness assured by the State guarantees also the exercise of "piety," i.e., of the Christian religion. Political peace is a prerequisite for the mission of the Church. Only then can God's plan of salvation be realized, the plan of him "who desires all men to be saved and to come to the knowledge of the truth" (1 Tim. 2:4).

The fulfillment of the obligation of fidelity to the State secures God's good pleasure (1 Tim. 2:3). The Church approves the State, in which she lives. Nevertheless, governments and kings stand in need of intercessory prayer, since they too need the grace and truth of God. The State shares in human inadequacy and is in need of divine assistance. It is not the Emperor who is Savior, as the cult of the ruler would have it; rather, it is God who is Savior, even of the Emperor (1 Tim. 2:6).

Accordingly it pertains to the duty of the bishop to admonish the congregation "to be submissive to the ruling authorities, to be obedient to them, to be ready for every good work, to speak evil of no one, and to be peaceable" (Titus 3:1-2). The admonition to revile no one (as godless) is to be understood as referring to one's attitude toward the civil authorities. It would be false to revile them indiscriminately as godless and as inimical to God. Civil authority is of God's ordaining. This it remains, even in the event of an official's misusing it. All this is required "because the goodness and loving kindness of God our Savior has appeared" (Tit. 3:4). Since God's mercy has been revealed in Christ, the Christian is obliged to practice similar kindness.[173]

In some passages of the Pastoral Epistles, exegesis asks whether the titles here applied to God and Christ are not perhaps intended to show a contrast for polemical purpose; thus, for example, with 1 Tim. 6:14f.; "until the appearing of our Lord Jesus Christ, which will be made manifest at its own time by the blessed and only Sovereign, the King of Kings and Lord of Lords"; or 2 Tim. 1:10: "the appearing of our Savior, Christ Jesus"; or Tit. 2:13: "We await our blessed hope and the appearing of the glory of our great God and Savior, Jesus Christ."

Even if such characteristic terms as ἐπιφάνεια, σωτήρ, and βασιλεύς τῶν βασιλέων are found also in the Septuagint, where they derive for the most part from an Old Testament Jewish context, nevertheless, their use in the Pastoral Epistles seems to provide them with a new emphasis; and probably we must acknowledge here a concurrent influence of the religious sentiments of Greece and the Orient, where this terminology was used in the mystery religions and also in the cult of the ruler. If the terms are likewise used in writings composed under the influence of Greek culture, such as the Pastoral Epistles, it is probably done so with one eye consciously turned toward that world.

The New Testament, then, does not simply appropriate the formulas as citations from the Old Testament; rather, it gives them an emphasis pertinent to its own times. Let it be said, then, that it is not the Emperor, but Christ, who is the Savior. In this way, mythological predicates were restored and replenished by biblical, salvation-historical predicates. Christians of the Greek world will have understood the new implications of these titles.[174]

New Testament exhortation is further occupied with the manifestly urgent question of the relationship of the community to the State. The congregation is admonished: "Be subject for the Lord's sake to every [divine] creation among men,[175] whether it be the Emperor as supreme, or to governors as sent by him to punish those who do wrong and to praise those who do right" (1 Peter 2:13-14). This passage of First Peter seems to be dependent upon Rom. 13:1-7, and in general the letter is clearly subject to Pauline influence. In both instances the State has its foundation in the creative will of God. Though couched in general terms, Paul's admonition clearly refers to the Roman government. In contrast to the admonition of Rom. 13:7, "to fear and honor all," 1 Peter 2:17 introduces some distinction and reservation: "fear God, honor the Emperor."

The tables of duties in 1 Peter 2:13–3:12 mention the State as the first order of creation, because it embraces and carries with it all others. Relationship to the State, however, is, for the Epistle, an inevitably difficult question. Although in the history of the community, conflicts with the authorities had already been occasioned now and then, the Church must now be prepared to expect more severe and more general oppression and persecution from the State. The letter speaks repeatedly (3:14, 17; 4:1, 12-19; 5:13) of this danger.

In 2:13-15 it is still confidently expected that the State is the guardian and protector of rights and goods. Chapters 3 and 4, however, are obliged to consider the possibility of the authorities' judging Christians unjustly. Christians still hope to experience justice from the State; for they themselves are firmly determined to live at peace with the State, perhaps, like Judaism, as a "tolerated religion." If the State inflicts injustice, then the Epistle can only counsel and admonish that it be borne patiently, as Christ bore it. The admonition to submissiveness still holds good. The letter has no thought of resistance (1 Peter 3:4-17). Thus do Christians come to the realization that they are but aliens in this world (1 Peter 1:1).

Ultimately, to be sure, the Epistle (5:13) characterizes Rome as a Babylon, just as the Apocalypse of John also does. 1 Peter, too, considers that the city of Rome, inimical as it is to God, must expect the judgment that befell Babylon. Toward the end of the New Testament period the circumstances of the Church's existence in, and co-existence with, the Roman Empire were radically changed. The Apocalypse of John is testimony to this. Former periods of oppression were of but short duration. Now the onslaughts against the Church have begun in earnest. The blood of martyrs is being poured out. The persecution was especially brutal in Asia Minor, where the Apocalypse of John was written.

The Apocalypse portrays in mythical images the struggle between God and Satan. This war, continuing from the very beginning to the end of the world, is now visible and is carried on in the struggle between Christianity and the Roman imperium. In this struggle Rome will make a general display of its governmental power. The dragon (Satan) comes forward and begins by pursuing the Messiah. When the latter is snatched up to the throne of God, the dragon pursues those who hold fast to the testimony of Christ, i.e., the Church (Apoc. 12).

Satan gives his strength to the "beast." The beast rises up out of the sea, i.e., the Mediterranean (Apoc. 13). Since it is from the Mediterranean that the beast comes, it comes from the West, from Rome. It has ten horns and seven heads; and on its horns there are ten crowns, and on its heads a blasphemous name. Probably this signifies the series of Roman Emperors. The beast itself is the Roman Empire (or better, the political power, inimical to God, displayed in the activities of the Roman Empire). The dragon loans his power to the beast and gives him his throne. "Men worshiped the dragon, because he had given his power to the beast; and they worshiped also the beast and said: 'Who is like the beast and who is able to fight against it?'" (Apoc. 13:4).

The power of Rome is borrowed from Satan. On the beast with the seven heads sits the whore of Babylon (Apoc. 17). "The seven heads are seven mountains, on which the woman sits" (Apoc. 17:9). Babylon on the seven mountains is the worldly city of Rome, built on seven hills. The whore, after the manner of prostitutes, is luxuriously clothed in purple and scarlet, bedecked with gold, precious stones, and pearls. She holds in her hand a golden cup which is full of abomination and the excrement of fornication (Apoc. 17:4). The sparkling culture of the Empire is but virulence of sins and abominations.

"The kings of the earth have fornicated with the whore, and they are drunk with the wine of her fornication" (Apoc. 17:2). The kings and lords of the world, dependent upon Rome, journey there and do everything to win the friendship of her that holds the power. With their masters, empire and world succumb to the seductive power of the imperial city. The political world is without direction. In the meaningless rotation of the constellations it seeks its fortune and worships its gods. "The woman is drunk with the blood of the saints and with the blood of the witnesses [martyrs] of Jesus" (Apoc. 17:6). The persecutions of Christians had already claimed the death of many martyrs.

Apocalypse 18 contains the proclamation and vision of Babylon's fall. The collapse of the city is not directly described, but indirectly, as in a purely vocal drama, in the laments of the friends of Babylon, the kings, merchants, shipmasters, who stand far off for fear that they might be dragged down along with her collapse.

Then with a terrifying symbolic gesture judgment is wrought. The angel casts a stone into the sea. It sinks and is seen no more (Apoc. 18:21). Finally the political sphere is unmasked. "Your merchants were the great men of the earth. By your sorcery were all nations seduced" (Apoc. 18:23). Not order, law, or culture, but money and profit are the essence of the grand polity. World domination was a calamity for the whole world.

After the judgment on Babylon, judgment is wrought on the beast and on the dragon. Beast and dragon together are flung into the lake of fire (Apoc. 19:20; 20:10). The virgin of Jerusalem, however, the antithesis of the whore of Babylon, celebrates her marriage with the Lamb, Christ, her Lord. On a renewed earth Christ will, with those who are his own, organize the new empire (Apoc. 21).

Christians live in the midst of the world, in that empire of injustice; and in the midst of this catastrophe they must exist. They do not worship the beast. Their faith is not to be brought low. Nevertheless, they do not reply to force with force. They are not revolutionaries. The arms of the Church are prayer and divine worship. Throughout the whole of the Apocalypse the Church is exhibited temperately as a community praying and celebrating. Her weapons, too, are her morally spotless behavior. Hope is her weapon — yes, the certainty that in the end the victory will be God's. Thus does the Church have eschatological assurance in her confrontation with the State.

Probably the Apocalypse of John expected the speedy collapse of Rome. It did not happen — at least not as it was expected. Is the judgment of the Apocalypse on the might of Rome justified? Is its judgment on the nature of politics valid?

In the New Testament the relation of Church to State is determined by her faith and by her hope. She believes that the kingdom of God has already begun, and she expects its full revelation to surmount all obstacles. In the course of the present period of expectation, the State, as a power directed toward orderliness, can realize the will of God; and in *that* it has the basis and the justification for its existence.

It is at the divine order and at the kingdom of God, however, that the State too has its boundaries. If it disavows or contests the kingdom, whether as to its present or its future existence, it is guilty and will be subject to judgment. If the State demands what is contrary to God's ordinance, it still holds good: "We must obey God rather than men" (Acts 4:19; 5:29). Faith must resist, even in the most extreme circumstances, when life itself is the price to be paid. But it will not take up the sword (Matthew 26:52). The Christian must decide whether he will say "yes" or "no" to the State. He must decide whether or not he will live his faith.

NOTES

[1] W. Beilner, *"Neutestamentliche Theologie,"* in *Dienst an der Lehre* (Festschrift for Franz Cardinal König), Vienna, 1965, pp. 145–165. G. Ebeling, *"Was heisst biblische Theologie?"*, in *Wort und Glaube*, 3rd ed., Tübingen, 1967, pp. 69–89 [trans. from the 1960 German edition, by J. W. Leitch, "The Meaning of Biblical Theology," in *Word and Faith*, Philadelphia, 1963, pp. 79–97]. K. Frör, *Wege zur Schriftauslegung*, 3rd ed., Düsseldorf, 1967. W. Joest (and others), *Was heisst Auslegung der Heiligen Schrift?*, Regensburg, 1966. H. Schlier, *Über Sinn und Aufgabe einer Theologie des Neuen Testaments*; and *Was heisst Auslegung der Heiligen Schrift?*, in *Besinning auf das Neue Testament*, Freiburg im Breisgau, 1964, pp. 7–24 and 35–62 [trans. under the title *The Relevance of the New Testament*, New York, 1968].

[2] A. Debrunner, H. Kleinknecht, O. Procksch, and G. Kittel, article λέγω, in *Theol. Dict. N.T.*, Vol. 4, 1967, pp. 69ff. R. Asting, *Die Verkündigung des Wortes Gottes im Urchristentum*, Stuttgart, 1939. D. Barsotti, *Christliches Mysterium und Wort Gottes*, Einsiedeln, 1957. R. Bultmann, *"Der Begriff des Wortes Gottes im Neuen Testament,"* in *Glauben und Verstehen*, Vol. 1, 6th ed., Tübingen, 1966, pp. 268–293 [trans. by L. P. Smith, "The Concept of the Word of God in the New Testament," in *Faith and Understanding*, Vol. 1, New York, 1969, pp. 286–312. K. H. Schelkle, *"Wort Gottes"* and *"Heilige Schrift und Wort Gottes,"* in *Wort und Schrift*, Düsseldorf, 1966, pp. 11–30 and 45–56. J. Schildenberger, *Das Geheimnis des Wortes Gottes*, Heidelberg, 1950. O. Semmelroth, *Wirkendes Wort*, Frankfurt, 1962 [trans. by J. J. Hughes, *The Preaching Word*, New York, 1965].

[3] Both principles of hermeneutics are enunciated in the dogmatic constitution of the Second Vatican Council, *On Divine Revelation (Dei Verbum)*, ch. 3, § 12. According to this constitution, exegesis must attend on the one hand to the historical and linguistic circumstances of the text and to the forms of thought and speech peculiar to the time in question, and on the other hand, "to the living tradition of the whole Church and the harmony which exists between the elements of the faith."

[4] A. M. Hunter, *The Work and Words of Jesus*, Philadelphia, 1950; and by the same author, *Introducing the New Testament*, 2nd ed., Philadelphia, 1957. A. Stock, *Einheit des Neuen Testaments*, Zürich, 1969.

[5] Dogmatics requires for each canonical writing of the New Testament — and the Old Testament too, of course — an express revelation of canonicity. Historical proofs will not serve as substitutes for such revelation. The inspiration of the New Testament (and in parenthetic fashion, of the Old Testament of which it makes use) is closely bound up with the inspiration and canonicity of the Apostolic Church, out of which the Bible arises; thus, Karl Rahner, *Über die Schrift-*

inspiration, Freiburg im Breisgau, 2nd ed., 1959 [trans. by C. H. Henkey, *Inspiration in the Bible*, New York, 1961].

⁶ Inasmuch as later writings expand and further develop the early Apostolic doctrine, I occasionally and without apology refer to them in connection with the latter. — For my interpretation of the literary and theological history of the New Testament, I refer the reader to my introduction: *Das Neue Testament*, 4th ed., Kevelaer, 1970.

⁷ K. Aland, *"Das Problem des neutestamentlichen Kanons,"* in *Zeitschrift für systematische Theologie*, Vol. 4 (1962), pp. 220–242. N. Appel, *Kirche und Kanon*, Paderborn, 1964. H. von Campenhausen, *Die Entstehung der christlichen Bibel*, Tübingen, 1968.

⁸ Thus with R. Bultmann, *"Weissagung und Erfüllung,"* in *Glauben und Verstehen* Vol. 3, 3rd ed., Tübingen, 1965, pp. 162–186.

⁹ James Barr, *Old and New in Interpretation*, New York, 1966. O. Cullman, *Christus und die Zeit*, 3rd ed., Zürich, 1962 [trans. by F. V. Filson, *Christ and Time*, Philadelphia, 1964]. G. von Rad, *Theologie des Alten Testaments*, Vol. 2, 4th ed., Munich, 1965, pp. 339–447 [trans. by D. M. G. Stalker, *Old Testament Theology*, Vol. 2, New York, 1965, pp. 319–409].

¹⁰ H. Schlier, *"Biblische und dogmatische Theologie,"* in *Besinnung auf das Neue Testament*, Freiburg im Breisgau, 1964, pp. 24–34. H. Vorgrimler (ed.), *Exegese und Dogmatik*, Mainz, 1962 [trans. under the title *Dogmatic vs. Biblical Theology*, Baltimore, 1965].

¹¹ K. Rahner, *"Theologie im Neuen Testament,"* in *Schriften zur Theologie*, Vol. 4, 5th ed., Einsiedeln, 1967, pp. 33–53. — The word *theology* was certainly possible in the New Testament, since the latter knows and constructs many compounds of θεός. In profane Greek literature, *theology* meant *mythology* (earliest certainly authentic usage in Plato). This being the case, perhaps Christians took special care to avoid using the word. It was accepted with some misgivings by Clement of Alexandria and Origen; later it was used more freely by Eusebius of Caesarea.

¹² Besides the general expositions of the theology of the New Testament already noted above on pp. 20–21, the following may be noted as pertaining particularly to biblical morality:

A. Dihle, *"Ethik,"* in *Reallexikon für Antike und Christentum*, Vol. 6 (1966), pp. 646–796. S. Bernfeld (ed.), *Die Lehren des Judentums nach den Quellen*, 3 vols., Berlin, 1920–1923. L. Dewar, *An Outline of New Testament Ethics*, London, 1949. C. H. Dodd, *Gospel and Law*, New York, 1951; and *Ethics and the Gospel*, London, 1960. N. Gäumann, *Taufe und Ethik*, Munich, 1967. W. Lillie, *Studies in New Testament Ethics*, Philadelphia, 1963. L. H. Marshall, *The Challenge of New Testament Ethics*, London, 1950. T. B. Masten, *Biblical Ethics*, Cleveland, 1967. E. Heuhäusler, *Anspruch und Antwort Gottes*, Düsseldorf, 1962. R. Schnackenburg, *Die sittliche Botschaft des Neuen Testaments*, 2nd ed., Munich, 1962 [trans. by J. Holland-Smith and W. J. O'Hara, *The Moral Teaching of the New Testament*, Freiburg, 1965]. And also by R. Schnackenburg, *Christliche*

Existenz nach dem Neuen Testament, 2 vols., Munich, 1967 and 1968 [trans. by F. Wieck, *Christian Existence in the New Testament*, 2 vols., Notre Dame, 1968 and 1969]. C. Spicq, *Théologie Morale du Nouveau Testament*, 2 vols., Paris, 1965 (major work). K. Barth, *Die kirchliche Dogmatik* I/2; II/2; III/4, Zollikon-Zürich, editions of 1957–1960 [trans. with same numbering of volumes by G. T. Thomson and others, *Church Dogmatics*, Edinburgh, 1936–1962]. D. Bonhoeffer, *Ethik*, edited by E. Bethge, 7th ed., Munich, 1966 [trans. by N. H. Smith, *Ethics*, New York, 1955]. F. Tillmann (ed.), *Die katholische Sittenlehre*, 5 vols., Düsseldorf, of which special note ought be made of F. Tillman, *Die Idee der Nachfolge Christi*, 2nd ed., 1939, and by the same author, *Die Verwirklichung der Nachfolge Christi*, 2 vols., 2nd ed., 1940. J. G. Ziegler, *Vom Gesetz zum Gewissen*, Freiburg im Breisgau, 1968.

[13] H. Gese, *Lehre und Wirklichkeit in der alttestamentlichen Weisheit*, Tübingen, 1958. H. H. Schmid, *Wesen und Geschichte der Weisheit*, Berlin, 1966.

[14] Questions pertaining to the post-Scriptural era are discussed by O. Michel in the article φιλοσοφία, in the *Theol. Dict. N.T.*, Vol 9; and by H. Köster in the article φύσις, *ibid*.

[15] In regard to the difficulties of Old Testament Jewish morality we may mention, besides J. Hempel and H. van Oyen, works already noted: H. Strack and P. Billerbeck, *Kommentar zum Neuen Testament aus Talmud und Midrasch*, Vol. 1, pp. 718ff., 902–905; W. Bousset, H. Gressmann, and E. Lohse, *Die Religion des Judentums im späthellenistischen Zeitalter*, 4th ed., Tübingen, 1966, pp. 409–431. The claim of observing all that God has enjoined and of keeping all his commands brought about in the Qumran community, for example, a mechanical equalizing of important and unimportant; see H. Braun, *Spätjüdisch-häretischer und frühchristlicher Radikalismus*, Vol. 1, 2nd edition, Tübingen, 1969, pp. 28ff.

[16] R. Bultmann, *Jesus*, Tübingen, 1951 [trans. by L. P. Smith, *Jesus and the Word*, New York, 1958].

[17] On the problem of formal and material ethics we may mention: K. Barth, *Die kirchliche Dogmatik*, Vol. III/4, 2nd ed., Zollikon-Zürich, 1957, pp. 1–34 [trans. by G. T. Thomson and others, *Church Dogmatics*, Vol. III/4, Edinburgh, 1961, pp. 3–46]. E. Brunner, *Das Gebot und die Ordnungen*, 4th ed., Zürich, 1939, pp. 116–123 [trans. by O. Wyon, *The Divine Imperative*, London, 1937, pp. 114–121]. K. Rahner, "*Über die Frage einer formalen Existentialethik*," in *Schriften zur Theologie*, Vol. 4, 5th ed., Einsiedeln, 1967, pp. 227–246.

[18] R. N. Flew, *Jesus and His Way*, London, 1963. T. W. Manson, *Ethics and the Gospel*, London, 1960. E. F. Scott, *The Ethical Teaching of Jesus*, New York, 1951. A. N. Wilder, *Eschatology and Ethics in the Teaching of Jesus*, 2nd ed., New York, 1950.

[19] G. Bouwman, *The Bible on the Imitation of Christ*, trans. by F. Vander Heijden, De Pere, Wis., 1965. E. Larsson, *Christus als Vorbild*, Uppsala, 1962.

[20] K. H. Schelkle, *Ihr alle seid Geistliche*, 3rd ed., Einsiedeln, 1967. K. Stalder, *Das Werk des Geistes in der Heiligung bei Paulus*, Zürich, 1962.

[21] M. E. Andrews, *The Ethical Teaching of Paul*, Baltimore, 1934. L. Cerfaux, *The Christian in the Theology of St. Paul*, trans. by Lilian Soiron, London, 1967. M. S. Enslin, *The Ethics of Paul*, New York, 1930.

N. Lazure, *Les valeurs morales de la théologie johannique*, Paris, 1965.

O. Prunet, *La morale chrétienne d'après les écrits johannique*, Paris, 1957.

[22] This saying of Jesus does not occur in the Gospels. It has, however, numerous parallels in ancient literature, and it may perhaps be a proverb placed in the mouth of Jesus. See J. Dupont, *Paulus an die Seelsorger* [trans.], Düsseldorf, 1966, pp. 225–234. J. Jeremias, *Unbekannte Jesusworte*, 3rd ed., Gütersloh, 1963, p. 37 [trans. by R. H. Fuller, *Unknown Sayings of Jesus*, 2nd Eng. ed., London, 1964, pp. 32–33].

[23] The schema of the Epistles' contents is incomplete. In the missionary preaching, monotheism must have been preached in opposition to the pagan polytheism. But in his letters Paul scarcely mentions it (1 Cor. 12:2; 1 Thess. 1:9). In his opening discourses, no doubt, Paul will have spoken at length of Jesus, the Christ. In the First Epistle of John there is scarcely a word about the history of Jesus; there is very much, however, in the Gospel of John. Is there perhaps a similar relationship between Paul's preaching of the gospel and his Epistles?

[24] A. Sand, *Der Begriff Fleisch in den paulinischen Hauptbriefen*, Munich, 1967. P. Schoonenberg, *Man and Sin; a Theological View*, trans. by Joseph Donceel, Notre Dame, Ind., 1965.

[25] "Adulterous" signifies "unfaithful" in the metaphorical language of the prophets, who designate God's covenant with Israel a "marriage," and Israel's disbelief as "adultery." See below, ch. 6.

[26] Mortal or deadly sin is originally a guilt which is expiated by the death penalty (Num. 18:22; Is. 22:14; Jer. 21, 22, *et al.*). In 1 John 5:16f., "sin unto death" is a sin which excludes from the life of God. Besides the usual commentaries, see also J. Herkenrath, "*Sünde zum Tode*," in *Aus Theologie und Philosophie* (Festschrift for F. Tillman), Düsseldorf, 1950, pp. 119–138.

[27] M. Hengel, *Nachfolge und Charisma*, Berlin, 1968. J. Moffat, *The Grace in the New Testament*, London, 1931. C. R. Smith, *The Bible Doctrine of Grace*, London, 1956.

[28] The original meaning of the word is the pleasantness and friendliness which a person is said to have when he evidences it in his dealings with another. It is in some way related to χαρὰ = joy. χάρις is what χαρὰ produces.

[29] For this interpretation, see below, ch. 11 (Peace).

[30] W. Pesch, *Der Lohngedanke in der Lehre Jesu*, Munich, 1955. H. Strack and P. Billerbeck, *Kommentar zum Neuen Testament aus Talmud und Midrasch*, Vol. 4, pp. 484–500.

[31] The translation "to suffer injury in the soul" is not correct. ζημιωθῆναι with the accusative does not signify "to be punished *in*," but "to be punished *to the extent of*." The punishment is not carried out now, but eschatologically. The passage concerns the coming of the Son of Man as Judge.

[32] *Gey-hinnom*, or the Valley of Hinnom, near Jerusalem, was an accursed place

because human sacrifices had been offered there (2 Kings 16:3; 21:6). The prophets threaten the place with judgment (Jer. 7:32; 19:6; Is. 31:9; 66:24). Late Jewish apocalyptic literature supposes that the fire of hell will be located in this place, after the final judgment (Ethiopic Henoch 90:26f.). From this, the name itself, Gehenna, came to be applied to the eschatological hell-fire (4 Esdras 7:36; and thus too in the New Testament).

[33] The figure is stylized. It is already used in Is. 66:24: "Where the worm does not die, and the fire is not extinguished." It appears frequently in the New Testament (Matthew 8:12; 13:42, 50; 24:51; 25:30; Luke 23:28). A similar description is found in 1 QS 4:11-14, wherein the angel of destruction thrusts the wicked "into the devastating shame, in the fire of the dark places. All times will be for them a sorrowful lament and bitter evil in dark disaster." If the Synoptics regularly speak of *the* weeping and *the* gnashing of teeth, the article is indicative of the fact that this is the lamenting so well known through biblical imagery. Such weeping can signify the creature's knowledge of his own lack of self-sufficiency. In this weeping, God is acknowledged and his justice is admitted. It includes the consciousness of "too late" and "in vain." The gnashing of teeth possibly represents the despairing regret which convulses their bodies.

[34] J. Behm, E. Würthwein, Art. μετανοέω, in *Theol. Dict. N.T.*, Vol. 4, 1967, pp. 975ff. A. Dirksen, *The New Testament Concept of Metanoia* (dissertation), Washington, 1932. J. Dupont, *"Repentir et Conversion d'après les Acts des Apôtres,"* in *Sciences ecclésiastiques*, Montreal, 1960, pp. 137-173. W. L. Holladay, *The Root Subh in the Old Testament*, Leiden, 1958. A Hulsbosch, *The Bible on Conversion*, trans. by F. Vander Heijden, De Pere, Wis., 1966.

[35] Strack and Billerbeck, *op. cit.*, Vol. 1, pp. 162-172.

[36] H. Braun, *"Umkehr in spätjüdisch-häretischer und in frühchristlicher Sicht,"* in *Gesammelte Studien zum Neuen Testament und seiner Umwelt*, Tübingen, 1967, pp. 70-85.

[37] P. Aubin, *Le problème de la 'conversion'. Étude sur un terme commun à l'hellénisme et christianisme des trois premiers siècles*, Paris, 1963.

[38] This is, after all, probably the way in which the announcement of calamities in Is. 6:9f. is to be understood, a passage which the New Testament Church used (Matthew 13:5; Mark 4:12; John 12:40; Acts 28:26f.) in attempting to explain the disbelief of Israel: "so that they will not (*or*: lest they might) understand with their hearts and turn about and I heal them."

[39] M. Buber, *Zwei Glaubensweisen*, Zürich, 1950 [trans. by N. P. Goldhawk, *Two types of Faith*, New York, 1951]. G. Ebeling, *Wort und Glaube*, 3rd ed., Tübingen, 1967 [trans. by J. W. Leitch, *Word and Faith*, Philadelphia, 1963]. E. D. O'Connor, *Faith in the Synoptic Gospels*, Notre Dame, 1961. A. Schlatter, *Der Glaube im Neuen Testament*, 4th ed., Stuttgart, 1927; reprinted at Darmstadt, 1963.

[40] *Translators Note*: The author remarks on the fact that even German translations have this in common with the Septuagint and other Greek translations,

that forms of a single word-stem supply for several Hebrew word-groups in the
conceptual area of faith. Thus in German the noun is *Glaube*, the verb *glauben*.
This is very nearly but not precisely the case with English, where we have a
choice of terms from two different roots, *faith* and *belief*. Thus πίστις =
Glaube = *faith* or *belief*; and πιστεύειν = *glauben* = *to believe* or *to have faith*.
In English, sometimes *faith* and *belief* are entirely synonymous, sometimes not.
When there is a difference, it is largely in the fact that *faith* is often more inten-
sive in its religious connotation than is *belief*.

⁴¹ The account is reminiscent of the imagery of the Old Testament as well as
of the Judaism of its own period. The pious man thinks he is sinking into the
watery depths, and he calls out for salvation by the hand of God on high (Pss.
18:17; 69:2f., 15f.; 144:7). According to the *Odes of Solomon* 39:57, the waters
of death are parted on this side and that. "But those who pass over in faith are
not engulfed. And they who enter them without fault have no fear." Other ancient narratives are drawn along similar lines. They too know about the rescuing
hand of the divinity. Thus, in Vergil, (*Aeneid*, 6, 370): "Stretch forth to me,
wretch that I am, your right hand, and take me with you through the billowing
waves!"

⁴² It is true that a saying of the Lord in Matthew 18:6 speaks of the "little ones,
who believe in me." But since the parallel saying in Mark 9:42 speaks only of
"those who believe," it may be that Matthew is a later interpretation, showing
certain inclinations and tendencies which have been furthered by tradition.

⁴³ M. Bonningues, *La foi dans l'Évangile de S. Jean*, Paris, 1955.

⁴⁴ O. Cullman, *Die ersten christlichen Glaubensbekenntnisses*, Zollikon-Zürich,
4th ed., 1949. J. N. D. Kelly, *Early Christian Creeds*, 2nd ed., London 1952. V. H.
Neufeld, *The Earliest Christian Confessions*, Leiden 1963.

⁴⁵ Besides the usual commentaries, see E. Grässer, *Der Glaube im Hebräerbrief*,
Marburg, 1964.

⁴⁶ K. H. Rengstorf and R. Bultmann, Art. ἐλπίς, in *Theol. Dict. N.T.*, Vol. 2,
1964, pp. 517ff. L. Boros, *Wir sind Zukunft*, Mainz, 1969 [trans. by W. J. O'Hara,
We Are Future, New York, 1970]. W. Grossouw, *"L'espérance dans le Nouveau
Testament,"* in *Revue Biblique*, Vol. 61 (1954), pp. 508–532. J. Moltmann, *The-
ologie der Hoffnung*, 7th ed., Munich, 1968 [in English under the title *Theology
of Hope*, New York, 1967]. W. Pannenberg, *"Der Gott der Hoffnung,"* in
Grundfragen systematischer Theologie, Göttingen, 1967, pp. 387–398 [trans. by
G. H. Kehm, "The God of Hope," in *Basic Questions in Theology*, Vol. 2,
Philadelphia, 1971, pp. 234–249].

⁴⁷ W. Foerster and G. Fohrer, Art. σωτήρ, in *Theol. Dict. N.T.*, Vol. 7, pp.
1003–1019.

⁴⁸ F. Nötscher, *Zur theologischen Terminologie der Qumran-Texte*, Bonn,
1956, pp. 149f., 161f.

⁴⁹ Besides the usual commentaries, see also E. Grässer, *Der Glaube im Hebräerbrief*, Marburg, 1965, pp. 203–214; and F. J. Schierse, *Verheissung und Heilsvollen-
dung*, Munich, 1955, pp. 80–127.

[50] The translation and explanation of the word ὑπόστασις (Heb. 11:1) is disputed. In reference to things, the word means "the foundation"; in reference to men, "the abiding beneath" some thing or some condition. The Protestant translation "confidence" is scarcely correct. Interpretations proposed are: "Faith is the *fundamental pledge* of what is hoped for"; and, "Faith is the *standing fast* by that for which one hopes."

[51] The symbol of the anchor is probably pre-Christian in origin. See A. Fichler, *"Der Hoffnungsanker,"* in *Zeitschrift des Deutschen Palästinavereins,* Vol. 59 (1956), pp. 208–214; and P. Stumpf, Art. *"Anker,"* in *Reallexikon für Antike und Christentum,* Vol. 1 (1950), pp. 440–443.

[52] K. Rahner, *"Theologische Prinzipien der Hermeneutik eschatologischer Aussagen,"* in *Schriften zur Theologie,* Vol. 4, 5th ed., Einsiedeln, 1967, pp. 401–428; and by the same author, *"Kirche und Parusie Christi,"* ibid., Vol. 6, Einsiedeln, 1965, pp. 348–368 [English translations in the series K. Rahner, *Theological Investigations,* trans. by C. Ernst et al., Baltimore, 1961–69].

[53] J. Coppens, *"La doctrine biblique sur l'amour de Dieu et du prochain,"* in *Ephemerides Theologicae Lovanienses,* Vol. 40 (1964), pp. 252–299. K. Rahner, *"Über die Einheit von Nächsten und Gottesliebe,"* in *Schriften zur Theologie* Vol. 6, Einsiedeln, 1965, pp. 277–298 [*"Reflections on the Unity of the Love of Neighbor and the Love of God,"* in *Theological Investigations,* Vol. 6, trans. by K.-H. and B. Kruger, London, 1969, pp. 231–249]. K. Romaniuk, *L'amour du Père et du Fils dans la sotèriologie de S. Paul,* Rome, 1961. C. Spicq, *Agapè. Prolégomènes à une étude de Théologie néo-testamentaire,* Louvain, 1955. Also by Spicq, *Agapè dans le Nouveau Testament,* 3 vols., Paris, 1958–1960.

[54] H. L. Strack and P. Billerbeck, *op. cit.,* Vol. 1, pp. 905–907.

[55] The three Synoptic accounts differ so widely from each other that it may perhaps be indicative of their dependence upon different sources. If the gospel history, prior to its actually being written down, were retained in a multiple tradition, this might indicate that narration in the community was an especially potent factor. See G. Bornkamm, *"Das Doppelgebot der Liebe,"* in *Gesammelte Aufsätze,* Vol. 3, Munich, 1968, pp. 37–45.

[56] H. U. von Balthasar, *Glaubhaft ist nur Liebe,* Einsiedeln, 1963 [trans. by A. Dru, *Love Alone,* New York, 1969]. A. Nygren, *Agape and Eros,* trans. by P. S. Watson, Philadelphia, 1953.

[57] H. Rusche, *"Gastfreundschaft im Alten Testament, im Spätjudentum und in den Evangelien,"* in *Zeitschrift für Missionswissenschaft,* Vol. 41 (1957), pp. 170–188.

[58] H. Braun, *Spätjüdisch-häretischer und frühchristlicher Radikalismus,* 2nd ed., Tübingen, 1968, Vol. 1, pp. 9, 37–39, 59–61, 121–130; Vol. 2, pp. 59–61, 83–99.

[59] Strack and Billerbeck, *op. cit.,* Vol. 4, pp. 536–610. A. Dihle, *Die goldene Regel,* Göttingen, 1962.

[60] A commandment to love oneself would be reasonable if men were inclined to regard their own lives as worthless, despising themselves and desiring to cast

themselves away. One who knows that he is loved by God cannot wish to destroy himself.

[61] W. Bauer, *"Das Gebot der Feindesliebe und die alten Christen,"* in *Aufsätze,* Tübingen, 1967, pp. 235–252. W. C. van Unnik, *"Die Motivierung der Feindesliebe in Lk 6, 32-35",* in *Novum Testamentum,* Vol. 8 (1966), pp. 284–300.

[62] C. Spicq, *Agapè. Prolégomènes à une étude de théologie néo-testamentaire,* Louvain, 1955, pp. 32–70.

[63] W. Grundmann, *"Das Wort von Jesu Freunden (Joh XV, 13-16) und das Herrenmahl,"* in *Novum Testamentum,* Vol. 3 (1959), pp. 62–69.

[64] Deserving of consideration are two possible interpretations of this short phras ، . Either love is the tie which binds together for perfection the other virtues, which, without love, would fall apart individually; or, love is the perfect bond of uni' in the Church.

[65] K. H. Schelkle, Art. *Bruder,* in *Reallexikon für Antike und Christentum,* Vol. 2 (1954), pp. 631–640.

[66] D. Nestle, Art. *Freiheit,* in *Reallexikon für Antike und Christentum,* Vol. 8 (1970), pp. 269–306. D. Nestle, *Eleutheria. Studien zum Wesen der Freiheit bei den Griechen und im Neuen Testament,* Vol. 1, Tübingen, 1967. K. Rahner, *"Die Freiheit in der Kirche,"* in *Schriften zur Theologie,* Vol. 2, 7th ed., Einsiedeln, 1967, pp. 95–114; and *"Theologie der Freiheit,"* in *Scriften zur Theologie,* Vol. 6, Einsiedeln, 1965, pp. 215–237 [translations in the series *Theological Investigations,* Baltimore, 1961–69]. H. R. Schlette, *Der Anspruch der Freiheit,* Munich, 1963.

[67] Of old Israel it is true enough: "The fundamental postulate of freedom appears in equal force alongside the religious conviction of the solitary efficacy of God without making any attempt at erecting a harmonious reconciliation between the two. It is a testimonial to the compelling power of the Old Testament experience of God that it was able to affirm both realities and to sustain their opposing pressures without in any way detracting from the unqualified validity of each" (W. Eichrodt, *Theologie des Alten Testaments,* Vol. 2, 4th ed., Stuttgart, 1961 p. 120 [trans. by J. A. Baker, *Theology of the Old Testament,* Vol. 2, Philadelphia, 1967, p. 179]).

[68] H. Schlier, Art. παρρησία, in *Theol. Dict. N.T.,* Vol. 5, 1967.

[69] G. von Rad and W. Foerster, Art. εἰρήνη, in *Theol. Dict. N.T.,* Vol. 2, 1964, pp. 400ff. E. Biser, *Der Sinn des Friedens,* Munich, 1960.

[70] R. E. Backherms, *Religious Joy in General in the New Testament and Its Sources in Particular,* (dissertation), Freiburg (Switzerland), 1963. P. Dacquino, *"Die menschliche Freude und das Jenseits in der Bibel,"* in *Concilium,* Vol. 4(1968), pp. 651–657.

[71] H. Strathmann and P. Keseling, Art. *Askese,* in *Reallexikon für Antike und Christentum.* Vol. 1 (1950), pp. 749–795. H. Chadwick, Art. *Enkrateia, ibid.,* Vol. 5 (1962), pp. 343–365. H. von Campenhausen, *"Die Askese im Urchristentum,"* in *Tradition und Leben,* Tübingen, 1960, pp. 114–156 [trans. by A. V. Littledale, "Early Christian Asceticism," in *Tradition and Life in the Early*

Church, Philadelphia, 1968, pp. 90–122]. H. Wennink, *The Bible on Asceticism*, trans. by F. Vander Heijden, De Pere, Wis., 1966.

[72] The Stoa produced numerous treatises with the title *On Asceticism*, and though such treatises may not have been preserved, they were, nevertheless, known to authors in antiquity. An example is Epictetus (*Diss.*, 3, 12): "On asceticism: One must not practice asceticism in a method or manner which is against nature or reason. . . . Without great and resolute asceticism it is not possible to curb one's appetites against failure of one's purpose, and to preserve abstemiousness against inconstancy." Similarly in Musonius (*Fragment 6*): "He encouraged his students with great emphasis to cling to asceticism, since virtue consists not only in theoretical knowledge but also in practical reality." Even expressions with the verb ἀσκέω (comparable to that in Acts 24:16) are used; thus, in Epictetus (*loc. cit.*): "Endeavor, when you are reviled, to bear it, and when you are despised, not to give way to anger."

[73] The commentaries mention the following illustrations: Artemidorus (*Dreambook*, 2, 56; *ca.* 250 A.D.), who explains; "If someone in a dream carries a god of the underworld, it means that he is to carry a cross. For the cross is a sign of death, and he that is to be nailed to it carries it beforehand." In the novel by Charito (4, 3, 10; *ca.* 200 A.D.) Chaireas laments: "I was sold because of you, was condemned, carried the cross, and was surrendered into the hands of the executioner." A midrash on Gen. 22:6 explains: "Isaac was like one who bears the cross."

Plato (*Republic*, 361E) describes the lot of the just man: "The just man will be scourged, tormented, put in chains, will be blinded in both eyes, and finally after every other torture he will be lifted up on a stake"; see E. Benz, *Der gekreuzigte Gerechte bei Platon, im Neuen Testament und in der alten Kirche*, Mainz, 1950, pp. 11–13. Benz conjectures that Plato depends upon a recollection of a historical publication of the suffering of Socrates.

It is to be noted that other explanations of the words of Mark 8:34 have been attempted. Originally there might have been a saying of the Lord like that in Matthew 11:29a: "take my yoke upon you." After the death of Jesus it might have been transformed into an invitation to take up the cross.

In Ezekiel 9:4-6 the elect are marked and protected with a *Tav*, the last letter of the Hebrew alphabet, shaped like an X or a T in certain more ancient forms of the alphabet. Accordingly, the disciples of Jesus might have regarded themselves as so marked. After the crucifixion the *Tav* would have become a reference to the historical cross of Jesus.

[74] ψυχή in Mark 8:35f means not *soul* but *life, a living being*. See the present work, Vol. 1, pp. 85–89, 98ff. In Mark 8:36 ζημιωθῆναι τὴν ψηχὴν does not mean *be punished in* but *be punished to the extent*; it is not to be translated *come to grief in the soul*, but *be punished to the extent of one's life*, = *to lose one's life*. See A. Stumpff, Art. ζημία, in *Theol. Dict. N.T.*, Vol. 2, 1964, pp. 888ff.

[75] E. Lövestam, *Spiritual Wakefulness in the New Testament*, Lund, 1963.

[76] V. C. Pfitzner, *Paul and the Agon-Motif*, Leiden, 1967.

[77] R. Baumann, *Mitte und Norm des Christlichen*, Münster i. W., 1968, pp. 386–304. K. H. Schelkle, *Die Passion Jesu in der Verkündigung des Neuen Testaments*, Heidelberg, 1949, pp. 217–238.

[78] R. Asting, *Die Heiligkeit im Urchristentum*, Stuttgart, 1930. S. Dillersberger, *Das Heilige im Neuen Testament*, Kufstein, 1926. E. Gaugler, *Die Heiligung im Zeugnis der Heiligen Schrift*, Bern, 1948.

[79] The term ἅγιος, meaning "holy," is the usual term used in the Greek Bible to translate the Hebrew term *qadosh*, which word is usually derived from the root *qd*, signifying "separating, parting, or detaching." *Qadosh*, accordingly, means "separated." The term ὅσιος is used infrequently in the New Testament. It has both the significance of the religio-moral and of the religio-legal. More frequent in both Old and New Testaments is the term ἱερός, which signifies "taboo," and in the New Testament especially refers to the holy things of Jews and pagans. It may be suggested that "holy" (heilig) means full of "prosperity" (*Heil*).

[80] C. H. W. Brekelmans, "The Saints of the Most High and Their Kingdom," in *Oudtestamentische Studien*, Vol. 14 (1965), pp. 305–329. O. Schilling, *Das Heilige und das Gute im Alten Testament*, Leipzig, 1956.

[81] F. Nötscher, *"Heiligkeit in den Qumranschriften,"* in *Vom Alten zum Neuen Testament*, Bonn, 1962, pp. 126–174.

[82] J. H. Elliot, *The Elect and the Holy. An Exegetical Examination of 1 Peter 2, 4-10*, Leiden, 1966.

[83] A. Descamps, *Les Justes et la Justice dans les evangiles et le christianisme primitif hormis la doctrine proprement paulinienne*, Louvain, 1950. K. Kertelge, *"Rechtfertigung" bei Paulus*, Münster i. W., 1967.

[84] J. Becker, *Das Heil Gottes, Heils- und Sündenbegriffe in den Qumrantexten und im Neuen Testament*, Göttingen, 1964. H. Braun, *"Römer 7, 7-25 und das Selbstverständnis der Qumranfrommen,"* in *Gesammelte Studien zum Neuen Testament und seiner Umwelt*, Tübingen, 1962, pp. 100–119.

[85] Since for Paul "righteousness through faith" is a solid principle, Rom. 1:17 is probably to be translated: "He who through faith is righteous shall live," and not, "The righteous man will live by faith." The Greek is ambiguous, admitting of either translation.

[86] The New Testament often speaks of the salvational action of Christ "for us." The potentiality and comprehension of this expression is to be explained in the treatment of New Testament Christology.

[87] K. H. Schelkle, *Paulus, Lehrer der Väter*, Düsseldorf, 2nd ed., 1959, pp. 111f.

[88] M. Dibelius, *Der Brief des Jakobus*, 8th ed. (edited by H. Greeven), Göttingen, 1956, pp. 163–168. W. Schmithals, *Paulus und Jakobus*, Göttingen, 1961 [trans. by D. M. Barton, *Paul and James*, Naperville, Ill., 1965].

[89] E. Käsemann, *Gottesgerechtigkeit bei Paulus. Exegetische Versuche und Besinnungen*, Vol. 2, 3rd ed., Göttingen, 1968, pp. 181–193. Following Käsemann, and occasionally taking exception to him, there is Ch. Müller, *Gottes Gerechtig-*

keit und Gottes Volk. Eine Untersuchung zu Römer 9–11, Göttingen, 1964; and P. Stuhlmacher, *Gerechtigkeit Gottes bei Paulus*, Göttingen, 1965.

[90] H. Braun, *Spätjüdisch-häretischer und frühchristlicher Radikalismus*, Vol. 1, pp. 113–119; Vol. 2, pp. 62–73, 2nd ed., Tübingen, 1968.

[91] R. Baumann, *Mitte und Norm des Christlichen*, Münster i. W., 1968, pp. 183–204. B. Rigaux, *"Révélation des mystères et perfection à Qumrân et dans le Nouveau Testament"*, in *New Testament Studies*, Vol. 4 (1957/58), pp. 237–262.

[92] U. Wilckens, *Weisheit und Torheit*, Tübingen, 1959.

[93] W. Trilling, *Das wahre Israel*, 3rd ed., Munich, 1964, pp. 192–196.

[94] Suitbertus a S. Johanne a Cruce, *"Die Vollkommenheitslehre des 1. Johannesbriefes,"* in *Biblica*, Vol. 39 (1958), pp. 319–333, 449–470.

[95] O. Michel, *Der Brief an die Hebräer*, 12th ed., Göttingen, 1966, pp. 145–149, 224–229. C. Spicq, *L'Épître aux Hébreux*, Vol. 2, Paris, 1953, pp. 214–225.

[96] R. Guardini, *Tugenden*, Würzburg, 1963 [trans. by S. Lange, *The Virtues*, Chicago, 1967], H. Klomps, *Tugenden des modernen Menschen*, Augsburg, 1969.

[97] J. Gnilka, in his *Die Philipperbrief*, Freiburg im Br., 1968, pp. 218–223, contends that Phil. 4:1 and 4:8f. belong together as the closing of a "Philippians B," distinct from our Epistle to the Philippians. The listing of virtues in 4:8f. would then be preceded by the admonition "to stand firm in the Lord" (4:1); and thus, even if this be the case, the list will have a New Testament orientation.

[98] E. Kamlah, *Die Form der katalogischen Paränese im Neuen Testament*, Tübingen 1964. S. Wibbing, *Die Tugend- und Lasterkataloge im Neuen Testament*, Berlin 1959.

[99] O. Merk, *Handeln aus Glauben*, Marburg 1968, pp. 214 224. H. Wendland, *"Zur socialethischen Bedeutung der neutestamentlichen Haustafeln"*, in *Die Leibhaftigkeit des Wortes* (Festschrift for A. Köberle), Hamburg 1958, pp. 34–46.

[100] L. Cerfaux (*et al.*), *La prière*, 2nd ed., Paris, 1965. A. Hamman, *La prière. 1: Le Nouveau Testament*, Tournai, 1959. J. M. Nielen, *Gebet und Gottesdienst im Neuen Testament*, 2nd ed., Freiburg im Br., 1963. J. M. Robinson, *"Die Hodajot-Formel in Gebet und Hymnus des Frühchristentums,"* in *Apophoreta* (Festschrift for E. Haenchen), Berlin, 1964, pp. 194–235.

[101] F. Hesse, *Die Fürbitte im Alten Testament*, Erlangen, 1951. L. Krinetzki, *Israels Gebet im Alten Testament*, Aschaffenburg, 1965.

[102] H. Kleinknecht, *Die Gebetsparodie in der Antike*, Stuttgart, 1937.

[103] W. Ott, *Gebet und Heil. Die Bedeutung der Gebetsparänese in der lukanischen Theologie*, Munich, 1965.

[104] H. von Soden, *"Sakrament und Ethik bei Paulus,"* in *Urchristentum und Geschichte*, Vol. 1, Tübingen, 1951, pp. 239–275. For further bibliography, see footnote 12 above.

[105] E. Käsemann, *"Gottesdienst im Alltag der Welt,"* in *Exegetische Versuche und Besinnungen*, Vol. 2, Göttingen, 1964, pp. 198–204.

[106] Although even non-Christian religious thought (see the present work, Vol. 1, pp. 103–106) can call God "Father," nevertheless, the prayerful address "Abba,

Father," is, in any case, in view of the security and confidence of which it is a reflection, something new and can probably be understood only as a continuation of the prayer and of the prayerful address of Jesus, after the example of Paul, who understands this address as prayer newly bestowed by the Spirit. The proposition, then, that the prayer of the disciples, "Our Father," may have been "Abba, Father" at its beginning as actual quotation, is very much deserving of consideration. See J. Jeremias, *Abba*, Göttingen, 1966, pp. 63–66. In regard to intercessory prayer, see A. Dietzel, *Die Gründe der Erlösungsgewissheit nach den Schriften des Neuen Testaments* (dissertation), Mainz, 1955. L. Kuppoldt, *Die theologische Grundlage des Bittgebets im Neuen Testament* (dissertation), Leipzig, 1953.

[107] D. Loenen, *"Eusebeia en de cardinale deugden,"* in *Mededelingen der Koniklijke Nederlandse Akademie van Wetenschapen*, new series, 23, 4, Amsterdam, 1960.

[108] J. N. Sevenster, *Leven en dood in de evangelien*, Amsterdam, 1952; also by Sevenster, *Leven en dood in de brieven van Paulus*, Amsterdam, 1955. H. Thielicke, *Tod und Leben*, Tübingen, 1946 [trans. by E. H. Schroeder, *Death and Life*, Philadelphia, 1970].

[109] G. Gloege, *Die Todesstrafe als theologisches Problem*, Cologne, 1966.

[110] U. Becker, *Jesus und die Ehebrecherin*, Berlin, 1963.

[111] Bear in mind that in modern discussions of the problem, attention is drawn to a recollection of the co-responsibility of society in the exercise of the death penalty.

[112] O. Bauernfeind, Art. πόλεμος, in *Theol. Dict. N.T.*, Vol. 6, 1968, pp. 502ff.

[113] A. Schweitzer, *Die Lehre von der Ehrfurcht vor dem Leben*, edited by H. W. Bähr, Munich, 1966.

[114] J. Dupont, *Mariage et divorce dans l'Évangile. Mt. 19, 3-12 et par.*, Bruges, 1959. L. Goessler, *Plutarchs Gedanken über die Ehe* (dissertation), Basel, 1962. H. Greeven, *"Zu der Aussage des Neuen Testaments über die Ehe,"* in *Zeitschrift für evangelische Ethik*, Vol. 1 (1957), pp. 109–125. P. Grelot, *Man and Wife in Scripture*, trans. by R. Brennan, New York, 1964. G. N. Vollebregt, *Die Ehe im Zeugnis der Bibel*, Salzburg, 1965 [trans. by R. A. Downie, *The Bible on Marriage*, De Pere, Wis., 1965]. L. Weber, *Mysterium Magnum*, Freiburg im Br., 2nd ed., 1965 [trans. by R. Brennan, *On Marriage, Sex, and Virginity*, New York, 1964].

[115] Besides the pertinent literature already mentioned in the note immediately preceding, see also H. Strack and P. Billerbeck, *op. cit.*, Vol. 1, pp. 303–321, 802f.; Vol. 2, pp. 372–390; Vol. 3, pp. 62–74, 343–358.

[116] In disputation, texts of Scripture are interpreted and played one against another. In such cases exegesis is inclined to suspect that what we have is actually the condensation of debates within the congregation. The frame of Mark 10:2, then, might well be a secondary structure. Mark 10:10-12 is an elucidation basted on as an instruction to the disciples; and its seam is showing. It can scarcely be denied that the congregation possessed an authentic remembrance of a saying of Jesus in reference to divorce, in which he condemned the same. This original

saying of Jesus became authentically interpreted in the community, in Mark 10:2-12. In contrast to Mark, the discussion in Matthew is constructed in a scripturally learned and logical fashion. Matthew is undoubtedly secondary. In Matthew 5:31f. the saying is included in the series of antitheses in the Sermon on the Mount. Matthew will have given it the form it has in that place. The saying is varied, inasmuch as it is set in relation (either by tradition or by the Evangelists) to the various existing legal ordinances in the Jewish or Greek milieu — ordinances applicable, therefore, in the congregation. According to Jewish law, only the husband could institute divorce proceedings (and thus in Matthew 5:32 and Luke 16:18); but in Greco-Roman law, either the husband or the wife could do so (Mark 10:11f.).

[117] *Two* is not to be found in the original Hebrew text; it is found, however, already in the Septuagint. The text is thereby interpreted in reference to the unity of marriage.

[118] Exegesis has come to grips in various ways with Matthew's unchastity clause. Catholic attempts to explain it seem to be influenced by the effort to explain the text in conformity with the accepted Canon Law, which permits no divorce. The clause is therefore interpreted to mean that even adultery is to be excluded as grounds for divorce. One might be obliged to take into account to some extent the gesture of Jesus which expressed the rejection. More recently the hypothesis has been advanced that in Matthew 5:32 and 19:9 (as in Acts 15:20, 29; 21:25; and Heb. 12:16), πορνεία does not mean unchastity, but a union forbidden by biblical law. This meaning, first assigned by J. Bonsirven (*Le divorce dans le Nouveau Testament*, Paris, 1948), is accepted in part and given a more detailed basis by H. Baltensweiler in *Die Ehe im Neuen Testament*, Zürich, 1967, pp. 87–102. Inasmuch, however, as this posits a totally unaccustomed meaning for πορνεία, the explanation remains highly questionable. And if, in fact, an illegal union had to be dissolved, no permission would then be required.

[119] Accordingly, a non-Christian marriage is dissolved "in favor of the faith" by the baptism of one of the spouses.

[120] Ecclesiastical marriage law, in order to take into account the circumstances of life, claims the right to make statutory certain possibilities of the dissolution of marriage. Solemn religious profession dissolves a valid, non-consummated marriage (CIC 1119). According to the "Petrine privilege," the Pope can, in certain circumstances, dissolve a non-Christian, half-Christian, even valid Catholic marriage, and can permit the Catholic partner to contract a new marriage (CIC 1127; see also, however, CIC 1118, where it is specified that the valid, consummated marriage in which both partners are baptized is absolutely indissoluble).

[121] J. Blinzler, in "'*Zur Ehe unfähig . . .*' *Auslegung von Matt. 19, 12*," in *Gesammelte Aufsätze*, Vol. 1, Stuttgart, 1969, pp. 20–39, is of the opinion that Jesus wanted to protect himself and his celibate disciples against slander. But were the disciples in fact celibate?

[122] Ever since the patristic age it has been customary, to be sure, to translate the passage so as to mean: "A father who gives his daughter in marriage does

well, but a father who does not give her in marriage does better." This interpretation is incorrect, as shown by the context and by the words themselves. Besides the more recent commentaries, see also W. G. Kümmel, *"Verlobung und Heirat bei Paulus (1 Cor. 7:36-38)"* in *Heilsgeschehen und Geschichte*, Marburg, 1965, pp. 310–327.

[123] J. Blinzler, *"Die 'Heiligkeit' der Kinder in der alten Kirche — Zur Auslegung von 1 Kor 7:14"* in *Gesammelte Aufsätze*, Vol. 1, Stuttgart, 1969, pp. 158–184.

[124] *Translator's note:* Yet, it must be affirmed that it is within Peter's jurisdiction to unite the vocations of priest and celibate. What a dismal prospect it would be if the Church were to be disallowed any progress from its first- and second-century positions. The union of priestly and celibate vocations begins to form in the third century and progresses historically until finally, for the Western Church, the high vocation of celibacy becomes prerequisite to the Church's issuing a call to priesthood. To return now to an early and freer discipline would constitute not reform but regression.

[125] *Translator's note:* No wonder, then, that the Church of the Apostolic age had not yet progressed to the position of demanding celibacy of its higher ministers, when there was already present the danger that the misguided might preach *general* celibacy as a salvational necessity!

[126] *Translator's Note:* The substitution of *days* for *years* is perhaps much more easily explained as a simple scribal misadventure when one considers how common a phrase *seven days* is, and especially in view of the fact that the word *days* occurs in the preceding clause of the same text. The reading *seven days* is found in certain Syriac manuscripts, and is the text quoted by St. Ephrem.

[127] *Translator's note:* There is a certain sophistry implied in this last paragraph, and the translator begs leave to make four observations: (1) He prefers to get his Christian principles from Trent rather than from Pythagoras. (2) There is no parallel between attendance at pagan shrines and reception of so great a sacrament as the Eucharist. (3) It remains to be demonstrated that the Fathers (who, with Scripture, constitute the source[s] of revelation), and many of them at that, shared an unbiblical and disparaging attitude toward marriage. (4) A certain abstinence in respect to food and drink is still required before reception of so great a sacrament as the Eucharist, which abstinence is never construed as disparaging to those who, in their normal daily lives, do sometimes partake of food and drink. If the translator does not err, the rationale for abstinence from food and drink before reception of the Eucharist is simply to impress upon us in a more remarkable manner the dignity of so great a sacrament. Possibly abstinence from conjugal communion, however good and holy that communion in marriage may be, might serve the same purpose of impressing upon the communicant the superior dignity of communion with Christ.

[128] U. Becker, *Jesus und die Ehebrecherin*, Berlin, 1963.

[129] S. Aalen, " 'Truth,' A Key Word in St. John's Gospel," in *Studia Evangelica*, Vol. 2, Berlin, 1964, pp. 3–24. M. A. Klopfenstein, *Die Lüge nach dem Alten Tes-*

tament, Zürich, 1964. J. Murphy-O'Connor, *"La 'vérité' chez St. Paul et à Qum-ran,"* in *Revue Biblique*, Vol. 72 (1965), pp. 29–76.

[180] The *Odes of Solomon* provide examples: "I hastened on the way of his salvation, on the way of truth" (11:3-5); "The light shall not be conquered by the darkness, though the lie yield in the face of truth" (18:6). Although the texts were written down later than the New Testament, the tradition may be older (see R. Bultmann, *Exegetica*, Tübingen, 1967, pp. 67–73). Mandaean literature too knows the pair of concepts "truth and lie"; thus, in *Mandäische Liturgien. Mitgeteilt, übersetzt, und erklärt von M. Lidzbarski*, Berlin, 1920, p. 77: "You show us the way of life and make us to walk the path of truth and faith."

[181] J. Amstutz, *Aplotes*, Bonn, 1968. C. Edlund, *Das Auge der Einfalt*, (*Acta Seminarii Neotestamentici Upsaliensis*, Vol. 19), 1952.

[182] In Deut. 5:20 the prohibition reads: "Thou shalt not give evidence against thy neighbor as a false witness." Is this a broadening and intensifying interpretation of the decalogue? Is the making of a false declaration in general forbidden, and not only the intentional and willful lie? Does Deuteronomy constitute a general condemnation of lies against one's neighbor, with the very intensification that is so often understood of the law? See M. A. Klopfenstein, *op. cit.*, pp. 18–21, 317.

[183] W. Beilner, *Christus und die Pharisäer*, Vienna, 1959, pp. 227–235. E. Neuhäusler, *Anspruch und Antwort Gottes*, Düsseldorf, 1962, pp. 63–76.

[184] H. Strack and P. Billerbeck, *op. cit.*, Vol. 1, pp. 328–336, 931f. O. Bauernfeind, *Eid und Friede*, Stuttgart, 1956.

[185] One cannot accuse Jesus of having been at variance with his own commandment when, as related in Matthew 26:64, he not only did not reprove the adjuration of the high priest, but acknowledged the demand of an oath and responded. In the law, under which the high priest was acting, an oath for the sake of finding the truth was not only permitted but prescribed. Only in the community of the disciples of the kingdom of God is oath-taking to be repudiated. Jesus could not, therefore, forbid the high priest's use of an oath. Jesus himself, however, took no oath in responding, and answered with a simple declaration.

[186] As with the whole lament against the Pharisees in Matthew 23:1-36, so too with the section Matthew 23:16-22, it must be asked whether or not a later altercation between Church and Synagogue has influenced the composition of the discourse, the debate then being placed on the lips of Jesus. Nevertheless, it would seem that the smaller section goes back to earlier times, since any cauistry over the temple would have become pointless with its destruction in the year 70 A.D. On the other hand, formulas which enter so much into particulars, as in Matthew 5:33f. and 23:16f., might be the result of halachist discussion. See W. Trilling, *Das wahre Israel*, 4th ed., Munich, 1959, p. 184.

[187] Heb. 6:13 refers to Gen. 22:16f. In reference to the same passage, Philo (*Leg. alleg.*, 3, 203) explains: "How excellent it is that the promise is confirmed with an oath, and indeed, with an oath that is appropriate to God; for God does

not swear by something else, which could not be stronger than he, but by himself, the ultimate of all that exists." Hebrews and Philo probably depend upon the same exegetical tradition. Philo, to be sure, adds: "Certainly some have said that it would be inappropriate for God to swear at all." There was, therefore, some criticism of the Old Testament exposition. Hebrews seems not to have been affected by such.

[138] Philo (*De somniis*, 1, 12) again expresses himself similarly in regard to the oath: "It is by an oath that things in doubt are decided: the uncertain is confirmed, and that which is not believable demands belief." Hebrews and Philo are both indebted to the conceptions and ideas of Hellenistic Judaism.

[139] M. D. Chenu, *The Theology of Work*, trans. by L. Soiron, Chicago, 1966. P. Schoonenberg, "*Die Welt der Arbeit*," in *Gottes werdende Welt*, Limburg, 1963, pp. 163–231 [in Eng. trans., "Labor and the World of Labor," in *God's World in the Making*, Pittsburgh, 1964, pp. 135–184].

[140] In Mark 6:3, Jesus is a carpenter; in the parallel passages, he is the carpenter's son (Matthew 13:55), and the son of Joseph (Luke 4:22). Was it a scandal to the pious that Jesus himself was a laborer, so that the later Gospels try to soften the facts? The Gospel seem to attach no great importance to Jesus' having worked with his hands until his thirtieth year. But if the preaching of the Apostles already understood the patient suffering of Christ as example of service and love (Mark 10:45; Gal. 2:20; Phil. 2:5; 1 Peter 2:21), it is surely possible also to present the example of Christ in the workshop as an example of Christian labor.

[141] O. Hofius, *Katapausis. Die Vorstellung vom endzeitlichen Ruheort im Hebräerbrief*, Tübingen, 1970.

[142] It must be asked whether the parable, especially in its disparagement of goods and possessions, as well as in its disparagement of marriage, does not already give evidence of later Christian asceticism. See above, ch. 20.

[143] In speaking of his ministry, Paul uses the words *kopian* and *kopos* nineteen times. Normally the terms refer to especially hard physical labor, the kind done by slaves.

[144] G. Kehnscherper, *Die Stellung der Bibel und der alten christlichen Kirche zur Sklaverei*, Halle, 1957. J. Vogt, *Sklaverei und Humanität*, Wiesbaden, 1965.

[145] J. van Gobry, *Als besässe man nicht*, "Düsseldorf, 1968. W. Kümmel, "*Der Begriff des Eigentums in Neuen Testament*" in *Heilsgeschehen und Geschichte*, Marburg, 1965, pp. 271–277. H. Vonhoff, *Herzen gegen die Not. Weltgeschichte der Barmherzigkeit*, Kassel, 1960.

[146] H. Strack and P. Billerbeck, *op. cit.*, Vol. 4, pp. 2, 536–610. H. J. Kandler, "*Die Bedeutung der Armut im Schrifttum von Qumran*," in *Judaica*, Vol. 13 (1957), pp. 193–209.

[147] H. Braun, *Spätjüdisch-häretischer und frühchristlicher Radikalismus*, 2nd ed., Tübingen, 1968, Vol. 1, pp. 58f., 77–80, 121–124; Vol. 2, pp. 73–80. J. Dupont,

Les Béatitudes, 2 vols., Bruges, 1958. E. Percy, *Die Botschaft Jesu*, Lund, 1953, pp. 40–108.

[148] Besides the usual commentaries, see also B. Noack, *"Jakobus wider die Reichen,"* in *Studia theologica*, Vol. 18 (1964), pp. 10–15.

[149] H. J. Degenhardt, *Lukas, Evangelist der Armen*, Stuttgart, 1965. R. Koch, *"Die Wertung des Besitzes im Lukasevangelium,"* in *Biblica*, Vol. 38 (1957), pp. 151–169.

[150] *Translators note:* See however Mark 10:21.

[151] The admonitions to official persons to be altruistic are continued in the *Didache* (11:9-12). In the *Letter to the Philippians* (11:1-4) Polycarp tells of a presbyter Valens in Philippi, who allowed himself to be led astray into embezzlement in the stewardship of his office.

[152] Even the rival Greek schools of philosophy reproach each other with charges of greed for money. See M. Dibelius, *An die Thessalonicher I. II*, 3rd ed., Tübingen, 1937, pp. 7f.

[153] The New Testament employs the terms δόξα and τιμή. In the New Testament and in biblical Greek in general, δόξα means, first of all, the majesty of God (Mark 8:38; Rom. 11:36), in which man can share in time and in eternity. God's glory, imparted to a man, is justification (Rom. 3:23f.; 8:18; 2 Cor. 3:18). Rarely does δόξα mean the honor or glory of men (Luke 14:10; 1 Thess. 2:6). τιμή indicates primarily the honor shown among men; but still, it can be used also for God's eschatological gift of salvation (Rom. 2:7, 10; 1 Peter 1:7; John 12:16), and even the very majesty of God (1 Tim. 1:17; Apoc. 4:9). In English, just as in German and Greek, the terms often overlap each other in their meanings. Even in the present brief note they are not entirely distinct from each other.

[154] "The commandment to attend to the honor of a man is binding in Judaism not only in a servant's dealings with his master, in the relationship of a child with his parents, for the citizen in respect to the king, but even for those of like station. Even the man of superior rank must not offend the dignity of his underlings. Judaism tries to ennoble human life, in that it demands self-respect and respect for others." — J. Lewkowitz, Art. *"Ehre,"* in *Jüdisches Lexikon*, Vol. 2, 1928, p. 275f.

[155] The two accounts, Matthew 21:15f. and Luke 19:37-40, are possibly doublets which have evolved one from the other. The Scriptural evidence adduced in Matthew 21:16 would then have resulted from the community's knowledge of Scripture.

[156] The interpretation is uncertain. Does it mean that elders who are administrators should be honored the more because of their double role of service; or does τιμή mean "honorarium, stipend," an occasional meaning of the term in biblical (Sir. 38:1) as well as in profane Greek?

[157] E. Deen, *Family Living in the Bible*, New York, 1963. J. Gamberoni, *"Das Elterngebot im Alten Testament,"* in *Biblische Zeitschrift*, new series Vol. 8 (1964), pp. 161–190.

[158] W. Trilling, *Hausordnung Gottes. Eine Auslegung von Mt 18*, Leipzig, 1960.

[159] K. H. Schelkle, Art. *"Bruder,"* in *Reallexikon für Antike und Christentum,* Vol. 2, 1954, pp. 631–640.

[160] C. H. Powell, *The Biblical Concept of Power,* London, 1963. K. H. Schelkle, *"Jerusalem und Rom im Neuen Testament"* in *Wort und Schrift,* Düsseldorf, 1966, pp. 126–144. W. Schweitzer, *Die Herrschaft Christi und der Staat im Neuen Testament,* Zürich, 1948.

[161] H. Fuchs, *Der geistige Widerstand gegen Rom in der antiken Welt,* 2nd ed., Berlin, 1964.

[162] O. Cullmann, *Jesus und der Revolutionären seiner Zeit,* Tübingen, 1970 trans. by G. Putnam, *Jesus and the Revolutionaries,* New York, 1970]. M. Hengel, *Die Zeloten,* Leiden, 1961; and also by Hengel, *War Jesus Revolutionär?,* Stuttgart, 1970.

[163] L. Goppelt, *"Die Freiheit zur Kaisersteuer. Zu Mk 12, 17 und Röm 13, 1-7"* in *Christologie und Ethik,* Göttingen, 1968, pp. 208–219.

[164] H. von Campenhausen, *"Zum Verständnis von Joh. 19, 11,"* in *Aus der Frühzeit des Christentums,* Tübingen, 1963, pp. 125–134.

[165] H. Conzelmann, *Die Mitte der Zeit,* 3rd ed., Tübingen, 1960, pp. 66–86, 128–135.

[166] Luke shares in a widespread tendency of primitive Christian narratives to exonerate the Romans while charging more and more to the account of the Jews. E. Lohse, *Die Geschichte des Leidens und Sterbens Jesu,* Göttingen, 1964, pp. 91–93 [trans. by M. O Dietrich, *History of the Suffering and Death of Jesus Christ,* Philadelphia, 1967, pp. 89–92].

[167] H. von Campenhausen, *"Zur Auslegung von Röm 13,"* in *Aus der Frühzeit des Christentums,* Tübingen, 1963, pp. 81–101. G. Delling, *Römer 13, 1-7 inner-halb der Briefe des Neuen Testaments,* Berlin, 1961.

[168] In Rom. 13:1 Paul speaks of the ἐξουσίαι, and in Rom. 13:4 of the ἄρχοντες. In 1 Cor. 15:24 the ἐξουσίαι are super-terrestrial powers; and in 1 Cor. 2:8 the ἄρχοντες τοῦ αἰῶνος τούτου are demoniacal powers in the world. In Col. 1:13, Christ delivers us from the ἐξουσίαι τοῦ σκότους τούτου. From such texts as these exegesis has attempted again and again to explain that even in Rom. 13:1f. Paul has in mind super-terrestrial powers which are represented in the State, but which have now been bound by Christ, and indeed, have even been obliged to serve him. The Gnosis already defended a similar interpretation; and Origen toyed with the idea; see K. H. Schelkle, *"Staat und Kirche in der patristischen Auslegung von Röm 13, 1-7"* in *Wort und Schrift,* Düsseldorf, 1966, pp. 228–230.

In our own time this explanation has been defended by not a few exegetes, among whom K. Barth and O. Cullmann might be mentioned as the more distinguished. Finally, it is defended by R. Walker, in *Studie zu Römer 13, 1-7,* Munich, 1966. The great majority of the commentaries reject this interpretation. The aforementioned exegesis could in fact explain some of the things in the text which seem surprising to us, as for example the unqualified recognition of the State; but in regard to some other matters, this exegesis becomes quite forced.

A. Strobel, in his article *"Zum Verständnis von Röm 13"*, in *Zeitschrift für die neutestamentliche Wissenschaft*, Vol. 47 (1956), pp. 67–93, seems to prove conclusively that Paul avails himself of the contemporary politico-legal terminology, and that he speaks therefore of the profane world and not of demoniacal powers. See also the comprehensive account of V. Zsifkovits, *Der Staatsgedanke nach Paulus in Römer 13, 1–7*, Vienna, 1966, pp. 59–64.

[169] E. Dinkler, *"Zum Problem der Ethik bei Paulus. Rechtsnahme und Rechtsverzicht (1 Kor 6, 1-11),"* in *Signum Crucis*, Tübingen, 1967, pp. 204–240.

[170] The political significance of the text is diminished by recent commentators. See the proper places in E. Lohmeyer, 11th ed., Göttingen, 1956, with the supplementary volume (1964); and J. Gnilka, Freiburg im Br., 1968.

[171] O. Cullmann, *"Eschatologie und Mission im Neuen Testament"* in *Vorträge und Aufsätze 1925-1962*, Tübingen, 1966, pp. 348–360.

[172] Similar formulations are frequent in Philo; thus, in *Conf. ling.*, 28: "Look upon the heavenly region, in which the wise dwell as citizens, as your fatherland; the earthly region, however, in which they dwell as sojourners, as a foreign land." Philo employs philosophical notions, whereas Paul's are eschatological. H. Strack and P. Billerbeck, *op. cit.*, Vol. 4, pp. 919–926.

[173] L. Biehl, *Das liturgische Gebet für Kaiser und Reich*, Paderborn, 1937. H. U. Instinsky, *Die alte Kirche und das Heil des Staates*, Munich, 1963, pp. 41–60.

[174] See the commentaries to the Pastoral Epistles, especially C. Spicq, *Les Épîtres Pastorales*, Paris, 1947, CLXII–CLXIV. G. Holtz, Berlin, 1965, pp. 145f., 158f.

[175] ἀνθρωπίνη κτίσις in 1 Peter 2:13 might, considering only the terms themselves, also be translated "creation made by men" or "human institution." However, the arrangements mentioned in 2:14 to 3:7 are not human institutions, but establishments of God. In the New Testament, κτίζειν and its derivatives are used only in reference to divine creation. Thus the passage must be rendered "divine creation among men."

GENERAL INDEX

Abraham, an example of faith, 42, 69, 83, 103f, 109, 154f, 179f, 199f, 204
Adam, sin of, 54, 106
Aeschylus, 193
Andromache, 245
Anna, 264
Antigone, 245
Antigonus of Socho, 66
Apostles' Creed, 93
Apphia, 259
Appolonius of Tyana, 162
Aquila, 258
Aristotle, 113, 178, 200
Artemis, cult of, 218
Asceticism, 160ff
Athenagoras, 154
Augustine, 95, 120, 177

Barth, Karl, 121
Bloch, Ernest, 112
Bonsirven, J., 20f
Book of Jubilees, 329f
Book of the Wars of Yahweh, 235
Bultmann, Rudolf, 20f, 30, 111f, 143, 190

Canon of biblical books, 9ff
Catechism of the Council of Trent, 265
Cato, 287
Christmann, Wolfgang Johannes, 19
Cicero, 287
Clement of Alexandria, 240, 257
Commentaries on Romans, 186
Commentary on Daniel, 343
Commentary on the Book of Habakkuk, 85
Conzelmann, Hans, 20f
Corpus Hermeticum, 83, 154, 200
Council of Jerusalem, 61

Cross of Christ, 164

Damascus Document, 244f, 282, 304, 308
Damascus (Zadokite) Fragment, 123
David, 277, 280
———, an example of faith, 42, 154f
Didache, 210f, 215, 278
Diogenes Laertius, 280
Divorce, 6, 33f, 243ff
Dogmatics, 14f
Drey, Johan Sebastian, 19f

Eighteen Benedictions, 74f, 138, 213, 336
Elijah, and the word of God 5f
Epicharmus, 99
Epictetus, 76, 139, 159, 193, 211, 245, 280
Epistle of Clement to the Corinthians, 211
Erasmus, 144
Esau, 276, 280
Essenes, 160, 282, 289
Ethik (philosophical ethics), 23ff
Ethiopic Henoch, 138, 146, 296, 306f, 329
Ethos (biblical morality), 23ff

Feine, P., 20f
Francis de Sales, 120
Francis of Assisi, 238

Gabler, Johann Philipp, 19
Gehenna of fire, 64f
Gnosticism, 270
God, as Creator of Life, 62
———, as Father, 35f
Good Samaritan parable, 121f, 125f
Grant, F. C., 21

Haymann, Carl, 19

371